the PARIS REVIEW
REVIEW
Interviews, I

the PARIS REVIEW

Interviews, I

WITH AN INTRODUCTION BY
PHILIP GOUREVITCH

CANON‖GATE
Edinburgh · London

Published in Great Britain in 2007 by
Canongate Books Ltd, 14 High Street.
Edinburgh, EH1 1TE

Published by arrangement with Picador
175 Fifth Avenue, New York, N.Y. 10010

www.canongate.tv

British Library Cataloguing-in-Publication Data
A catalogue record for this book is available on
request from the British Library

ISBN 978 1 84195 925 2

Printed and bound in Great Britain
by Clays Ltd, St Ives plc

Contents

Introduction

by Philip Gourevitch

Question and answer—the form is primal. It was there at the beginning of our literature: *"Who told you that you were naked? Have you eaten of the tree of which I commanded you not to eat?"*

Interrogation or dialogue—*"Where do you come from Socrates?"*—call it what you like, the ancients understood the dramatic force and intimacy of direct colloquy. Call and response, give and take: the reader becomes engrossed as an eavesdropper, and every thought gleaned, every argument or story overheard acquires an extra jolt of vividness and of surprise. The conversational transcript seems the most natural sort of writing, yet the interview as a genre of literature unto itself is a distinctly modern phenomenon, a mode of expression that, to a large degree, came into its own during the second half of the twentieth century in the pages of a literary magazine of decidedly modest circulation called *The Paris Review*.

Like many great innovations that later appear inevitable and indispensable, the *Paris Review* interviews got started without any notion that they might one day be acclaimed as canonical. On the contrary, the young Americans who started the magazine, in the city that gave it its name, imagined the interviews as an antidote to the academic formalism that dominated other literary journals. At that time—the early 1950s—such publications were largely preoccupied with criticism, and their editorial boards tended to be allied with one or another aesthetic stance or political creed by which they set their agendas. The men who started *The Paris Review* took the dissenting view that instead of pontificating about writing they should simply publish the stuff: fiction and poetry, nonfiction and plays. Who needed a theory, much less a dogma? "The literary magazines seem today on the verge of doing away with literature, not with any philistine bludgeon but by smothering it under the weight of learned chatter," William Styron (at the age of twenty-seven, one of the elders of the original *Paris Review* circle) declared in a sort of antimanifesto in the inaugural issue. He called for the magazine to devote its pages simply to "the good writers and good poets, the non-drumbeaters and non-axe-grinders."

Excellence, then, would be the magazine's only editorial requirement, and the interviews were conceived as the best way to discuss writing and the writing life in their own terms—by letting writers speak for themselves about their work. It didn't hurt that conducting a sustained Q&A with an established master offered a new, virtually penniless and unheard of "little magazine" the additional advantage of publishing the biggest names in contemporary literature. In 1953 the first issue of the magazine carried an interview with E. M. Forster, and just five years later, when the Viking Press published the first collection of *Paris Review* interviews under the title "Writers at Work," the table of contents boasted, in addition to Forster, Nelson Algren, Truman Capote, Joyce Cary, William Faulkner, François Mauriac, Alberto Moravia, Frank O'Connor, Dorothy Parker, Françoise Sagan, Georges Simenon, William Styron, James Thurber, Robert Penn Warren, Thornton Wilder, and Angus Wilson. The magazine was only publishing twice a year during much of that period, yet the interview archive was already so rich that there wasn't room in that first collection for Isak Dinesen, Ralph Ellison, or Graham Greene.

So it has gone ever since at *The Paris Review*—issue by issue, year by year, decade by decade—and there are now more than three hundred interviews from which the selection in this book was chosen. When they appear in the magazine, the interviews are tagged according to the writer's main body of work, most of them falling under the rubrics Art of Fiction, Art of Poetry, and Art of Theater. With time, the categories have proliferated to include: Art of Biography, Art of Criticism, Art of the Diary, Art of the Essay, Art of Humor, Art of the Musical, Art of Screenwriting, and Art of Translation, as well as

Art of Editing and Art of Publishing. To chose the best—a greatest hits list—from this extraordinary trove is an inherently absurd and arbitrary task: for every writer I've had the delight of including here, there are a handful of others I'm pained not to have had room for. The consolation is that this is but the first book of a three-volume set, and in choosing its content I have sought not only to pick exceptionally strong examples of what can fairly be called the art of the interview—but also to make this a book that reflects the scope and depth and variety of the interview archive as a whole.

What draws so many of the world's best writers to talk to *The Paris Review* is an understanding of the seriousness and care with which the interviews are conducted and edited, the way they are constructed to stand as testimonials for the ages—if not as definitive portraits of each artist, then as a significant contribution to such an ultimate portrait, with the added fascination that they are in large measure self-portraits. A *Paris Review* interview is always a collaboration, not a confrontation. In the beginning, before there were tape recorders, the interviewers worked in teams of two—"like FBI agents," as Malcolm Cowley observed. Each person would scribble down the writer's remarks as fast as possible, and later they would coordinate their notes to create a master transcript that would be trimmed and shaped and reorganized into a cohesive, fluent whole—"a dramatic form in itself," said George Plimpton, who edited the magazine for its first fifty years and made the interviews what they are. With the advent of the tape recorder, the task became at once more efficient and more cumbersome, since the volume of words recorded was far greater and the cruel literalism of verbatim transcripts requires particular editorial vigilance to safeguard against what the journalist Janet Malcolm calls "tape-recorderese"—"the bizarre syntax, the hesitations, the circumlocutions, the repetitions, the contradictions, the lacunae in almost every non-sentence we speak." In shaping a *Paris Review* interview, Plimpton said, "One's tools are very much the dramatic devices: character buildup, surprise, argument even. The best interviews not only divulge something about the character of the writer, but have a surprise or two in them, and maybe even a plot."

Along the way, during the editing process, or at least before the interview finally goes to press, the writer who has been interviewed is given the text to review and revise. This collaborative approach to the final product is unapologetically at odds with journalistic practice, where it is presumed that the reporter's accuracy depends on strict independence from the subject's influence. *The Paris Review*'s purpose is not to catch writers off guard, but to elicit from them the fullest possible reckoning of what interests them most—their lives and work as writers, who they are and where they came from, and how they go about doing what they do all day. A few *Paris Review* interviews were accomplished in a single sitting, but it is far more common for them to be conducted over several seasons, even several years, with multiple sessions in person and many rounds of written correspondence as well. And just as there is no attempt to play "gotcha" with the subject, the interviewer in the most successful final edits never shows off, never appears self-serious, and is never afraid to sound dumb in the cause of asking what may be a fruitful question about writerly process and craft (the sort of question that the novelist William Gaddis, in his *Paris Review* interview, described jokingly: "On which side of the paper do you write?").

The best *Paris Review* interviews—there are many, and every one in this book is of that number—are at once fine entertainments and profound soundings of the writer's soul. They may contain gossip or bile or rhapsodies or love stories or medical complaints or a lot of jokes, or all of these things—and they are bound to be seething with strong opinions strongly expressed—but they are also discussions of the making of literature that frequently attain the quality of literature itself. And although the writers who reveal themselves in these pages all did so willingly and had the opportunity to clarify, correct, retract, and amplify their remarks, they never used that opportunity to hide themselves better—but rather, whether knowingly or inadvertently, the deeper they got into rendering their accounts the more they tended to unmask themselves.

When *The Paris Review* began interviewing writers, the exercise was something of a novelty. This was before the publishing industry had discovered the book tour, before television and radio appearances were the hope of every aspiring sonnet writer. You could be an extremely famous author, with a vast international readership, without really having been heard from except in your books. If the *Paris Review* interviews helped to change that (Hugh Hefner at *Playboy* and Andy Warhol when he launched *Interview* both pointed to Plimpton's quarterly as a driving inspiration), the Writers at Work series has nevertheless retained its freshness and timeless appeal—for writers and readers equally—in our media-dizzied age. Indeed, a *Paris Review* interview has become a sort of international laurel for writers, a recognition of a mature life's work, and an occasion to reflect on what has been achieved and how it has been achieved. And even now, in a world where authors are chattering all over the radio and television dial and in nearly every bookstore and library, the *Paris Review* interview is one of the few occasions, outside of a book, where a writer with something to say can really hope to be heard.

What makes writers different from everyone else is that they write, day after day, year after year, decade after decade, story after story, book after book. The writers whose voices are collected in these pages could hardly make up a more various and eclectic company, and their interviews reflect all their differences—but what binds them together is that they all do it, they write and keep writing, whatever it takes. Most of them will tell you, at first, that it's not terribly interesting to observe what they do when they're doing it—but for half a century now one of the ways writers learned how to do it, felt less alone doing it, or found affirmation in their solitude while doing it is by observing their fellow writers as they describe themselves at work in the *Paris Review* interviews. There is hardly a more enjoyable way to spend one's time, when not writing, than in the company of so much sheer intelligence demanding the best of itself.

the PARIS REVIEW

REVIEW

Interviews, I

Dorothy Parker

The Art of Fiction

At the time of this interview, Mrs. Parker was living in a midtown New York hotel. She shared her small apartment with a youthful poodle that had the run of the place and had caused it to look, as Mrs. Parker said apologetically, somewhat "Hogarthian": newspapers spread about the floor, picked lamb chops here and there, and a rubber doll—its throat torn from ear to ear—which Mrs. Parker lobbed left-handed from her chair into corners of the room for the poodle to retrieve—as it did, never tiring of the opportunity. The room was sparsely decorated, its one overpowering fixture being a large dog portrait, not of the poodle, but of a sheepdog owned by the author Philip Wylie, and painted by his wife. The portrait indicated a dog of such size that if it were real, would have dwarfed Mrs. Parker, who was a small woman, her voice gentle, her tone often apologetic, but occasionally, given the opportunity to comment on matters she felt strongly about, she spoke almost harshly, and her sentences were punctuated with observations phrased with lethal force. Hers was still the wit that made her a legend as a member of the Round Table of the Algonquin—a humor whose particular quality seemed a coupling of brilliant social commentary with a mind of devastating inventiveness. She seemed able to produce the well-turned phrase for any occasion. A friend remembered sitting next to her at the theater when the news was announced of the death of the stolid Calvin Coolidge. "How can they tell?" whispered Mrs. Parker.

Readers of this interview, however, will find that Mrs. Parker had

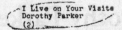

I Live on Your Visits
Dorothy Parker
(2)

and, on consoles and desk and table, photographs of himself at two
and-a-half and five and seven and nine, framed in broad mirror
bands. Whenever his mother settled in a new domicile, and she
removed often, those photographs were the first things out of the
luggage. The boy hated them. He had had to pass his fifteenth
birthday before his body had caught up with his head; *there was that head* in these
presentments of his former selves, that pale, enormous blob.
Once he had asked his mother to put the pictures somewhere else -
preferably some small, dark place that could be locked. But he
had had the bad fortune to make his request on one of the occasions
when she was given to weeping suddenly and long. So the photographs stood out on parade, with their frames twinkling away.

There were twinkings, too, to the silver top of the
fat crystal cocktail shaker, but the liquid low within the crystal
was pale and dull. There was no shine, either, to the glass his
mother held. It was cloudy from the clutch of her
hand, and on the inside there were oily dribbles of what it had
contained.

His mother shut the door by which she had admitted him
and followed him into the room. She looked at him with her head
tilted to the side.

"Well, aren't you going to kiss me?" she said in a
charming, wheedling voice, the voice of a little, little girl.
"Aren't you, you beautiful big ox, you?"

"Sure," he said. He bent down toward her, but she
stepped suddenly away. A sharp change came over her. She drew
herself tall, with her shoulders back and her head flung high.
Her upper lip lifted over her teeth, and her gaze came cold beneath

A manuscript page from "I Live on Your Visits" by Dorothy Parker.

only contempt for the eager reception accorded her wit. "Why, it got so bad," she had said bitterly, "that they began to laugh before I opened my mouth." And she had a similar attitude toward her value as a serious writer. But Mrs. Parker was her own worst critic. Her three books of poetry may have established her reputation as a master of light verse, but her short stories were essentially serious in tone—serious in that they reflected her own life, which was in many ways an unhappy one—and also serious in their intention. Franklin P. Adams described them in an introduction to her work: "Nobody can write such ironic things unless he has a deep sense of injustice—injustice to those members of the race who are the victims of the stupid, the pretentious and the hypocritical."

—Marion Capron, 1956

INTERVIEWER

Your first job was on *Vogue*, wasn't it? How did you go about getting hired, and why *Vogue*?

DOROTHY PARKER

After my father died there wasn't any money. I had to work, you see, and Mr. Crowninshield, God rest his soul, paid twelve dollars for a small verse of mine and gave me a job at ten dollars a week. Well, I thought I was Edith Sitwell. I lived in a boardinghouse at 103rd and Broadway, paying eight dollars a week for my room and two meals, breakfast and dinner. Thorne Smith was there, and another man. We used to sit around in the evening and talk. There was no money, but, Jesus, we had fun.

INTERVIEWER

What kind of work did you do at *Vogue*?

PARKER

I wrote captions. "This little pink dress will win you a beau," that sort of thing. Funny, they were plain women working at *Vogue*, not chic. They were decent, nice women—the nicest women I ever met—

but they had no business on such a magazine. They wore funny little bonnets and in the pages of their magazine they virginized the models from tough babes into exquisite little loves. Now the editors are what they should be: all chic and worldly; most of the models are out of the mind of a Bram Stoker, and as for the caption writers—my old job— they're recommending mink covers at seventy-five dollars apiece for the wooden ends of golf clubs "—for the friend who has everything." Civilization is coming to an end, you understand.

INTERVIEWER

Why did you change to *Vanity Fair*?

PARKER

Mr. Crowninshield wanted me to. Mr. Sherwood and Mr. Benchley—we always called each other by our last names—were there. Our office was across from the Hippodrome. The midgets would come out and frighten Mr. Sherwood. He was about seven feet tall and they were always sneaking up behind him and asking him how the weather was up there. Walk down the street with me, he'd ask, and Mr. Benchley and I would leave our jobs and guide him down the street. I can't tell you, we had more fun. Both Mr. Benchley and I subscribed to two undertaking magazines: *The Casket* and *Sunnyside*. Steel yourself: *Sunnyside* had a joke column called "From Grave to Gay." I cut a picture out of one of them, in color, of how and where to inject embalming fluid, and had it hung over my desk until Mr. Crowninshield asked me if I could possibly take it down. Mr. Crowninshield was a lovely man, but puzzled. I must say we behaved extremely badly. Albert Lee, one of the editors, had a map over his desk with little flags on it to show where our troops were fighting during the First World War. Every day he would get the news and move the flags around. I was married, my husband was overseas, and since I didn't have anything better to do I'd get up half an hour early and go down and change his flags. Later on, Lee would come in, look at his map, and he'd get very serious about spies—shout, and spend his morning moving his little pins back into position.

How long did you stay at *Vanity Fair*?

PARKER
Four years. I'd taken over the drama criticism from P. G. Wodehouse. Then I fixed three plays—one of them *Caesar's Wife*, with Billie Burke in it—and as a result I was fired.

INTERVIEWER
You *fixed* three plays?

PARKER
Well, *panned*. The plays closed and the producers, who were the big boys—Dillingham, Ziegfeld, and Belasco—didn't like it, you know. *Vanity Fair* was a magazine of no opinion, but I had opinions. So I was fired. And Mr. Sherwood and Mr. Benchley resigned their jobs. It was all right for Mr. Sherwood, but Mr. Benchley had a family—two children. It was the greatest act of friendship I'd known. Mr. Benchley did a sign, CONTRIBUTIONS FOR MISS BILLIE BURKE, and on our way out we left it in the hall of *Vanity Fair*. We behaved very badly. We made ourselves discharge chevrons and wore them.

INTERVIEWER
Where did you all go after *Vanity Fair*?

PARKER
Mr. Sherwood became the motion-picture critic for the old *Life*. Mr. Benchley did the drama reviews. He and I had an office so tiny that an inch smaller and it would have been adultery. We had *Parkbench* for a cable address, but no one ever sent us one. It was so long ago—before you were a gleam in someone's eyes—that I doubt there was a cable.

INTERVIEWER

It's a popular supposition that there was much more communication between writers in the twenties. The Round Table discussions in the Algonquin, for example.

PARKER

I wasn't there very often—it cost too much. Others went. Kaufman was there. I guess he was sort of funny. Mr. Benchley and Mr. Sherwood went when they had a nickel. Franklin P. Adams, whose column was widely read by people who wanted to write, would sit in occasionally. And Harold Ross, the *New Yorker* editor. He was a professional lunatic, but I don't know if he was a great man. He had a profound ignorance. On one of Mr. Benchley's manuscripts he wrote in the margin opposite "Andromache," "Who he?" Mr. Benchley wrote back, "You keep out of this." The only one with stature who came to the Round Table was Heywood Broun.

INTERVIEWER

What was it about the twenties that inspired people like yourself and Broun?

PARKER

Gertrude Stein did us the most harm when she said, "You're all a lost generation." That got around to certain people and we all said, Whee! We're lost. Perhaps it suddenly brought to us the sense of change. Or irresponsibility. But don't forget that, though the people in the twenties seemed like flops, they weren't. Fitzgerald, the rest of them, reckless as they were, drinkers as they were, they worked damn hard and all the time.

INTERVIEWER

Did the "lost generation" attitude you speak of have a detrimental effect on your own work?

PARKER

Silly of me to blame it on dates, but so it happened to be. Dammit, it *was* the twenties and we had to be smarty. I *wanted* to be cute. That's the terrible thing. I should have had more sense.

INTERVIEWER

And during this time you were writing poems?

PARKER

My verses. I cannot say poems. Like everybody was then, I was following in the exquisite footsteps of Miss Millay, unhappily in my own horrible sneakers. My verses are no damn good. Let's face it, honey, my verse is terribly dated—as anything once fashionable is dreadful now. I gave it up, knowing it wasn't getting any better, but nobody seemed to notice my magnificent gesture.

INTERVIEWER

Do you think your verse writing has been of any benefit to your prose?

PARKER

Franklin P. Adams once gave me a book of French verse forms and told me to copy their design, that by copying them I would get precision in prose. The men you imitate in verse influence your prose, and what I got out of it was precision, all I realize I've ever had in prose writing.

INTERVIEWER

How did you get started in writing?

PARKER

I fell into writing, I suppose, being one of those awful children who wrote verses. I went to a convent in New York—the Blessed Sacrament. Convents do the same things progressive schools do, only they don't know it. They don't teach you how to read; you have to find out for yourself. At my convent we *did* have a textbook, one that devoted a page and a half to Adelaide Ann Proctor; but we couldn't read Dickens; he was vulgar, you know. But I read him and Thackeray, and I'm the one woman you'll ever know who's read every word of Charles Reade, the author of *The Cloister and the Hearth*. But as for helping me in the outside world, the convent taught me only that if you spit on a pencil eraser it will erase ink. And I remember the smell of oilcloth, the smell of nuns' garb. I was fired from there, finally, for a lot of things, among them my insistence that the Immaculate Conception was spontaneous combustion.

INTERVIEWER

Have you ever drawn from those years for story material?

PARKER

All those writers who write about their childhood! Gentle God, if I wrote about mine you wouldn't sit in the same room with me.

INTERVIEWER

What, then, would you say is the source of most of your work?

PARKER

Need of money, dear.

INTERVIEWER

And besides that?

PARKER

It's easier to write about those you hate—just as it's easier to criticize a bad play or a bad book.

INTERVIEWER

What about "Big Blonde"? Where did the idea for that come from?

PARKER

I knew a lady—a friend of mine who went through holy hell. Just say I knew a woman once. The purpose of the writer is to say what he feels and sees. To those who write fantasies—the Misses Baldwin, Ferber, Norris—I am not at home.

INTERVIEWER

That's not showing much respect for your fellow women, at least not the writers.

PARKER

As artists they're not, but as providers they're oil wells; they gush. Norris said she never wrote a story unless it was fun to do. I understand Ferber whistles at her typewriter. And there was that poor sucker Flaubert rolling around on his floor for three days looking for the right word. I'm a feminist, and God knows I'm loyal to my sex, and you must remember that from my very early days, when this city was scarcely safe from buffaloes, I was in the struggle for equal rights for women. But when we paraded through the catcalls of men and when we chained ourselves to lampposts to try to get our equality— dear child, we didn't foresee *those* female writers. Or Clare Boothe Luce, or Perle Mesta, or Oveta Culp Hobby.

INTERVIEWER

You have an extensive reputation as a wit. Has this interfered, do you think, with your acceptance as a serious writer?

PARKER

I don't want to be classed as a humorist. It makes me feel guilty. I've never read a good tough quotable female humorist, and I never was one myself. I couldn't do it. A "smartcracker" they called me, and that makes me sick and unhappy. There's a hell of a distance between wisecracking and wit. Wit has truth in it; wisecracking is simply calisthenics with words. I didn't mind so much when they were good, but for a long time anything that was called a crack was attributed to me—and then they got the shaggy dogs.

INTERVIEWER

How about satire?

PARKER

Ah, satire. That's another matter. They're the big boys. If I'd been called a satirist there'd be no living with me. But by satirist I mean those boys in the other centuries. The people we call satirists now are those who make cracks at topical topics and consider themselves satirists—creatures like George S. Kaufman and such who don't even know what satire is. Lord knows, a writer should show his times, but not show them in wisecracks. Their stuff is not satire; it's as dull as yesterday's newspaper. Successful satire has got to be pretty good the day after tomorrow.

INTERVIEWER

And how about contemporary humorists? Do you feel about them as you do about satirists?

PARKER

You get to a certain age and only the tired writers are funny. I read my verses now and I ain't funny. I haven't been funny for twenty years. But anyway there aren't any humorists anymore, except for Perelman. There's no need for them. Perelman must be very lonely.

INTERVIEWER

Why is there no need for the humorist?

PARKER

It's a question of supply and demand. If we needed them, we'd have them. The new crop of would-be humorists doesn't count. They're like the would-be satirists. They write about topical topics.

Not like Thurber and Mr. Benchley. Those two were damn well-read and, though I hate the word, they were cultured. What sets them apart is that they both had a point of view to express. That is important to all good writing. It's the difference between Paddy Chayefsky, who just puts down lines, and Clifford Odets, who in his early plays not only sees but has a point of view. The writer must be aware of life around him. Carson McCullers is good, or she used to be, but now she's withdrawn from life and writes about freaks. Her characters are grotesques.

INTERVIEWER

Speaking of Chayefsky and McCullers, do you read much of your own or the present generation of writers?

PARKER

I will say of the writers of today that some of them, thank God, have the sense to adapt to their times. Mailer's *The Naked and the Dead* is a great book. And I thought William Styron's *Lie Down in Darkness* an extraordinary thing. The start of it took your heart and flung it over there. He writes like a god. But for most of my reading I go back to the old ones—for comfort. As you get older you go much farther back. I read *Vanity Fair* about a dozen times a year. I was a woman of eleven when I first read it—the thrill of that line "George Osborne lay dead with a bullet through his heart." Sometimes I read, as an elegant friend of mine calls them, "who-did-its." I love Sherlock Holmes. My life is so untidy and he's so neat. But as for living novelists, I suppose E. M. Forster is the best, not knowing what that is, but at least he's a semifinalist, wouldn't you think? Somerset Maugham once said to me, "We have a novelist over here, E. M. Forster, though I don't suppose he's familiar to you." Well, I could have kicked him. Did he think I carried a papoose on my back? Why, I'd go on my hands and knees to get to Forster. He once wrote something I've always remembered: "It has never happened to me that I've had to choose between betraying a friend and betraying my country, but if it ever does so happen I hope I have the guts to betray my country." Now doesn't that make the Fifth Amendment look like a bum?

INTERVIEWER

Could I ask you some technical questions? How do you actually write out a story? Do you write out a draft and then go over it or what?

PARKER

It takes me six months to do a story. I think it out and then write it sentence by sentence—no first draft. I can't write five words but that I change seven.

INTERVIEWER

How do you name your characters?

PARKER

The telephone book and from the obituary columns.

INTERVIEWER

Do you keep a notebook?

PARKER

I tried to keep one, but I never could remember where I put the damn thing. I always say I'm going to keep one tomorrow.

INTERVIEWER

How do you get the story down on paper?

PARKER

I wrote in longhand at first, but I've lost it. I use two fingers on the typewriter. I think it's unkind of you to ask. I know so little about the typewriter that once I bought a new one because I couldn't change the ribbon on the one I had.

INTERVIEWER

You're working on a play now, aren't you?

PARKER

Yes, collaborating with Arnaud d'Usseau. I'd like to do a play more than anything. First night is the most exciting thing in the world. It's wonderful to hear your words spoken. Unhappily, our first play, *The Ladies of the Corridor*, was not a success, but writing that play was the best time I ever had, both for the privilege and the stimulation of working with Mr. d'Usseau and because that play was the only thing I have ever done in which I had great pride.

INTERVIEWER

How about the novel? Have you ever tried that form?

PARKER

I wish to God I could do one, but I haven't got the nerve.

INTERVIEWER

And short stories? Are you still doing them?

PARKER

I'm trying now to do a story that's purely narrative. I think narrative stories are the best, though my past stories make themselves stories by telling themselves through what people say. I haven't got a visual mind. I hear things. But I'm not going to do those *he-said, she-said* things anymore, they're over, honey, they're over. I want to do the story that can only be told in the narrative form, and though they're going to scream about the rent, I'm going to do it.

INTERVIEWER

Do you think economic security an advantage to the writer?

PARKER

Yes. Being in a garret doesn't do you any good unless you're some sort of a Keats. The people who lived and wrote well in the twenties were comfortable and easy living. They were able to find stories and novels, and good ones, in conflicts that came out of two million dollars a year, not a garret. As for me, I'd like to have money. And I'd like to be a good writer. These two can come together, and I hope they will, but if that's too adorable, I'd rather have money. I hate almost all rich people, but I think I'd be darling at it. At the moment, however, I like to think of Maurice Baring's remark: "If you would know what the Lord God thinks of money, you have only to look at those to whom he gives it." I realize that's not much help when the wolf comes scratching at the door, but it's a comfort.

INTERVIEWER

What do you think about the artist being supported by the state?

PARKER

Naturally, when penniless, I think it's superb. I think that the art of the country so immeasurably adds to its prestige that if you want the country to have writers and artists—persons who live precariously in our country—the state must help. I do not think that any kind of artist thrives under charity, by which I mean one person or organization giving him money. Here and there, this and that—that's no good. The difference between the state giving and the individual patron is that one is charity and the other isn't. Charity is murder and you know it. But I do think that if the government supports its artists, they need have no feeling of gratitude—the meanest and most sniveling attribute in the world—or baskets being brought to them, or apple polishing. Working for the state—for Christ's sake, are you grateful to your employers? Let the state see what its artists are trying to do—like France with the Académie Française. The artists are a part of their country and their country should recognize this, so both it and the artists can take pride in their efforts. Now I mean that, my dear.

INTERVIEWER

How about Hollywood as provider for the artist?

PARKER

Hollywood money isn't money. It's congealed snow, melts in your hand, and there you are. I can't talk about Hollywood. It was a horror to me when I was there and it's a horror to look back on. I can't imagine how I did it. When I got away from it I couldn't even refer to the place by name. "Out there," I called it. You want to know what "out there" means to me? Once I was coming down a street in Beverly Hills and I saw a Cadillac about a block long, and out of the side window was a wonderfully slinky mink, and an arm, and at the end of the arm a hand in a white suede glove wrinkled around the wrist, and in the hand was a bagel with a bite out of it.

INTERVIEWER

Do you think Hollywood destroys the artist's talent?

PARKER

No, no, no. I think nobody on earth writes down. Garbage though they turn out, Hollywood writers aren't writing down. That is their best. If you're going to write, don't pretend to write down. It's going to be the best you can do, and it's the fact that it's the best you can do that kills you. I want so much to write well, though I know I don't, and that I didn't make it. But during and at the end of my life, I will adore those who have.

INTERVIEWER

Then what is it that's the evil in Hollywood?

PARKER

It's the people. Like the director who put his finger in Scott Fitzgerald's face and complained, Pay *you*. Why, you ought to pay us. It was terrible about Scott; if you'd seen him you'd have been sick. When he died no one went to the funeral, not a single soul came, or even sent a flower. I said, "Poor son of a bitch," a quote right out of *The Great Gatsby*, and everyone thought it was another wisecrack.

But it was said in dead seriousness. Sickening about Scott. And it wasn't only the people, but also the indignity to which your ability was put. There was a picture in which Mr. Benchley had a part. In it Monty Woolley had a scene in which he had to enter a room through a door on which was balanced a bucket of water. He came into the room covered with water and muttered to Mr. Benchley, who had a part in the scene, "Benchley? Benchley of *Harvard*?" "Yes," mumbled Mr. Benchley and he asked, "Woolley? Woolley of *Yale*?"

INTERVIEWER

How about your political views? Have they made any difference to you professionally?

PARKER

Oh, certainly. Though I don't think this "blacklist" business extends to the theater or certain of the magazines, in Hollywood it exists because several gentlemen felt it best to drop names like marbles which bounced back like rubber balls about people they'd seen in the company of what they charmingly called "commies." You can't go back thirty years to Sacco and Vanzetti. I won't do it. Well, well, well, that's the way it is. If all this means something to the good of the movies, I don't know what it is. Sam Goldwyn said, How'm I gonna do decent pictures when all my good writers are in jail? Then he added, the infallible Goldwyn, Don't misunderstand me, they all ought to be hung. Mr. Goldwyn didn't know about "hanged." That's all there is to say. It's not the tragedies that kill us, it's the messes. I can't stand messes. I'm not being a smartcracker. You know I'm not when you meet me—don't you, honey?

Truman Capote

The Art of Fiction

Truman Capote lives in a big yellow house in Brooklyn Heights, which he has recently restored with the taste and elegance that is generally characteristic of his undertakings. As I entered he was head and shoulders inside a newly arrived crate containing a wooden lion.

"There!" he cried as he tugged it out to a fine birth amid a welter of sawdust and shavings. "Did you ever see anything so splendid? Well, that's that. I saw him and I bought him. Now he's all mine."

"He's large," I said. "Where are you going to put him?"

"Why, in the fireplace, of course," said Capote. "Now come along into the parlor while I get someone to clear away this mess."

The parlor is Victorian in character and contains Capote's most intimate collection of art objects and personal treasures, which, for all their orderly arrangement on polished tables and bamboo bookcases, somehow remind you of the contents of a very astute little boy's pockets. There is, for instance, a golden Easter egg brought back from Russia, an iron dog, somewhat the worse for wear, a Fabergé pillbox, some marbles, blue ceramic fruit, paperweights, Battersea boxes, picture postcards, and old photographs. In short everything that might seem useful or handy in a day's adventuring around the world.

Capote himself fits in very well with this impression at first glance. He is small and blond, with a forelock that persists in falling down into his eyes, and his smile is sudden and sunny. His approach to

9 7.

She spent entire days mopping
about in her tiny, sweet box kitchen
(José says I'm a fabulous cook,
Better than the Colony. Who would
have thought I had such a great
natural talent. A month ago I couldn't
scramble eggs.") And she still
couldn't, for that matter. The simpler
dishes, steak, a proper salad, were
beyond her; instead, she fed José
outré soups (brandied black Terrapin
poured into avocado shells), dubious
innovations (chicken and rice served with
a chocolate sauce: An East Indian specialty, darling."), Moorish novelties

A manuscript page from Truman Capote's short novel
Breakfast at Tiffany's.

anyone new is one of open curiosity and friendliness. He might be taken in by anything and, in fact, seems only too ready to be. There is something about him, though, that makes you feel that for all his willingness it would be hard to pull any wool over his eyes and maybe it is better not to try.

There was a sound of scuffling in the hall and Capote came in, preceded by a large bulldog with a white face.

"This is Bunky," he said.

Bunky sniffed me over and we sat down.

—Pati Hill, 1957

INTERVIEWER

When did you first start writing?

CAPOTE

When I was a child of about ten or eleven and lived near Mobile. I had to go into town on Saturdays to the dentist and I joined the Sunshine Club that was organized by the Mobile Press Register. There was a children's page with contests for writing and for coloring pictures, and then every Saturday afternoon they had a party with free Nehi and Coca-Cola. The prize for the short-story writing contest was either a pony or a dog, I've forgotten which, but I wanted it badly. I had been noticing the activities of some neighbors who were up to no good, so I wrote a kind of roman à clef called "Old Mr. Busybody" and entered it in the contest. The first installment appeared one Sunday, under my real name of Truman Streckfus Persons. Only somebody suddenly realized that I was serving up a local scandal as fiction, and the second installment never appeared. Naturally, I didn't win a thing.

INTERVIEWER

Were you sure then that you wanted to be a writer?

CAPOTE

I realized that I *wanted* to be a writer. But I wasn't sure I *would* be until I was fifteen or so. At that time I had immodestly started sending stories to magazines and literary quarterlies. Of course no writer ever forgets his first acceptance; but one fine day when I was seventeen, I had my first, second, and third, all in the same morning's mail. Oh, I'm here to tell you, dizzy with excitement is no mere phrase!

INTERVIEWER

What did you first write?

CAPOTE

Short stories. And my more unswerving ambitions still revolve around this form. When seriously explored, the short story seems to me the most difficult and disciplining form of prose writing extant. Whatever control and technique I may have I owe entirely to my training in this medium.

INTERVIEWER

What do you mean exactly by "control"?

CAPOTE

I mean maintaining a stylistic and emotional upper hand over your material. Call it precious and go to hell, but I believe a story can be wrecked by a faulty rhythm in a sentence—especially if it occurs toward the end—or a mistake in paragraphing, even punctuation. Henry James is the maestro of the semicolon. Hemingway is a first-rate paragrapher. From the point of view of ear, Virginia Woolf never wrote a bad sentence. I don't mean to imply that I successfully practice what I preach. I try, that's all.

INTERVIEWER

How does one arrive at short-story technique?

CAPOTE

Since each story presents its own technical problems, obviously one can't generalize about them on a two-times-two-equals-four basis. Finding the right form for your story is simply to realize the most *natural* way of telling the story. The test of whether or not a writer has divined the natural shape of his story is just this: After reading it, can you imagine it differently, or does it silence your imagination and seem to you absolute and final? As an orange is final. As an orange is something nature has made just right.

INTERVIEWER

Are there devices one can use in improving one's technique?

CAPOTE

Work is the only device I know of. Writing has laws of perspective, of light and shade, just as painting does, or music. If you are born knowing them, fine. If not, learn them. Then rearrange the rules to suit yourself. Even Joyce, our most extreme disregarder, was a superb craftsman; he could write *Ulysses because* he could write *Dubliners*. Too many writers seem to consider the writing of short stories as a kind of finger exercise. Well, in such cases, it is certainly only their fingers they are exercising.

INTERVIEWER

Did you have much encouragement in those early days, and if so, by whom?

CAPOTE

Good Lord! I'm afraid you've let yourself in for quite a saga. The answer is a snake's nest of No's and a few Yes's. You see, not altogether but by and large, my childhood was spent in parts of the country and among people unprovided with any semblance of a cultural attitude. Which was probably not a bad thing, in the long view. It toughened me rather too soon to swim against the current—indeed, in some areas I developed the muscles of a veritable barracuda, especially in the art of dealing with one's enemies, an art no less necessary than knowing how to appreciate one's friends. But to go back. Naturally, in the milieu aforesaid, I was thought somewhat *eccentric*, which was fair enough, and *stupid*, which I suitably resented. Still, I despised school—or schools, for I was always changing from one to another—and year after year failed the simplest subjects out of loathing and boredom. I played hooky at least twice a week and was always running away from home. Once I ran away with a friend who lived across the street—a girl much older than myself who in later life achieved a certain fame. Because she murdered a half-dozen people and was electrocuted at Sing Sing. Someone wrote a book about her. They called her the Lonely Hearts Killer. But there, I'm wandering again. Well, finally, I guess I was around twelve, the principal at the school I was attending paid a call on my family, and told them that in his opinion, and in the opinion of the faculty, I was "subnormal." He thought it would be sensible, the humane action, to send me to some special school equipped to handle backward brats. Whatever they may have privately felt, my family as a whole took official umbrage, and in an effort to prove I wasn't subnormal, pronto packed me off to a psychiatric study clinic at a university in the East where I had my IQ inspected. I enjoyed it thoroughly and—guess what?—came home a genius, so proclaimed by science. I don't know who was the more appalled: my former teachers, who refused to believe it, or my family, who didn't want to believe it—they'd just hoped to be told I was a nice normal boy. Ha ha! But as for me, I was exceedingly pleased— went around staring at myself in mirrors and sucking in my cheeks and thinking over in my mind, my lad, you and Flaubert—or Maupassant or Mansfield or Proust or Chekhov or Wolfe, whoever was the idol of the moment.

I began writing in fearful earnest—my mind zoomed all night every night, and I don't think I really slept for several years. Not until I discovered that whiskey could relax me. I was too young, fifteen, to buy it myself, but I had a few older friends who were most obliging in this respect and I soon accumulated a suitcase full of bottles, everything from blackberry brandy to bourbon. I kept the suitcase hidden in a closet. Most of my drinking was done in the late afternoon; then I'd chew a handful of Sen Sen and go down to dinner, where my behavior, my glazed silences, gradually grew into a source of general consternation. One of my relatives used to say, Really, if I didn't know better, I'd swear he was dead drunk. Well, of course, this little comedy, if such it was, ended in discovery and some disaster, and it was many a moon before I touched another drop. But I seem to be off the track again. You asked about encouragement. The first person who ever really helped me was, strangely, a teacher. An English teacher I had in high school, Catherine Wood, who backed my ambitions in every way, and to whom I shall always be grateful. Later on, from the time I first began to publish, I had all the encouragement anyone could ever want, notably from Margarita Smith, fiction editor of *Mademoiselle*, Mary Louise Aswell of *Harper's Bazaar*, and Robert Linscott of Random House. You would have to be a glutton indeed to ask for more good luck and fortune than I had at the beginning of my career.

INTERVIEWER

Did the three editors you mention encourage you simply by buying your work, or did they offer criticism, too?

CAPOTE

Well, I can't imagine anything *more* encouraging than having someone buy your work. I never write—indeed, am physically incapable of writing—anything that I don't think will be paid for. But, as a matter of fact, the persons mentioned, and some others as well, were all very generous with advice.

INTERVIEWER

Do you like anything you wrote long ago as well as what you write now?

CAPOTE

Yes. For instance, last summer I read my novel *Other Voices, Other Rooms* for the first time since it was published eight years ago, and it was quite as though I were reading something by a stranger. The truth is, I am a stranger to that book; the person who wrote it seems to have so little in common with my present self. Our mentalities, our interior temperatures are entirely different. Despite awkwardness, it has an amazing intensity, a real voltage. I am very pleased I was able to write the book when I did, otherwise it would never have been written. I like *The Grass Harp* too, and several of my short stories, though not "Miriam," which is a good stunt but nothing more. No, I prefer "Children on Their Birthdays" and "Shut a Final Door," and oh, some others, especially a story not too many people seemed to care for, "Master Misery," which was in my collection *A Tree of Night*.

INTERVIEWER

You recently published a book about the *Porgy and Bess* trip to Russia. One of the most interesting things about the style was its unusual detachment, even by comparison to the reporting of journalists who have spent many years recording events in an impartial way. One had the impression that this version must have been as close to the truth as it is possible to get through another person's eyes, which is surprising when you consider that most of your work has been characterized by its very personal quality.

CAPOTE

Actually, I don't consider the style of this book, *The Muses Are Heard*, as markedly different from my fictional style. Perhaps the content, the fact that it is about real events, makes it seem so. After all, *Muses* is straight reporting, and in reporting one is occupied with literalness and surfaces, with implication without comment—one can't achieve immediate depths the way one may in fiction. However, one of the reasons I've wanted to do reportage was to prove that I could apply my style to the realities of journalism. But I believe my fictional method is equally detached—emotionality makes me lose writing control: I have to exhaust the emotion before I feel clinical enough to analyze and project it, and as far as I'm concerned that's one of the laws of achieving true technique. If my fiction seems more personal it is because it depends on the artist's most personal and revealing area: his imagination.

INTERVIEWER

How do you exhaust the emotion? Is it only a matter of thinking about the story over a certain length of time, or are there other considerations?

CAPOTE

No, I don't think it is merely a matter of time. Suppose you ate nothing but apples for a week. Unquestionably you would exhaust your appetite for apples and most certainly know what they taste like. By the time I write a story I may no longer have any hunger for it, but I feel that I thoroughly know its flavor. The *Porgy and Bess* articles are not relevant to this issue. That was reporting, and "emotions" were not much involved—at least not the difficult and personal territories of feeling that I mean. I seem to remember reading that Dickens, as he wrote, choked with laughter over his own humor and dripped tears all over the page when one of his characters died. My own theory is that the writer should have considered his wit and dried his tears long, long before setting out to evoke similar reactions in a reader. In other words, I believe the greatest intensity in art in all its shapes is achieved with a deliberate, hard, and cool head. For example, Flaubert's *A Simple Heart*. A warm story, warmly written; but it could only be the work of an artist muchly aware of true techniques, i.e., necessities. I'm sure, at some point, Flaubert must have felt the story very deeply—but *not* when he wrote it. Or, for a more contemporary example, take that marvelous short novel of Katherine Anne Porter's, *Noon Wine*. It has such intensity, such a sense of happening now, yet the writing is so controlled, the inner rhythms of the story so immaculate, that I feel fairly certain Miss Porter was at some distance *from* her material.

INTERVIEWER

Have your best stories or books been written at a comparatively tranquil moment in your life or do you work better because, or in spite, of emotional stress?

CAPOTE

I feel slightly as though I've never lived a tranquil moment, unless you count what an occasional Nembutal induces. Though, come to think of it, I spent two years in a very romantic house on top of a mountain in Sicily, and I guess this period could be called tranquil.

God knows, it was quiet. That's where I wrote *The Grass Harp*. But I must say an iota of stress, striving toward deadlines, does me good.

INTERVIEWER

You have lived abroad for the last eight years. Why did you decide to return to America?

CAPOTE

Because I'm an American, and never could be, and have no desire to be, anything else. Besides, I like cities, and New York is the only real city-city. Except for a two-year stretch, I came back to America every one of those eight years, and I never entertained expatriate notions. For me, Europe was a method of acquiring perspective and an education, a stepping stone toward maturity. But there *is* the law of diminishing returns, and about two years ago it began to set in: Europe had given me an enormous lot, but suddenly I felt as though the process were reversing itself—there seemed to be a taking away. So I came home, feeling quite grown up and able to settle down where I belong—which doesn't mean I've bought a rocking chair and turned to stone. No indeed. I intend to have footloose escapades as long as frontiers stay open.

INTERVIEWER

Do you read a great deal?

CAPOTE

Too much. And anything, including labels and recipes and advertisements. I have a passion for newspapers—read all the New York dailies every day, and the Sunday editions, and several foreign magazines too. The ones I don't buy I read standing at newsstands. I average about five books a week—the normal-length novel takes me about two hours. I enjoy thrillers and would like someday to write one. Though I prefer first-rate fiction, for the last few years my reading seems to have been concentrated on letters and journals and biographies. It doesn't bother me to read while I am writing—I mean, I don't suddenly find another writer's style seeping out of my pen.

Though once, during a lengthy spell of James, my own sentences *did* get awfully long.

What writers have influenced you the most?

So far as I consciously know, I've never been aware of direct literary influence, though several critics have informed me that my early works owe a debt to Faulkner and Welty and McCullers. Possibly. I'm a great admirer of all three; and Katherine Anne Porter, too. Though I don't think, when really examined, that they have much in common with each other, or me, except that we were all born in the South. Between thirteen and sixteen are the ideal if not the only ages for succumbing to Thomas Wolfe—he seemed to me a great genius then, and still does, though I can't read a line of it now. Just as other youthful flames have guttered: Poe, Dickens, Stevenson. I love them in memory, but find them unreadable. These are the enthusiasms that remain constant: Flaubert, Turgenev, Chekhov, Jane Austen, James, E. M. Forster, Maupassant, Rilke, Proust, Shaw, Willa Cather—oh the list is too long, so I'll end with James Agee, a beautiful writer whose death over two years ago was a real loss. Agee's work, by the way, was much influenced by the films. I think most of the younger writers have learned and borrowed from the visual, structural side of movie technique. I have.

You've written for the films, haven't you? What was that like?

A lark. At least the one picture I wrote, *Beat the Devil*, was tremendous fun. I worked on it with John Huston while the picture was actually being made on location in Italy. Sometimes scenes that were just about to be shot were written right on the set. The cast were completely bewildered—sometimes even Huston didn't seem to know what was going on. Naturally the scenes had to be written out of a sequence, and there were peculiar moments when I was carrying around in my head the only real outline of the so-called plot. You never saw it? Oh, you should. It's a marvelous joke. Though I'm afraid the producer didn't laugh. The hell with them. Whenever there's a revival I go to see it and have a fine time. Seriously, though, I don't think a writer stands much chance of imposing himself on a film unless he works in the warmest rapport with the director or is himself the director. It's so much a director's medium that the movies have developed only one writer who, working exclusively as a scenarist, could be called a film genius. I mean that shy, delightful little peasant, Zavattini. What a visual sense! Eighty percent of the good Italian movies were made from Zavattini scripts—all of the De Sica pictures, for instance. De Sica is a charming man, a gifted and deeply sophisticated person; nevertheless he's mostly a megaphone for Zavattini, his pictures are absolutely Zavattini's creations: every nuance, mood, every bit of business is clearly indicated in Zavattini's scripts.

INTERVIEWER

What are some of your writing habits? Do you use a desk? Do you write on a machine?

CAPOTE

I am a completely horizontal author. I can't think unless I'm lying down, either in bed or stretched on a couch and with a cigarette and coffee handy. I've got to be puffing and sipping. As the afternoon wears on, I shift from coffee to mint tea to sherry to martinis. No, I don't use a typewriter. Not in the beginning. I write my first version in longhand (pencil). Then I do a complete revision, also in longhand. Essentially I think of myself as a stylist, and stylists can become notoriously obsessed with the placing of a comma, the weight of a semicolon. Obsessions of this sort, and the time I take over them, irritate me beyond endurance.

INTERVIEWER

You seem to make a distinction between writers who are stylists and writers who aren't. Which writers would you call stylists and which not?

CAPOTE

What is style? And what, as the Zen koan asks, is the sound of one hand? No one really *knows*; yet either you *know* or you don't. For myself, if you will excuse a rather cheap little image, I suppose style is the mirror of an artist's sensibility—more so than the *content* of his work. To some degree all writers have style—Ronald Firbank, bless his heart, had little else, and thank God he realized it. But the possession of style, *a* style, is often a hindrance, a negative force, not as it should be, and as it is—with, say, E. M. Forster and Colette and Flaubert and Mark Twain and Hemingway and Isak Dinesen—a reinforcement. Dreiser, for instance, has *a* style—but oh, *Dio buono*! And Eugene O'Neill. And Faulkner, brilliant as he is. They all seem to me triumphs over strong but negative styles, styles that do not really add to the communication between writer and reader. Then there is the styleless stylist—which is very difficult, very admirable, and *always* very popular: Graham Greene, Maugham, Thornton Wilder, John Hersey, Willa Cather, Thurber, Sartre (remember, we're *not* discussing content), J. P. Marquand, and so on. But yes, there *is* such an animal as a nonstylist. Only they're not writers; they're typists. Sweaty typists blacking up pounds of bond paper with formless, eyeless, earless messages. Well, who are some of the younger writers who seem to know that style exists? P. H. Newby, Françoise Sagan, somewhat. Bill Styron, Flannery O'Connor—she has some fine moments, that girl. James Merrill. William Goyen—if he'd stop being hysterical. J. D. Salinger—especially in the colloquial tradition. Colin Wilson? Another typist.

INTERVIEWER

You say that Ronald Firbank had little else but style. Do you think that style alone can make a writer a great one?

CAPOTE

No, I don't think so—though, it could be argued, what happens to Proust if you separate him from his style? Style has never been a strong point with American writers. This though some of the best have been Americans. Hawthorne got us off to a fine start. For the past thirty years Hemingway, stylistically speaking, has influenced more writers on a world scale than anyone else. At the moment, I think our own Miss Porter knows as well as anyone what it's all about.

INTERVIEWER

Can a writer learn style?

CAPOTE

No, I don't think that style is consciously arrived at, any more than one arrives at the color of one's eyes. After all, your style *is* you. At the end the personality of a writer has so much to do with the work. The personality has to be humanly there. Personality is a debased word, I know, but it's what I mean. The writer's individual humanity, his word or gesture toward the world, has to appear almost like a character that makes contact with the reader. If the personality is vague or confused or merely literary, *ça ne va pas*. Faulkner, McCullers—they project their personality at once.

INTERVIEWER

It is interesting that your work has been so widely appreciated in France. Do you think style can be translated?

CAPOTE

Why not? Provided the author and the translator are artistic twins.

INTERVIEWER

Well, I'm afraid I interrupted you with your short story still in penciled manuscript. What happens next?

CAPOTE

Let's see, that was the second draft. Then I type a third draft on yellow paper, a very special certain kind of yellow paper. No, I don't get out of bed to do this. I balance the machine on my knees. Sure, it works fine; I can manage a hundred words a minute. Well, when the yellow draft is finished, I put the manuscript away for a while, a week, a month, sometimes longer. When I take it out again, I read it as coldly as possible, then read it aloud to a friend or two, and decide what changes I want to make and whether or not I want to publish it. I've thrown away rather a few short stories, an entire novel, and half of another. But if all goes well, I type the final version on white paper and that's that.

INTERVIEWER

Is the book organized completely in your head before you begin it or does it unfold, surprising you as you go along?

CAPOTE

Both. I invariably have the illusion that the whole play of a story, its start and middle and finish, occur in my mind simultaneously—that I'm seeing it in one flash. But in the working-out, the writing-out, infinite surprises happen. Thank God, because the surprise, the twist, the phrase that comes at the right moment out of nowhere, is the unexpected dividend, that joyful little push that keeps a writer going.

At one time I used to keep notebooks with outlines for stories. But I found doing this somehow deadened the idea in my imagination. If the notion is good enough, if it truly belongs to *you*, then you can't forget it—it will haunt you till it's written.

INTERVIEWER

How much of your work is autobiographical?

CAPOTE

Very little, really. A little is *suggested* by real incidents or person-ages, although everything a writer writes is in some way autobio-graphical. *The Grass Harp* is the only true thing I ever wrote, and naturally everybody thought it all invented, and imagined *Other Voices, Other Rooms* to be autobiographical.

INTERVIEWER

Do you have any definite ideas or projects for the future?

CAPOTE

Well, yes, I believe so. I have always written what was easiest for me until now: I want to try something else, a kind of controlled extravagance. I want to use my mind more, use many more colors. Hemingway once said anybody can write a novel in the first person. I know now exactly what he means.

INTERVIEWER

Were you ever tempted by any of the other arts?

CAPOTE

I don't know if it's art, but I was stagestruck for years and more than anything I wanted to be a tap dancer. I used to practice my buck-and-wing until everybody in the house was ready to kill me. Later on, I longed to play the guitar and sing in nightclubs. So I saved up for a guitar and took lessons for one whole winter, but in the end the only tune I could really play was a beginner's thing called "I Wish I Were Single Again." I got so tired of it that one day I just gave the guitar to a stranger in a bus station. I was also interested in painting, and studied for three years, but I'm afraid the fervor, *la vrai chose*, wasn't there.

INTERVIEWER

Do you think criticism helps any?

CAPOTE

Before publication, and if provided by persons whose judgment you trust, yes, of course criticism helps. But after something is published, all I want to read or hear is praise. Anything less is a bore, and I'll give you fifty dollars if you produced a writer who can honestly say he was ever helped by the prissy carpings and condescensions of reviewers. I don't mean to say that none of the professional critics are worth paying attention to—but few of the good ones review on a regular basis. Most of all, I believe in hardening yourself against opinion. I've had, and continue to receive, my full share of abuse, some of it extremely personal, but it doesn't faze me any more. I can read the most outrageous libel about myself and never skip a pulse-beat. And in this connection there is one piece of advice I strongly urge: Never demean yourself by talking back to a critic, never. Write those letters to the editor in your head, but don't put them on paper.

INTERVIEWER

What are some of your personal quirks?

CAPOTE

I suppose my superstitiousness could be termed a quirk. I have to add up all numbers: there are some people I never telephone because their number adds up to an unlucky figure. Or I won't accept a hotel room for the same reason. I will not tolerate the presence of yellow roses—which is sad because they're my favorite flower. I can't allow three cigarette butts in the same ashtray. Won't travel on a plane with two nuns. Won't begin or end anything on a Friday. It's endless, the things I can't and won't. But I derive some curious comfort from obeying these primitive concepts.

INTERVIEWER

You have been quoted as saying your preferred pastimes are "conversation, reading, travel, and writing, in that order." Do you mean that literally?

CAPOTE

I think so. At least I'm pretty sure conversation will always come first with me. I like to listen, and I like to talk. Heavens, girl, can't you *see* I like to talk?

Issue 16, 1957

Ernest Hemingway

The Art of Fiction

HEMINGWAY

You go to the races?

INTERVIEWER

Yes, occasionally.

HEMINGWAY

Then you read the *Racing Form*. . . .
There you have the true art of fiction.

—*Conversation in a Madrid café, May 1954*

Ernest Hemingway writes in the bedroom of his house in the Havana suburb of San Francisco de Paula. He has a special workroom prepared for him in a square tower at the southwest corner of the house, but prefers to work in his bedroom, climbing to the tower room only when "characters" drive him up there.

The bedroom is on the ground floor and connects with the main room of the house. The door between the two is kept ajar by a heavy volume listing and describing *The World's Aircraft Engines*. The bedroom is large, sunny, the windows facing east and south letting in the day's light on white walls and a yellow-tinged tile floor.

The room is divided into two alcoves by a pair of chest-high bookcases that stand out into the room at right angles from opposite walls. A large and low double bed dominates one section, oversized slippers and loafers neatly arranged at the foot, the two bedside tables at the head piled seven-high with books. In the other alcove stands a massive flat-top desk with a chair at either side, its surface an ordered clutter of papers and mementos. Beyond it, at the far end of the room, is an armoire with a leopard skin draped across the top. The other walls are lined with white-painted bookcases from which books overflow to the floor, and are piled on top among old newspapers, bullfight journals, and stacks of letters bound together by rubber bands.

It is on the top of one of these cluttered bookcases—the one against the wall by the east window and three feet or so from his bed—that Hemingway has his "work desk"—a square foot of cramped area hemmed in by books on one side and on the other by a newspaper-covered heap of papers, manuscripts, and pamphlets. There is just enough space left on top of the bookcase for a typewriter, surmounted by a wooden reading board, five or six pencils, and a chunk of copper ore to weight down papers when the wind blows in from the east window.

A working habit he has had from the beginning, Hemingway stands when he writes. He stands in a pair of his oversized loafers on the worn skin of a lesser kudu—the typewriter and the reading board chest-high opposite him.

When Hemingway starts on a project he always begins with a pencil, using the reading board to write on onionskin typewriter paper. He keeps a sheaf of the blank paper on a clipboard to the left of the typewriter, extracting the paper a sheet at a time from under a metal clip that reads "These Must Be Paid." He places the paper slantwise on the reading board, leans against the board with his left arm, steadying the paper with his hand, and fills the paper with handwriting that through the years has become larger, more boyish, with a paucity of punctuation, very few capitals, and often the period marked with an X. The page completed, he clips it facedown on another clipboard that he places off to the right of the typewriter.

Hemingway shifts to the typewriter, lifting off the reading board, only when the writing is going fast and well, or when the writing is, for him at least, simple—dialogue, for instance.

He keeps track of his daily progress—"so as not to kid myself"—on a large chart made out of the side of a cardboard packing case and set up against the wall under the nose of a mounted gazelle head. The numbers on the chart showing the daily output of words differ from four hundred and fifty, five hundred and seventy-five, four hundred and sixty-two, twelve hundred and fifty, back to five hundred and twelve, the higher figures on days Hemingway puts in extra work so he won't feel guilty spending the following day fishing on the Gulf Stream.

A man of habit, Hemingway does not use the perfectly suitable desk in the other alcove. Though it allows more space for writing, it too has its miscellany: stacks of letters; a stuffed toy lion of the type sold in Broadway nighteries; a small burlap bag full of carnivore teeth; shotgun shells; a shoehorn; wood carvings of a lion, a rhino, two zebras, and a warthog—these last set in a neat row across the surface of the desk. And, of course, books: piled on the desk, beside tables, jamming the shelves in indiscriminate order—novels, histories, collections of poetry, drama, essays. A look at their titles shows their variety. On the shelf opposite Hemingway's knee as he stands up to his "work desk" are Virginia Woolf's *The Common Reader*, Ben Ames Williams's *House Divided*, *The Partisan Reader*, Charles A. Beard's *The Republic*, Tarle's *Napoleon's Invasion of Russia*, *How Young You Look* by Peggy Wood, Alden Brooks's *Will Shakespeare and the Dyer's Hand*, Baldwin's *African Hunting*, T. S. Eliot's *Collected Poems*, and two books on General Custer's fall at the battle of the Little Big Horn.

The room, however, for all the disorder sensed at first sight, indicates on inspection an owner who is basically neat but cannot bear to throw anything away—especially if sentimental value is attached. One bookcase top has an odd assortment of mementos: a giraffe made of wood beads; a little cast-iron turtle; tiny models of a locomotive; two jeeps and a Venetian gondola; a toy bear with a key in its back; a monkey carrying a pair of cymbals; a miniature guitar; and a little tin model of a U.S. Navy biplane (one wheel missing) resting awry on a circular straw place mat—the quality of the collection that of the odds and ends which turn up in a shoebox at the back of a small boy's closet. It is evident, though, that these tokens have their value, just as three buffalo horns Hemingway keeps in his bedroom have a value dependent not on size but because during the acquiring of them things went badly in the bush, yet ultimately turned out well. "It cheers me up to look at them," he says.

Hemingway may admit superstitions of this sort, but he prefers not to talk about them, feeling that whatever value they may have can be talked away. He has much the same attitude about writing. Many times during the making of this interview he stressed that the craft of writing should not be tampered with by an excess of scrutiny—"that though there is one part of writing that is solid and you do it no harm by talking about it, the other is fragile, and if you talk about it, the structure cracks and you have nothing."

As a result, though a wonderful raconteur, a man of rich humor, and possessed of an amazing fund of knowledge on subjects that interest him, Hemingway finds it difficult to talk about writing—not because he has few ideas on the subject, but rather because he feels so strongly that such ideas should remain unexpressed, that to be asked questions on them "spooks" him (to use one of his favorite expressions) to the point where he is almost inarticulate. Many of the replies in this interview he preferred to work out on his reading board. The occasional waspish tone of the answers is also part of this strong feeling that writing is a private, lonely occupation with no need for witnesses until the final work is done.

This dedication to his art may suggest a personality at odds with the rambunctious, carefree, world-wheeling Hemingway-at-play of popular conception. The fact is that Hemingway, while obviously enjoying life, brings an equivalent dedication to everything he does—an outlook that is essentially serious, with a horror of the inaccurate, the fraudulent, the deceptive, the half-baked.

Nowhere is the dedication he gives his art more evident than in the yellow-tiled bedroom—where early in the morning Hemingway gets up to stand in absolute concentration in front of his reading board, moving only to shift weight from one foot to another, perspiring heavily when the work is going well, excited as a boy, fretful, miserable when the artistic touch momentarily vanishes—slave of a self-imposed discipline, which lasts until about noon when he takes a knotted walking stick and leaves the house for the swimming pool where he takes his daily half-mile swim.

—George Plimpton, 1958

INTERVIEWER

Are these hours during the actual process of writing pleasurable?

ERNEST HEMINGWAY

Very.

INTERVIEWER

Could you say something of this process? When do you work? Do you keep to a strict schedule?

HEMINGWAY

When I am working on a book or a story I write every morning as soon after first light as possible. There is no one to disturb you and it is cool or cold and you come to your work and warm as you write. You read what you have written and, as you always stop when you know what is going to happen next, you go on from there. You write until you come to a place where you still have your juice and know what will happen next and you stop and try to live through until the next day when you hit it again. You have started at six in the morning, say, and may go on until noon or be through before that. When you stop you are as empty, and at the same time never empty but filling, as when you have made love to someone you love. Nothing can hurt you, nothing can happen, nothing means anything until the next day when you do it again. It is the wait until the next day that is hard to get through.

INTERVIEWER

Can you dismiss from your mind whatever project you're on when you're away from the typewriter?

HEMINGWAY

Of course. But it takes discipline to do it, and this discipline is acquired. It has to be.

INTERVIEWER

Do you do any rewriting as you read up to the place you left off the day before? Or does that come later, when the whole is finished?

HEMINGWAY

I always rewrite each day up to the point where I stopped. When it is all finished, naturally you go over it. You get another chance to correct and rewrite when someone else types it, and you see it clean in type. The last chance is in the proofs. You're grateful for these different chances.

INTERVIEWER

How much rewriting do you do?

HEMINGWAY

It depends. I rewrote the ending to *Farewell to Arms*, the last page of it, thirty-nine times before I was satisfied.

INTERVIEWER

Was there some technical problem there? What was it that had stumped you?

HEMINGWAY

Getting the words right.

INTERVIEWER

Is it the rereading that gets the "juice" up?

HEMINGWAY

Rereading places you at the point where it *has* to go on, knowing it is as good as you can get it up to there. There is always juice somewhere.

INTERVIEWER

But are there times when the inspiration isn't there at all?

HEMINGWAY

Naturally. But if you stopped when you knew what would happen
next, you can go on. As long as you can start, you are all right. The
juice will come.

INTERVIEWER

Thornton Wilder speaks of mnemonic devices that get the writer
going on his day's work. He says you once told him you sharpened
twenty pencils.

HEMINGWAY

I don't think I ever owned twenty pencils at one time. Wearing
down seven number-two pencils is a good day's work.

INTERVIEWER

Where are some of the places you have found most advantageous
to work? The Ambos Mundos Hotel must have been one, judging
from the number of books you did there. Or do surroundings have
little effect on the work?

HEMINGWAY

The Ambos Mundos in Havana was a very good place to work in.
This Finca is a splendid place, or was. But I have worked well everywhere. I mean I have been able to work as well as I can under varied
circumstances. The telephone and visitors are the work destroyers.

INTERVIEWER

Is emotional stability necessary to write well? You told me once
that you could only write well when you were in love. Could you expound on that a bit more?

HEMINGWAY

What a question. But full marks for trying. You can write any time people will leave you alone and not interrupt you. Or rather you can if you will be ruthless enough about it. But the best writing is certainly when you are in love. If it is all the same to you I would rather not expound on that.

INTERVIEWER

How about financial security? Can that be a detriment to good writing?

HEMINGWAY

If it came early enough and you loved life as much as you loved your work it would take much character to resist the temptations. Once writing has become your major vice and greatest pleasure, only death can stop it. Financial security then is a great help as it keeps you from worrying. Worry destroys the ability to write. Ill health is bad in the ratio that it produces worry that attacks your subconscious and destroys your reserves.

INTERVIEWER

Can you recall an exact moment when you decided to become a writer?

HEMINGWAY

No, I always wanted to be a writer.

INTERVIEWER

Philip Young in his book on you suggests that the traumatic shock of your severe 1918 mortar wound had a great influence on you as a writer. I remember in Madrid you talked briefly about his thesis, finding little in it, and going on to say that you thought the artist's equipment was not an acquired characteristic, but inherited, in the Mendelian sense.

HEMINGWAY

Evidently in Madrid that year my mind could not be called very sound. The only thing to recommend it would be that I spoke only briefly about Mr. Young's book and his trauma theory of literature. Perhaps the two concussions and a skull fracture of that year had made me irresponsible in my statements. I do remember telling you that I believed imagination could be the result of inherited racial experience. It sounds all right in good jolly post-concussion talk, but I think that is more or less where it belongs. So until the next liberation trauma, let's leave it there. Do you agree? But thanks for leaving out the names of any relatives I might have implicated. The fun of talk is to explore, but much of it and all that is irresponsible should not be written. Once written you have to stand by it. You may have said it to see whether you believed it or not. On the question you raised, the effects of wounds vary greatly. Simple wounds that do not break bone are of little account. They sometimes give confidence. Wounds that do extensive bone and nerve damage are not good for writers, nor anybody else.

INTERVIEWER

What would you consider the best intellectual training for the would-be writer?

HEMINGWAY

Let's say that he should go out and hang himself because he finds that writing well is impossibly difficult. Then he should be cut down without mercy and forced by his own self to write as well as he can for the rest of his life. At least he will have the story of the hanging to commence with.

INTERVIEWER

How about people who've gone into the academic career? Do you think the large numbers of writers who hold teaching positions have compromised their literary careers?

HEMINGWAY

It depends on what you call compromise. Is the usage that of a woman who has been compromised? Or is it the compromise of the statesman? Or the compromise made with your grocer or your tailor that you will pay a little more but will pay it later? A writer who can both write and teach should be able to do both. Many competent writers have proved it could be done. I could not do it, I know, and I admire those who have been able to. I would think though that the academic life could put a period to outside experience that might possibly limit growth of knowledge of the world. Knowledge, however, demands more responsibility of a writer and makes writing more difficult. Trying to write something of permanent value is a full-time job even though only a few hours a day are spent on the actual writing. A writer can be compared to a well. There are as many kinds of wells as there are writers. The important thing is to have good water in the well, and it is better to take a regular amount out than to pump the well dry and wait for it to refill. I see I am getting away from the question, but the question was not very interesting.

INTERVIEWER

Would you suggest newspaper work for the young writer? How helpful was the training you had with *The Kansas City Star*?

HEMINGWAY

On the *Star* you were forced to learn to write a simple declarative sentence. This is useful to anyone. Newspaper work will not harm a young writer and could help him if he gets out of it in time. This is one of the dustiest clichés there is and I apologize for it. But when you ask someone old, tired questions you are apt to receive old, tired answers.

INTERVIEWER

You once wrote in the *Transatlantic Review* that the only reason for writing journalism was to be well paid. You said, "And when you destroy the valuable things you have by writing about them, you want to get big money for it." Do you think of writing as a type of self-destruction?

HEMINGWAY

I do not remember ever writing that. But it sounds silly and violent enough for me to have said it to avoid having to bite on the nail and make a sensible statement. I certainly do not think of writing as a type of self-destruction, though journalism, after a point has been reached, can be a daily self-destruction for a serious creative writer.

INTERVIEWER

Do you think the intellectual stimulus of the company of other writers is of any value to an author?

HEMINGWAY

Certainly.

INTERVIEWER

In the Paris of the twenties did you have any sense of "group feeling" with other writers and artists?

HEMINGWAY

No. There was no group feeling. We had respect for each other. I respected a lot of painters, some of my own age, others older—Gris, Picasso, Braque, Monet (who was still alive then)—and a few writers: Joyce, Ezra, the good of Stein. . . .

INTERVIEWER

When you are writing, do you ever find yourself influenced by what you're reading at the time?

HEMINGWAY

Not since Joyce was writing *Ulysses*. His was not a direct influence. But in those days when words we knew were barred to us, and we had to fight for a single word, the influence of his work was what changed everything, and made it possible for us to break away from the restrictions.

INTERVIEWER

Could you learn anything about writing from the writers? You were telling me yesterday that Joyce, for example, couldn't bear to talk about writing.

HEMINGWAY

In company with people of your own trade you ordinarily speak of other writers' books. The better the writers, the less they will speak about what they have written themselves. Joyce was a very great writer and he would only explain what he was doing to jerks. Other writers that he respected were supposed to be able to know what he was doing by reading it.

INTERVIEWER

You seem to have avoided the company of writers in late years. Why?

HEMINGWAY

That is more complicated. The further you go in writing, the more alone you are. Most of your best and oldest friends die. Others move away. You do not see them except rarely, but you write and have much the same contact with them as though you were together at the café in the old days. You exchange comic, sometimes cheerfully obscene and irresponsible letters, and it is almost as good as talking. But you are more alone because that is how you must work and the time to work is shorter all the time and if you waste it you feel you have committed a sin for which there is no forgiveness.

INTERVIEWER

What about the influence of some of these people—your contemporaries—on your work? What was Gertrude Stein's contribution, if any? Or Ezra Pound's? Or Max Perkins's?

HEMINGWAY

I'm sorry, but I am no good at these postmortems. There are coroners, literary and nonliterary, provided to deal with such matters. Miss Stein wrote at some length and with considerable inaccuracy about her influence on my work. It was necessary for her to do this after she had learned to write dialogue from a book called *The Sun Also Rises*. I was very fond of her and thought it was splendid she had learned to write conversation. It was no new thing to me to learn from everyone I could, living or dead, and I had no idea it would affect Gertrude so violently. She already wrote very well in other ways. Ezra was extremely intelligent on the subjects he really knew. Doesn't this sort of talk bore you? This backyard literary gossip while washing out the dirty clothes of thirty-five years ago is disgusting to me. It would be different if one had tried to tell the whole truth. That would have some value. Here it is simpler and better to thank Gertrude for everything I learned from her about the abstract relationship of words, say how fond I was of her, reaffirm my loyalty to Ezra as a great poet and a loyal friend, and say that I cared so much for Max Perkins that I have never been able to accept that he is dead. He never asked me to change anything I wrote except to remove certain words that were not then publishable. Blanks were left, and anyone who knew the words would know what they were. For me he was not an editor. He was a wise friend and a wonderful companion. I liked the way he wore his hat and the strange way his lips moved.

INTERVIEWER

Who would you say are your literary forebears—those you have learned the most from?

HEMINGWAY

Mark Twain, Flaubert, Stendhal, Bach, Turgenev, Tolstoy, Dostoyevsky, Chekhov, Andrew Marvell, John Donne, Maupassant, the good Kipling, Thoreau, Captain Marryat, Shakespeare, Mozart, Quevedo, Dante, Virgil, Tintoretto, Hieronymus Bosch, Brueghel, Patinir, Goya, Giotto, Cézanne, Van Gogh, Gauguin, San Juan de la

Cruz, Góngora—it would take a day to remember everyone. Then it would sound as though I were claiming an erudition I did not possess instead of trying to remember all the people who have been an influence on my life and work. This isn't an old dull question. It is a very good but a solemn question and requires an examination of conscience. I put in painters, or started to, because I learn as much from painters about how to write as from writers. You ask how this is done? It would take another day of explaining. I should think what one learns from composers and from the study of harmony and counterpoint would be obvious.

Did you even play a musical instrument?

I used to play cello. My mother kept me out of school a whole year to study music and counterpoint. She thought I had ability, but I was absolutely without talent. We played chamber music—someone came in to play the violin; my sister played the viola, and mother the piano. That cello—I played it worse than anyone on earth. Of course, that year I was out doing other things too.

Do you reread the authors of your list? Twain, for instance?

You have to wait two or three years with Twain. You remember too well. I read some Shakespeare every year, *Lear* always. Cheers you up if you read that.

Reading, then, is a constant occupation and pleasure.

I'm always reading books—as many as there are. I ration myself on them so that I'll always be in supply.

INTERVIEWER

Do you ever read manuscripts?

HEMINGWAY

You can get into trouble doing that unless you know the author personally. Some years ago I was sued for plagiarism by a man who claimed that I'd lifted *For Whom the Bell Tolls* from an unpublished screen scenario he'd written. He'd read this scenario at some Hollywood party. I was there, he said, at least there was a fellow called Ernie there listening to the reading, and that was enough for him to sue for a million dollars. At the same time he sued the producers of the motion pictures *Northwest Mounted Police* and the *Cisco Kid*, claiming that these, as well, had been stolen from that same unpublished scenario. We went to court and, of course, won the case. The man turned out to be insolvent.

INTERVIEWER

Well, could we go back to that list and take one of the painters—Hieronymus Bosch, for instance? The nightmare symbolic quality of his work seems so far removed from your own.

HEMINGWAY

I have the nightmares and know about the ones other people have. But you do not have to write them down. Anything you can omit that you know you still have in the writing and its quality will show. When a writer omits things he does not know, they show like holes in his writing.

INTERVIEWER

Does that mean that a close knowledge of the works of the people on your list helps fill the "well" you were speaking of a while back? Or were they consciously a help in developing the techniques of writing?

HEMINGWAY

They were a part of learning to see, to hear, to think, to feel and not feel, and to write. The well is where your "juice" is. Nobody knows what it is made of, least of all yourself. What you know is if you have it, or you have to wait for it to come back.

INTERVIEWER

Would you admit to there being symbolism in your novels?

HEMINGWAY

I suppose there are symbols since critics keep finding them. If you do not mind, I dislike talking about them and being questioned about them. It is hard enough to write books and stories without being asked to explain them as well. Also it deprives the explainers of work. If five or six or more good explainers can keep going why should I interfere with them? Read anything I write for the pleasure of reading it. Whatever else you find will be the measure of what you brought to the reading.

INTERVIEWER

Continuing with just one question on this line: One of the advisory staff editors wonders about a parallel he feels he's found in *The Sun Also Rises* between the dramatis personae of the bull ring and the characters of the novel itself. He points out that the first sentence of the book tells us Robert Cohn is a boxer; later, during the *desencajonada*, the bull is described as using his horns like a boxer, hooking and jabbing. And just as the bull is attracted and pacified by the presence of a steer, Robert Cohn defers to Jake who is emasculated precisely as is a steer. He sees Mike as the picador, baiting Cohn repeatedly. The editor's thesis goes on, but he wondered if it was your conscious intention to inform the novel with the tragic structure of the bullfight ritual.

HEMINGWAY

It sounds as though the advisory staff editor was a little bit screwy. Whoever said Jake was "emasculated precisely as is a steer"? Actually he had been wounded in quite a different way and his testicles were intact and not damaged. Thus he was capable of all normal feelings as a *man* but incapable of consummating them. The important distinction is that his wound was physical and not psychological and that he was not emasculated.

INTERVIEWER

These questions that inquire into craftsmanship really are an annoyance.

HEMINGWAY

A sensible question is neither a delight nor an annoyance. I still believe, though, that it is very bad for a writer to talk about how he writes. He writes to be read by the eye and no explanations or dissertations should be necessary. You can be sure that there is much more there than will be read at any first reading and having made this it is not the writer's province to explain it or to run guided tours through the more difficult country of his work.

INTERVIEWER

In connection with this, I remember you have also warned that it is dangerous for a writer to talk about a work in progress, that he can "talk it out" so to speak. Why should this be so? I only ask because there are so many writers—Twain, Wilde, Thurber, Steffens come to mind—who would seem to have polished their material by testing it on listeners.

HEMINGWAY

I cannot believe Twain ever "tested out" *Huckleberry Finn* on listeners. If he did they probably had him cut out good things and put in the bad parts. Wilde was said by people who knew him to have been a better talker than a writer. Steffens talked better than he wrote.

Both his writing and his talking were sometimes hard to believe, and I heard many stories change as he grew older. If Thurber can talk as well as he writes he must be one of the greatest and least boring talkers. The man I know who talks best about his own trade and has the pleasantest and most wicked tongue is Juan Belmonte, the matador.

INTERVIEWER

Could you say how much thought-out effort went into the evolvement of your distinctive style?

HEMINGWAY

That is a long-term tiring question and if you spent a couple of days answering it you would be so self-conscious that you could not write. I might say that what amateurs call a style is usually only the unavoidable awkwardnesses in first trying to make something that has not heretofore been made. Almost no new classics resemble other previous classics. At first people can see only the awkwardness. Then they are not so perceptible. When they show so very awkwardly people think these awkwardnesses are the style and many copy them. This is regrettable.

INTERVIEWER

You once wrote me that the simple circumstances under which various pieces of fiction were written could be instructive. Could you apply this to "The Killers"—you said that you had written it, "Ten Indians," and "Today Is Friday" in one day—and perhaps to your first novel, *The Sun Also Rises*?

HEMINGWAY

Let's see. *The Sun Also Rises* I started in Valencia on my birthday, July 21. Hadley, my wife, and I had gone to Valencia early to get good tickets for the *feria* there that started the twenty-fourth of July. Everybody my age had written a novel and I was still having a difficult time writing a paragraph. So I started the book on my birthday, wrote all through the *feria*, in bed in the morning, went on to Madrid and wrote there. There was no *feria* there, so we had a room with a table and I wrote in great luxury on the table and around the corner from the hotel in a beer place in the Pasaje Alvarez where it was cool. It finally got too hot to write and we went to Hendaye. There was a small cheap hotel there on the big long lovely beach and I worked very well there and then went up to Paris and finished the first draft in the apartment over the sawmill at 113 rue Notre-Dame-des-Champs six weeks from the day I started it. I showed the first draft to Nathan Asch, the novelist, who then had quite a strong accent, and he said, Hem, vaht do you mean saying you wrote a novel? A novel huh. Hem you are riding a travhel büch. I was not too discouraged by Nathan and rewrote the book, keeping in the travel (that was the part about the fishing trip and Pamplona) at Schruns in the Vorarlberg at the Hotel Taube.

The stories you mention I wrote in one day in Madrid on May 16 when it snowed out the San Isidro bullfights. First I wrote "The Killers," which I'd tried to write before and failed. Then after lunch I got in bed to keep warm and wrote "Today Is Friday." I had so much juice I thought maybe I was going crazy and I had about six other stories to write. So I got dressed and walked to Fornos, the old bullfighters' café, and drank coffee and then came back and wrote "Ten Indians." This made me very sad and I drank some brandy and went to sleep. I'd forgotten to eat and one of the waiters brought me up some *bacalao* and a small steak and fried potatoes and a bottle of Valdepeñas.

The woman who ran the pension was always worried that I did not eat enough and she had sent the waiter. I remember sitting up in bed and eating and drinking the Valdepeñas. The waiter said he would bring up another bottle. He said the señora wanted to know if I was going to write all night. I said no, I thought I would lay off for a while. Why don't you try to write just one more, the waiter asked. I'm only supposed to write one, I said. Nonsense, he said. You could write six. I'll try tomorrow, I said. Try it tonight, he said. What do you think the old woman sent the food up for?

I'm tired, I told him. Nonsense, he said (the word was not *nonsense*). You tired after three miserable little stories. Translate me one.

Leave me alone, I said. How am I going to write it if you don't leave me alone? So I sat up in bed and drank the Valdepeñas and thought what a hell of a writer I was if the first story was as good as I'd hoped.

INTERVIEWER

How complete in your own mind is the conception of a short story? Does the theme, or the plot, or a character change as you go along?

HEMINGWAY

Sometimes you know the story. Sometimes you make it up as you go along and have no idea how it will come out. Everything changes as it moves. That is what makes the movement which makes the story. Sometimes the movement is so slow it does not seem to be moving. But there is always change and always movement.

INTERVIEWER

Is it the same with the novel, or do you work out the whole plan before you start and adhere to it rigorously?

HEMINGWAY

For Whom the Bell Tolls was a problem that I carried on each day. I knew what was going to happen in principle. But I invented what happened each day I wrote.

INTERVIEWER

Were *The Green Hills of Africa, To Have and Have Not*, and *Across the River and Into the Trees* all started as short stories and developed into novels? If so, are the two forms so similar that the writer can pass from one to the other without completely revamping his approach?

HEMINGWAY

No, that is not true. *The Green Hills of Africa* is not a novel, but was written in an attempt to write an absolutely true book to see whether the shape of a country and the pattern of a month's action could, if truly presented, compete with a work of the imagination.

After I had written it I wrote two short stories, "The Snows of Kilimanjaro" and "The Short Happy Life of Francis Macomber." These were stories that I invented from the knowledge and experience acquired on the same long hunting trip one month of which I had tried to write a truthful account of in *The Green Hills*. *To Have and Have Not* and *Across the River and Into the Trees* were both started as short stories.

INTERVIEWER

Do you find it easy to shift from one literary project to another, or do you continue through to finish what you start?

HEMINGWAY

The fact that I am interrupting serious work to answer these questions proves that I am so stupid that I should be penalized severely. I will be. Don't worry.

INTERVIEWER

Do you think of yourself in competition with other writers?

HEMINGWAY

Never. I used to try to write better than certain dead writers of whose value I was certain. For a long time now I have tried simply to write the best I can. Sometimes I have good luck and write better than I can.

INTERVIEWER

Do you think a writer's power diminishes as he grows older? In *The Green Hills of Africa* you mention that American writers at a certain age change into Old Mother Hubbards.

HEMINGWAY

I don't know about that. People who know what they are doing should last as long as their heads last. In that book you mention, if you look it up, you'll see I was sounding off about American literature with a humorless Austrian character who was forcing me to talk when

I wanted to do something else. I wrote an accurate account of the conversation. Not to make deathless pronouncements. A fair percent of the pronouncements are good enough.

INTERVIEWER

We've not discussed character. Are the characters of your work taken without exception from real life?

HEMINGWAY

Of course they are not. *Some* come from real life. Mostly you invent people from a knowledge and understanding and experience of people.

INTERVIEWER

Could you say something about the process of turning a real-life character into a fictional one?

HEMINGWAY

If I explained how that is sometimes done, it would be a handbook for libel lawyers.

INTERVIEWER

Do you make a distinction—as E. M. Forster does—between "flat" and "round" characters?

HEMINGWAY

If you describe someone, it is flat, as a photograph is, and from my standpoint a failure. If you make him up from what you know, there should be all the dimensions.

INTERVIEWER

Which of your characters do you look back on with particular affection?

HEMINGWAY

That would make too long a list.

INTERVIEWER

Then you enjoy reading over your own books—without feeling there are changes you would like to make?

HEMINGWAY

I read them sometimes to cheer me up when it is hard to write and then I remember that it was always difficult and how nearly impossible it was sometimes.

INTERVIEWER

How do you name your characters?

HEMINGWAY

The best I can.

INTERVIEWER

Do the titles come to you while you're in the process of doing the story?

HEMINGWAY

No. I make a list of titles *after* I've finished the story or the book—sometimes as many as a hundred. Then I start eliminating them, sometimes all of them.

INTERVIEWER

And you do this even with a story whose title is supplied from the text—"Hills Like White Elephants," for example?

HEMINGWAY

Yes. The title comes afterwards. I met a girl in Prunier where I'd gone to eat oysters before lunch. I knew she'd had an abortion. I went over and we talked, not about that, but on the way home I thought of the story, skipped lunch, and spent that afternoon writing it.

INTERVIEWER

So when you're not writing, you remain constantly the observer, looking for something which can be of use.

HEMINGWAY

Surely. If a writer stops observing he is finished. But he does not have to observe consciously nor think how it will be useful. Perhaps that would be true at the beginning. But later everything he sees goes into the great reserve of things he knows or has seen. If it is any use to know it, I always try to write on the principle of the iceberg. There is seven-eighths of it underwater for every part that shows. Anything you know you can eliminate and it only strengthens your iceberg. It is the part that doesn't show. If a writer omits something because he does not know it then there is a hole in the story.

The Old Man and the Sea could have been over a thousand pages long and had every character in the village in it and all the processes of how they made their living, were born, educated, bore children, et cetera. That is done excellently and well by other writers. In writing you are limited by what has already been done satisfactorily. So I have tried to learn to do something else. First I have tried to eliminate everything unnecessary to conveying experience to the reader so that after he or she has read something it will become a part of his or her experience and seem actually to have happened. This is very hard to do and I've worked at it very hard.

Anyway, to skip how it is done, I had unbelievable luck this time and could convey the experience completely and have it be one that no one had ever conveyed. The luck was that I had a good man and a good boy and lately writers have forgotten there still are such things. Then the ocean is worth writing about just as man is. So I was lucky there. I've seen the marlin mate and know about that. So I leave that out. I've seen a school (or pod) of more than fifty sperm whales in that same stretch of water and once harpooned one nearly sixty feet in length and lost him. So I left that out. All the stories I know from the fishing village I leave out. But the knowledge is what makes the underwater part of the iceberg.

Archibald MacLeish has spoken of a method of conveying experience to a reader that he said you developed while covering baseball games back in those *Kansas City Star* days. It was simply that experience is communicated by small details, intimately preserved, which have the effect of indicating the whole by making the reader conscious of what he had been aware of only subconsciously . . .

HEMINGWAY

The anecdote is apocryphal. I never wrote baseball for the *Star*. What Archie was trying to remember was how I was trying to learn in Chicago in around 1920 and was searching for the unnoticed things that made emotions, such as the way an outfielder tossed his glove without looking back to where it fell, the squeak of resin on canvas under a fighter's flat-soled gym shoes, the gray color of Jack Blackburn's skin when he had just come out of stir, and other things I noted as a painter sketches. You saw Blackburn's strange color and the old razor cuts and the way he spun a man before you knew his history. These were the things that moved you before you knew the story.

INTERVIEWER

Have you ever described any type of situation of which you had no personal knowledge?

HEMINGWAY

That is a strange question. By personal knowledge, do you mean carnal knowledge? In that case the answer is positive. A writer, if he is any good, does not describe. He invents or *makes* out of knowledge personal and impersonal and sometimes he seems to have unexplained knowledge which could come from forgotten racial or family experience. Who teaches the homing pigeon to fly as he does; where does a fighting bull get his bravery, or a hunting dog his nose? This is an elaboration or a condensation on that stuff we were talking about in Madrid that time when my head was not to be trusted.

INTERVIEWER

How detached must you be from an experience before you can write about it in fictional terms? The African air crashes you were involved in, for instance?

HEMINGWAY

It depends on the experience. One part of you sees it with complete detachment from the start. Another part is very involved. I think there is no rule about how soon one should write about it. It would depend on how well adjusted the individual was and on his or her recuperative powers. Certainly it is valuable to a trained writer to crash in an aircraft that burns. He learns several important things very quickly. Whether they will be of use to him is conditioned by survival. Survival, with honor, that outmoded and all-important word, is as difficult as ever and as all-important to a writer. Those who do not last are always more beloved since no one has to see them in their long, dull, unrelenting, no-quarter-given-and-no-quarter-received fights that they make to do something as they believe it should be done before they die. Those who die or quit early and easy and with every good reason are preferred because they are understandable and human. Failure and well-disguised cowardice are more human and more beloved.

INTERVIEWER

Could I ask you to what extent you think the writer should concern himself with the sociopolitical problems of his times?

HEMINGWAY

Everyone has his own conscience, and there should be no rules about how a conscience should function. All you can be sure about in a political-minded writer is that if his work should last you will have to skip the politics when you read it. Many of the so-called politically enlisted writers change their politics frequently. This is very exciting to them and to their political-literary reviews. Sometimes they even have to rewrite their viewpoints . . . and in a hurry. Perhaps it can be respected as a form of the pursuit of happiness.

INTERVIEWER

Has the political influence of Ezra Pound on the segregationist Kasper had any effect on your belief that the poet ought to be released from St. Elizabeth's Hospital?

HEMINGWAY

No. None at all. I believe Ezra should be released and allowed to write poetry in Italy on an undertaking by him to abstain from any politics. I would be happy to see Kasper jailed as soon as possible. Great poets are not necessarily Girl Guides nor scoutmasters nor splendid influences on youth. To name a few: Verlaine, Rimbaud, Shelley, Byron, Baudelaire, Proust, Gide should not have been confined to prevent them from being aped in their thinking, their manners or their morals, by local Kaspers. I am sure that it will take a footnote to this paragraph in ten years to explain who Kasper was.

INTERVIEWER

Would you say, ever, that there is any didactic intention in your work?

HEMINGWAY

Didactic is a word that has been misused and has spoiled. *Death in the Afternoon* is an instructive book.

INTERVIEWER

It has been said that a writer only deals with one or two ideas throughout his work. Would you say your work reflects one or two ideas?

HEMINGWAY

Who said that? It sounds much too simple. The man who said it possibly *had* only one or two ideas.

INTERVIEWER

Well, perhaps it would be better put this way: Graham Greene said that a ruling passion gives to a shelf of novels the unity of a system. You yourself have said, I believe, that great writing comes out of a sense of injustice. Do you consider it important that a novelist be dominated in this way—by some such compelling sense?

HEMINGWAY

Mr. Greene has a facility for making statements that I do not possess. It would be impossible for me to make generalizations about a shelf of novels or a wisp of snipe or a gaggle of geese. I'll try a generalization though. A writer without a sense of justice and of injustice would be better off editing the yearbook of a school for exceptional children than writing novels. Another generalization. You see, they are not so difficult when they are sufficiently obvious. The most essential gift for a good writer is a built-in, shockproof, shit detector. This is the writer's radar and all great writers have had it.

INTERVIEWER

Finally, a fundamental question: As a creative writer what do you think is the function of your art? Why a representation of fact, rather than fact itself?

HEMINGWAY

Why be puzzled by that? From things that have happened and from things as they exist and from all things that you know and all those you cannot know, you make something through your invention that is not a representation but a whole new thing truer than anything true and alive, and you make it alive, and if you make it well enough, you give it immortality. That is why you write and for no other reason that you know of. But what about all the reasons that no one knows?

T. S. Eliot

The Art of Poetry

T he interview took place in New York, at the apartment of Mrs. Louis Henry Cohn, of House of Books, Ltd., who is a friend of Mr. and Mrs. Eliot. The bookcases of the attractive living room contain a remarkable collection of modern authors. On a wall near the entrance hangs a drawing of Mr. Eliot, done by his sister-in-law, Mrs. Henry Ware Eliot. An inscribed wedding photograph of the Eliots stands in a silver frame on a table. Mrs. Cohn and Mrs. Eliot sat on a sofa at one end of the room, while Mr. Eliot and the interviewer faced each other in the center. The microphone of a tape recorder lay on the floor between them.

Mr. Eliot looked particularly well. He was visiting the United States briefly on his way back to London from a holiday in Nassau. He was tanned, and he seemed to have put on weight in the three years since the interviewer had seen him. Altogether, he looked younger and seemed jollier. He frequently glanced at Mrs. Eliot during the interview, as if he were sharing with her an answer which he was not making.

The interviewer had talked with Mr. Eliot previously in London. The small office at Faber and Faber, a few flights above Russell Square, displays a gallery of photographs on its walls: here is a large picture of Virginia Woolf, with an inset portrait of Pius XII; here are I. A. Richards, Paul Valéry, W. B. Yeats, Goethe, Marianne Moore, Charles Whibley, Djuna Barnes, and others. Many young poets have stared at the faces there, during a talk with Mr. Eliot. One of them has

2.

he was exploring his own mind also.   The compositions in verse and
in prose fiction ~~to which I have just referred~~ may I think be ignored, except for ~~the~~ such information they can yield about their author; and his other writings, those concerned directly with theo-
logical, social or political matter, should be ~~considered~~ conside.
as by-products of a mind of which the primary activity was litera
criticism.

I ~~first~~ met Middleton Murry ~~by~~ appointment at some meeting
place whence he was to conduct me to his home for dinner and a
discussion of his projects for <u>The Athenaeum</u>, a defunct weekly
which was to be revived under his editorship.   I had heard of
him earlier, in the circle of Lady Ottoline Morrell where I had
already met Katharine Mansfield on one occasion, but we had held
no communication ~~until~~ before he wrote to ~~invite me to~~ propose this a meeting.   I do
not know what he had been told about me; what is important is that
he had read (having had it brought to his attention no doubt) at
Garsington) my first ~~volume~~ book of Verse, <u>Prufrock</u>, and that it was
entirely because of ~~him this verse~~ his this verse that he wished to ask me to
become Assistant Editor ~~of The Athenaeum under him.~~   Of my critical writings he knew nothing: I gave him some copies of <u>The
Egoist</u> to enable him to judge of my abilities.   It speaks of the
man, however, that he had made up his mind that he wanted my help
in his editorial and
~~with~~ this venture without having seen any criticism of mine, ~~and~~
wholly on the strength of <u>Prufrock</u>.   After a good deal of hesitation I declined; and I think that I was wise to do so, and to
remain for some years at my desk in the City.   I did however
become one of Murry's regular contributors, reviewing some book

Part of a manuscript by T. S. Eliot.

told a story that illustrates some of the unsuspected in Mr. Eliot's conversation. After an hour of serious literary discussion, Mr. Eliot paused to think if he had a final word of advice; the young poet, an American, was about to go up to Oxford as Mr. Eliot had done forty years before. Then, as gravely as if he were recommending salvation, Mr. Eliot advised the purchase of long woolen underwear because of Oxford's damp stone. Mr. Eliot is able to be avuncular while he is quite aware of comic disproportion between manner and message.

Similar combinations modified many of the comments that are reported here, and the ironies of gesture are invisible on the page. At times, actually, the interview moved from the ironic and the mildly comic to the hilarious. The tape is punctuated by the head-back boom-boom of Mr. Eliot's laughter, particularly in response to mention of his early derogation of Ezra Pound, and to a question about the unpublished and, one gathers, improper, King Bolo poems of his Harvard days.

—Donald Hall, 1959

INTERVIEWER

Perhaps I can begin at the beginning. Do you remember the circumstances under which you began to write poetry in St. Louis when you were a boy?

T. S. ELIOT

I began I think about the age of fourteen, under the inspiration of Fitzgerald's *Omar Khayyam*, to write a number of very gloomy and atheistical and despairing quatrains in the same style, which fortunately I suppressed completely—so completely that they don't exist. I never showed them to anybody. The first poem that shows is one that appeared first in the *Smith Academy Record*, and later in *The Harvard Advocate*, which was written as an exercise for my English teacher and was an imitation of Ben Johnson. He thought it very good for a boy of fifteen or sixteen. Then I wrote a few at Harvard, just enough to qualify for election to an editorship on *The Harvard Advocate*, which I enjoyed. Then I had an outburst during my junior and senior years. I became much more prolific, under the influence first of Baudelaire and then of Jules Laforgue, whom I discovered I think in my junior year at Harvard.

Did anyone in particular introduce you to the French poets? Not Irving Babbitt, I suppose.

No, Babbitt would be the last person! The one poem that Babbitt always held up for admiration was Gray's *Elegy*. And that's a fine poem, but I think this shows certain limitations on Babbitt's part, God bless him. I have advertised my source, I think; it's Arthur Symons's book on French poetry, which I came across in the Harvard Union. In those days the Harvard Union was a meeting place for any undergraduate who chose to belong to it. They had a very nice little library, like the libraries in many Harvard houses now. I liked his quotations and I went to a foreign bookshop somewhere in Boston (I've forgotten the name and I don't know whether it still exists) that specialized in French and German and other foreign books and found Laforgue, and other poets. I can't imagine why that bookshop should have had a few poets like Laforgue in stock. Goodness knows how long they'd had them or whether there were any other demands for them.

When you were an undergraduate, were you aware of the dominating presence of any older poets? Today the poet in his youth is writing in the age of Eliot and Pound and Stevens. Can you remember your own sense of the literary times? I wonder if your situation may not have been extremely different.

I think it was rather an advantage not having any living poets in England or America in whom one took any particular interest. I don't know what it would be like, but I think it would be a rather troublesome distraction to have such a lot of dominating presences, as you call them, about. Fortunately we weren't bothered by each other.

Were you aware of people like Hardy or Robinson at all?

I was slightly aware of Robinson because I read an article about him in *The Atlantic Monthly* that quoted some of his poems, and that wasn't my cup of tea at all. Hardy was hardly known to be a poet at that time. One read his novels, but his poetry only really became conspicuous to a later generation. Then there was Yeats, but it was the early Yeats. It was too much Celtic twilight for me. There was really nothing except the people of the nineties who had all died of drink or suicide or one thing or another.

Did you and Conrad Aiken help each other with your poems when you were coeditors on the *Advocate?*

We were friends, but I don't think we influenced each other at all. When it came to foreign writers, he was more interested in Italian and Spanish, and I was all for the French.

Were there any other friends who read your poems and helped you?

Well, yes. There was a man who was a friend of my brother's, a man named Thomas H. Thomas who lived in Cambridge and who saw some of my poems in *The Harvard Advocate*. He wrote me a most enthusiastic letter and cheered me up. And I wish I had his letters still. I was very grateful to him for giving me that encouragement.

INTERVIEWER

I understand that it was Conrad Aiken who introduced you and your work to Pound.

ELIOT

Yes it was. Aiken was a very generous friend. He tried to place some of my poems in London, one summer when he was over, with Harold Monro and others. Nobody would think of publishing them. He brought them back to me. Then in 1914, I think, we were both in London in the summer. He said, You go to Pound. Show him your poems. He thought Pound might like them. Aiken liked them, though they were very different from his.

INTERVIEWER

Do you remember the circumstances of your first meeting with Pound?

ELIOT

I think I went to call on him first. I think I made a good impression, in his little triangular sitting room in Kensington. He said, Send me your poems. And he wrote back, This is as good as anything I've seen. Come around and have a talk about them. Then he pushed them on Harriet Monroe, which took a little time.

INTERVIEWER

In an article about your *Advocate* days, for the book in honor of your sixtieth birthday, Aiken quotes an early letter from England in which you refer to Pound's verse as "touchingly incompetent." I wonder when you changed your mind.

ELIOT

Hah! That was a bit brash, wasn't it? Pound's verse was first shown me by an editor of *The Harvard Advocate*, W. G. Tinckom-Fernandez, who was a crony of mine and Conrad Aiken's and the other Signet poets of the period. He showed me those little things of Elkin Mathews, *Exultations* and *Personae*. He said, This is up your street; you ought to like this. Well, I didn't, really. It seemed to me rather fancy, old-fashioned, romantic stuff, cloak-and-dagger kind of stuff. I wasn't very much impressed by it. When I went to see Pound, I was not particularly an admirer of his work, and though I now regard the work I saw then as very accomplished, I am certain that in his later work is to be found the grand stuff.

INTERVIEWER

You have mentioned in print that Pound cut *The Waste Land* from a much larger poem into its present form. Were you benefited by his criticism of your poems in general? Did he cut other poems?

ELIOT

Yes. At that period, yes. He was a marvelous critic because he didn't try to turn you into an imitation of himself. He tried to see what you were trying to do.

INTERVIEWER

Have you helped to rewrite any of your friends' poems? Ezra Pound's, for instance?

ELIOT

I can't think of any instances. Of course I have made innumerable suggestions on manuscripts of young poets in the last twenty-five years or so.

INTERVIEWER

Does the manuscript of the·original, uncut *Waste Land* exist?

ELIOT

Don't ask me. That's one of the things I don't know. It's an unsolved mystery. I sold it to John Quinn. I also gave him a notebook of unpublished poems, because he had been kind to me in various affairs. That's the last I heard of them. Then he died and they didn't turn up at the sale.

INTERVIEWER

What sort of thing did Pound cut from *The Waste Land*? Did he cut whole sections?

ELIOT

Whole sections, yes. There was a long section about a shipwreck. I don't know what that had to do with anything else, but it was rather inspired by the Ulysses canto in *The Inferno*, I think. Then there was another section that was an imitation *Rape of the Lock*. Pound said, It's no use trying to do something that somebody else has done as well as it can be done. Do something different.

INTERVIEWER

Did the excisions change the intellectual structure of the poem?

ELIOT

No. I think it was just as structureless, only in a more futile way, in the longer version.

INTERVIEWER

I have a question about the poem, which is related to its composition. In *Thoughts after Lambeth* you denied the allegation of critics who said that you expressed "the disillusionment of a generation" in *The Waste Land*, or you denied that it was your intention. Now F. R. Leavis, I believe, has said that the poem exhibits no progression; yet on the other hand, more recent critics, writing after your later poetry, found *The Waste Land* Christian. I wonder if this was part of your intention.

ELIOT

No, it wasn't part of my conscious intention. I think that in *Thoughts after Lambeth*, I was speaking of intentions more in a negative than in a positive sense, to say what was not my intention. I wonder what an *intention* means! One wants to get something off one's chest. One doesn't know quite what it is that one wants to get off the chest until one's got it off. But I couldn't apply the word *intention* positively to any of my poems. Or to any poem.

INTERVIEWER

I have another question about you and Pound and your earlier career. I have read somewhere that you and Pound decided to write quatrains, in the late teens, because vers libre had gone far enough.

ELIOT

I think that's something Pound said. And the suggestion of writing quatrains was his. He put me onto *Emaux et camées*.*

INTERVIEWER

I wonder about your ideas about the relation of form to subject. Would you then have chosen the form before you knew quite what you were going to write in it?

ELIOT

Yes, in a way. One studied originals. We studied Gautier's poems and then we thought, Have I anything to say in which this form will be useful? And we experimented. The form gave the impetus to the content.

INTERVIEWER

Why was vers libre the form you chose to use in your early poems?

ELIOT

My early vers libre, of course, was started under the endeavor to practice the same form as Laforgue. This meant merely rhyming lines of irregular length, with the rhymes coming in irregular places. It wasn't quite so libre as much vers, especially the sort which Ezra

*Poems by Théophile Gautier.

called Amygism.* Then, of course, there were things in the next phase which were freer, like "Rhapsody on a Windy Night." I don't know whether I had any sort of model or practice in mind when I did that. It just came that way.

Did you feel, possibly, that you were writing against something, more than from any model? Against the poet laureate perhaps?

No, no, no. I don't think one was constantly trying to reject things, but just trying to find out what was right for oneself. One really ignored poet laureates as such, the Robert Bridges. I don't think good poetry can be produced in a kind of political attempt to overthrow some existing form. I think it just supersedes. People find a way in which they can say something—I can't say it that way, what way can I find that will do? One didn't really *bother* about the existing modes.

I think it was after "Prufrock" and before "Gerontion" that you wrote the poems in French that appear in your *Collected Poems*. I wonder how you happened to write them. Have you written any since?

No, and I never shall. That was a very curious thing which I can't altogether explain. At that period I thought I'd dried up completely. I hadn't written anything for some time and was rather desperate. I started writing a few things in French and found I *could*, at that period. I think it was that when I was writing in French I didn't take the poems so seriously, and that, not taking them seriously, I wasn't so worried about not being able to write. I did these things as a sort of tour de force to see what I could do. That went on for some months.

*A reference to Amy Lowell.

The best of them have been printed. I must say that Ezra Pound went through them, and Edmond Dulac, a Frenchman we knew in London, helped with them a bit. We left out some, and I suppose they disappeared completely. Then I suddenly began writing in English again and lost all desire to go on with French. I think it was just something that helped me get started again.

INTERVIEWER

Did you think at all about becoming a French symbolist poet like the two Americans of the last century?

ELIOT

Stuart Merrill and Viélé-Griffin. I only did that during the romantic year I spent in Paris after Harvard. I had at that time the idea of giving up English and trying to settle down and scrape along in Paris and gradually write French. But it would have been a foolish idea even if I'd been much more bilingual than I ever was, because, for one thing, I don't think that one can be a bilingual poet. I don't know of any case in which a man wrote great or even fine poems equally well in two languages. I think one language must be the one you express yourself in, in poetry, and you've got to give up the other for that purpose. And I think that the English language really has more resources in some respects than the French. I think, in other words, I've probably done better in English than I ever would have in French even if I'd become as proficient in French as the poets you mentioned.

INTERVIEWER

Can I ask you if you have any plans for poems now?

ELIOT

No, I haven't any plans for anything at the moment, except that I think I would like, having just got rid of *The Elder Statesman* (I only passed the final proofs just before we left London), to do a little prose writing of a critical sort. I never think more than one step ahead. Do I want to do another play or do I want to do more poems? I don't know until I find I want to do it.

INTERVIEWER

Do you have any unfinished poems that you look at occasionally?

ELIOT

I haven't much in that way, no. As a rule, with me an unfinished thing is a thing that might as well be rubbed out. It's better, if there's something good in it that I might make use of elsewhere, to leave it at the back of my mind than on paper in a drawer. If I leave it in a drawer it remains the same thing but if it's in the memory it becomes transformed into something else. As I have said before, *Burnt Norton* began with bits that had to be cut out of *Murder in the Cathedral*. I learned in *Murder in the Cathedral* that it's no use putting in nice lines that you think are good poetry if they don't get the action on at all. That was when Martin Browne was useful. He would say, There are very nice lines here, but they've nothing to do with what's going on on stage.

INTERVIEWER

Are any of your minor poems actually sections cut out of longer works? There are two that sound like "The Hollow Men."

ELIOT

Oh, those were the preliminary sketches. Those things were earlier. Others I published in periodicals but not in my collected poems. You don't want to say the same thing twice in one book.

INTERVIEWER

You seem often to have written poems in sections. Did they begin as separate poems? I am thinking of "Ash Wednesday," in particular.

ELIOT

Yes, like "The Hollow Men," it originated out of separate poems. As I recall, one or two early drafts of parts of "Ash Wednesday" appeared in *Commerce* and elsewhere. Then gradually I came to see it as a sequence. That's one way in which my mind does seem to have worked throughout the years poetically—doing things separately and then seeing the possibility of fusing them together, altering them, and making a kind of whole of them.

INTERVIEWER

Do you write anything now in the vein of *Old Possum's Book of Practical Cats* or *King Bolo*?

ELIOT

Those things do come from time to time! I keep a few notes of such verse, and there are one or two incomplete cats that probably will never be written. There's one about a glamour cat. It turned out too sad. This would never do. I can't make my children weep over a cat who's gone wrong. She had a very questionable career, did this cat. It wouldn't do for the audience of my previous volume of cats. I've never done any dogs. Of course dogs don't seem to lend themselves to verse quite so well, collectively, as cats. I may eventually do an enlarged edition of my cats. That's more likely than another volume. I did add one poem, which was originally done as an advertisement for Faber and Faber. It seemed to be fairly successful. Oh, yes, one wants to keep one's hand in, you know, in every type of poem, serious and frivolous and proper and improper. One doesn't want to lose one's skill.

INTERVIEWER

There's a good deal of interest now in the process of writing. I wonder if you could talk more about your actual habits in writing verse. I've heard you composed on the typewriter.

ELIOT

Partly on the typewriter. A great deal of my new play, *The Elder Statesman*, was produced in pencil and paper, very roughly. Then I typed it myself first before my wife got to work on it. In typing myself I make alterations, very considerable ones. But whether I write or type, composition of any length, a play for example, means for me regular hours, say ten to one. I found that three hours a day is about all I can do of actual composing. I could do polishing perhaps later. I sometimes found at first that I wanted to go on longer, but when I looked at the stuff the next day, what I'd done after the three hours were up was never satisfactory. It's much better to stop and think about something else quite different.

INTERVIEWER

Did you ever write any of your nondramatic poems on schedule? Perhaps the *Four Quartets*?

ELIOT

Only "occasional" verse. The *Quartets* were not on schedule. Of course the first one was written in '35, but the three that were written during the war were more in fits and starts. In 1939, if there hadn't been a war I would probably have tried to write another play. And I think it's a very good thing I didn't have the opportunity. From my personal point of view, the one good thing the war did was to prevent me from writing another play too soon. I saw some of the things that were wrong with *Family Reunion*, but I think it was much better that any possible play was blocked for five years or so to get up a head of steam. The form of the *Quartets* fitted in very nicely to the conditions under which I was writing, or could write at all. I could write them in sections and I didn't have to have quite the same continuity; it didn't matter if a day or two elapsed when I did not write, as they frequently did, while I did war jobs.

INTERVIEWER

We have been mentioning your plays without talking about them. In *Poetry and Drama* you talked about your first plays. I wonder if you could tell us something about your intentions in *The Elder Statesman*.

ELIOT

I said something, I think, in *Poetry and Drama* about my ideal aims, which I never expect fully to realize. I started, really, from *The Family Reunion*, because *Murder in the Cathedral* is a period piece and something out of the ordinary. It is written in rather a special language, as you do when you're dealing with another period. It didn't solve any of the problems I was interested in. Later I thought that in *The Family Reunion* I was giving so much attention to the versification that I neglected the structure of the play. I think *The Family Reunion* is still the best of my plays in the way of poetry, although it's not very well constructed.

In *The Cocktail Party* and again in *The Confidential Clerk*, I went further in the way of structure. *The Cocktail Party* wasn't altogether satisfactory in that respect. It sometimes happens, disconcertingly, at any rate with a practitioner like myself, that it isn't always the things constructed most according to plan that are the most successful. People criticized the third act of *The Cocktail Party* as being rather an epilogue, so in *The Confidential Clerk* I wanted things to turn up in the third act that were fresh events. Of course, *The Confidential Clerk* was so well constructed in some ways that people thought it was just meant to be farce.

I wanted to get to learn the technique of the theater so well that I could then forget about it. I always feel it's not wise to violate rules until you know how to observe them.

I hope that *The Elder Statesman* goes further in getting more poetry in, at any rate, than *The Confidential Clerk* did. I don't feel that I've got to the point I aim at and I don't think I ever will, but I would like to feel I was getting a little nearer to it each time.

INTERVIEWER

Do you have a Greek model behind *The Elder Statesman?*

ELIOT

The play in the background is the *Oedipus at Colonus.* But I wouldn't like to refer to my Greek originals as models. I have always regarded them more as points of departure. That was one of the weaknesses of *The Family Reunion*; it was rather too close to the *Eumenides.* I tried to follow my original too literally and in that way led to confusion by mixing pre-Christian and post-Christian attitudes about matters of conscience and sin and guilt.

So in the subsequent three I have tried to take the Greek myth as a sort of springboard, you see. After all, what one gets essential and permanent, I think, in the old plays, is a situation. You can take the situation, rethink it in modern terms, develop your own characters from it, and let another plot develop out of that. Actually you get further and further away from the original. *The Cocktail Party* had to do with Alcestis simply because the question arose in my mind, what would the life of Admetus and Alcestis be, after she'd come back from the dead; I mean if there'd been a break like that, it couldn't go on just as before. Those two people were the center of the thing when I started and the other characters only developed out of it. The character of Celia, who came to be really the most important character in the play, was originally an appendage to a domestic situation.

INTERVIEWER

Do you still hold to the theory of levels in poetic drama (plot, character, diction, rhythm, meaning) that you put forward in 1932?

ELIOT

I am no longer very much interested in my own theories about poetic drama, especially those put forward before 1934. I have thought less about theories since I have given more time to writing for the theater.

INTERVIEWER

How does the writing of a play differ from the writing of poems?

ELIOT

I feel that they take quite different approaches. There is all the difference in the world between writing a play for an audience and writing a poem, in which you're writing primarily for yourself—although obviously you wouldn't be satisfied if the poem didn't mean something to other people afterward. With a poem you can say, I got my feeling into words for myself. I now have the equivalent in words for that much of what I have felt. Also in a poem you're writing for your own voice, which is very important. You're thinking in terms of your own voice, whereas in a play from the beginning you have to realize that you're preparing something that is going into the hands of other people, unknown at the time you're writing it. Of course I won't say there aren't moments in a play when the two approaches may not converge, when I think ideally they *should*. Very often in Shakespeare they do, when he is writing a poem and thinking in terms of the theater and the actors and the audience all at once. And the two things are one. That's wonderful when you can get that. With me it only happens at odd moments.

INTERVIEWER

Have you tried at all to control the speaking of your verse by the actors? To make it seem more like verse?

ELIOT

I leave that primarily to the producer. The important thing is to have a producer who has the feeling of verse and who can guide them in just how emphatic to make the verse, just how far to depart from prose or how far to approach it. I only guide the actors if they ask me questions directly. Otherwise I think that they should get their advice through the producer. The important thing is to arrive at an agreement with him first, and then leave it to him.

INTERVIEWER

Do you feel that there's been a general tendency in your work, even in your poems, to move from a narrower to a larger audience?

ELIOT

I think that there are two elements in this. One is that I think that writing plays—that is, *Murder in the Cathedral* and *The Family Reunion*—made a difference to the writing of the *Four Quartets*. I think that it led to a greater simplification of language and to speaking in a way which is more like conversing with your reader. I see the later *Quartets* as being much simpler and easier to understand than *The Waste Land* and "Ash Wednesday." Sometimes the thing I'm trying to say, the subject matter, may be difficult, but it seems to me that I'm saying it in a simpler way.

The other element that enters into it, I think, is just experience and maturity. I think that in the early poems it was a question of not being able to—of having more to say than one knew how to say, and having something one wanted to put into words and rhythm which one didn't have the command of words and rhythm to put in a way immediately apprehensible.

That type of obscurity comes when the poet is still at the stage of learning how to use language. You have to say the thing the difficult way. The only alternative is not saying it at all, at that stage. By the time of the *Four Quartets*, I couldn't have written in the style of *The Waste Land*. In *The Waste Land*, I wasn't even bothering whether I understood what I was saying. These things, however, become easier to people with time. You get used to having *The Waste Land*, or *Ulysses*, about.

INTERVIEWER

Do you feel that the *Four Quartets* are your best work?

ELIOT

Yes, and I'd like to feel that they get better as they go on. The second is better than the first, the third is better than the second, and the fourth is the best of all. At any rate, that's the way I flatter myself.

INTERVIEWER

This is a very general question, but I wonder if you could give advice to a young poet about what disciplines or attitudes he might cultivate to improve his art.

ELIOT

I think it's awfully dangerous to give general advice. I think the best one can do for a young poet is to criticize in detail a particular poem of his. Argue it with him if necessary; give him your opinion, and if there are any generalizations to be made, let him do them himself. I've found that different people have different ways of working and things come to them in different ways. You're never sure when you're uttering a statement that's generally valid for all poets or when it's something that only applies to yourself. I think nothing is worse than to try to form people in your own image.

INTERVIEWER

Do you think there's any possible generalization to be made about the fact that all the better poets now, younger than you, seem to be teachers?

ELIOT

I don't know. I think the only generalization that can be made of any value will be one which will be made a generation later. All you can say at this point is that at different times there are different possibilities of making a living, or different limitations on making a living. Obviously a poet has got to find a way of making a living apart from his poetry. After all, artists do a great deal of teaching, and musicians too.

INTERVIEWER

Do you think that the optimal career for a poet would involve no work at all but writing and reading?

ELIOT

No, I think that would be . . . But there again one can only talk about oneself. It is very dangerous to give an optimal career for everybody, but I feel quite sure that if I'd started by having independent means, if I hadn't had to bother about earning a living and could have given all my time to poetry, it would have had a deadening influence on me.

INTERVIEWER

Why?

ELIOT

I think that for me it's been very useful to exercise other activities, such as working in a bank, or publishing even. And I think also that the difficulty of not having as much time as I would like has given me a greater pressure of concentration. I mean it has prevented me from writing too much. The danger, as a rule, of having nothing else to do is that one might write too much rather than concentrating and perfecting smaller amounts. That would be *my* danger.

INTERVIEWER

Do you consciously attempt, now, to keep up with the poetry that is being written by young men in England and America?

ELIOT

I don't now, not with any conscientiousness. I did at one time when I was reading little reviews and looking out for new talent as a publisher. But as one gets older, one is not quite confident in one's own ability to distinguish new genius among younger men. You're always afraid that you are going as you have seen your elders go. At Faber and Faber now I have a younger colleague who reads poetry manuscripts. But even before that, when I came across new stuff that I thought had real merit, I would show it to younger friends whose critical judgment I trusted and get their opinion. But of course there is always the danger that there is merit where you don't see it. So I'd rather have younger people to look at things first. If they like it, they will show it to me, and see whether I like it too. When you get something that knocks over younger people of taste and judgment and older people as well, then that's likely to be something important. Sometimes there's a lot of resistance. I shouldn't like to feel that I was resisting, as my work was resisted when it was new, by people who thought that it was imposture of some kind or other.

INTERVIEWER

Do you feel that younger poets in general have repudiated the experimentalism of the early poetry of this century? Few poets now seem to be resisted the way you were resisted, but some older critics like Herbert Read believe that poetry after you has been a regression to outdated modes. When you talked about Milton the second time, you spoke of the function of poetry as a retarder of change, as well as a maker of change, in language.

ELIOT

Yes, I don't think you want a revolution every ten years.

INTERVIEWER

But is it possible to think that there has been a counterrevolution rather than an exploration of new possibilities?

ELIOT

No, I don't see anything that looks to me like a counterrevolution. After a period of getting away from the traditional forms, comes a period of curiosity in making new experiments with traditional forms. This can produce very good work if what has happened in between has made a difference: when it's not merely going back, but taking up an old form, which has been out of use for a time, and making something new with it. That is not counterrevolution. Nor does mere regression deserve the name. There is a tendency in some quarters to revert to Georgian scenery and sentiments; and among the public there are always people who prefer mediocrity, and when they get it, say, What a relief! Here's some real poetry again. And there are also people who like poetry to be modern but for whom the really creative stuff is too strong—they need something diluted.

What seems to me the best of what I've seen in young poets is not reaction at all. I'm not going to mention any names, for I don't like to make public judgments about younger poets. The best stuff is a further development of a less revolutionary character than what appeared in earlier years of the century.

INTERVIEWER

I have some unrelated questions that I'd like to end with. In 1945 you wrote, "A poet must take as his material his own language as it is actually spoken around him." And later you wrote, "The music of poetry, then, will be a music latent in the common speech of his time." After the second remark, you disparaged "standardized BBC English." Now isn't one of the changes of the last fifty years, and perhaps even more of the last five years, the growing dominance of commercial speech through the means of communication? What you referred to as "BBC English" has become immensely more powerful through the ITA and BBC television, not to speak of CBS, NBC, and ABC. Does this development make the problem of the poet and his relationship to common speech more difficult?

ELIOT

You've raised a very good point there. I think you're right, it does make it more difficult.

INTERVIEWER

I wanted *you* to make the point.

ELIOT

Yes, but you wanted the point to be *made*. So I'll take the responsibility of making it: I do think that where you have these modern means of communication and means of imposing the speech and idioms of a small number on the mass of people at large, it does complicate the problem very much. I don't know to what extent that goes for film speech, but obviously radio speech has done much more.

INTERVIEWER

I wonder if there's a possibility that what you mean by common speech will disappear.

ELIOT

That is a very gloomy prospect. But very likely indeed.

INTERVIEWER

Are there other problems for a writer in our time that are unique? Does the prospect of human annihilation have any particular effect on the poet?

ELIOT

I don't see why the prospect of human annihilation should affect the poet differently from men of other vocations. It will affect him as a human being, no doubt in proportion to his sensitiveness.

INTERVIEWER

Another unrelated question: I can see why a man's criticism is better for his being a practicing poet, better, although subject to his own prejudices. But do you feel that writing criticism has helped you as a poet?

ELIOT

In an indirect way it has helped me somehow as a poet—to put down in writing my critical valuation of the poets who have influenced me and whom I admire. It is merely making an influence more conscious and more articulate. It's been a rather natural impulse. I think probably my best critical essays are essays on the poets who had influenced me, so to speak, long before I thought of writing essays about them. They're of more value, probably, than any of my more generalized remarks.

INTERVIEWER

G. S. Fraser wonders, in an essay about the two of you, whether you ever met Yeats. From remarks in your talk about him, it would seem that you did. Could you tell us the circumstances?

ELIOT

Of course I had met Yeats many times. Yeats was always very gracious when one met him and had the art of treating younger writers as if they were his equals and contemporaries. I can't remember any one particular occasion.

INTERVIEWER

I have heard that you consider that your poetry belongs in the tradition of American literature. Could you tell us why?

ELIOT

I'd say that my poetry has obviously more in common with my distinguished contemporaries in America than with anything written in my generation in England. That I'm sure of.

INTERVIEWER

Do you think there's a connection with the American past?

ELIOT

Yes, but I couldn't put it any more definitely than that, you see. It wouldn't be what it is, and I imagine it wouldn't be so good; putting it as modestly as I can, it wouldn't be what it is if I'd been born in England, and it wouldn't be what it is if I'd stayed in America. It's a combination of things. But in its sources, in its emotional springs, it comes from America.

INTERVIEWER

One last thing. Seventeen years ago you said, "No honest poet can ever feel quite sure of the permanent value of what he has written. He may have wasted his time and messed up his life for nothing." Do you feel the same now, at seventy?

ELIOT

There may be honest poets who do feel sure. I don't.

Issue 21, 1959

Saul Bellow

The Art of Fiction

T he interview "took place" over a period of several weeks. Beginning with some exploratory discussions during May of 1965, it was shelved during the summer, and actually accomplished during September and October. Two recording sessions were held, totaling about an hour and a half, but this was only a small part of the effort Mr. Bellow gave to this interview. A series of meetings, for over five weeks, was devoted to the most careful revision of the original material. Recognizing at the outset the effort he would make for such an interview, he had real reluctance about beginning it at all. Once his decision had been reached, however, he gave a remarkable amount of his time freely to the task—up to two hours a day, at least twice and often three times a week throughout the entire five-week period. It had become an opportunity, as he put it, to say some things which were important but which weren't being said.

Certain types of questions were ruled out in early discussions. Mr. Bellow was not interested in responding to criticisms of his work that he found trivial or stupid. He quoted the Jewish proverb that a fool can throw a stone into the water that ten wise men cannot recover. Nor did he wish to discuss what he considered his personal writing habits, whether he used a pen or typewriter, how hard he pressed on the page. For the artist to give such loving attention to his own shoelaces was dangerous, even immoral. Finally, there were certain questions that led into too "wide spaces" for this interview, subjects for fuller treatment on other occasions.

Then she came to a decision and turned to him again with the same abruptness. She was a pretty woman, but stiff, very stiff, bony looking ~~without~~ self confidence.

96 ——

HERZOG 10|12|24 TR-OS (VIKING)　　　　　　4591

what did he call it?

"We're all right."

"Comfortably settled? Liking Chicago? Little Ephraim still in the Lab School?"

"Yes."

"And the Temple? I see that Val taped a program with Rabbi Itzkowitz—Hasidic Judaism, Martin Buber, *I and Thou*. He's very thick with these rabbis. Maybe he wants to swap wives with a rabbi. He'll work his way round from 'I and Thou' to 'Me and You'— 'You and Me, Kid!') I suppose you wouldn't go along with everything."

Still the Buber-kick!

But

'd draw the line there ① you

Phoebe made no answer and remained standing.

"Maybe you think I'll leave sooner if you don't sit. Come, Phoebe, sit down. I promise you I haven't come to make scenes. I have only one purpose here, in addition to wanting to see an old friend. . . ."

"We're not really old friends."

"Not by calendar years. But we were so close out in Ludeyville. That is true. You have to think of duration—Bergsonian duration. We have known each other in duration. Some people are *sentenced* to certain relationships." *Maybe every relationship is either a joy or a sentence?*

"You earned your own sentence, if that's how you want to think about it. We had a quiet life till you and Madeleine descended on Ludeyville and forced yourself on me." Phoebe, her face thin but hot, eyelids unmoving, sat down on the edge of the chair Herzog had drawn forward for her.

Say what you think, Phoebe. That's what I want.

"Good. Sit back. Don't be afraid. I'm not looking for trouble. We've got a problem in common."

Phoebe denied this. She shook her head, with a stubborn look, all too vigorously. "I'm a plain woman. Valentine is from upstate New York."

Didn't even know how to deal a number.

"Just a rube. Yes. Knows nothing about fancy vices from the big city. Had to be led step by step into degeneracy by me—Moses E. Herzog."

Stiff and hesitant, she turned her body aside in her abrupt way, then ~~her decision reached~~, turned just as abruptly to him again. "You never understood a thing about him. He fell for you. Adored you. Tried to become an intellectual because he wanted to help you—saw what a terrible thing you had done in giving up your respectable university position and how reckless you were, rushing out to the country with Madeleine. He thought she was ruining you and tried to set you on the right track again. He read all those books so you'd have somebody to talk to, out in the sticks, Moses. Because you needed help, praise, flattery, support, affection. It never was enough. You wore him out." *It nearly killed him, trying to buck you up.*

she came to a

"Yes. ? What else? Go on," said Herzog.

"It's still not enough. What do you want from him now? What are you here for? More excitement? Are you still greedy for ~~kit~~ *excitement?*"

Herzog no longer smiled. "Some of what you say is right enough, Phoebe. I was certainly floundering in Ludeyville. But you take the wind out of me when you say you were leading a perfectly

Final galley proof of *Herzog*.

The two tapes were made in Bellow's University of Chicago office on the fifth floor of the Social Sciences Building. The office, though large, is fairly typical of those on the main quadrangles: much of it rather dark with one brightly lighted area, occupied by his desk, immediately before a set of three dormer windows; dark-green metal bookcases line the walls, casually used as storage for a miscellany of books, magazines, and correspondence. A set of *The Complete Works of Rudyard Kipling* ("it was given to me") shares space with examination copies of new novels and with a few of Bellow's own books, including recent French and Italian translations of *Herzog*. A table, a couple of typing stands, and various decrepit and mismatched chairs are scattered in apparently haphazard fashion throughout the room. A wall rack just inside the door holds his jaunty black felt hat and his walking cane. There is a general sense of disarray, with stacks of papers, books, and letters lying everywhere. When one comes to the door, Bellow is frequently at his typing stand, rapidly pounding out on a portable machine responses to some of the many letters he gets daily. Occasionally a secretary enters and proceeds to type away on some project at the far end of the room.

During the two sessions with the tape recorder, Bellow sat at his desk, between the eaves that project prominently into the room, backlighted by the dormer windows that let in the bright afternoon sun from the south. Four stories below lie Fifty-ninth Street and the Midway, their automobile and human noises continually penetrating the office. As the questions were asked, Bellow listened carefully and often developed an answer slowly, pausing frequently to think out the exact phrasing he sought. His answers were serious, but full of his special quality of humor. He took obvious pleasure in the amusing turns of thought with which he often concluded an answer. Throughout, he was at great pains to make his ideas transparent to the interviewer, asking repeatedly if this was clear or if he should say more on the subject. His concentration during these sessions was intense enough to be tiring, and both tapes were brought to a close with his confessing to some exhaustion.

Following each taping session, a typescript of his remarks was prepared. Bellow worked over these typed sheets extensively with pen and ink, taking as many as three separate meetings to do a complete revision. Then another typescript was made, and the process started over. This work was done when the interviewer could be present, and again the changes were frequently tested on him. Generally these sessions occurred at Bellow's office or at his apartment, overlooking the Outer Drive and Lake Michigan. Once, however, revisions were made while he and the interviewer sat on a Jackson Park bench on a fine October afternoon, and one typescript was worked on along with beer and hamburgers at a local bar.

Revisions were of various sorts. Frequently there were slight changes in meaning: "That's what I really meant to say." Other alterations tightened up his language or were in the nature of stylistic improvements. Any sections that he judged to be excursions from the main topic were deleted. Most regretted by the interviewer were prunings that eliminated certain samples of the characteristic Bellow wit: in a few places he came to feel he was simply "exhibiting" himself, and these were scratched out. On the other hand, whenever he could substitute for conventional literary diction an unexpected colloquial turn of phrase—which often proved humorous in context—he did so.

—*Gordon Lloyd Harper, 1966*

INTERVIEWER

Some critics have felt that your work falls within the tradition of American naturalism, possibly because of some things you've said about Dreiser. I was wondering if you saw yourself in a particular literary tradition?

SAUL BELLOW

Well, I think that the development of realism in the nineteenth century is still the major event of modern literature. Dreiser, a realist of course, had elements of genius. He was clumsy, cumbersome, and in some respects a poor thinker. But he was rich in a kind of feeling that has been ruled off the grounds by many contemporary writers— the kind of feeling that every human being intuitively recognizes as primary. Dreiser has more open access to primary feelings than any American writer of the twentieth century. It makes a good many people uncomfortable that his emotion has not found a more developed literary form. It's true his art may be too "natural." He sometimes conveys his understanding by masses of words, verbal approximations. He blunders, but generally in the direction of truth. The result is that we are moved in an unmediated way by his characters, as by life, and then we say that his novels are simply torn from the side of life, and therefore not novels. But we can't escape reading them. He somehow conveys, without much refinement, depths of feeling that we usually associate with Balzac or Shakespeare.

INTERVIEWER

This realism, then, is a particular kind of sensibility, rather than a technique?

BELLOW

Realism specializes in *apparently* unmediated experiences. What stirred Dreiser was simply the idea that you could bring unmediated feeling to the novel. He took it up naively without going to the trouble of mastering an art. We don't see this because he makes so many familiar "art" gestures, borrowed from the art-fashions of his day, and even from the slick magazines, but he is really a natural, a primitive. I have great respect for his simplicities and I think they are worth more than much that has been praised as high art in the American novel.

INTERVIEWER

Could you give me an example of what you mean?

BELLOW

In a book like *Jennie Gerhardt*, the delicacy with which Jennie allows Lester Kane to pursue his conventional life while she herself lives unrecognized with her illegitimate daughter, the depth of her understanding, and the depth of her sympathy and of her truthfulness impress me. She is not a sentimental figure. She has a natural sort of honor.

INTERVIEWER

Has recent American fiction pretty much followed this direction?

BELLOW

Well, among his heirs there are those who believe that clumsiness and truthfulness go together. But cumbersomeness does not necessarily imply a sincere heart. Most of the Dreiserians lack talent. On the other hand, people who put Dreiser down, adhering to a "high art" standard for the novel, miss the point.

INTERVIEWER

Aside from Dreiser, what other American writers do you find particularly of interest?

BELLOW

I like Hemingway, Faulkner, and Fitzgerald. I think of Hemingway as a man who developed a significant manner as an artist, a lifestyle that is important. For his generation, his language created a lifestyle, one that pathetic old gentlemen are still found clinging to. I don't think of Hemingway as a great novelist. I like Fitzgerald's novels better, but I often feel about Fitzgerald that he couldn't distinguish between innocence and social climbing. I am thinking of *The Great Gatsby*.

INTERVIEWER

If we go outside American literature, you've mentioned that you read the nineteenth-century Russian writers with a good deal of interest. Is there anything particular about them that attracts you?

BELLOW

Well, the Russians have an immediate charismatic appeal—excuse the Max Weberism. Their conventions allow them to express freely their feelings about nature and human beings. We have inherited a more restricted and imprisoning attitude toward the emotions. We have to work around puritanical and stoical restraints. We lack the Russian openness. Our path is narrower.

INTERVIEWER

In what other writers do you take special interest?

BELLOW

I have a special interest in Joyce; I have a special interest in Lawrence. I read certain poets over and over again. I can't say where they belong in my theoretical scheme; I only know that I have an attachment to them. Yeats is one such poet. Hart Crane is another. Hardy and Walter de la Mare. I don't know what these have in common—probably nothing. I know that I am drawn repeatedly to these men.

INTERVIEWER

It's been said that one can't like *both* Lawrence and Joyce, that one has to choose between them. You don't feel this way?

BELLOW

No. Because I really don't take Lawrence's sexual theories very seriously. I take his art seriously, not his doctrine. But he himself warned us repeatedly not to trust the artist. He said trust the work itself. So I have little use for the Lawrence who wrote *The Plumed Serpent* and great admiration for the Lawrence who wrote *The Lost Girl*.

INTERVIEWER

Does Lawrence at all share the special feeling you find attractive in Dreiser?

BELLOW

A certain openness to experience, yes. And a willingness to trust one's instinct, to follow it freely—that Lawrence has.

INTERVIEWER

You mentioned before the interview that you would prefer not to talk about your early novels, that you feel you are a different person now from what you were then. I wonder if this is all you want to say, or if you can say something about how you have changed.

BELLOW

I think that when I wrote those early books I was timid. I still felt the incredible effrontery of announcing myself to the world (in part I mean the WASP world) as a writer and an artist. I had to touch a great many bases, demonstrate my abilities, pay my respects to formal requirements. In short, I was afraid to let myself go.

INTERVIEWER

When do you find a significant change occurring?

BELLOW

When I began to write *Augie March*. I took off many of these restraints. I think I took off too many, and went too far, but I was feeling the excitement of discovery. I had just increased my freedom, and like any emancipated plebeian I abused it at once.

INTERVIEWER

What were these restraints that you took off in *Augie March*?

BELLOW

My first two books are well made. I wrote the first quickly but took great pains with it. I labored with the second and tried to make it letter-perfect. In writing *The Victim* I accepted a Flaubertian standard. Not a bad standard, to be sure, but one which, in the end, I found repressive—repressive because of the circumstances of my life and because of my upbringing in Chicago as the son of immigrants. I could not, with such an instrument as I developed in the first two books, express a variety of things I knew intimately. Those books, though useful, did not give me a form in which I felt comfortable. A writer should be able to express himself easily, naturally, copiously in a form that frees his mind, his energies. Why should he hobble himself with formalities? With a borrowed sensibility? With the desire to be "correct"? Why should I force myself to write like an Englishman or a contributor to *The New Yorker*? I soon saw that it was simply not in me to be a mandarin. I should add that for a young man in my position there were social inhibitions too. I had good reason to fear that I would be put down as a foreigner, an interloper. It was made clear to me when I studied literature in the university that as a Jew and the son of Russian Jews I would probably never have the right *feeling* for Anglo-Saxon traditions, for English words. I realized even in college that the people who told me this were not necessarily disinterested friends. But they had an effect on me, nevertheless. This was something from which I had to free myself. I fought free because I had to.

INTERVIEWER

Are these social inhibitors as powerful today as they were when you wrote *Dangling Man*?

BELLOW

I think I was lucky to have grown up in the Midwest, where such influences are less strong. If I'd grown up in the East and attended an Ivy League university, I might have been damaged more badly. Puritan and Protestant America carries less weight in Illinois than in Massachusetts. But I don't bother much with such things now.

INTERVIEWER

Did another change in your writing occur between *Augie March* and *Herzog*? You've mentioned writing *Augie March* with a great sense of freedom, but I take it that *Herzog* was a very difficult book to write.

BELLOW

It was. I had to tame and restrain the style I developed in *Augie March* in order to write *Henderson* and *Herzog*. I think both those books reflect that change in style. I wouldn't really know how to describe it. I don't care to trouble my mind to find an exact description for it, but it has something to do with a kind of readiness to record impressions arising from a source of which we know little. I suppose that all of us have a primitive prompter or commentator within, who from earliest years has been advising us, telling us what the real world is. There is such a commentator in me. I have to prepare the ground for him. From this source come words, phrases, syllables; sometimes only sounds, which I try to interpret, sometimes whole paragraphs, fully punctuated. When E. M. Forster said, "How do I know what I think until I see what I say?" he was perhaps referring to his own prompter. There is that observing instrument in us—in childhood at any rate. At the sight of a man's face, his shoes, the color of light, a woman's mouth or perhaps her ear, one receives a word, a phrase, at times nothing but a nonsense syllable from the primitive commentator.

INTERVIEWER

So this change in your writing—

BELLOW

—was an attempt to get nearer to that primitive commentator.

INTERVIEWER

How do you go about getting nearer to him, preparing the way for him?

BELLOW

When I say the commentator is primitive, I don't mean that he's crude; God knows he's often fastidious. But he won't talk until the situation's right. And if you prepare the ground for him with too many difficulties underfoot, he won't say anything. I must be terribly given to fraud and deceit because I sometimes have great difficulty preparing a suitable ground. This is why I've had so much trouble with my last two novels. I appealed directly to my prompter. The prompter, however, has to find the occasion perfect—that is to say, truthful, and necessary. If there is any superfluity or inner falsehood in the preparations, he is aware of it. I have to stop. Often I have to begin again, with the first word. I can't remember how many times I wrote *Herzog*. But at last I did find the acceptable ground for it.

Do these preparations include your coming to some general conception of the work?

Well, I don't know exactly how it's done. I let it alone a good deal. I try to avoid common forms of strain and distortion. For a long time, perhaps from the middle of the nineteenth century, writers have not been satisfied to regard themselves simply as writers. They have required also a theoretical framework. Most often they have been their own theoreticians, have created their own ground as artists, and have provided an exegesis for their own works. They have found it necessary to take a position, not merely to write novels. In bed last night I was reading a collection of articles by Stendhal. One of them amused me very much, touched me. Stendhal was saying how lucky writers were in the age of Louis XIV not to have anyone take them very seriously. Their obscurity was very valuable. Corneille had been dead for several days before anyone at court considered the fact important enough to mention. In the nineteenth century, says Stendhal, there would have been several public orations, Corneille's funeral covered by all the papers. There are great advantages in not being taken *too* seriously. Some writers are excessively serious about themselves. They accept the ideas of the "cultivated public." There is such a thing as overcapitalizing the *A* in artist. Certain writers and musicians understand this. Stravinsky says the composer should practice his trade exactly as a shoemaker does. Mozart and Haydn accepted commissions—wrote to order. In the nineteenth century, the artist loftily waited for *inspiration*. Once you elevate yourself to the rank of a cultural institution, you're in for a lot of trouble.

Then there is a minor modern disorder—the disease of people who live by an image of themselves created by papers, television, Broadway, Sardi's, gossip, or the public need for celebrities. Even buffoons, prizefighters, and movie stars have caught the bug. I avoid these "images." I have a longing, not for downright obscurity—I'm too egotistical for that—but for peace, and freedom from meddling.

INTERVIEWER

In line with this, the enthusiastic response to *Herzog* must have affected your life considerably. Do you have any thoughts as to why this book became and remained the bestseller it did?

BELLOW

I don't like to agree with the going view that if you write a bestseller it's because you betrayed an important principle or sold your soul. I know that sophisticated opinion believes this. And although I don't take much stock in sophisticated opinion, I have examined my conscience. I've tried to find out whether I had unwittingly done wrong. But I haven't yet discovered the sin. I do think that a book like *Herzog*, which ought to have been an obscure book with a total sale of eight thousand, has such a reception because it appeals to the unconscious sympathies of many people. I know from the mail I've received that the book described a common predicament. *Herzog* appealed to Jewish readers, to those who have been divorced, to those who talk to themselves, to college graduates, readers of paperbacks, autodidacts, to those who yet hope to live awhile, etc.

INTERVIEWER

Do you feel there were deliberate attempts at lionizing by the literary tastemakers? I was thinking that the recent deaths of Faulkner and Hemingway have been seen as creating a vacuum in American letters, which we all know is abhorrent.

BELLOW

Well, I don't know whether I would say a vacuum. Perhaps a pigeonhole. I agree that there is a need to keep the pigeonholes filled and that people are uneasy when there are vacancies. Also the mass media demand material—grist—and literary journalists have to create a major-league atmosphere in literature. The writers don't offer to fill the pigeonholes. It's the critics who want figures in the pantheon. But there are many people who assume that every writer must be bucking for the niche. Why should writers wish to be rated—seeded—like tennis players? Handicapped like racehorses? What an epitaph for a novelist: He won all the polls!

INTERVIEWER

How much are you conscious of the reader when you write? Is there an ideal audience that you write for?

BELLOW

I have in mind another human being who will understand me. I count on this. Not on perfect understanding, which is Cartesian, but on approximate understanding, which is Jewish. And on a meeting of sympathies, which is human. But I have no ideal reader in my head, no. Let me just say this, too. I seem to have the blind self-acceptance of the eccentric who can't conceive that his eccentricities are not clearly understood.

INTERVIEWER

So there isn't a great deal of calculation about rhetoric?

BELLOW

These are things that can't really be contrived. People who talk about contrivance must think that a novelist is a man capable of building a skyscraper to conceal a dead mouse. Skyscrapers are not raised simply to conceal mice.

INTERVIEWER

It's been said that contemporary fiction sees man as a victim. You gave this title to one of your early novels, yet there seems to be very strong opposition in your fiction to seeing man as simply determined or futile. Do you see any truth to this claim about contemporary fiction?

BELLOW

Oh, I think that realistic literature from the first has been a victim literature. Pit any ordinary individual—and realistic literature concerns itself with ordinary individuals—against the external world, and the external world will conquer him, of course. Everything that people believed in the nineteenth century about determinism, about man's place in nature, about the power of productive forces in society, made it inevitable that the hero of the realistic novel should not be a hero but a sufferer who is eventually overcome. So I was doing nothing very original by writing another realistic novel about a common man and calling it *The Victim*. I suppose I was discovering independently the essence of much of modern realism. In my innocence, I put my finger on it. Serious realism also contrasts the common man with aristocratic greatness. He is overborne by fate, just as the great are in Shakespeare or Sophocles. But this contrast, inherent in literary tradition, always damages him. In the end the force of tradition carries realism into parody, satire, mock epic—Leopold Bloom.

INTERVIEWER

Haven't you yourself moved away from the suggestion of plebeian tragedy toward a treatment of the sufferer that has greater comic elements? Although the concerns and difficulties are still fundamentally serious, the comic elements in *Henderson*, in *Herzog*, even in *Seize the Day* seem much more prominent than in *Dangling Man* or *The Victim*.

BELLOW

Yes, because I got very tired of the solemnity of complaint, altogether impatient with complaint. Obliged to choose between complaint and comedy, I choose comedy, as more energetic, wiser, and manlier. This is really one reason why I dislike my own early novels. I find them plaintive, sometimes querulous. *Herzog* makes comic use of complaint.

INTERVIEWER

When you say that you are obliged to choose between complaint and comedy, does it mean this is the only choice—that you are limited to choosing between just these two alternatives?

BELLOW

I'm not inclined to predict what will happen. I may feel drawn to comedy again, I may not. But modern literature was dominated by a tone of elegy from the twenties to the fifties, the atmosphere of Eliot in *The Waste Land* and that of Joyce in *A Portrait of the Artist as a Young Man*. Sensibility absorbed this sadness, this view of the artist as the only contemporary link with an age of gold, forced to watch the sewage flowing in the Thames, every aspect of modern civilization doing violence to his (artist-patrician) feelings. This went much farther than it should have been allowed to go. It descended to absurdities, of which I think we have had enough.

INTERVIEWER

I wonder if you could say something about how important the environments are in your works. I take it that for the realist tradition the context in which the action occurs is of vital importance. You set your novels in Chicago, New York, as far away as Africa. How important are these settings for the fiction?

BELLOW

Well, you present me with a problem to which I think no one has the answer. People write realistically but at the same time they want to create environments that are somehow desirable, which are surrounded by atmospheres in which behavior becomes significant, which display the charm of life. What is literature without these things? Dickens's London is gloomy, but also cozy. And yet realism has always offered to annihilate precisely such qualities. That is to say, if you want to be ultimately realistic you bring artistic space itself in danger. In Dickens, there is no void beyond the fog. The environment is human, at all times. Do you follow me?

INTERVIEWER

I'm not sure I do.

BELLOW

The realistic tendency is to challenge the human significance of things. The more realistic you are the more you threaten the grounds of your own art. Realism has always both accepted and rejected the circumstances of ordinary life. It accepted the task of writing about ordinary life and tried to meet it in some extraordinary fashion. As Flaubert did. The subject might be common, low, degrading; all this was to be redeemed by art. I really do see those Chicago environments as I represent them. They suggest their own style of presentation. I elaborate it.

INTERVIEWER

Then you aren't especially disturbed by readers of *Henderson*, for example, who say that Africa really isn't like that? One sort of realist would require a writer to spend several years on location before daring to place his characters there. You're not troubled by him, I take it?

BELLOW

Perhaps you should say "factualist" rather than "realist." Years ago, I studied African ethnography with the late Professor Herskovits. Later he scolded me for writing a book like *Henderson*. He said the subject was much too serious for such fooling. I felt that my fooling was fairly serious. Literalism, factualism, will smother the imagination altogether.

INTERVIEWER

You have on occasion divided recent American fiction into what you call the "cleans" and the "dirties." The former, I gather, tend to be conservative and easily optimistic, the latter the eternal naysayers, rebels, iconoclasts. Do you feel this is still pretty much the picture of American fiction today?

BELLOW

I feel that both choices are rudimentary and pitiful, and though I know the uselessness of advocating any given path to other novelists, I am still inclined to say, Leave both these extremes. They are useless, childish. No wonder the really powerful men in our society, whether politicians or scientists, hold writers and poets in contempt. They do it because they get no evidence from modern literature that anybody is thinking about any significant question. What does the radicalism of radical writers nowadays amount to? Most of it is hand-me-down bohemianism, sentimental populism, D. H. Lawrence-and-water, or imitation Sartre. For American writers radicalism is a question of honor. They must be radicals for the sake of their dignity. They see it as their function, and a noble function, to say *nay*, and to bite not only the hand that feeds them (and feeds them with comic abundance, I might add) but almost any other hand held out to them. Their radicalism, however, is contentless. A genuine radicalism, which truly challenges authority, we need desperately. But a radicalism of posture is easy and banal. Radical criticism requires knowledge, not posture, not slogans, not rant. People who maintain their dignity as artists, in a small way, by being mischievous on television, simply delight the networks and the public. True radicalism requires homework—thought. Of the cleans, on the other hand, there isn't much to say. They seem faded.

INTERVIEWER

Your context is essentially that of the modern city, isn't it? Is there a reason for this beyond the fact that you come out of an urban experience?

BELLOW

Well, I don't know how I could possibly separate my knowledge of life, such as it is, from the city. I could no more tell you how deeply it's gotten into my bones than the lady who paints radium dials in the clock factory can tell you.

INTERVIEWER

You've mentioned the distractive character of modern life. Would this be most intense in the city?

BELLOW

The volume of judgments one is called upon to make depends upon the receptivity of the observer, and if one is very receptive, one has a terrifying number of opinions to render—what do you think about this, about that, about Vietnam, about city planning, about expressways, or garbage disposal, or democracy, or Plato, or pop art, or welfare states, or literacy in a "mass society"? I wonder whether there will ever be enough tranquillity under modern circumstances to allow our contemporary Wordsworth to recollect anything. I feel that art has something to do with the achievement of stillness in the midst of chaos. A stillness that characterizes prayer, too, and the eye of the storm. I think that art has something to do with an arrest of attention in the midst of distraction.

INTERVIEWER

I believe you once said that it is the novel that must deal particularly with this kind of chaos, and that as a consequence certain forms appropriate to poetry or to music are not available to the novelist.

BELLOW

I'm no longer so sure of that. I think the novelist can avail himself of similar privileges. It's just that he can't act with the same purity or economy of means as the poet. He has to traverse a very muddy and noisy territory before he can arrive at a pure conclusion. He's more exposed to the details of life.

INTERVIEWER

Is there anything peculiar about the *kind* of distractions you see the novelist having to confront today? Is it just that there are more details, or is their quality different today from what it used to be?

BELLOW

The modern masterpiece of confusion is Joyce's *Ulysses*. There the mind is unable to resist experience. Experience in all its diversity, its pleasure and horror, passes through Bloom's head like an ocean through a sponge. The sponge can't resist; it has to accept whatever the waters bring. It also notes every microorganism that passes through it. This is what I mean. How much of this must the spirit suffer, in what detail is it obliged to receive this ocean with its human plankton? Sometimes it looks as if the power of the mind has been nullified by the volume of experiences. But of course this is assuming the degree of passivity that Joyce assumes in *Ulysses*. Stronger, more purposeful minds can demand order, impose order, select, disregard, but there is still the threat of disintegration under the particulars. A Faustian artist is unwilling to surrender to the mass of particulars.

INTERVIEWER

Some people have felt your protagonists are seeking the answer to a question that might be phrased: How is it possible today for a good man to live? I wonder if you feel there is any single recurring question like this in the novels?

BELLOW

I don't think that I've represented any really good men; no one is thoroughly admirable in any of my novels. Realism has restrained me too much for that. I should *like* to represent good men. I long to know who and what they are and what their condition might be. I often represent men who desire such qualities but seem unable to achieve them on any significant scale. I criticize this in myself. I find it a limitation.

INTERVIEWER

I'm sorry; what exactly is this limitation?

BELLOW

The fact that I have not discerned those qualities or that I have not shown them in action. Herzog wants very much to have effective virtues. But that's a source of comedy in the book. I think I am far more concerned with another matter, and I don't approach this as a problem with a ready answer. I see it rather as a piece of research, having to do with human characteristics or qualities that have no need of justification. It's an odd thing to do; it shouldn't be necessary to "justify" certain things. But there are many skeptical, rebellious, or simply nervous writers all around us, who, having existed a full twenty or thirty years in this universe, denounce or reject life because it fails to meet their standards as philosophical intellectuals. It seems to me that they can't know enough about it for confident denial. The mystery is too great. So when they knock at the door of mystery with the knuckles of cognition it is quite right that the door should open and some mysterious power should squirt them in the eye. I think a good deal of *Herzog* can be explained simply by the implicit assumption that existence, quite apart from any of our judgments, has value, that existence is worthful. Here it is possible, however, that the desire to go on with his creaturely career vulgarly betrays Herzog. He wants to live? What of it! The clay that frames him contains this common want. Simple *aviditas vitae*. Does a man deserve any credit for this?

INTERVIEWER

Would this help to explain, then, why many of the difficulties that Herzog's mind throws up for him throughout the novel don't ever seem to be *intellectually* resolved?

BELLOW

The book is not anti-intellectual, as some have said. It simply points to the comic impossibility of arriving at a synthesis that can satisfy modern demands. That is to say, full awareness of all major problems, together with the necessary knowledge of history, of science and philosophy. That's why Herzog paraphrases Thomas

Marshall, Woodrow Wilson's vice president, who said what this country needs is a good five-cent cigar. (I think it was Bugs Baer who said it first.) Herzog's version: What this country needs is a good five-cent synthesis.

INTERVIEWER

Do you find many contemporary writers attempting to develop such syntheses or insisting that significant fiction provide them?

BELLOW

Well, I don't know that too many American novelists, young or old, are tormenting their minds with these problems. Europeans do. I don't know that they can ever reach satisfactory results on the grounds they have chosen. At any rate, they write few good novels. But that leads us into some very wide spaces.

INTERVIEWER

Do the ideas in *Herzog* have any other major roles to play? The "anti-intellectual" charge seems to come from people who don't feel the ideas are essential either in motivating the action, the decisions Herzog makes, or in helping him to come through at the end.

BELLOW

To begin with, I suppose I should say something about the difference in the role ideas play in American literature. European literature—I speak now of the Continent—is intellectual in a different sense from ours. The intellectual hero of a French or a German novel is likely to be a philosophical intellectual, an ideological intellectual. We here, intellectuals—or the educated public—know that in our liberal democracy ideas become effective within an entirely different tradition. The lines are less clearly drawn. We do not expect thought to have results, say, in the moral sphere, or in the political, in quite the way a Frenchman would. To be an intellectual in the United States sometimes means to be immured in a private life in which one thinks, but thinks with some humiliating sense of how little thought can accomplish. To call therefore for a dramatic resolution in terms of ideas in an American novel is to demand something for which there is scarcely any precedent. My novel deals with the humiliating sense that results from the American mixture of private concerns and intellectual interests. This is something that most readers of the book seem utterly to have missed. Some, fortunately, have caught it. But in part *Herzog* is intended to bring to an end, under blinding light, a certain course of development. Many people feel a "private life" to be an affliction. In some sense it is a genuine affliction; it cuts one off from a common life. To me, a significant theme of *Herzog* is the imprisonment of the individual in a shameful and impotent privacy. He feels humiliated by it; he struggles comically with it; and he comes to realize at last that what he considered his intellectual "privilege" has proved to be another form of bondage. Anyone who misses this misses the point of the book. So that to say that Herzog is not motivated in his acts by ideas is entirely false. Any bildungsroman—and *Herzog* is, to use that heavy German term, a bildungsroman—concludes with the first step. The first *real* step. Any man who has rid himself of superfluous ideas in order to take that first step has done something significant. When people complain of a lack of ideas in novels, they may mean that they do not find familiar ideas, fashionable ideas. Ideas outside the "canon" they don't recognize. So, if what they mean is ideas à la Sartre or ideas à la Camus, they are quite right: there are few such in *Herzog*. Perhaps they mean that the thoughts of a man fighting for sanity and life are not suitable for framing.

INTERVIEWER

Herzog rejects certain of these fashionable ideas, doesn't he—the ideas à la Sartre or à la Camus?

BELLOW

I think he tests them first upon his own sense of life and against his own desperate need for clarity. With him these thoughts are not a game. Though he may laugh as he thinks them, his survival depends upon them. I didn't have him engage in full combat with figures like Sartre. If he had chosen to debate with Sartre in typical Herzogian fashion, he would perhaps have begun with Sartre's proposition that Jews exist only because of anti-Semitism, that the Jew has to choose between authentic and inauthentic existence, that authentic existence can never be detached from this anti-Semitism which determines it. Herzog might have remembered that for Sartre, the Jew exists because he is hated, not because he has a history, not because he has origins of his own—but simply because he is designated, created, in his Jewishness by an outrageous evil. Sartre offers a remedy for those Jews who are prepared to make the authentic choice: he extends to them the invitation to become Frenchmen. If this great prince of contemporary European philosophy offers Herzog ideas such as this to embrace (or dispute), who can blame him for his skepticism toward what is called, so respectfully, *thought*, toward contemporary intellectual fare? Often Herzog deals with ideas in negative fashion. He needs to dismiss a great mass of irrelevancy and nonsense in order to survive. Perhaps this was what I meant earlier when I said that we were called upon to make innumerable judgments. We can be consumed simply by the necessity to discriminate between multitudes of propositions. We have to dismiss a great number of thoughts if we are to have any creaturely or human life at all. It seems at times that we are on trial seven days a week answering the questions, giving a clear account of ourselves. But when does one live? How does one live if it is necessary to render ceaseless judgments?

INTERVIEWER

Herzog's rejection of certain ideas has been widely recognized, but—

BELLOW

—why he rejects them is not at all clear. Herzog's skepticism toward ideas is very deep. Though Jews are often accused of being "rootless" rationalists, a man like Herzog knows very well that habit, custom, tendency, temperament, inheritance, and the power to recognize real and human facts have equal weight with ideas.

INTERVIEWER

You've spoken also of the disabling effects of basing a novel on ideas. Does this mean structuring a novel according to a philosophical conception?

BELLOW

No, I have no objection to that, nor do I have any objection to basing novels on philosophical conceptions or anything else that works. But let us look at one of the dominant ideas of the century, accepted by many modern artists—the idea that humankind has reached a terminal point. We find this terminal assumption in writers like Joyce, Céline, Thomas Mann. In *Doktor Faustus* politics and art are joined in the destruction of civilization. Now here is an idea, found in some of the greatest novelists of the twentieth century. How good is this idea? Frightful things have happened, but is the apocalyptic interpretation true? The terminations did not fully terminate. Civilization is still here. The prophecies have not been borne out. Novelists are wrong to put an interpretation of history at the base of artistic creation—to speak "the last word." It is better that the novelist should trust his own sense of life. Less ambitious. More likely to tell the truth.

INTERVIEWER

Frequently in your fiction the hero strives to avoid being swallowed up by other people's ideas or versions of reality. On occasion you seem to present him with something like the whole range of contemporary alternatives—say, in *Augie March* or *Herzog*. Was this one of your intentions?

BELLOW

All these matters are really so complicated. Of course these books are somewhat concerned with free choice. I don't think that they pose the question successfully—the terms are not broad enough. I think I have let myself off easily. I seem to have asked in my books, How can one resist the controls of this vast society *without* turning into a nihilist, avoiding the absurdity of empty rebellion? I have asked, Are there other, more good-natured forms of resistance and free choice? And I suppose that, like most Americans, I have involuntarily favored the more comforting or melioristic side of the question. I don't mean that I ought to have been more "pessimistic," because I have found "pessimism" to be in most of its forms nearly as empty as "optimism." But I am obliged to admit that I have not followed these questions to the necessary depth. I can't blame myself for not having been a stern moralist; I can always use the excuse that I'm after all nothing but a writer of fiction. But I don't feel satisfied with what I have done to date, except in the comic form. There is, however, this to be added—that our French friends invariably see the answers to such questions, and all questions of truth, to be overwhelmingly formidable, uncongenial, hostile to us. It may be, however, that truth is not always so punitive. I've tried to suggest this in my books. There may be truths on the side of life. I am quite prepared to admit that being habitual liars and self-deluders, we have good cause to fear the truth, but I'm not at all ready to stop hoping. There may be some truths that are, after all, our friends in the universe.

Jorge Luis Borges

The Art of Fiction

This interview was conducted in July of 1966, in conversations I held with Borges at his office in the Biblioteca Nacional, of which he is the director. The room, recalling an older Buenos Aires, is not really an office at all but a large, ornate, high-ceilinged chamber in the newly renovated library. On the walls—but far too high to be easily read, as if hung with diffidence—are various academic certificates and literary citations. There are also several Piranesi etchings, bringing to mind the nightmarish Piranesi ruin in Borges's story "The Immortal." Over the fireplace is a large portrait; when I asked Borges's secretary, Miss Susana Quinteros, about the portrait, she responded in a fitting, if unintentional echo of a basic Borgesean theme: "No importa. It's a reproduction of another painting."

At diagonally opposite corners of the room are two large, revolving bookcases that contain, Miss Quinteros explained, books Borges frequently consults, all arranged in a certain order and never varied so that Borges, who is nearly blind, can find them by position and size. The dictionaries, for instance, are set together, among them an old, sturdily rebacked, well-worn copy of *Webster's Encyclopedic Dictionary of the English Language* and an equally well-worn Anglo-Saxon dictionary. Among the other volumes, ranging from books in German and English on theology and philosophy to literature and history, are the complete *Pelican Guide to English Literature*, the Modern Library's *Selected Writings* of Francis Bacon, Hollander's *The Poetic Edda*, *The Poems of Catullus*, Forsyth's *Geometry of Four*

Research notes for "The Cult of the Phoenix," a short story by
Jorge Luis Borges.

Dimensions, several volumes of Harrap's English Classics, Park-
man's *The Conspiracy of Pontiac*, and the Chambers edition of *Beowulf*. Recently, Miss Quinteros said, Borges had been reading *The
American Heritage Picture History of the Civil War*, and just the
night before he had taken to his home—where his mother, who is in
her nineties, reads aloud to him—Washington Irving's *The Life of
Mahomet*.

Each day, late in the afternoon, Borges arrives at the library where
it is now his custom to dictate letters and poems, which Miss Quinteros types and reads back to him. Following his revisions, she
makes two or three, sometimes four, copies of each poem before
Borges is satisfied. Some afternoons she reads to him, and he carefully corrects her English pronunciation. Occasionally, when he
wants to think, Borges leaves his office and slowly circles the library's rotunda, high above the readers at the tables below. But he is
not always serious, Miss Quinteros stressed, confirming what one
might expect from his writing: "Always there are jokes, little practical jokes."

When Borges enters the library, wearing a beret and a dark gray
flannel suit hanging loosely from his shoulders and sagging over his
shoes, everyone stops talking for a moment, pausing perhaps out of
respect, perhaps out of empathetic hesitation for a man who is not entirely blind. His walk is tentative, and he carries a cane, which he uses
like a divining rod. He is short, with hair that looks slightly unreal in
the way it rises from his head. His features are vague, softened by age,
partially erased by the paleness of his skin. His voice, too, is unem-
phatic, almost a drone, seeming, possibly because of the unfocused
expression of his eyes, to come from another person behind the face;
his gestures and expressions are lethargic—characteristic is the invol-
untary droop of one eyelid. But when he laughs—and he laughs
often—his features wrinkle into what actually resembles a wry question mark; and he is apt to make a sweeping or clearing gesture with
his arm and to bring his hand down on the table. Most of his statements take the form of rhetorical questions, but in asking a genuine
question, Borges displays now a looming curiosity, now a shy, almost

pathetic incredulity. When he chooses, as in telling a joke, he adopts a crisp, dramatic tone; his quotation of a line from Oscar Wilde would do justice to an Edwardian actor. His accent defies easy classification: a cosmopolitan diction emerging from a Spanish background, educated by correct English speech and influenced by American movies. (Certainly no Englishman ever pronounced *piano* as "pieano," and no American says "a-nee-hilates" for *annihilates*.) The predominant quality of his articulation is the way his words slur softly into one another, allowing suffixes to dwindle so that *couldn't* and *could* are virtually indistinguishable. Slangy and informal when he wants to be, more typically he is formal and bookish in his English speech, relying, quite naturally, on phrases like "that is to say" and "wherein." Always his sentences are linked by the narrative "and then" or the logical "consequently."

But most of all, Borges is shy. Retiring, even self-obliterating, he avoids personal statement as much as possible and obliquely answers questions about himself by talking of other writers, using their words and even their books as emblems of his own thought.

In this interview it has been attempted to preserve the colloquial quality of his English speech—an illuminating contrast to his writings and a revelation of his intimacy with a language that has figured so importantly in the development of his writing.

—*Ronald Christ, 1967*

INTERVIEWER

You don't object to my recording our conversations?

JORGE LUIS BORGES

No, no. You fix the gadgets. They are a hindrance, but I will try to talk as if they're not there. Now where are you from?

INTERVIEWER

From New York.

BORGES

Ah, New York. I was there, and I liked it very much—I said to myself, Well, I have made this; this is my work.

INTERVIEWER

You mean the walls of the high buildings, the maze of streets?

BORGES

Yes. I rambled about the streets—Fifth Avenue—and got lost, but the people were always kind. I remember answering many questions about my work from tall, shy young men. In Texas they had told me to be afraid of New York, but I liked it. Well, are you ready?

INTERVIEWER

Yes, the machine is already working.

BORGES

Now, before we start, what kind of questions are they?

INTERVIEWER

Mostly about your own work and about English writers you have expressed an interest in.

BORGES

Ah, that's right. Because if you ask me questions about the younger contemporary writers, I'm afraid I know very little about them. For about the last seven years I've been doing my best to know something of Old English and Old Norse. Consequently, that's a long way off in time and space from the Argentine, from Argentine writers, no? But if I have to speak to you about the *Finnsburg Fragment* or the elegies or the *Battle of Brunanburg* . . .

INTERVIEWER

Would you like to talk about those?

No, not especially.

What made you decide to study Anglo-Saxon and Old Norse?

I began by being very interested in metaphor. And then in some book or other—I think in Andrew Lang's *History of English Literature*—I read about the kennings, metaphors of Old English, and in a far more complex fashion of Old Norse poetry. Then I went in for the study of Old English. Nowadays, or rather today, after several years of study, I'm no longer interested in the metaphors because I think that they were rather a weariness of the flesh to the poets themselves—at least to the Old English poets.

To repeat them, you mean?

To repeat them, to use them over and over again and to keep on speaking of the *hranrād, waelrād,* or "road of the whale" instead of "the sea"—that kind of thing—and "the seawood," "the stallion of the sea" instead of "the ship." So I decided finally to stop using them, the metaphors, that is; but in the meanwhile I had begun studying the language, and I fell in love with it. Now I have formed a group—we're about six or seven students—and we study almost every day. We've been going through the highlights in *Beowulf,* the *Finnsburg Fragment,* and *The Dream of the Rood.* Also, we've gotten into King Alfred's prose. Now we've begun learning Old Norse, which is rather akin to Old English. I mean the vocabularies are not really very different; Old English is a kind of halfway house between the Low German and the Scandinavian.

INTERVIEWER
Epic literature has always interested you very much, hasn't it?

BORGES
Always, yes. For example, there are many people who go to the cinema and cry. That has always happened; it has happened to me also. But I have never cried over sob stuff, or the pathetic episodes. But, for example, when I saw the first gangster films of Joseph von Sternberg, I remember that when there was anything epic about them—I mean Chicago gangsters dying bravely—well, I felt that my eyes were full of tears. I have felt epic poetry far more than lyric or elegy. I always felt that. Now that may be, perhaps, because I come from military stock. My grandfather, Colonel Francisco Borges Lafinur, fought in the border warfare with the Indians, and he died in a revolution; my great-grandfather, Colonel Suárez, led a Peruvian cavalry charge in one of the last great battles against the Spaniards; another great-great-uncle of mine led the vanguard of San Martin's army—that kind of thing. And I had, well, one of my great-great-grandmothers was a sister of Rosas*—I'm not especially proud of that relationship because I think of Rosas as being a kind of Perón in his day; but still all those things link me with Argentine history and also with the idea of a man's having to be brave, no?

INTERVIEWER
But the characters you pick as your epic heroes—the gangster, for example—are not usually thought of as epic, are they? Yet you seem to find the epic there?

BORGES
I think there is a kind of, perhaps, of low epic in him—no?

*Rosas, Juan Manuel de (1793–1877), an Argentine military dictator.

INTERVIEWER

Do you mean that since the old kind of epic is apparently no longer possible for us, we must look to this kind of character for our heroes?

BORGES

I think that as to epic poetry or as to epic literature, rather—if we except such writers as T. E. Lawrence in his *Seven Pillars of Wisdom* or some poets like Kipling, for example, in "Harp Song of the Dane Women" or even in the stories—I think nowadays, while literary men seem to have neglected their epic duties, the epic has been saved for us, strangely enough, by the Westerns.

INTERVIEWER

I have heard that you have seen the film *West Side Story* many times.

BORGES

Many times, yes. Of course, *West Side Story* is not a Western.

INTERVIEWER

No, but for you it has the same epic qualities?

BORGES

I think it has, yes. During this century, as I say, the epic tradition has been saved for the world by, of all places, Hollywood. When I went to Paris, I felt I wanted to shock people, and when they asked me—they knew that I was interested in the films, or that I had been, because my eyesight is very dim now—and they asked me, What kind of film do you like? And I said, Candidly, what I most enjoy are the Westerns. They were all Frenchmen; they fully agreed with me. They said, Of course we see such films as *Hiroshima mon amour* or *L'Année dernière à Marienbad* out of a sense of duty, but when we want to amuse ourselves, when we want to enjoy ourselves, when we want, well, to get a real kick, then we see American films.

INTERVIEWER

Then it is the content, the "literary" content of the film, rather than any of the technical aspects, that interests you?

BORGES

I know very little about the technical part of movies.

INTERVIEWER

If I may change the subject to your own fiction, I would like to ask about your having said that you were very timid about beginning to write stories.

BORGES

Yes, I was very timid because when I was young I thought of myself as a poet. So I thought, If I write a story, everybody will know I'm an outsider, that I am intruding in forbidden ground. Then I had an accident. You can feel the scar. If you touch my head here, you will see. Feel all those mountains, bumps? Then I spent a fortnight in a hospital. I had nightmares and sleeplessness—insomnia. After that they told me that I had been in danger, well, of dying, that it was really a wonderful thing that the operation had been successful. I began to fear for my mental integrity—I said, Maybe I can't write anymore. Then my life would have been practically over because literature is very important to me. Not because I think my own stuff particularly good, but because I know that I can't get along without writing. If I don't write, I feel, well, a kind of remorse, no? Then I thought I would try my hand at writing an article or a poem. But I thought, I have written hundreds of articles and poems. If I can't do it, then I'll know at once that I am done for, that everything is over with me. So I thought I'd try my hand at something I hadn't done; if I couldn't do it, there would be nothing strange about it because why should I write short stories? It would prepare me for the final overwhelming blow: knowing that I was at the end of my tether. I wrote a story called, let me see, I think, "Hombre de la esquina rosada,"* and everyone enjoyed it very much. It was a great relief to me. If it hadn't been for that particular knock on the head I got, perhaps I would never have written short stories.

INTERVIEWER

And perhaps you would never have been translated?

BORGES

And no one would have thought of translating me. So it was a blessing in disguise. Those stories, somehow or other, made their way: They got translated into French, I won the Prix Formentor, and then I seemed to be translated into many tongues. The first translator was Ibarra. He was a close friend of mine, and he translated the stories into French. I think he greatly improved upon them, no?

INTERVIEWER

Ibarra, not Caillois, was the first translator?

BORGES

He and Roger Caillois.† At a ripe old age, I began to find that many people were interested in my work all over the world. It seems strange, many of my writings have been done into English, into Swedish, into French, into Italian, into German, into Portuguese, into some of the Slav languages, into Danish. And always this comes as a great surprise to me because I remember I published a book—

---

*This is, perhaps, a slip of memory: the story was "Pierre Menard, autor del Quijote," published in *Sur*, number 56 (May 1939). Borges had, in fact, written two short stories before this story—"The Approach to Al-Mu'lasim" (1938), a review of a book that did not exist (similar to the "Pierre Menard" story), and "Hombre de la esquina rosada," his first short story, originally published in *A Universal History of Iniquity* in 1935. The Prix Formentor, mentioned later in this interview, was for Borges story collection *Ficciones*, which did not include "Hombre de la esquina rosada."
†Caillois was the publisher.

that must have been way back in 1932, I think*—and at the end of the year I found out that no less than thirty-seven copies had been sold!

Was that the *Universal History of Infamy*?

No, no. *History of Eternity*. At first I wanted to find every single one of the buyers to apologize because of the book and also to thank them for what they had done. There is an explanation for that. If you think of thirty-seven people—those people are real, I mean every one of them has a face of his own, a family, he lives on his own particular street. Why, if you sell, say two thousand copies, it is the same thing as if you had sold nothing at all because two thousand is too vast—I mean, for the imagination to grasp. While thirty-seven people—perhaps thirty-seven are too many, perhaps seventeen would have been better, or even seven—but still thirty-seven are still within the scope of one's imagination.

Speaking of numbers, I notice in your stories that certain numbers occur repeatedly.

Oh, yes. I'm awfully superstitious. I'm ashamed about it. I tell myself that after all, superstition is, I suppose, a slight form of madness, no?

Or of religion?

*It was 1936.

BORGES

Well, religion, but . . . I suppose that if one attained one hundred and fifty years of age, one would be quite mad, no? Because all those small symptoms would have been growing. Still, I see my mother, who is ninety, and she has far fewer superstitions than I have. Now, when I was reading, for the tenth time, I suppose, Boswell's *Johnson*, I found that he was full of superstition, and at the same time, that he had a great fear of madness. In the prayers he composed, one of the things he asked God was that he should not be a madman, so he must have been worried about it.

INTERVIEWER

Would you say that it is the same reason—superstition—that causes you to use the same colors—red, yellow, green—again and again?

BORGES

But do I use green?

INTERVIEWER

Not as often as the others. But you see I did a rather trivial thing, I counted the colors in . . .

BORGES

No, no. That is called *estilística*; here it is studied. No, I think you'll find yellow.

INTERVIEWER

But red, too, often moving, fading into rose.

BORGES

Really? Well, I never knew that.

INTERVIEWER

It's as if the world today were a cinder of yesterday's fire—that's a metaphor you use. You speak of "Red Adam," for example.

BORGES

Well, the word *Adam*, I think, in the Hebrew means "red earth."
Besides it sounds well, no? *Rojo Adán*.

INTERVIEWER

Yes it does. But that's not something you intend to show: the degeneration of the world by the metaphorical use of color?

BORGES

I don't intend to show anything. [*Laughter.*] I have no intentions.

INTERVIEWER

Just to describe?

BORGES

I describe. I write. Now as for the color yellow, there is a physical
explanation of that. When I began to lose my sight, the last color I
saw, or the last color, rather, that stood out, because of course now I
know that your coat is not the same color as this table or of the wood-
work behind you—the last color to stand out was yellow because it is
the most vivid of colors. That's why you have the Yellow Cab Company in the United States. At first they thought of making the cars
scarlet. Then somebody found out that at night or when there was a
fog that yellow stood out in a more vivid way than scarlet. So you have
yellow cabs because anybody can pick them out. Now when I began
to lose my eyesight, when the world began to fade away from me,
there was a time among my friends . . . well they made, they poked
fun at me because I was always wearing yellow neckties. Then they
thought I really liked yellow, although it really was too glaring. I said,
Yes, to you, but not to me, because it is the only color I can see, practically! I live in a gray world, rather like the silver-screen world. But
yellow stands out. That might account for it. I remember a joke of Oscar Wilde's: a friend of his had a tie with yellow, red, and so on, in it,
and Wilde said, Oh, my dear fellow, only a deaf man could wear a tie
like that!

INTERVIEWER

He might have been talking about the yellow necktie I have on now.

BORGES

Ah, well. I remember telling that story to a lady who missed the whole point. She said, Of course, it must be because being deaf he couldn't hear what people were saying about his necktie. That might have amused Oscar Wilde, no?

INTERVIEWER

I'd like to have heard his reply to that.

BORGES

Yes, of course. I never heard of such a case of something being so perfectly misunderstood. The perfection of stupidity. Of course, Wilde's remark is a witty translation of an idea; in Spanish as well as English you speak of a "loud color." A "loud color" is a common phrase, but then the things that are said in literature are always the same. What is important is the way they are said. Looking for metaphors, for example: When I was a young man I was always hunting for new metaphors. Then I found out that really good metaphors are always the same. I mean you compare time to a road, death to sleeping, life to dreaming, and those are the great metaphors in literature because they correspond to something essential. If you invent metaphors, they are apt to be surprising during the fraction of a second, but they strike no deep emotion whatever. If you think of life as a dream, that is a thought, a thought that is real, or at least that most men are bound to have, no? "What oft was thought, but ne'er so well expressed." I think that's better than the idea of shocking people, than finding connections between things that have never been connected before, because there is no real connection, so the whole thing is a kind of juggling.

INTERVIEWER

Juggling just words?

BORGES

Just words. I wouldn't even call them real metaphors because in a real metaphor both terms are really linked together. I have found one exception—a strange, new, and beautiful metaphor from Old Norse poetry. In Old English poetry a battle is spoken of as the "play of swords" or the "encounter of spears." But in Old Norse, and I think, also, in Celtic poetry, a battle is called a "web of men." That is strange, no? Because in a web you have a pattern, a weaving of men, *un tejido*. I suppose in medieval battle you got a kind of web because of having the swords and spears on opposite sides and so on. So there you have, I think, a new metaphor; and, of course, with a nightmare touch about it, no? The idea of a web made of living men, of living things, and still being a web, still being a pattern. It is a strange idea, no?

INTERVIEWER

It corresponds, in a general way, to the metaphor George Eliot uses in *Middlemarch*, that society is a web and one cannot disentangle a strand without touching all the others.

BORGES

[*With great interest.*] Who said that?

INTERVIEWER

George Eliot, in *Middlemarch*.

BORGES

Ah, *Middlemarch*! Yes, of course! You mean the whole universe is linked together—everything linked. Well that's one of the reasons the Stoic philosophers had for believing in omens. There's a paper, a very interesting paper, as all of his are, by De Quincey on modern superstition, and there he gives the Stoic theory. The idea is that since the whole universe is one living thing, then there is a kinship between things that seem far off. For example, if thirteen people dine together, one of them is bound to die within the year. Not merely because of

Jesus Christ and the Last Supper, but also because *all* things are bound together. He said—I wonder how that sentence runs—that everything in the world is a secret glass or secret mirror of the universe.

INTERVIEWER

You have often spoken of the people who have influenced you, like De Quincey . . .

BORGES

De Quincey greatly, yes, and Schopenhauer in German. Yes, in fact, during the First World War, I was led by Carlyle—Carlyle, I rather dislike him; I think he invented Nazism and so on, one of the fathers or forefathers of such things—well, I was led by Carlyle to a study of German, and I tried my hand at Kant's *Critique of Pure Reason*. Of course, I got bogged down as most people do—as most Germans do. Then I said, Well, I'll try their poetry, because poetry has to be shorter because of the verse. I got hold of a copy of Heine's *Lyrisches Intermezzo* and an English-German dictionary, and at the end of two or three months I found I could get on fairly well without the aid of a dictionary.

I remember the first novel in English I read through was a Scottish novel called *The House with the Green Shutters*.

INTERVIEWER

Who wrote that?

BORGES

A man called Douglas. Then that was plagiarized by the man who wrote *Hatters Castle*—Cronin—there was the same plot, practically. The book was written in the Scots dialect—I mean, people instead of saying *money* speak of *bawbees* or instead of *children*, *bairns* (that's an Old English and Norse word also) and they say *nicht* for *night*, that's Old English.

INTERVIEWER

And how old were you when you read that?

I must have been about—there were many things I didn't
understand—I must have been about ten or eleven. Before that, of
course, I had read *The Jungle Book*, and I had read Stevenson's *Trea-
sure Island*, a very fine book. But the first real novel was that novel.
When I read that, I wanted to be Scotch, and then I asked my grandmother, and she was very indignant about it. She said, Thank goodness that you're not! Of course, maybe she was wrong. She came from
Northumberland; they must have had some Scottish blood in them.
Perhaps even Danish blood way back.

INTERVIEWER
With this long interest in English and your great love of it . . .

BORGES
Look here, I'm talking to an American: there's a book I *must* speak
about—nothing unexpected about it—that book is *Huckleberry Finn*.
I thoroughly dislike Tom Sawyer. I think that Tom Sawyer spoils the
last chapters of *Huckleberry Finn*. All those silly jokes. They are all
pointless jokes; but I suppose Mark Twain thought it was his duty to
be funny even when he wasn't in the mood. The jokes had to be
worked in somehow. According to what George Moore said, the English always thought "better a bad joke than no joke."

I think that Mark Twain was one of the really great writers, but I
think he was rather unaware of the fact. But perhaps in order to write
a really great book, you *must* be rather unaware of the fact. You can
slave away at it and change every adjective to some other adjective,
but perhaps you can write better if you leave the mistakes. I remember what Bernard Shaw said, that as to style, a writer has as much style
as his conviction will give him and not more. Shaw thought that the
idea of a game of style was quite nonsensical, quite meaningless. He
thought of Bunyan, for example, as a great writer because he was
convinced of what he was saying. If a writer disbelieves what he is
writing, then he can hardly expect his readers to believe it. In this
country, though, there is a tendency to regard any kind of writing—

especially the writing of poetry—as a game of style. I have known many poets here who have written well—very fine stuff—with delicate moods and so on—but if you talk with them, the only thing they tell you is smutty stories or they speak of politics in the way that everybody does, so that really their writing turns out to be kind of a sideshow. They had learned writing in the way that a man might learn to play chess or to play bridge. They were not really poets or writers at all. It was a trick they had learned, and they had learned it thoroughly. They had the whole thing at their finger ends. But most of them—except four or five, I should say—seemed to think of life as having nothing poetic or mysterious about it. They take things for granted. They know that when they have to write, then, well, they have to suddenly become rather sad or ironic.

INTERVIEWER

To put on their writer's hat?

BORGES

Yes, put on the writer's hat and get into a right mood, and then write. Afterward, they fall back on current politics.

SUSANA QUINTEROS [*Entering.*]

Excuse me. Señor Campbell is waiting.

BORGES

Ah, please ask him to wait a moment. Well, there's a Mr. Campbell waiting; the Campbells are coming.

INTERVIEWER

When you wrote your stories, did you revise a great deal?

BORGES

At first I did. Then I found out that when a man reaches a certain age, he has found his real tone. Nowadays, I try to go over what I've written after a fortnight or so, and of course there are many slips and repetitions to be avoided, certain favorite tricks that should not be overworked. But I think that what I write nowadays is always on a certain level and that I can't better it very much, nor can I spoil it very much, either. Consequently I let it go, forget all about it, and think about what I'm doing at the time. The last things I have been writing are *milongas*, popular songs.

Yes, I saw a volume of them, a beautiful book.

Yes, *Para las seis cuerdas*, meaning, of course, the guitar. The guitar was a popular instrument when I was a boy. Then you would find people strumming the guitar, not too skillfully, at nearly every street corner of every town. Some of the best tangos were composed by people who couldn't write them or read them. But of course they had music in their souls, as Shakespeare might have said. So they dictated them to somebody; they were played on the piano, and they got written down, and they were published for the literate people. I remember I met one of them—Ernesto Poncio. He wrote "Don Juan," one of the best tangos before the tangos were spoiled by the Italians in La Boca and so on—I mean, when the tangos came from the *criolla*. He once said to me, I have been in jail many times, Señor Borges, but always for manslaughter! What he meant to say was that he wasn't a thief or a pimp.

In your *Antología Personal* . . .

Look here, I want to say that that book is full of misprints. My eyesight is very dim, and the proofreading had to be done by somebody else.

I see, but those are only minor errors, aren't they?

BORGES

Yes, I know, but they creep in, and they worry the writer, not the reader. The reader accepts anything, no? Even the starkest nonsense.

INTERVIEWER

What was your principle of selection in that book?

BORGES

My principle of selection was simply that I felt the stuff was better than what I had left out. Of course, if I had been cleverer, I would have insisted on leaving out those stories, and then after my death someone would have found out that what had been left out was really good. That would have been a cleverer thing to do, no? I mean, to publish all the weak stuff, then to let somebody find out that I had left out the real things.

INTERVIEWER

You like jokes very much, don't you?

BORGES

Yes, I do, yes.

INTERVIEWER

But the people who write about your books, your fiction in particular . . .

BORGES

No, no—they write far too seriously.

INTERVIEWER

They seldom seem to recognize that some of them are very funny.

BORGES

They are meant to be funny. Now a book will come out called *Cronícas de Bustos Domecq*, written with Adolfo Bioy Casares. That book will be about architects, poets, novelists, sculptors, and so on. All the characters are imaginary, and they are all very up-to-date, very modern; they take themselves very seriously; so does the writer, but they are not actually parodies of anybody. We are simply going as far as a certain thing can be done. For example, many writers from here tell me, We would like to have your message. You see, we have no message at all. When I write, I write because a thing has to be done. I don't think a writer should meddle too much with his own work. He should let the work write itself, no?

INTERVIEWER

You have said that a writer should never be judged by his ideas.

BORGES

No, I don't think ideas are important.

INTERVIEWER

Well, then, what should he be judged by?

BORGES

He should be judged by the enjoyment he gives and by the emotions one gets. As to ideas, after all it is not very important whether a writer has some political opinion or other because a work will come through despite them, as in the case of Kipling's *Kim*. Suppose you consider the idea of the empire of the English—well, in *Kim* I think the characters one really is fond of are not the English, but many of the Indians, the Mussulmans. I think they're nicer people. And that's because he thought them—no! no! not because he *thought* them nicer—because he *felt* them nicer.

INTERVIEWER

What about metaphysical ideas, then?

BORGES

Ah, well, metaphysical ideas, yes. They can be worked into parables and so on.

INTERVIEWER

Readers very often call your stories parables. Do you like that description?

BORGES

No, no. They're not meant to be parables. I mean if they are parables [*long pause*], that is, if they are parables, they have *happened* to be parables, but my intention has never been to write parables.

INTERVIEWER

Not like Kafka's parables, then?

BORGES

In the case of Kafka, we know very little. We only know that he was very dissatisfied with his own work. Of course, when he told his friend Max Brod that he wanted his manuscripts to be burned, as Virgil did, I suppose he knew that his friend wouldn't do that. If a man wants to destroy his own work, he throws it into a fire, and there it goes. When he tells a close friend of his, I want all the manuscripts to be destroyed, he knows that the friend will never do that, and the friend knows that he knows, and that he knows that the other knows that he knows, and so on and so forth.

INTERVIEWER

It's all very Jamesian.

BORGES

Yes, of course. I think that the whole world of Kafka is to be found in a far more complex way in the stories of Henry James. I think that they both thought of the world as being at the same time complex and meaningless.

INTERVIEWER

Meaningless?

BORGES

Don't you think so?

INTERVIEWER

No, I don't really think so. In the case of James . . .

BORGES

But in the case of James, yes. In the case of James, yes. I don't think he thought the world had any moral purpose. I think he disbelieved in God. In fact, I think there's a letter written to his brother, the psychologist William James, wherein he says that the world is a diamond museum, let's say a collection of oddities, no? I suppose he meant that. Now in the case of Kafka, I think Kafka was looking for something.

INTERVIEWER

For some meaning?

BORGES

For some meaning, yes; and not finding it, perhaps. But I think that they both lived in a kind of maze, no?

INTERVIEWER

I would agree to that. A book like *The Sacred Fount*, for example.

BORGES

Yes, *The Sacred Fount* and many short stories. For example, "The Abasement of the Northmores," where the whole story is a beautiful revenge, but a revenge that the reader never knows will happen or not. The woman is very sure that her husband's work, which nobody seems to have read or cares about, is far better than the work of his famous friend. But maybe the whole thing is untrue. Maybe she was just led by her love for him. One doesn't know whether those letters, when they are published, will really come to anything. Of course James was trying to write two or three stories at one time. That's the reason why he never gave any explanation. The explanation would have made the story poorer. He said *The Turn of the Screw* was just a potboiler, don't worry about it. But I don't think that was the truth. For instance, he said, Well, if I give explanations, then the story will be poorer because the alternative explanations will be left out. I think he did that on purpose.

INTERVIEWER

I agree; people shouldn't know.

BORGES

People shouldn't know, and perhaps he didn't know himself!

INTERVIEWER

Do you like to have the same effect on your readers?

BORGES

Oh, yes. Of course I do. But I think the stories of Henry James are far above his novels. What's important in the stories of Henry James are the situations created, not the characters. *The Sacred Fount* would be far better if you could tell one character from the other. But you have to wade through some three hundred pages in order to find out who Lady So-and-so's lover was, and then at the end you may guess that it was So-and-so and not What's-his-name. You can't tell them apart; they all speak in the same way; there are no real characters. Only the American seems to stand out. If you think of Dickens, well, while the characters don't seem to stand out, they are far more important than the plot.

INTERVIEWER

Would you say that your own stories have their point of origin in a situation, not in a character?

In a situation, right. Except for the idea of bravery, of which I'm very fond. Bravery, perhaps, because I'm not very brave myself.

Is that why there are so many knives and swords and guns in your stories?

Yes, that may be. Oh, but there are two causes there. First, seeing the swords at home because of my grandfather and my great-grandfather and so on. Seeing all those swords. Then I was bred in Palermo; it all was a slum then, and people always thought of themselves—I don't say that it was true but that they always thought of themselves—as being better than the people who lived on a different side of the town, as being better fighters and that kind of thing. Of course, that may have been rubbish. I don't think they were especially brave. To call a man, or to think of him, as a coward—that was the last thing; that's the kind of thing he couldn't stand. I have even known of a case of a man coming from the southern side of the town in order to pick a quarrel with somebody who was famous as a knifer on the north side and getting killed for his pains. They had no real reason to quarrel; they had never seen each other before; there was no question of money or women or anything of the kind. I suppose it was the same thing in the West in the States. Here the thing wasn't done with guns, but with knives.

Using the knife takes the deed back to an older form of behavior?

An older form, yes. Also, it is a more personal idea of courage. Because you can be a good marksman and not especially brave. But if you're going to fight your man at close quarters, and you have knives . . . I remember I once saw a man challenging another to fight, and the other caved in. But he caved in, I think, because of a trick. One was an old hand, he was seventy, and the other was a young and vigorous man, he must have been between twenty-five and thirty. Then the old man, he begged your pardon, he came back with two daggers, and one was a span longer than the other. He said, Here, choose your weapon. So he gave the other the chance of choosing the longer weapon, and having an advantage over him; but that also meant that he felt so sure of himself that he could afford that handicap. The other apologized and caved in, of course. I remember that a brave man, when I was a young man in the slums, he was always supposed to carry a *short* dagger, and it was worn here. Like this [*pointing to his armpit*], so it could be taken out at moment's notice, and the slum word for the knife—or one of the slum words—well, one was *el fierro*, but of course that means nothing special. But one of the names, and that has been quite lost—it's a pity—was *el vaivén*, the "come and go." In the word *come-and-go* [*making gesture*] you see the flash of the knife, the sudden flash.

INTERVIEWER

It's like a gangster's holster?

BORGES

Exactly, yes, like a holster—on the left side. Then it could be taken out at a moment's notice, and you scored *el vaivén*. It was spelled as one word and everyone knew it meant *knife*. *El fierro* is rather poor as a name because to call it *the iron* or *the steel* means nothing, while *el vaivén* does.

SUSANA QUINTEROS [*Entering again.*]

Señor Campbell is still waiting.

BORGES

Yes, yes, we know. The Campbells are coming!

INTERVIEWER

Two writers I wanted to ask you about are Joyce and Eliot. You were one of the first readers of Joyce, and you even translated part of *Ulysses* into Spanish, didn't you?

BORGES

Yes, I'm afraid I undertook a very faulty translation of the last page of *Ulysses*. Now as to Eliot, at first I thought of him as being a finer critic than a poet; now I think that sometimes he is a very fine poet, but as a critic I find that he's too apt to be always drawing fine distinctions. If you take a great critic, let's say, Emerson or Coleridge, you feel that he has read a writer, and that his criticism comes from his personal experience of him, while in the case of Eliot you always think—at least I always feel—that he's agreeing with some professor or slightly disagreeing with another. Consequently, he's not creative. He's an intelligent man who's drawing fine distinctions, and I suppose he's right; but at the same time after reading, to take a stock example, Coleridge on Shakespeare, especially on the character of Hamlet, a new Hamlet had been created for you, or after reading Emerson on Montaigne or whoever it may be. In Eliot there are no such acts of creation. You feel that he has read many books on the subject—he's agreeing or disagreeing—sometimes making slightly nasty remarks, no?

INTERVIEWER

Yes, that he takes back later.

BORGES

Yes, yes, that he takes back later. Of course, he took those remarks back later because at first he was what might be called nowadays "an angry young man." In the end, I suppose he thought of himself as being an English classic, and then he found that he had to be polite to his fellow classics, so that afterwards he took back most of the things he had said about Milton or even against Shakespeare.

After all, he felt that in some ideal way they were all sharing the same academy.

INTERVIEWER

Did Eliot's work, his poetry, have any effect on your own writing?

BORGES

No, I don't think so.

INTERVIEWER

I have been struck by certain resemblances between *The Waste Land* and your story "The Immortal."

BORGES

Well, there may be something there, but in that case I'm quite unaware of it because he's not one of the poets I love. I should rank Yeats far above him. In fact, if you don't mind my saying so, I think Frost is a finer poet than Eliot. I mean, a finer *poet*. But I suppose Eliot was a far more intelligent man; however, intelligence has little to do with poetry. Poetry springs from something deeper; it's beyond intelligence. It may not even be linked with wisdom. It's a thing of its own; it has a nature of its own. Undefinable. I remember—of course I was a young man—I was even angry when Eliot spoke in a slighting way of Sandburg. I remember he said that classicism is good—I'm not quoting his words, but the drift of them—because it enabled us to deal with such writers as Mr. Carl Sandburg. When one calls a poet *mister* [*laughter*], it's a word of haughty feelings; it means Mr. So-and-so who has found his way into poetry and has no right to be there, who is really an outsider. In Spanish it's still worse because sometimes when we speak of a poet we say, El Doctor So-and-so. Then that annihilates him, that blots him out.

INTERVIEWER

You like Sandburg, then?

BORGES

Yes, I do. Of course, I think Whitman is far more important than Sandburg, but when you read Whitman, you think of him as a literary, perhaps a not-too-learned man of letters, who is doing his best to write in the vernacular, and who is using slang as much as he can. In Sandburg the slang seems to come naturally. Now of course there are two Sandburgs: there is the *rough*, but there is also a very delicate Sandburg, especially when he deals with landscapes. Sometimes when he is describing the fog, for example, you are reminded of a Chinese painting. While in other poems of Sandburg you rather think of, well, gangsters, hoodlums, that kind of people. But I suppose he could be both, and I think he was equally sincere—when he was doing his best to be the poet of Chicago and when he wrote in quite a different mood. Another thing that I find strange in Sandburg is that in Whitman—but of course Whitman is Sandburg's father—Whitman is full of hope, while Sandburg writes as if he were writing in the two or three centuries to come. When he writes of the American expeditionary forces, or when he writes about empire or the war or so on, he writes as if all those things were dead and gone by.

INTERVIEWER

There is an element of fantasy in his work, then—which leads me to ask you about the fantastic. You use the word a great deal in your writing, and I remember that you call *Green Mansions*, for example, a fantastic novel.

BORGES

Well, it is.

INTERVIEWER

How would you define *fantastic*, then?

BORGES

I wonder if you *can* define it. I think it's rather an intention in a writer. I remember a very deep remark of Joseph Conrad—he is one of my favorite authors—I think it is in the foreword to something like *The Dark Line*, but it's not that . . .

INTERVIEWER

The Shadow Line?

BORGES

The Shadow Line. In that foreword he said that some people have thought that the story was a fantastic story because of the captain's ghost stopping the ship. He wrote—and that struck me because I write fantastic stories myself—that to deliberately write a fantastic story was not to feel that the whole universe is fantastic and mysterious; nor that it meant a lack of sensibility for a person to sit down and write something deliberately fantastic. Conrad thought that when one wrote, even in a realistic way, about the world, one was writing a fantastic story because the world itself is fantastic and unfathomable and mysterious.

INTERVIEWER

You share this belief?

BORGES

Yes. I found that he was right. I talked to Bioy Casares, who also writes fantastic stories—very, very fine stories—and he said, I think Conrad is right; really, nobody knows whether the world is realistic or fantastic, that is to say, whether the world is a natural process or whether it is a kind of dream, a dream that we may or may not share with others.

INTERVIEWER

You have often collaborated with Bioy Casares, haven't you?

BORGES

Yes, I have always collaborated with him. Every night I dine at his house, and then after dinner we sit down and write.

INTERVIEWER

Would you describe your method of collaboration?

BORGES

Well, it's rather queer. When we write together, when we collaborate, we call ourselves H. Bustos Domecq. Bustos was a great-great-grandfather of mine, and Domecq was a great-great-grandfather of his. Now, the queer thing is that when we write, and we write mostly humorous stuff—even if the stories are tragic, they are told in a humorous way, or they are told as if the teller hardly understood what he was saying—when we write together, what comes of the writing, if we are successful, and sometimes we are—why not? after all, I'm speaking in the plural, no?—when our writing is successful, then what comes out is something quite different from Bioy Casares's stuff and my stuff, even the jokes are different. So we have created between us a kind of third person; we have somehow begotten a third person that is quite unlike us.

INTERVIEWER

A fantastic author?

BORGES

Yes, a fantastic author with his likes, his dislikes, and a personal style that is meant to be ridiculous; but still, it is a style of his own, quite different from the kind of style I write when I try to create a ridiculous character. I think that's the only way of collaborating. Generally speaking, we go over the plot together before we set pen to paper—rather, I should talk about typewriters because he has a typewriter. Before we begin writing, we discuss the whole story; then we go over the details, we change them, of course. We think of a beginning, and then we think the beginning might be the end or that it might be more striking if somebody said nothing at all or said something quite outside the mark. Once the story is written, if you ask us whether this adjective or this particular sentence came from Bioy or from me, we can't tell.

INTERVIEWER

It comes from the third person.

BORGES

Yes. I think that's the only way of collaborating because I have tried collaborating with other people. Sometimes it works out all right, but sometimes one feels that the collaborator is a kind of rival. Or, if not— as in the case of Peyrou—we began collaborating, but he is timid and a very courteous, a very polite kind of person, and consequently, if he says anything, and you make any objections, he feels hurt, and he takes it back. He says, Oh, yes, of course, of course, yes, I was quite wrong. It was a blunder. Or if you propose anything, he says, Oh, that's wonderful! Now that kind of thing can't be done. In the case of me and Casares, we don't feel as if we are two rivals, or even as if we were two men who play chess. There's no case of winning or losing. What we're thinking of is the story itself, the stuff itself.

INTERVIEWER

I'm sorry, I'm not familiar with the second writer you named.

BORGES

Peyrou. He began by imitating Chesterton and writing stories, detective stories, not unworthy, and even worthy of Chesterton. But now he's struck a new line of novels whose aim is to show what this country was like during Perón's time and after Perón took to flight. I don't care very much for that kind of writing. I understand that his novels are fine; but, I should say, from the historical, even the journalistic point of view. When he began writing stories after Chesterton, and then he wrote some very fine stories—one of them made me cry, but of course, perhaps it made me cry because he spoke of the quarter I was bred in, Palermo, and of hoodlums of those days—a book called *La Noche repetida*, with very, very fine stories about gangsters, hoodlums, holdup men, that kind of thing. And all that way back, let's say, well, at the beginning of the century. Now he has started this new kind of novel wherein he wants to show what the country was like.

INTERVIEWER

Local color, more or less?

BORGES

Local color and local politics. Then his characters are very interested, well, in graft, in loot, making money, and so on. As I am less interested in those subjects, maybe it's my fault, not his, if I prefer his early stuff. But I always think of him as a great writer, an important writer, and an old friend of mine.

INTERVIEWER

You have said that your own work has moved from, in the early times, *expression*, to, in the later times, *allusion*.

BORGES

Yes.

INTERVIEWER

What do you mean by *allusion*?

BORGES

Look, I mean to say this: when I began writing, I thought that everything should be defined by the writer. For example, to say "the moon" was strictly forbidden; that one had to find an adjective, an epithet for the moon. (Of course, I'm simplifying things. I know it because many times I have written *la luna*, but this is a kind of symbol of what I was doing.) Well, I thought everything had to be defined and that no common turns of phrase should be used. I would never have said, So-and-so came in and sat down, because that was far too simple and far too easy. I thought I had to find out some fancy way of saying it. Now I find out that those things are generally annoyances to the reader. But I think the whole root of the matter lies in the fact that when a writer is young he feels somehow that what he is going to say is rather silly or obvious or commonplace, and then he tries to hide it under baroque ornament, under words taken from the seventeenth-century writers; or, if not, and he sets out to be modern, then he does the contrary: he's inventing words all the time, or alluding to airplanes, railway trains, or the telegraph and telephone because he's doing his best to be modern. Then as time goes on, one feels that one's ideas, good or bad, should be plainly expressed, because if you have an idea you must try to get that idea or that feeling or that mood into the mind of the reader. If, at the same time, you are trying to be, let's say, Sir Thomas Browne or Ezra Pound, then it can't be done. So that I think a writer always begins by being too complicated—he's playing at several games at the same time. He wants to convey a peculiar mood; at the same time he must be a contemporary, and if not a contemporary, then he's a reactionary and a classic. As to the vocabulary, the first thing a young writer, at least in this country, sets out to do is to show his readers that he possesses a dictionary, that he knows all the synonyms; so we get, for example, in one line, *red*, then we get *scarlet*, then we get other different words, more or less, for the same color—*purple*.

INTERVIEWER

You've worked, then, toward a kind of classical prose?

BORGES

Yes, I do my best now. Whenever I find an out-of-the-way word, that is to say, a word that may be used by the Spanish classics or a word used in the slums of Buenos Aires, I mean, a word that is different from the others, then I strike it out, and I use a common word. I remember that Stevenson wrote that in a well-written page all the words should look the same way. If you write an uncouth word or an astonishing or an archaic word, then the rule is broken; and what is far more important, the attention of the reader is distracted by the word. One should be able to read smoothly in it even if you're writing metaphysics or philosophy or whatever.

Dr. Johnson said something similar to that.

Yes, he must have said it; in any case, he must have agreed with that. Look, his own English was rather cumbersome, and the first thing you feel is that he is writing in a cumbersome English—that there are far too many Latin words in it—but if you reread what is written, you find that behind those involutions of phrase there is always a meaning, generally an interesting and a new meaning.

A personal one?

Yes, a personal one. So even though he wrote in a Latin style, I think he is the most English of writers. I think of him as—this is a blasphemy, of course, but why not be blasphemous while we're about it?—I think that Johnson was a far more English writer than Shakespeare. Because if there's one thing typical of Englishmen, it's their habit of understatement. Well, in the case of Shakespeare, there are no understatements. On the contrary, he is piling on the agonies, as I think the American said. I think Johnson, who wrote a Latin kind of English, and Wordsworth, who wrote more Saxon words, and there is a third writer whose name I can't recall—well—let's say Johnson, Wordsworth, and Kipling also, I think they're far more typically English than Shakespeare. I don't know why, but I always feel something Italian, something Jewish about Shakespeare, and perhaps Englishmen admire him because of that, because it's so unlike them.

And why the French dislike him to the extent that they do; because he's so bombastic.

BORGES

He *was* very bombastic. I remember I saw a film some days ago—not too good a film—called *Darling*. There some verses of Shakespeare are quoted. Now those verses are always better when they are quoted because he is defining England, and he calls it, for example, "This other Eden, demi-paradise . . . This precious stone set in the silver sea," and so on, and in the end he says something like, "this realm, this England." Now when that quotation is made, the reader stops there, but in the text I think the verses go on so that the whole point is lost. The real point would have been the idea of a man trying to define England, loving her very much and finding at the end that the only thing he can do is to say *England* outright—as if you said *America*. But if he says "this realm, this land, this England," and then goes on "this demi-paradise" and so on, the whole point is lost because *England* should be the last word. Well, I suppose Shakespeare always wrote in a hurry, as the player said to Ben Jonson, and so be it. You've no time to feel that that would have been the last word, the word England, summing up and blotting out all the others, saying, Well, I've been attempting something that is impossible. But he went on with it, with his metaphors and his bombast, because he was bombastic. Even in such a famous phrase as Hamlet's last words, I think, "The rest is silence." There is something phony about it; it's meant to impress. I don't think anybody would say anything like that.

INTERVIEWER

In the context of the play, my favorite line in *Hamlet* occurs just after Claudius's praying scene when Hamlet enters his mother's chamber and says, "Now, Mother, what's the matter?"

BORGES

"What's the matter?" is the opposite of "The rest is silence." At least for me, "The rest is silence" has a hollow ring about it. One feels that Shakespeare is thinking, Well, now Prince Hamlet of Denmark is dying; he must say something impressive. So he ekes out that phrase

"The rest is silence." Now that may be impressive, but it is not true! He was working away at his job of poet and not thinking of the real character, of Hamlet the Dane.

INTERVIEWER

When you are working, what kind of reader do you imagine you are writing for, if you do imagine it? Who would be your ideal audience?

BORGES

Perhaps a few personal friends of mine. Not myself because I never reread what I've written. I'm far too afraid to feel ashamed of what I've done.

INTERVIEWER

Do you expect the many people who read your work to catch the allusions and references?

BORGES

No. Most of those allusions and references are merely put there as a kind of private joke.

INTERVIEWER

A *private* joke?

BORGES

A joke not to be shared with other people. I mean, if they share it, all the better; but if they don't, I don't care a hang about it.

INTERVIEWER

Then it's the opposite approach to allusion from, say, Eliot in *The Waste Land*.

BORGES

I think that Eliot and Joyce wanted their readers to be rather mystified and so to be worrying out the sense of what they had done.

INTERVIEWER

You seem to have read as much, if not more, nonfiction or factual material as fiction and poetry. Is that true? For example, you apparently like to read encyclopedias.

BORGES

Ah, yes. I'm very fond of that. I remember a time when I used to come here to read. I was a very young man, and I was far too timid to ask for a book. Then I was rather, I won't say poor, but I wasn't too wealthy in those days—so I used to come every night here and pick out a volume of the *Encyclopaedia Britannica*, the old edition.

INTERVIEWER

The eleventh?

BORGES

The eleventh or twelfth because those editions are far above the new ones. They were meant to be *read*. Now they are merely reference books. While in the eleventh or twelfth edition of the *Encyclopaedia Britannica*, you had long articles by Macaulay, by Coleridge; no, not by Coleridge by . . .

INTERVIEWER

By De Quincey?

BORGES

Yes, by De Quincey, and so on. So that I used to take any volume from the shelves—there was no need to ask for them; they were reference books—and then I opened the book till I found an article that interested me, for example, about the Mormons or about any particular writer. I sat down and read it because those articles were really monographs, really books or short books. The same goes for the German encyclopedias—*Brockhaus* or *Meyers*. When we got the new copy, I thought that was what they call the *The Baby Brockhaus*, but it wasn't. It was explained to me that because people live in small flats there is

no longer room for books in thirty volumes. Encyclopedias have suffered greatly; they have been packed in.

SUSANA QUINTEROS [*Interrupting.*]

I'm sorry. *Está esperando el Señor Campbell.*

BORGES

Ah, please ask him to wait just a moment more. Those Campbells
keep coming.

INTERVIEWER

May I ask just a few more questions?

BORGES

Yes, please, of course.

INTERVIEWER

Some readers have found that your stories are cold, impersonal,
rather like some of the newer French writers. Is that your intention?

BORGES

No. [*Sadly.*] If that has happened, it is out of mere clumsiness. Because I have felt them very deeply. I have felt them so deeply that I
have told them, well, using strange symbols so that people might not
find out that they were all more or less autobiographical. The stories
were about myself, my personal experiences. I suppose it's the English diffidence, no?

INTERVIEWER

Then a book like the little volume called *Everness* would be a good
book for someone to read about your work?

BORGES

I think it is. Besides, the lady who wrote it is a close friend of mine.
I found that word in *Roget's Thesaurus.* Then I thought that word was
invented by Bishop Wilkins, who invented an artificial language.

You've written about that.

Yes, I wrote about Wilkins. But he also invented a wonderful word that strangely enough has never been used by English poets—an awful word, really, a terrible word. *Everness*, of course, is better than *eternity* because *eternity* is rather worn now. *Ever-r-ness* is far better than the German *Ewigkeit*, the same word. But he also created a beautiful word, a word that's a poem in itself, full of hopelessness, sadness, and despair—the word *neverness*. A beautiful word, no? He invented it, and I don't know why the poets left it lying about and never used it.

Have you used it?

No, no, never. I used *everness*, but *neverness* is very beautiful. There is something hopeless about it, no? And there is no word with the same meaning in any other language, or in English. You might say *impossibility*, but that's very tame for *neverness*—the Saxon ending in *-ness*. *Neverness*. Keats uses *nothingness*: "Till love and fame to nothingness do sink"; but *nothingness*, I think, is weaker than *neverness*. You have in Spanish *nadería*—many similar words—but nothing like *neverness*. So if you're a poet, you should use that word. It's a pity for that word to be lost in the pages of a dictionary. I don't think it's ever been used. It may have been used by some theologian; it might. I suppose Jonathan Edwards would have enjoyed that kind of word or Sir Thomas Browne, perhaps, and Shakespeare, of course, because he was very fond of words.

You respond to English so well, you love it so much, how is it you have written so little in English?

BORGES

Why? Why, I'm afraid. Fear. But next year, those lectures of mine that I shall deliver, I'll write them in English. I already wrote to Harvard.

INTERVIEWER

You're coming to Harvard next year?

BORGES

Yes. I'm going to deliver a course of lectures on poetry. And as I think that poetry is more or less untranslatable, and as I think English literature—and that includes America—is by far the richest in the world, I will take most, if not all, of my examples, from English poetry. Of course, as I have my hobby, I'll try to work in some Old English verses, but that's English also! In fact, according to some of my students, it's far more English than Chaucer's English!

INTERVIEWER

To get back to your own work for a moment: I have often wondered how you go about arranging works in those collections. Obviously the principle is not chronological. Is it similarity of theme?

BORGES

No, not chronology; but sometimes I find out that I've written the same parable or story twice over, or that two different stories carry the same meaning, and so I try to put them alongside each other. That's the only principle. Because, for example, once it happened to me to write a poem, a not too good poem, and then to rewrite it many years afterwards. After the poem was written, some of my friends told me, Well, that's the same poem you published some five years ago. And I said, Well, so it is! But I hadn't the faintest notion that it was. After all, I think that a poet has maybe five or six poems to write and not more than that. He's trying his hand at rewriting them from different angles and perhaps with different plots and in different ages and different characters, but the poems are essentially and innerly the same.

INTERVIEWER

You have written many reviews and journal articles.

BORGES

Well, I had to do it.

INTERVIEWER

Did you choose the books you wanted to review?

BORGES

Yes, I generally did.

INTERVIEWER

So the choice does express your own tastes?

BORGES

Oh yes, yes. For example, when somebody told me to write a review of a certain history of literature, I found there were so many howlers and blunders, and as I greatly admire the author as a poet, I said, No, I don't want to write about it, because if I write about it I shall write against it. I don't like to attack people, especially now—when I was a young man, yes, I was very fond of it, but as time goes on, one finds that it is no good. When people write in favor or against anybody, that hardly helps or hurts them. I think that a man can be helped, well, the man can be done or undone by his *own* writing, not by what other people say of him, so that even if you brag a lot and people say that you are a genius—well, you'll be found out.

INTERVIEWER

Do you have any particular method for the naming of your characters?

BORGES

I have two methods. One of them is to work in the names of my grandfathers, great-grandfathers, and so on. To give them a kind of, well, I won't say immortality, but that's one of the methods. The other is to use names that somehow strike me. For example, in a story of mine, one of the characters who comes and goes is called Yarmolinsky because the name struck me—it's a strange word, no? Then another character is called Red Scharlach because Scharlach means *scarlet* in German, and he was a murderer; he was doubly red, no? Red Scharlach, Red Scarlet.

INTERVIEWER

What about the princess with the beautiful name who occurs in two of your stories?

BORGES

Faucigny Lucinge? Well, she's a great friend of mine. She's an Argentine lady. She married a French prince, and as the name is very beautiful, as most French titles are, especially if you cut out the Faucigny, as she does. She calls herself La Princesse de Lucinge. It's a beautiful word.

INTERVIEWER

What about Tlön and Uqbar?

BORGES

Oh, well, those are merely meant to be uncouth. So *u-q-b-a-r*.

INTERVIEWER

Unpronounceable, in a way?

BORGES

Yes, more or less unpronounceable, and then *Tlön*: *t-l* is rather an uncommon combination, no? Then *ö*. The Latin *Orbis Tertius*—one can say that swimmingly, no? Perhaps in *Tlön* I may have been thinking of *Traum*, the same word as the English *dream*. But then it would have to be *Tröme*, but *Tröme* might remind the reader of a railway train: *t-l* was a queerer combination. I thought I had invented a word for imagined objects called *hrön*. Yet when I began learning Old English, I found that *hrān* was one of the words for whale. There were two words, *wael* and *hrān*, so the *hranrād* is the "whale road," that is to say "the sea" in Old English poetry.

INTERVIEWER

Then the word you invented to describe an object perpetrated on reality by the imagination, that word had already been invented and was, in fact, *a hran*?

BORGES

Yes, yes, it came to me. I would like to think that it came from my ancestors of ten centuries ago—that's a probable explanation, no?

INTERVIEWER

Would you say that in your stories you have tried to hybridize the short story and the essay?

BORGES

Yes—but I have done that on purpose. The first to point that out to me was Casares. He said that I had written short stories that were really sort of halfway houses between an essay and a story.

INTERVIEWER

Was that partly to compensate for your timidity about writing narratives?

BORGES

Yes, it may have been. Yes, because nowadays, or at least today, I began writing that series of stories about hoodlums of Buenos Aires: those are straightforward stories. There is nothing of the essay about them or even of poetry. The story is told in a straightforward way, and those stories are in a sense sad, perhaps horrible. They are always understated. They are told by people who are also hoodlums, and you can hardly understand them. They may be tragedies, but tragedy is not felt by them. They merely tell the story, and the reader is, I suppose, made to feel that the story goes deeper than the story itself. Nothing is said of the sentiments of the characters—I got that out of the Old Norse saga—the idea that one should know a character by his words and by his deeds, but that one shouldn't get inside his skull and say what he was thinking.

So they are nonpsychological rather than impersonal?

Yes, but there is a hidden psychology behind the story because, if not, the characters would be mere puppets.

What about the Cabala? When did you first get interested in that?

I think it was through De Quincey, through his idea that the whole world was a set of symbols, or that everything meant something else. Then when I lived in Geneva, I had two personal, two great friends—Maurice Abramowicz and Simon Jichlinski—their names tell you the stock they sprang from; they were Polish Jews. I greatly admired Switzerland and the nation itself, not merely the scenery and the towns; but the Swiss are very standoffish; one can hardly have a Swiss friend because as they have to live on foreigners, I suppose they dislike them. That would be the same case with the Mexicans. They chiefly live on Americans, on American tourists, and I don't think anybody likes to be a hotel keeper even though there's nothing dishonorable about it. But if you are a hotel keeper, if you have to entertain many people from other countries, well, you feel that they are different from you, and you may dislike them in the long run.

Have you tried to make your own stories Cabalistic?

BORGES

Yes, sometimes I have.

INTERVIEWER

Using traditional Cabalistic interpretations?

BORGES

No. I read a book called *Major Trends in Jewish Mysticism*.

INTERVIEWER

The one by Scholem?

BORGES

Yes, by Scholem and another book by Trachtenberg on Jewish superstitions. Then I have read all the books of the Cabala I have found and all the articles in the encyclopedias and so on. But I have no Hebrew whatever. I may have Jewish ancestors, but I can't tell. My mother's name is Acevedo: Acevedo may be a name for a Portuguese Jew, but again, it may not. Now if you're called Abraham, I think there is no doubt whatever about it, but as the Jews took Italian, Spanish, Portuguese names, it does not necessarily follow that if you have one of those names you come from Jewish stock. The word *acevedo*, of course, means a kind of tree; the word is not especially Jewish, though many Jews are called Acevedo. I can't tell. I wish I had some Jewish forefathers.

INTERVIEWER

You once wrote that all men are either Platonists or Aristotelians.

BORGES

I didn't say that. Coleridge said it.

INTERVIEWER

But you quoted him.

BORGES

Yes, I quoted him.

INTERVIEWER

And which are you?

BORGES

I think I'm Aristotelian, but I wish it were the other way. I think it's the English strain that makes me think of particular things and persons being real rather than general ideas being real. But I'm afraid now that the Campbells are coming.

INTERVIEWER

Before I go, would you mind signing my copy of *Labyrinths*?

BORGES

I'll be glad to. Ah yes, I know this book. There's my picture—but do I really look like this? I don't like that picture. I'm not so gloomy? So beaten down?

INTERVIEWER

Don't you think it looks pensive?

BORGES

Perhaps. But so dark? So heavy? The brow . . . oh, well.

INTERVIEWER

Do you like this edition of your writings?

BORGES

A good translation, no? Except that there are too many Latin words in it. For example, if I wrote, just say, *habitación oscura* (I wouldn't, of course, have written *that*, but *cuarto oscuro*, but just say that I did), then the temptation is to translate *habitación* with *habita-*

tion, a word which sounds close to the original. But the word I want is *room*: it is more definite, simpler, better. You know, English is a beautiful language, but the older languages are even more beautiful: they had *vowels*. Vowels in modern English have lost their value, their color. My hope for English—for the English language—is America. Americans speak clearly. When I go to the movies now, I can't see much, but in the American movies, I understand every word. In the English movies I can't understand as well. Do you ever find it so?

INTERVIEWER

Sometimes, particularly in comedies. The English actors seem to speak too fast.

BORGES

Exactly! Exactly. Too fast with too little emphasis. They blur the words, the sounds. A fast blur. No, America must save the language; and, do you know, I think the same is true for Spanish? I prefer South American speech. I always have. I suppose you in America don't read Ring Lardner or Bret Harte much anymore?

INTERVIEWER

They are read, but mostly in the secondary schools.

BORGES

What about O. Henry?

INTERVIEWER

Again, mostly in the schools.

BORGES

And I suppose there mostly for the technique, the surprise ending. I don't like that trick, do you? Oh, it's all right in theory; in practice, that's something else. You can read them only once if there is just the surprise. You remember what Pope said: "the art of sinking." Now in the detective story, that's different. The surprise is there, too, but there are also the characters; the scene or the landscape to satisfy us. But now I remember that the Campbells are coming, the Campbells are coming. They are supposed to be a ferocious tribe. Where are they?

Issue 40, 1967

Kurt Vonnegut

The Art of Fiction

This interview with Kurt Vonnegut was originally a composite of four interviews done with the author over the past decade. The composite has gone through an extensive working over by the subject himself, who looks upon his own spoken words on the page with considerable misgivings . . . Indeed, what follows can be considered an interview conducted with himself, by himself.

The introduction to the first of the incorporated interviews (done in West Barnstable, Massachusetts, when Vonnegut was forty-four) reads: "He is a veteran and a family man, large-boned, loose-jointed, at ease. He camps in an armchair in a shaggy tweed jacket, Cambridge gray flannels, a blue Brooks Brothers shirt, slouched down, his hands stuffed into his pockets. He shells the interview with explosive coughs and sneezes, windages of an autumn cold and a lifetime of heavy cigarette smoking. His voice is a resonant baritone, Midwestern, wry in its inflections. From time to time he issues the open, alert smile of a man who has seen and reserved within himself almost everything: depression, war, the possibility of violent death, the inanities of corporate public relations, six children, an irregular income, long-delayed recognition."

The last of the interviews that made up the composite was conducted during the summer of 1976, years after the first. The description of him at this time reads: ". . . he moves with the low-keyed amiability of an old family dog. In general, his appearance is tousled: the long curly hair, mustache, and sympathetic smile suggest a man at

SPIT AND IMAGE

<u>I N T R O D U C T I O N</u>

It was the childishness of my father, finally, that spoiled
Heaven for me.   We could be any age we wished back there, provided we had actually attained that age in life on Earth.   I
myself elected to be thirty-three most of the time, which would
have been a comfortable way to spend Eternity -- if only Father
hadn't tagged after me everywhere in the shape of a runty, unhap
nine-year-old.

"Father," I would say to him in Heaven, "for the love of God
grow up!"

But he would not grow up.

So, just to get away from him, I volunteered to return to Ear
as a doppelganger, a spook whose business it is to let certain
people know that they are about to die.

I make myself into a near-double of a doomed person, and then
show myself to him very briefly.   He invariably gets my message
That he is about to die.

• •

Yes, and about once every six months I turn into a poltergeis
which is simply a spook who throws a tantrum.   Suddenly I can't
stand the Universe and my place in it, and the way it's being ru
So I ~~were~~ become invisible, and go into somebody's house or apar
ment, and dump tables and chairs and breakfronts and so on, and
throw books and bric-a-brac around.

A manuscript page from *Spit and Image*, an unpublished novel by
Kurt Vonnegut.

once amused and saddened by the world around him. He has rented the Gerald Murphy house for the summer. He works in the little bedroom at the end of a hall where Murphy, artist, bon vivant, and friend to the artistic great, died in 1964. From his desk Vonnegut can look out onto the front lawn through a small window; behind him is a large, white canopy bed. On the desk next to the typewriter is a copy of Andy Warhol's *Interview*, Clancy Sigal's *Zone of the Interior*, and several discarded cigarette packs.

"Vonnegut has chain-smoked Pall Malls since 1936 and during the course of the interview he smokes the better part of one pack. His voice is low and gravelly, and as he speaks, the incessant procedure of lighting the cigarettes and exhaling smoke is like punctuation in his conversation. Other distractions, such as the jangle of the telephone and the barking of a small, shaggy dog named Pumpkin, do not detract from Vonnegut's good-natured disposition. Indeed, as Dan Wakefield once said of his fellow Shortridge High School alumnus, 'He laughed a lot and was kind to everyone.'"

—*David Hayman, David Michaelis,*
George Plimpton, Richard L. Rhodes, 1977

INTERVIEWER

You are a veteran of the Second World War?

KURT VONNEGUT, JR.

Yes. I want a military funeral when I die—the bugler, the flag on the casket, the ceremonial firing squad, the hallowed ground.

INTERVIEWER

Why?

VONNEGUT

It will be a way of achieving what I've always wanted more than anything—something I could have had, if only I'd managed to get myself killed in the war.

Which is—?

VONNEGUT
The unqualified approval of my community.

INTERVIEWER
You don't feel that you have that now?

VONNEGUT
My relatives say that they are glad I'm rich, but that they simply cannot read me.

INTERVIEWER
You were an infantry battalion scout in the war?

VONNEGUT
Yes, but I took my basic training on the 240-millimeter howitzer.

INTERVIEWER
A rather large weapon.

VONNEGUT
The largest mobile fieldpiece in the army at that time. This weapon came in six pieces, each piece dragged wallowingly by a Caterpillar tractor. Whenever we were told to fire it, we had to build it first. We practically had to invent it. We lowered one piece on top of another, using cranes and jacks. The shell itself was about nine and a half inches in diameter and weighed three hundred pounds. We constructed a miniature railway which would allow us to deliver the shell from the ground to the breech, which was about eight feet above grade. The breechblock was like the door on the vault of a savings and loan association in Peru, Indiana, say.

INTERVIEWER

It must have been a thrill to fire such a weapon.

VONNEGUT

Not really. We would put the shell in there, and then we would throw in bags of very slow and patient explosives. They were damp dog biscuits, I think. We would close the breech, and then trip a hammer which hit a fulminate of mercury percussion cap, which spit fire at the damp dog biscuits. The main idea, I think, was to generate steam. After a while, we could hear these cooking sounds. It was a lot like cooking a turkey. In utter safety, I think, we could have opened the breechblock from time to time, and basted the shell. Eventually, though, the howitzer always got restless. And finally it would heave back on its recoil mechanism, and it would have to expectorate the shell. The shell would come floating out like the Goodyear blimp. If we had had a stepladder, we could have painted "Fuck Hitler" on the shell as it left the gun. Helicopters could have taken after it and shot it down.

INTERVIEWER

The ultimate terror weapon.

VONNEGUT

Of the Franco-Prussian War.

INTERVIEWER

But you were ultimately sent overseas not with this instrument but with the 106th Infantry Division—

VONNEGUT

"The Bag Lunch Division." They used to feed us a lot of bag lunches. Salami sandwiches. An orange.

INTERVIEWER

In combat?

VONNEGUT

When we were still in the States.

INTERVIEWER

While they trained you for the infantry?

VONNEGUT

I was never trained for the infantry. Battalion scouts were elite troops, see. There were only six in each battalion, and nobody was very sure about what they were supposed to do. So we would march over to the rec room every morning and play Ping-Pong and fill out applications for Officer Candidate School.

INTERVIEWER

During your basic training, though, you must have been familiarized with weapons other than the howitzer.

VONNEGUT

If you study the 240-millimeter howitzer, you don't even have time left over for a venereal-disease film.

INTERVIEWER

What happened when you reached the front?

VONNEGUT

I imitated various war movies I'd seen.

INTERVIEWER

Did you shoot anybody in the war?

VONNEGUT

I thought about it. I did fix my bayonet once, fully expecting to charge.

INTERVIEWER

Did you charge?

VONNEGUT

No. If everybody else had charged, I would have charged, too. But we decided not to charge. We couldn't see anybody.

INTERVIEWER

This was during the Battle of the Bulge, wasn't it? It was the largest defeat of American arms in history.

VONNEGUT

Probably. My last mission as a scout was to find our own artillery. Usually, scouts go out and look for enemy stuff. Things got so bad that we were finally looking for our own stuff. If I'd found our own battalion commander, everybody would have thought that was pretty swell.

INTERVIEWER

Do you mind describing your capture by the Germans?

VONNEGUT

Gladly. We were in this gully about as deep as a World War I trench. There was snow all around. Somebody said we were probably in Luxembourg. We were out of food.

INTERVIEWER

Who was "we"?

VONNEGUT

Our battalion scouting unit. All six of us. And about fifty people we'd never met before. The Germans could see us, because they were talking to us through a loudspeaker. They told us our situation was hopeless, and so on. That was when we fixed bayonets. It was nice there for a few minutes.

INTERVIEWER

How so?

VONNEGUT

Being a porcupine with all those steel quills. I pitied anybody who had to come in after us.

INTERVIEWER

But they came in anyway?

VONNEGUT

No. They sent in eighty-eight millimeter shells instead. The shells burst in the treetops right over us. Those were very loud bangs right over our heads. We were showered with splintered steel. Some people got hit. Then the Germans told us again to come out. We didn't yell "Nuts" or anything like that. We said, "OK" and "Take it easy," and so on. When the Germans finally showed themselves, we saw they were wearing white camouflage suits. We didn't have anything like that. We were olive drab. No matter what season it was, we were olive drab.

INTERVIEWER

What did the Germans say?

VONNEGUT

They said the war was all over for us, that we were lucky, that we could now be sure we would live through the war, which was more than they could be sure of. As a matter of fact, they were probably killed or captured by Patton's Third Army within the next few days. Wheels within wheels.

INTERVIEWER

Did you speak any German?

VONNEGUT

I had heard my parents speak it a lot. They hadn't taught me how to do it, since there had been such bitterness in America against all things German during the First World War. I tried a few words I knew on our captors, and they asked me if I was of German ancestry, and I said, Yes. They wanted to know why I was making war against my brothers.

INTERVIEWER

And you said—?

VONNEGUT

I honestly found the question ignorant and comical. My parents had separated me so thoroughly from my Germanic past that my captors might as well have been Bolivians or Tibetans, for all they meant to me.

INTERVIEWER

After you were captured, you were shipped to Dresden?

VONNEGUT.

In the same boxcars that had brought up the troops that captured us—probably in the same boxcars that had delivered Jews and Gypsies and Jehovah's Witnesses and so on to the extermination camps. Rolling stock is rolling stock. British mosquito bombers attacked us at night a few times. I guess they thought we were strategic materials of some kind. They hit a car containing most of the officers from our battalion. Every time I say I hate officers, which I still do fairly frequently, I have to remind myself that practically none of the officers I served under survived. Christmas was in there somewhere.

INTERVIEWER

And you finally arrived in Dresden.

VONNEGUT

In a huge prison camp south of Dresden first. The privates were separated from the noncoms and officers. Under the articles of the Geneva Convention, which is a very Edwardian document, privates were required to work for their keep. Everybody else got to languish in prison. As a private, I was shipped to Dresden . . .

INTERVIEWER

What were your impressions of the city itself before the bombing?

VONNEGUT

The first fancy city I'd ever seen. A city full of statues and zoos, like Paris. We were living in a slaughterhouse, in a nice new cement-block hog barn. They put bunks and straw mattresses in the barn, and we went to work every morning as contract labor in a malt-syrup factory. The syrup was for pregnant women. The damned sirens would go off and we'd hear some other city getting it—*whump a whump a whumpa whump*. We never expected to get it. There were very few air-raid shelters in town and no war industries, just cigarette factories, hospitals, clarinet factories. Then a siren went off—it was February 13, 1945—and we went down two stories under the pavement into a big meat locker. It was cool there, with cadavers hanging all around. When we came up the city was gone.

INTERVIEWER

You didn't suffocate in the meat locker?

VONNEGUT

No. It was quite large, and there weren't very many of us. The attack didn't sound like a hell of a lot either. *Whump.* They went over with high explosives first to loosen things up, and then scattered incendiaries. When the war started, incendiaries were fairly sizable, about as long as a shoebox. By the time Dresden got it, they were tiny little things. They burnt the whole damn town down.

INTERVIEWER

What happened when you came up?

VONNEGUT

Our guards were noncoms—a sergeant, a corporal, and four privates—and leaderless. Cityless, too, because they were Dresdeners who'd been shot up on the front and sent home for easy duty. They kept us at attention for a couple of hours. They didn't know what else to do. They'd go over and talk to each other. Finally we trekked across the rubble and they quartered us with some South Africans in a suburb. Every day we walked into the city and dug into basements and shelters to get the corpses out, as a sanitary measure. When we went into them, a typical shelter, an ordinary basement usually, looked like a streetcar full of people who'd simultaneously had heart failure. Just people sitting there in their chairs, all dead. A firestorm is an amazing thing. It doesn't occur in nature. It's fed by the tornadoes that occur in the midst of it and there isn't a damned thing to breathe. We brought the dead out. They were loaded on wagons and taken to parks, large, open areas in the city that weren't filled with rubble. The Germans got funeral pyres going, burning the bodies to keep them from stinking and from spreading disease. One hundred thirty thousand corpses were hidden underground. It was a terribly elaborate Easter-egg hunt. We went to work through cordons of German soldiers. Civilians didn't get to see what we were up to. After a few days the city began to smell, and a new technique was invented. Necessity is the mother of invention. We would bust into the shelter, gather up valuables from people's laps without attempting identification, and turn the valuables over to guards. Then soldiers would come in with a flamethrower and stand in the door and cremate the people inside. Get the gold and jewelry out and then burn everybody inside.

INTERVIEWER

What an impression on someone thinking of becoming a writer!

VONNEGUT

It was a fancy thing to see, a startling thing. It was a moment of truth, too, because American civilians and ground troops didn't know American bombers were engaged in saturation bombing. It was kept a secret until very close to the end of the war. One reason they burned down Dresden is that they'd already burned down everything else. You know: What're we going to do tonight? Here was everybody all set to go, and Germany still fighting, and this machinery for burning down cities was being used. It was a secret, burning down cities—boiling pisspots and flaming prams. There was all this hokum about the Norden bomb sight. You'd see a newsreel showing a bombardier with an MP on either side of him holding a drawn .45. That sort of nonsense, and hell, all they were doing was just flying over cities, hundreds of airplanes, and dropping everything. When I went to the University of Chicago after the war the guy who interviewed me for admission had bombed Dresden. He got to that part of my life story and he said, Well, we hated to do it. The comment sticks in my mind.

INTERVIEWER

Another reaction would be, We were ordered to do it.

VONNEGUT

His was more humane. I think he felt the bombing was necessary, and it may have been. One thing everybody learned is how fast you can rebuild a city. The engineers said it would take five hundred years to rebuild Germany. Actually it took about eighteen weeks.

INTERVIEWER

Did you intend to write about it as soon as you went through the experience?

VONNEGUT

When the city was demolished I had no idea of the scale of the thing . . . Whether this was what Bremen looked like or Hamburg,

Coventry . . . I'd never seen Coventry, so I had no scale except for what I'd seen in movies. When I got home (I was a writer since I had been on the *Cornell Sun*, except that was the extent of my writing) I thought of writing my war story, too. All my friends were home; they'd had wonderful adventures, too. I went down to the newspaper office, the *Indianapolis News*, and looked to find out what they had about Dresden. There was an item about half an inch long, which said our planes had been over Dresden and two had been lost. And so I figured, well, this really was the most minor sort of detail in World War II. Others had so much more to write about. I remember envying Andy Rooney, who jumped into print at that time; I didn't know him, but I think he was the first guy to publish his war story after the war; it was called *Air Gunner*. Hell, I never had any classy adventure like that. But every so often I would meet a European and we would be talking about the war and I would say I was in Dresden; he'd be astonished that I'd been there, and he'd always want to know more. Then a book by David Irving was published about Dresden, saying it was the largest massacre in European history. I said, By God, I saw something after all! I would try to write my war story, whether it was interesting or not, and try to make something out of it. I describe that process a little in the beginning of *Slaughterhouse Five*; I saw it as starring John Wayne and Frank Sinatra. Finally, a girl called Mary O'Hare, the wife of a friend of mine who'd been there with me, said, You were just children then. It's not fair to pretend that you were men like Wayne and Sinatra, and it's not fair to future generations, because you're going to make war look good. That was a very important clue to me.

INTERVIEWER

That sort of shifted the whole focus . . .

VONNEGUT

She freed me to write about what infants we really were: seventeen, eighteen, nineteen, twenty, twenty-one. We were baby faced, and as a prisoner of war I don't think I had to shave very often. I don't recall that that was a problem.

INTERVIEWER

One more war question: Do you still think about the firebombing of Dresden at all?

VONNEGUT

I wrote a book about it, called *Slaughterhouse Five*. The book is still in print, and I have to do something about it as a businessman now and then. Marcel Ophuls asked me to be in his film, *The Memory of Justice*. He wanted me to talk about Dresden as an atrocity. I told him to talk to my friend Bernard V. O'Hare, Mary's husband, instead, which he did. O'Hare was a fellow battalion scout, and then a fellow prisoner of war. He's a lawyer in Pennsylvania now.

INTERVIEWER

Why didn't you wish to testify?

VONNEGUT

I had a German name. I didn't want to argue with people who thought Dresden should have been bombed to hell. All I ever said in my book was that Dresden, willy-nilly, *was* bombed to hell.

INTERVIEWER

It was the largest massacre in European history?

VONNEGUT

It was the fastest killing of large numbers of people—one hundred and thirty-five thousand people in a matter of hours. There were slower schemes for killing, of course.

INTERVIEWER

The death camps.

VONNEGUT

Yes—in which millions were eventually killed. Many people see the Dresden massacre as correct and quite minimal revenge for what had been done by the camps. Maybe so. As I say, I never argue that point. I do note in passing that the death penalty was applied to absolutely anybody who happened to be in the undefended city—babies, old people, the zoo animals, and thousands upon thousands of rabid Nazis, of course, and, among others, my best friend Bernard V. O'Hare and me. By all rights, O'Hare and I should have been part of the body count. The more bodies, the more correct the revenge.

INTERVIEWER

The Franklin Library is bringing out a deluxe edition of *Slaughterhouse Five*, I believe.

VONNEGUT

Yes. I was required to write a new introduction for it.

INTERVIEWER

Did you have any new thoughts?

VONNEGUT

I said that only one person on the entire planet benefited from the raid, which must have cost tens of millions of dollars. The raid didn't shorten the war by half a second, didn't weaken a German defense or attack anywhere, didn't free a single person from a death camp. Only one person benefited—not two or five or ten. Just one.

INTERVIEWER

And who was that?

VONNEGUT

Me. I got three dollars for each person killed. Imagine that.

INTERVIEWER

How much affinity do you feel toward your contemporaries?

VONNEGUT

My brother and sister writers? Friendly, certainly. It's hard for me to talk to some of them, since we seem to be in very different sorts of businesses. This was a mystery to me for a while, but then Saul Steinberg—

INTERVIEWER

The graphic artist?

VONNEGUT

Indeed. He said that in almost all arts, there were some people who responded strongly to art history, to triumphs and fiascoes and experiments of the past, and others who did not. I fell into the second group, and had to. I couldn't play games with my literary ancestors, since I had never studied them systematically. My education was as a chemist at Cornell and then an anthropologist at the University of Chicago. Christ—I was thirty-five before I went crazy about Blake, forty before I read *Madame Bovary*, forty-five before I'd even heard of Céline. Through dumb luck, I read *Look Homeward, Angel* exactly when I was supposed to.

INTERVIEWER

When?

VONNEGUT

At the age of eighteen.

INTERVIEWER

So you've always been a reader?

VONNEGUT

Yes. I grew up in a house crammed with books. But I never had to read a book for academic credit, never had to write a paper about it, never had to prove I'd understood it in a seminar. I am a hopelessly clumsy discusser of books. My experience is nil.

INTERVIEWER

Which member of your family had the most influence on you as a writer?

VONNEGUT

My mother, I guess. Edith Lieber Vonnegut. After our family lost almost all of its money in the Great Depression, my mother thought she might make a new fortune by writing for the slick magazines. She took short-story courses at night. She studied magazines the way gamblers study racing forms.

INTERVIEWER

She'd been rich at one time?

VONNEGUT

My father, an architect of modest means, married one of the richest girls in town. It was a brewing fortune based on Lieber Lager Beer and then Gold Medal Beer. Lieber Lager became Gold Medal after winning a prize at some Paris exposition.

INTERVIEWER

It must have been a very good beer.

VONNEGUT

Long before my time. I never tasted any. It had a secret ingredient, I know. My grandfather and his brewmaster wouldn't let anybody watch while they put it in.

INTERVIEWER

Do you know what it was?

VONNEGUT

Coffee.

INTERVIEWER

So your mother studied short-story writing—

VONNEGUT

And my father painted pictures in a studio he'd set up on the top floor of the house. There wasn't much work for architects during the Great Depression—not much work for anybody. Strangely enough, though, Mother was right: Even mediocre magazine writers were making money hand over fist.

INTERVIEWER

So your mother took a very practical attitude toward writing.

VONNEGUT

Not to say crass. She was a highly intelligent, cultivated woman, by the way. She went to the same high school I did, and was one of the few people who got nothing but A-pluses while she was there. She went east to a finishing school after that, and then traveled all over Europe. She was fluent in German and French. I still have her high-school report cards somewhere. A-plus, A-plus, A-plus . . . She was a good writer, it turned out, but she had no talent for the vulgarity the slick magazines required. Fortunately, I was loaded with vulgarity, so when I grew up I was able to make her dream come true. Writing for *Collier's* and *The Saturday Evening Post* and *Cosmopolitan* and *Ladies' Home Journal* and so on was as easy as falling off a log for me. I only wish she'd lived to see it. I only wish she'd lived to see all her grandchildren. She has ten. She didn't even get to see the first one. I made another one of her dreams come true: I lived on Cape Cod for many years. She always wanted to live on Cape Cod.

It's probably very common for sons to try to make their mothers' impossible dreams come true. I adopted my sister's sons after she died, and it's spooky to watch them try to make her impossible dreams come true.

What were your sister's dreams like?

She wanted to live like a member of *The Swiss Family Robinson*, with impossibly friendly animals in impossibly congenial isolation. Her oldest son, Jim, has been a goat farmer on a mountaintop in Jamaica for the past eight years. No telephone. No electricity.

The Indianapolis high school you and your mother attended—

And my father. Shortridge High.

It had a daily paper, I believe.

Yes. The *Shortridge Daily Echo*. There was a print shop right in the school. Students wrote the paper. Students set the type. After school.

You just laughed about something.

It was something dumb I remembered about high school. It doesn't have anything to do with writing.

INTERVIEWER

You care to share it with us anyway?

VONNEGUT

Oh—I just remembered something that happened in a high-school course on civics, on how our government worked. The teacher asked each of us to stand up in turn and tell what we did after school. I was sitting in the back of the room, sitting next to a guy named J. T. Alburger. He later became an insurance man in Los Angeles. He died fairly recently. Anyway—he kept nudging me, urging me, daring me to tell the truth about what I did after school. He offered me five dollars to tell the truth. He wanted me to stand up and say, I make model airplanes and jerk off.

INTERVIEWER

I see.

VONNEGUT

I also worked on the *Shortridge Daily Echo*.

INTERVIEWER

Was that fun?

VONNEGUT

Fun and easy. I've always found it easy to write. Also, I learned to write for peers rather than for teachers. Most beginning writers don't get to write for peers—to catch hell from peers.

INTERVIEWER

So every afternoon you would go to the *Echo* office—

VONNEGUT

Yeah. And one time, while I was writing, I happened to sniff my armpits absentmindedly. Several people saw me do it, and thought it was funny—and ever after that I was given the name "Snarf." In the annual for my graduating class, the class of 1940, I'm listed as "Kurt Snarfield Vonnegut, Jr." Technically, I wasn't really a snarf. A snarf was a person who went around sniffing girls' bicycle saddles. I didn't do that. *Twerp* also had a very specific meaning, which few people know now. Through careless usage, twerp is a pretty formless insult now.

INTERVIEWER

What is a twerp in the strictest sense, in the original sense?

VONNEGUT

It's a person who inserts a set of false teeth between the cheeks of his ass.

INTERVIEWER

I see.

VONNEGUT

I beg your pardon; between the cheeks of his or *her* ass. I'm always offending feminists that way.

INTERVIEWER

I don't quite understand why someone would do that with false teeth.

VONNEGUT

In order to bite the buttons off the backseats of taxicabs. That's the only reason twerps do it. It's all that turns them on.

INTERVIEWER

You went to Cornell University after Shortridge?

VONNEGUT

I imagine.

INTERVIEWER

You imagine?

VONNEGUT

I had a friend who was a heavy drinker. If somebody asked him if he'd been drunk the night before, he would always answer offhand-edly, Oh, I imagine. I've always liked that answer. It acknowledges life as a dream. Cornell was a boozy dream, partly because of booze itself, and partly because I was enrolled exclusively in courses I had no talent for. My father and brother agreed that I should study chemistry, since my brother had done so well with chemicals at MIT. He's eight years older than I am. Funnier, too. His most fa-mous discovery is that silver iodide will sometimes make it rain or snow.

INTERVIEWER

Was your sister funny, too?

VONNEGUT

Oh, yes. There was an odd cruel streak to her sense of humor, though, which didn't fit in with the rest of her character somehow. She thought it was terribly funny whenever anybody fell down. One time she saw a woman come out of a streetcar horizontally, and she laughed for weeks after that.

INTERVIEWER

Horizontally?

VONNEGUT

Yes. This woman must have caught her heels somehow. Anyway, the streetcar door opened, and my sister happened to be watching from the sidewalk, and then she saw this woman come out horizontally—as straight as a board, face down, and about two feet off the ground.

INTERVIEWER

Slapstick?

VONNEGUT

Sure. We loved Laurel and Hardy. You know what one of the funniest things is that can happen in a film?

INTERVIEWER

No.

VONNEGUT

To have somebody walk through what looks like a shallow little puddle, but which is actually six feet deep. I remember a movie where Cary Grant was loping across lawns at night. He came to a low hedge, which he cleared ever so gracefully, only there was a twenty-foot drop on the other side. But the thing my sister and I loved best was when somebody in a movie would tell everybody off, and then make a grand exit into the coat closet. He had to come out again, of course, all tangled in coat hangers and scarves.

INTERVIEWER

Did you take a degree in chemistry at Cornell?

VONNEGUT

I was flunking everything by the middle of my junior year. I was delighted to join the army and go to war. After the war, I went to the University of Chicago, where I was pleased to study anthropology, a science that was mostly poetry, that involved almost no math at all. I was married by then, and soon had one kid, who was Mark. He would later go crazy, of course, and write a fine book about it—*The Eden Express*. He has just fathered a kid himself, my first grandchild, a boy named Zachary. Mark is finishing his second year in Harvard Medical School, and will be about the only member of his class not to be in debt when he graduates—because of the book. That's a pretty decent recovery from a crack-up, I'd say.

INTERVIEWER

Did the study of anthropology later color your writings?

VONNEGUT

It confirmed my atheism, which was the faith of my fathers anyway. Religions were exhibited and studied as the Rube Goldberg inventions I'd always thought they were. We weren't allowed to find one culture superior to any other. We caught hell if we mentioned races much. It was highly idealistic.

INTERVIEWER

Almost a religion?

VONNEGUT

Exactly. And the only one for me. So far.

INTERVIEWER

What was your dissertation?

VONNEGUT

Cat's Cradle.

INTERVIEWER

But you wrote that years after you left Chicago, didn't you?

VONNEGUT

I left Chicago without writing a dissertation—and without a degree. All my ideas for dissertations had been rejected, and I was broke, so I took a job as a PR man for General Electric in Schenectady. Twenty years later, I got a letter from a new dean at Chicago, who had been looking through my dossier. Under the rules of the university, he said, a published work of high quality could be substituted for a dissertation, so I was entitled to an M.A. He had shown *Cat's Cradle* to the anthropology department, and they had said it was halfway decent anthropology, so they were mailing me my degree. I'm class of 1972 or so.

INTERVIEWER

Congratulations.

VONNEGUT

It was nothing, really. A piece of cake.

INTERVIEWER

Some of the characters in *Cat's Cradle* were based on people you knew at GE, isn't that so?

VONNEGUT

Dr. Felix Hoenikker, the absentminded scientist, was a caricature of Dr. Irving Langmuir, the star of the GE research laboratory. I knew him some. My brother worked with him. Langmuir was wonderfully absentminded. He wondered out loud one time whether, when turtles pulled in their heads, their spines buckled or contracted. I put that in the book. One time he left a tip under his plate after his wife served him breakfast at home. I put that in. His most important contribution, though, was the idea for what I called "Ice-9," a form of frozen water that was stable at room temperature. He didn't tell it directly to me. It was a legend around the laboratory—about the time H. G. Wells came to Schenectady. That was long before my time. I was just a little boy when it happened—listening to the radio, building model airplanes.

INTERVIEWER

Yes?

VONNEGUT

Anyway—Wells came to Schenectady, and Langmuir was told to be his host. Langmuir thought he might entertain Wells with an idea for a science-fiction story—about a form of ice that was stable at room temperature. Wells was uninterested, or at least never used the idea. And then Wells died, and then, finally, Langmuir died. I thought to myself: Finders, keepers—the idea is mine. Langmuir, incidentally, was the first scientist in private industry to win a Nobel Prize.

INTERVIEWER

How do you feel about Bellow's winning the Nobel Prize for Literature?

VONNEGUT

It was the best possible way to honor our entire literature.

INTERVIEWER

Do you find it easy to talk to him?

VONNEGUT

Yes. I've had about three opportunities. I was his host one time at the University of Iowa, where I was teaching and he was lecturing. It went very well. We had one thing in common, anyway—

INTERVIEWER

Which was—?

VONNEGUT

We were both products of the anthropology department of the University of Chicago. So far as I know, he never went on any anthropological expeditions, and neither did I. We invented preindustrial peoples instead—I in *Cat's Cradle* and he in *Henderson the Rain King*.

INTERVIEWER

So he is a fellow scientist.

VONNEGUT

I'm no scientist at all. I'm glad, though, now, that I was pressured into becoming a scientist by my father and my brother. I understand how scientific reasoning and playfulness work, even though I have no talent for joining in. I enjoy the company of scientists, am easily excited and entertained when they tell me what they're doing. I've spent a lot more time with scientists than with literary people, my brother's friends, mostly. I enjoy plumbers and carpenters and automobile mechanics, too. I didn't get to know any literary people until the last ten years, starting with two years of teaching at Iowa. There at Iowa, I was suddenly friends with Nelson Algren and José Donoso and Vance Bourjaily and Donald Justice and George Starbuck and Marvin Bell, and so on. I was amazed. Now, judging from the reviews my latest book, *Slapstick*, has received, people would like to bounce me out of the literary establishment—send me back where I came from.

INTERVIEWER

There were some bad reviews?

VONNEGUT

Only in *The New York Times*, *TIME*, *Newsweek*, *The New York Review of Books*, *The Village Voice*, and *Rolling Stone*. They loved me in Medicine Hat.

INTERVIEWER

To what do you attribute this rancor?

VONNEGUT

Slapstick may be a very bad book. I am perfectly willing to believe that. Everybody else writes lousy books, so why shouldn't I? What was unusual about the reviews was that they wanted people to admit now that I had never been any good. The reviewer for the Sunday *Times* actually asked critics who had praised me in the past to now admit in public how wrong they'd been. My publisher, Sam Lawrence, tried to comfort me by saying that authors were invariably attacked when they became fabulously well-to-do.

INTERVIEWER

You needed comforting?

VONNEGUT

I never felt worse in my life. I felt as though I were sleeping standing up on a boxcar in Germany again.

INTERVIEWER

That bad?

VONNEGUT

No. But bad enough. All of a sudden, critics wanted me squashed
like a bug. And it wasn't just that I had money all of a sudden, either.
The hidden complaint was that I was barbarous, that I wrote without
having made a systematic study of great literature, that I was no gentleman, since I had done hack writing so cheerfully for vulgar
magazines—that I had not paid my academic dues.

INTERVIEWER

You had not suffered?

VONNEGUT

I had suffered, all right—but as a badly educated person in vulgar
company and in a vulgar trade. It was dishonorable enough that I per-
verted art for money. I then topped that felony by becoming, as I say,
fabulously well-to-do. Well, that's just too damn bad for me and for
everybody. I'm completely in print, so we're all stuck with me and
stuck with my books.

INTERVIEWER

Do you mean to fight back?

VONNEGUT

In a way. I'm on the New York State Council for the Arts now, and
every so often some other member talks about sending notices to college English departments about some literary opportunity, and I say,
Send them to the chemistry departments, send them to the zoology

departments, send them to the anthropology departments and the astronomy departments and physics departments, and all the medical and law schools. That's where the writers are most likely to be.

INTERVIEWER

You believe that?

VONNEGUT

I think it can be tremendously refreshing if a creator of literature has something on his mind other than the history of literature so far. Literature should not disappear up its own asshole, so to speak.

INTERVIEWER

Let's talk about the women in your books.

VONNEGUT

There aren't any. No real women, no love.

INTERVIEWER

Is this worth expounding upon?

VONNEGUT

It's a mechanical problem. So much of what happens in storytelling is mechanical, has to do with the technical problems of how to make a story work. Cowboy stories and policeman stories end in shoot-outs, for example, because shoot-outs are the most reliable mechanisms for making such stories end. There is nothing like death to say what is always such an artificial thing to say: The end. I try to keep deep love out of my stories because, once that particular subject comes up, it is almost impossible to talk about anything else. Readers don't want to hear about anything else. They go gaga about love. If a lover in a story wins his true love, that's the end of the tale, even if World War III is about to begin, and the sky is black with flying saucers.

INTERVIEWER

So you keep love out.

VONNEGUT

I have other things I want to talk about. Ralph Ellison did the same thing in *Invisible Man*. If the hero in that magnificent book had found somebody worth loving, somebody who was crazy about him, that would have been the end of the story. Céline did the same thing in *Journey to the End of Night*: he excluded the possibility of true and final love—so that the story could go on and on and on.

INTERVIEWER

Not many writers talk about the mechanics of stories.

VONNEGUT

I am such a barbarous technocrat that I believe they can be tinkered with like Model T Fords.

INTERVIEWER

To what end?

VONNEGUT

To give the reader pleasure.

INTERVIEWER

Will you ever write a love story, do you think?

VONNEGUT

Maybe. I lead a loving life. I really do. Even when I'm leading that loving life, though, and it's going so well, I sometimes find myself thinking, My goodness, couldn't we talk about something else for just a little while? You know what's really funny?

INTERVIEWER

No.

VONNEGUT

My books are being thrown out of school libraries all over the country—because they're supposedly obscene. I've seen letters to small-town newspapers that put *Slaughterhouse Five* in the same class with *Deep Throat* and *Hustler* magazine. How could anybody masturbate to *Slaughterhouse Five*?

INTERVIEWER

It takes all kinds.

VONNEGUT

Well, that kind doesn't exist. It's my religion the censors hate. They find me disrespectful toward their idea of God Almighty. They think it's the proper business of government to protect the reputation of God. All I can say is, Good luck to them, and good luck to the government, and good luck to God. You know what H. L. Mencken said one time about religious people? He said he'd been greatly misunderstood. He said he didn't hate them. He simply found them comical.

INTERVIEWER

When I asked you a while back which member of your family had influenced you most as a writer, you said your mother. I had expected you to say your sister, since you talked so much about her in *Slapstick*.

VONNEGUT

I said in *Slapstick* that she was the person I wrote for—that every successful creative person creates with an audience of one in mind. That's the secret of artistic unity. Anybody can achieve it, if he or she will make something with only one person in mind. I didn't realize that she was the person I wrote for until after she died.

INTERVIEWER

She loved literature?

VONNEGUT

She wrote wonderfully well. She didn't read much—but then again, neither in later years did Henry David Thoreau. My father was the same way: he didn't read much, but he could write like a dream. Such letters my father and sister wrote! When I compare their prose with mine, I am ashamed.

INTERVIEWER

Did your sister try to write for money, too?

VONNEGUT

No. She could have been a remarkable sculptor, too. I bawled her out one time for not doing more with the talents she had. She replied that having talent doesn't carry with it the obligation that something has to be done with it. This was startling news to me. I thought people were supposed to grab their talents and run as far and fast as they could.

INTERVIEWER

What do you think now?

VONNEGUT

Well—what my sister said now seems a peculiarly feminine sort of wisdom. I have two daughters who are as talented as she was, and both of them are damned if they are going to lose their poise and senses of humor by snatching up their talents and desperately running as far and as fast as they can. They saw me run as far and as fast as I could—and it must have looked like quite a crazy performance to them. And this is the worst possible metaphor, for what they actually saw was a man sitting still for decades.

INTERVIEWER

At a typewriter.

VONNEGUT

Yes, and smoking his fool head off.

INTERVIEWER

Have you ever stopped smoking?

VONNEGUT

Twice. Once I did it cold turkey, and turned into Santa Claus. I became roly-poly. I was approaching two hundred and fifty pounds. I stopped for almost a year, and then the University of Hawaii brought me to Oahu to speak. I was drinking out of a coconut on the roof of the Ili Kai one night, and all I had to do to complete the ring of my happiness was to smoke a cigarette. Which I did.

INTERVIEWER

The second time?

VONNEGUT

Very recently—last year. I paid Smokenders a hundred and fifty dollars to help me quit, over a period of six weeks. It was exactly as they had promised—easy and instructive. I won my graduation certificate and recognition pin. The only trouble was that I had also gone insane. I was supremely happy and proud, but those around me found me unbearably opinionated and abrupt and boisterous. Also: I had stopped writing. I didn't even write letters anymore. I had made a bad trade, evidently. So I started smoking again. As the National Association of Manufacturers used to say, There's no such thing as a free lunch.

INTERVIEWER

Do you really think creative writing can be taught?

VONNEGUT

About the same way golf can be taught. A pro can point out obvious flaws in your swing. I did that well, I think, at the University of

Iowa for two years. Gail Godwin and John Irving and Jonathan Penner and Bruce Dobler and John Casey and Jane Casey were all students of mine out there. They've all published wonderful stuff since then. I taught creative writing badly at Harvard—because my marriage was breaking up, and because I was commuting every week to Cambridge from New York. I taught even worse at City College a couple of years ago. I had too many other projects going on at the same time. I don't have the will to teach anymore. I only know the theory.

INTERVIEWER

Could you put the theory into a few words?

VONNEGUT

It was stated by Paul Engle—the founder of the Writers' Workshop at Iowa. He told me that, if the workshop ever got a building of its own, these words should be inscribed over the entrance: Don't take it all so seriously.

INTERVIEWER

And how would that be helpful?

VONNEGUT

It would remind the students that they were learning to play practical jokes.

INTERVIEWER

Practical jokes?

VONNEGUT

If you make people laugh or cry about little black marks on sheets of white paper, what is that but a practical joke? All the great story lines are great practical jokes that people fall for over and over again.

INTERVIEWER

Can you give an example?

VONNEGUT

The Gothic novel. Dozens of the things are published every year, and they all sell. My friend Borden Deal recently wrote a Gothic novel for the fun of it, and I asked him what the plot was, and he said, A young woman takes a job in an old house and gets the pants scared off her.

INTERVIEWER

Some more examples?

VONNEGUT

The others aren't that much fun to describe: somebody gets into trouble, and then gets out again; somebody loses something and gets it back; somebody is wronged and gets revenge; Cinderella; somebody hits the skids and just goes down, down, down; people fall in love with each other, and a lot of other people get in the way; a virtuous person is falsely accused of sin; a sinful person is believed to be virtuous; a person faces a challenge bravely, and succeeds or fails; a person lies, a person steals, a person kills, a person commits fornication.

INTERVIEWER

If you will pardon my saying so, these are very old-fashioned plots.

VONNEGUT

I guarantee you that no modern story scheme, even plotlessness, will give a reader genuine satisfaction, unless one of those old-fashioned plots is smuggled in somewhere. I don't praise plots as accurate representations of life, but as ways to keep readers reading. When I used to teach creative writing, I would tell the students to make their characters want something right away—even if it's only a glass of water. Characters paralyzed by the meaninglessness of modern life still have to drink water from time to time. One of my students wrote a story about a nun who got a piece of dental floss stuck between her lower left molars, and who couldn't get it out all day long. I thought that was wonderful. The story dealt with issues a lot more important than dental floss, but what kept readers going was anxiety about when the dental floss would finally be removed. Nobody could read that story without fishing around in his mouth with a finger. Now there's an admirable practical joke for you. When you exclude plot, when you exclude anyone's wanting anything, you exclude the reader, which is a mean-spirited thing to do. You can also exclude the reader by not telling him immediately where the story is taking place, and who the people are—

INTERVIEWER

And what they want.

VONNEGUT

Yes. And you can put him to sleep by never having characters confront each other. Students like to say that they stage no confrontations because people avoid confrontations in modern life. Modern life is so lonely, they say. This is laziness. It's the writer's job to stage confrontations, so the characters will say surprising and revealing things, and educate and entertain us all. If a writer can't or won't do that, he should withdraw from the trade.

INTERVIEWER

Trade?

VONNEGUT

Trade. Carpenters build houses. Storytellers use a reader's leisure time in such a way that the reader will not feel that his time has been wasted. Mechanics fix automobiles.

INTERVIEWER

Surely talent is required?

VONNEGUT

In all those fields. I was a Saab dealer on Cape Cod for a while, and I enrolled in their mechanic's school, and they threw me out of their mechanic's school. No talent.

INTERVIEWER

How common is storytelling talent?

VONNEGUT

In a creative writing class of twenty people anywhere in this country, six students will be startlingly talented. Two of those might actually publish something by and by.

INTERVIEWER

What distinguishes those two from the rest?

VONNEGUT

They will have something other than literature itself on their minds. They will probably be hustlers, too. I mean that they won't want to wait passively for somebody to discover them. They will insist on being read.

INTERVIEWER

You have been a public relations man and an advertising man—

VONNEGUT

Oh, I imagine.

INTERVIEWER

Was this painful? I mean—did you feel your talent was being wasted, being crippled?

VONNEGUT

No. That's romance—that work of that sort damages a writer's soul. At Iowa, Dick Yates and I used to give a lecture each year on the writer and the free-enterprise system. The students hated it. We would talk about all the hack jobs writers could take in case they found themselves starving to death, or in case they wanted to accumulate enough capital to finance the writing of a book. Since publishers aren't putting money into first novels anymore, and since the magazines have died, and since television isn't buying from young freelancers anymore, and since the foundations give grants only to old poops like me, young writers are going to have to support themselves as shameless hacks. Otherwise, we are soon going to find ourselves without a contemporary literature. There is only one genuinely ghastly thing hack jobs do to writers, and that is to waste their precious time.

INTERVIEWER

No joke.

VONNEGUT

A tragedy. I just keep trying to think of ways, even horrible ways, for young writers to somehow hang on.

INTERVIEWER

Should young writers be subsidized?

VONNEGUT

Something's got to be done, now that free enterprise has made it impossible for them to support themselves through free enterprise. I was a sensational businessman in the beginning—for the simple reason that there was so much business to be done. When I was working for General Electric, I wrote a story, "Report on the Barnhouse Effect," the first story I ever wrote. I mailed it off to *Collier's*. Knox Burger was fiction editor there. Knox told me what was wrong with it and how to fix it. I did what he said, and he bought the story for seven hundred and fifty dollars, six weeks' pay at GE. I wrote another, and he paid me nine hundred and fifty dollars, and suggested that it was perhaps time for me to quit GE. Which I did. I moved to Province-town. Eventually, my price for a short story got up to twenty-nine hundred dollars a crack. Think of that. And Knox got me a couple of agents who were as shrewd about storytelling as he was—Kenneth Littauer, who had been his predecessor at *Collier's*, and Max Wilkin-son, who had been a story editor for MGM. And let it be put on the record here that Knox Burger, who is about my age, discovered and encouraged more good young writers than any other editor of his time. I don't think that's ever been written down anywhere. It's a fact known only to writers, and one that could easily vanish, if it isn't somewhere written down.

INTERVIEWER

Where is Knox Burger now?

VONNEGUT

He's a literary agent. He represents my son Mark, in fact.

INTERVIEWER

And Littauer and Wilkinson?

VONNEGUT

Littauer died ten years ago or so. He was a colonel in the Lafayette Escadrille, by the way, at the age of twenty-three—and the first man to strafe a trench. He was my mentor. Max Wilkinson has retired to Florida. It always embarrassed him to be an agent. If some stranger asked him what he did for a living, he always said he was a cotton planter.

INTERVIEWER

Do you have a new mentor now?

VONNEGUT

No. I guess I'm too old to find one. Whatever I write now is set in type without comment by my publisher, who is younger than I am, by editors, by anyone. I don't have my sister to write for anymore. Suddenly, there are all these unfilled jobs in my life.

INTERVIEWER

Do you feel as though you're up there without a net under you?

VONNEGUT

And without a balancing pole, either. It gives me the heebie-jeebies sometimes.

INTERVIEWER

Is there anything else you'd like to add?

VONNEGUT

You know the panic bars they have on the main doors of schools and theaters? If you get slammed into the door, the door will fly open?

INTERVIEWER

Yes.

VONNEGUT

The brand name on most of them is "Von Duprin." The "Von" is for Vonnegut. A relative of mine was caught in the Iroquois Theater Fire in Chicago a long time ago, and he invented the panic bar along with two other guys. "Prin" was Prinzler. I forget who "Du" was.

INTERVIEWER

OK.

VONNEGUT

And I want to say, too, that humorists are very commonly the youngest children in their families. When I was the littlest kid at our supper table, there was only one way I could get anybody's attention, and that was to be funny. I had to specialize. I used to listen to radio comedians very intently, so I could learn how to make jokes. And that's what my books are, now that I'm a grownup—mosaics of jokes.

INTERVIEWER

Do you have any favorite jokes?

VONNEGUT

My sister and I used to argue about what the funniest joke in the world was—next to a guy storming into a coat closet, of course. When the two of us worked together, incidentally, we could be almost as funny as Laurel and Hardy. That's basically what *Slapstick* was about.

INTERVIEWER

Did you finally agree on the world's champion joke?

VONNEGUT

We finally settled on two. It's sort of hard to tell either one just flat-footed like this.

INTERVIEWER

Do it anyway.

VONNEGUT

Well—you won't laugh. Nobody ever laughs. But one is an old Two Black Crows joke. The Two Black Crows were white guys in blackface—named Moran and Mack. They made phonograph records of their routines, two supposedly black guys talking lazily to each other. Anyway, one of them says, "Last night I dreamed I was eating flannel cakes." The other one says, "Is that so?" And the first one says, "And when I woke up, the blanket was gone."

INTERVIEWER

Um.

VONNEGUT

I told you you wouldn't laugh. The other champion joke requires your cooperation. I will ask you a question, and you will have to say "No."

INTERVIEWER

OK.

VONNEGUT

Do you know why cream is so much more expensive than milk?

INTERVIEWER

No.

VONNEGUT

Because the cows hate to squat on those little bottles. See, you didn't laugh again, but I give you my sacred word of honor that those are splendid jokes. Exquisite craftsmanship.

INTERVIEWER

You seem to prefer Laurel and Hardy over Chaplin. Is that so?

VONNEGUT

I'm crazy about Chaplin, but there's too much distance between him and his audience. He is too obviously a genius. In his own way, he's as brilliant as Picasso, and this is intimidating to me.

INTERVIEWER

Will you ever write another short story?

VONNEGUT

Maybe. I wrote what I thought would be my last one about eight years ago. Harlan Ellison asked me to contribute to a collection he was making. The story's called "The Big Space Fuck." I think I am the first writer to use "fuck" in a title. It was about firing a spaceship with a warhead full of jizzum at Andromeda. Which reminds me of my good Indianapolis friend, about the only Indianapolis friend I've got left—William Failey. When we got into the Second World War, and everybody was supposed to give blood, he wondered if he couldn't give a pint of jizzum instead.

INTERVIEWER

If your parents hadn't lost all their money, what would you be doing now?

VONNEGUT

I'd be an Indianapolis architect—like my father and grandfather. And very happy, too. I still wish that had happened. One thing, anyway: One of the best young architects out there lives in a house my father built for our family the year I was born—1922. My initials, and my sister's initials, and my brother's initials are all written in leaded glass in the three little windows by the front door.

INTERVIEWER

So you have good old days you hanker for.

VONNEGUT

Yes. Whenever I go to Indianapolis, the same question asks itself over and over again in my head: Where's my bed, where's my bed? And if my father's and grandfather's ghosts haunt that town, they must be wondering where all their buildings have gone to. The center of the city, where most of their buildings were, has been turned into parking lots. They must be wondering where all their relatives went, too. They grew up in a huge extended family which is no more. I got the slightest taste of that—the big family thing. And when I went to the University of Chicago, and I heard the head of the Department of Anthropology, Robert Redfield, lecture on the folk society, which was essentially a stable, isolated extended family, he did not have to tell me how nice that could be.

INTERVIEWER

Anything else?

VONNEGUT

Well—I just discovered a prayer for writers. I'd heard of prayers for sailors and kings and soldiers and so on—but never of a prayer for writers. Could I put that in here?

INTERVIEWER

Certainly.

VONNEGUT

It was written by Samuel Johnson on April 3, 1753, the day on which he signed a contract that required him to write the first complete dictionary of the English language. He was praying for himself. Perhaps April third should be celebrated as Writers' Day. Anyway, this is the prayer: "O God, who hast hitherto supported me, enable me to proceed in this labor, and in the whole task of my present state; that when I shall render up, at the last day, an account of the talent committed to me, I may receive pardon, for the sake of Jesus Christ. Amen."

INTERVIEWER

That seems to be a wish to carry his talent as far and as fast as he can.

VONNEGUT

Yes. He was a notorious hack.

INTERVIEWER

And you consider yourself a hack?

VONNEGUT

Of a sort.

INTERVIEWER

What sort?

VONNEGUT

A child of the Great Depression. And perhaps we should say something at this point how this interview itself was done—unless candor would somehow spoil everything.

INTERVIEWER

Let the chips fall where they may.

VONNEGUT

Four different interviews with me were submitted to *The Paris Review*. These were patched together to form a single interview, which was shown to me. This scheme worked only fairly well, so I called in yet another interviewer to make it all of a piece. I was that person. With utmost tenderness, I interviewed myself.

INTERVIEWER

I see. Our last question. If you were Commissar of Publishing in the United States, what would you do to alleviate the present deplorable situation?

VONNEGUT

There is no shortage of wonderful writers. What we lack is a dependable mass of readers.

INTERVIEWER

So—?

VONNEGUT

I propose that every person out of work be required to submit a book report before he or she gets his or her welfare check.

INTERVIEWER

Thank you.

VONNEGUT

Thank *you*.

Issue 69, 1977

James M. Cain

The Art of Fiction

J ames M. Cain, best known as the author of *The Postman Always Rings Twice, Double Indemnity*, and *Mildred Pierce*, was born in Maryland in 1892. After an army career and early aspirations of becoming a singer, as his mother had been, he was a reporter and journalist for many years in Baltimore and New York. His first story was published in H. L. Mencken's *American Mercury*. When *The Postman Always Rings Twice* appeared in print in 1934, it became an immediate bestseller. The next year *Double Indemnity* was equivalently successful, and Cain became known for something more than his early journalism or his Hollywood scripts. Today it is perhaps more through the films of his novels that we remember Cain: *The Postman Always Rings Twice* was filmed with Lana Turner and John Garfield in Hollywood, and later (without authorization) in Italy served as the basis of Luschine Visconti's first film *Ossessione*. Billy Wilder's *Double Indemnity*, with a script by Raymond Chandler, is a classic thriller; Joan Crawford won an Academy Award for the lead role in *Mildred Pierce*.

Cain died October 31, 1977, in University Park, Maryland, near where he grew up, went to college, and taught. This interview was conducted on January 7, 1977, at his home, a small two-story frame house on a quiet street. The sitting room was furnished simply; an upright piano stood against a wall. Then eighty-five, Cain was gaunt, his voice raspy, but mentally he gave nothing away to his years. He lived alone in Hyattsville. His stationery bore a notice suggesting the reclusive and quiet nature of his last years: to those trying to get in

Cain

J. M. Cain,
616 East 10th St.,
Burbank. Calif.   BAR-B-C
                By James M. Cain

They threw me off the hay truck about noon. I
had swung on the night before, down at the border, and as
soon as I got up there under the canvas, I went to sleep.
I needed plenty of that, after three weeks in Tia Juana, and
I was still getting it when they pulled off to one side
to let the engine cool. Then they saw a foot sticking out
and threw me off. I tried some comical stuff, but all I
got was a dead pan, so that gag was out. They gave me
a cigarette, though, and I hiked down the road to find something
to eat.

        That was when I hit this Twin Oaks Tavern. It was
nothing but a roadside sandwich joint, like a million others
in California. There was a lunchroom part, and over that
the house part, where they lived, and off to one side a
filling station, and out back a half dozen shacks that they
called an auto court. I blew in there in a hurry and began
looking down the road. When the Greek showed, I asked if a guy
had been by in a cadillac. He was to pick me up here, I said,
and we were to have lunch. Not today, said the Greek. He
layed a place at one of the tables and asked me what I was going
to have. I said orange juice, corn flakes, fried eggs and
bacon, enchilada, flapjacks, and coffee. Pretty soon he came
out with the orange juice and the corn flakes.

        "Hold on, now. One thing I got to tell you. If this
guy don't show up, you'll have to trust me for it. This was to

A manuscript page from James M. Cain's "Bar-B-Q," an early draft
of his novel *The Postman Always Rings Twice*.

touch with him by phone he had printed on the bottom of each page, "Station to station does it—there's nobody here but me."

—*David L. Zinsser, 1978*

INTERVIEWER

So this is where you grew up?

JAMES M. CAIN

I was born in Annapolis. I lived there eleven years and then my father, who had been vice president and a professor of English at St. John's College, became president of Washington College across the bay, which is still there. It's one of the old ones; George Washington contributed to its endowment. And that's where I went to college. The next four years I had a pretty rough time because I didn't know, nor did anyone else, that I was due to become a writer. I had several jobs that just made no sense. Suddenly I decided to be a singer, sending my mother nuts. She said I had nothing for it. Turned out she was right but she should have kept her flap shut and let me find out for myself. But then one day, just for no reason, I was sitting in Lafayette Park, and I heard my own voice telling me, You're going to be a writer. For no reason at all. Just like that. Now there had been signs. One sign nobody paid any attention to was when I was maybe ten years old. My father smoked Turkish Trophy cigarettes. At first he rolled his own, and then he bought ready-mades. Each pack was in a black and red box; they were oval cigarettes with coupons in each pack. For seventy of these things you could get a fountain pen. I would send off seventy of these things and got a succession of fountain pens. You know how you filled fountain pens at that time, don't you? You unscrewed them and filled it with an eyedropper. Today, whenever I take out the clinical thermometer to take my temperature, I think of those pens and the eyedroppers. So the succession of fountain pens may have been an omen at the age of ten.

INTERVIEWER

Were there other signs?

CAIN

Well, when I went to Baltimore to work for the gas company, the first of the meaningless jobs I held when I was just out of college, I kept going down to this whorehouse on Saturday nights. I never did go upstairs, though twice I wanted to. One night I met this girl who was awful pretty, and she had pretty legs. I badly wanted to go upstairs with her, but I was afraid because of the disease that I imagined she had. (In Paris during the war I bumped into a girl, and I was horribly lonely, didn't particularly crave her physically, but she approached me, and asked me to spend the night, and I'm glad I didn't because I think she would have had my wallet with everything else.) But during this six months I worked for the gas company, I kept going down to that area around Josephine Street. At one of these places you could buy a bottle of beer for fifty cents. "Small as a whorehouse beer" was an expression then. They'd serve them up in glasses so small that thimbles were twice as big. For that fifty cents you were welcome to do anything, downstairs—get along with the girls, stick around—I was just eighteen years old. I listened a lot downstairs. Upstairs was another matter. I was a potential customer, of course. I guess the things you didn't do . . .

INTERVIEWER

What prompted your move to New York City, away from the Baltimore papers?

CAIN

In 1924, I had met Mencken in Baltimore. He gave me a lot of encouragement and published some pieces of mine in *American Mercury*. It's funny; people always take him at his own evaluation—an iconoclast, a mocker, a heaver of dead cats into the sanctuary. That's the way he put it one time, and he was certainly all those things. But a man who writes words knows that there comes a point when you have to ask: What's this guy for, what's he in favor of? I don't think Mencken would have lifted a finger to defend the rights of some colored man in Baltimore to get up and make a speech against the white society. But anyway, he knew I wanted to work in New York, at the

World. Actually, I talked myself into a job there by seeing Arthur Krock. I wanted to get this job on my own cheek; the guy respects you for that. Another thing, you get a much better job on your own cheek than if the guy gives you a job as a favor to whoever wrote the letter. Mencken gave me a letter of introduction that I never presented. But he loused me up. Without my knowing, he wrote Krock with the best intentions in the world, as he just loved me, and that crossed me up because I didn't get the job on my own after all. So Krock took me in to see Walter Lippmann. Lippmann wanted to know what I could do for a job, so I started talking with him. I told him I'd noticed that they didn't seem to have any articles on the editorial page of *The New York World*. I was just out of the lung house—I'd had tuberculosis—and I had to have a job that wouldn't involve too much walking around. So I suggested a job where I would just sit around and *think up* articles, ideas. I said I knew articles didn't grow on trees. Surely it was practically a full-time job, thinking up articles for a newspaper. I went on like this, with Lippmann staring at me while I tried to talk myself into a job. I knew I was getting somewhere in a direction altogether different, that he was listening to what I had to say, and though disregarding it, he was meditating. I thought, What the hell is with this guy? He interrupted to ask if I had any specimens of my writing. Writing, I thought, what has writing got to do with it? I was still talking about thinking up articles. Later, when we got to be easy friends, I asked him about this first interview and he said, I began to realize as I listened to you talk, that none of your infinitives were split, all of your pronouns were correct, and that none of your participles dangled. That was true. I talked the way my father had beat into me; he was a shot for style, and that's what got me a job.

INTERVIEWER

Don't you ever speak like your characters?

CAIN

I slip into the vulgate every once in a while—an affectation I only half-understand. There I am speaking impeccable English and suddenly I lingo it up.

What were your impressions of Lippmann?

Nothing startling about him except the difference between the man and his literary style. On paper, Lippmann was always to my eye and ear a bit literary. He was so described when he died—people doubtless thought of him as a small nervous man. He was not small—but a big, stocky guy, very powerful, with thick, strong hands. He wrote in a microscopic hand, so small the printers had to put a glass on it to read it.

What did he have you do on the *World*?

I wrote editorials. Now this was tough, because I'd never read an editorial. Now this might amuse you: the first editorial I ever wrote. Miss Lasham, his tiny secretary, gave me a stack of New York papers to give me an idea, and an office and a typewriter. At least, the typewriter was an Underwood, which is the kind I like. Mr. Highland, from the typesetting office, said, Now here's a subject for you to write about—the Ruhr. Well, I said, sure I could write about it soon as I found out where it is. So I sat there in my office thinking, never read any goddamn editorials yet, and now I'm supposed to be *writing* one. Then it flitted through my mind what we always said in Sun City: Editorials (we called them idiotorials) were written by trained seals whose only qualifications were that they be in favor of motherhood and against the man-eating shark. So I wrote this editorial: We're all in favor of motherhood, I said, but what's with this fish? Why should we be against the man-eating shark? It's a very well-behaved fish, I said, given to no unseemly outcries, which doesn't attack unless attack-ted (I put that in). Leave us never forget, I said, that the man-eating shark is a fish that brings forth its young alive. It's been doing this for two million years, long before the human race had ever been heard of, they were mothers long before we were. Obviously the man-eating shark in a very real sense *is* motherhood. So that was the first one. I'd put those things into the secretary's basket and sneak down the stairs.

INTERVIEWER

What was Lippmann's opinion of your editorials?

CAIN

Well, he read them at least. He once asked me if I realized that forty percent of the allusions in my editorials were to Lewis Carroll and W. S. Gilbert. But Mencken! Did you know that he never even read *Alice in Wonderland*? Imagine: Henry Mencken never read the greatest novel in the English language.

INTERVIEWER

After the *World* you went to *The New Yorker*, didn't you? You were the managing editor there.

CAIN

I needed a good salary because I had been working for the *World*, doing editorials and features, as well as writing in the weekend magazine. Combined, I got two hundred and fifty dollars, a nice wage in those days. With the *New Yorker* job, I got the same thing.

INTERVIEWER

What was your recollection of working with Harold Ross?

CAIN

If I started talking about it I would sound as if I were a guy who virtuously knew all the right answers and that Ross could not accept my superior wisdom. But I have to preface that by saying that it was a job that I was weirdly unqualified for temperamentally. I wasn't a flop at the job, but it meant nothing to me; I couldn't take any pride in it. I did well enough.

Ross had a streak that nobody who writes him up ever mentions. I don't think Thurber had any idea this streak in Ross existed that I had to battle morning, noon, and night. I'll tell you what the streak was. He had this reputation, you know, of getting out the most sophisticated magazine in the world, yet he'd talk like a Colorado hillbilly; he'd say to me, We gotta get this place organized. I didn't quite know what he meant, but after being there a couple of weeks, I began to detect this uneasy improvisation . . . things getting lost, nobody quite knowing how to go about things, and I began to get what he was talking about. My first realization came from my own experience. I'd inherited a girl from Ogden Nash, a secretary, and I discovered I was spending my days not doing my work but telling her how to do hers. Finally, after making an inquiry about it, and finding out she came from a family comfortably situated here in New York and wouldn't starve if she got let out, I let her out and told Ross, I'm getting a new girl. The trouble with this girl is that she's no good because you don't pay her enough, only about twenty-two dollars a week. You can't get a good girl for twenty-two dollars; I'm going to pay thirty-five dollars. In the depths of the Depression, thirty-five dollars a week was quite nice pay for a secretary. He gulped and looked rather strange. Ross had this idea about "talent," meaning only writers and artists. He was wonderful up there at 21, his table was a hub—they just doted on him. Sitting down with him for five minutes, he was the big gun; you can't imagine his magnetism, the inspiration he was to these people. But he regarded secretaries and "nontalent" functionaries around the magazine, accountants and things like that, as practically thieves, probably with their hands in the till. He begrudged them every dime they made. One time he said to me, Plugs, Cain, plugs. I can't get a *writer* except by watching everywhere and grabbing him off. But I can get a line around the block of these secretaries just by putting an ad in the paper. They're all plugs. Human ciphers, he meant. I said, Look, to me they're all human beings and there's no such thing as a plug. But for the sake of argument, let's call them plugs. They're good plugs and bad plugs. And there are plugs competent to do their work and those that aren't. By getting competent secretaries and paying them enough that they do their work, you'll save money; you won't need as many editors. That wasn't the only battle I had with him. He was inclined to make his decisions without consulting me. I didn't ask for approval, but if something was going across my desk I had to know. He made deals I didn't even know about. The thing that finally brought me up tight was the case of John O'Hara. O'Hara wanted an advance from the magazine; Ross promised it to him. When I heard about it, I made an issue of it. I said, Goddam it, you cannot do things like that without my knowing. Then Ross withdrew the advance from O'Hara, or said he did. And I then thought, Why in hell do I make an issue of these things? Here's a man, O'Hara, you have every admiration for, who's personally fairly cold, but who is a very gifted writer. He ought to be in this magazine. And yet you're making an issue of the thing. What the hell are you doing this god-dam job for anyway? It happened that my agent had been making noises about getting me a Hollywood offer; I had lunch with him the day this O'Hara business came up, and I said, OK, you've been talking a Hollywood offer. If you can get it, I'm receptive. I guess I'm ready to go out there. He had the offer by three o'clock that afternoon. So that's how I quit *The New Yorker*.

INTERVIEWER

What was Ross like personally?

CAIN

After six o'clock Ross was a nice guy. He had a gummy, toothy grin, like Caruso. And he listened to other men's jokes. But I didn't like it. New York is not even a city, it's a congerie of rotten villages. Besides, I had come from a newspaper where the ideal was informa-tion. *The New Yorker*'s ideal was entertainment. I earned my money, but I had no pride or satisfaction.

INTERVIEWER

So you had no regrets at leaving?

CAIN

One personal reason for being pleased at being in California was that I couldn't seem to write about New York. Those funny New York taxi drivers weren't funny to me. I couldn't manage the New

York idiom. If you can't write like New York, you have no business living in New York and making New York the locale of your stories. There would be a falsity to it. When I got out to California, I found the people there spoke my lingo. They use a little better grammar in California than they do in Maryland, but what was even better for me was the roughneck who uses fairly good grammar. I found by putting the story in his mouth it wasn't so knobby and gnarled for the reader. It would kind of go along . . . easy reading. So, suddenly, out there in California I began writing in the local idiom. Everything broke for me.

INTERVIEWER

You were nearly in your forties then. Wasn't this quite late to think of becoming a novelist?

CAIN

A lot of novelists start late—Conrad, Pirandello, even Mark Twain. When you're young, chess is all right, and music and poetry. But novel-writing is something else. It has to be learned, but it can't be taught. This bunkum and stinkum of college creative-writing courses! The academics don't know that the only thing you can do for someone who wants to write is to buy him a typewriter.

INTERVIEWER

Do you have any memory of the origins of *The Postman Always Rings Twice*?

CAIN

Oh yes, I can remember the beginning of *The Postman*. It was based on the Snyder-Gray case, which was in the papers about then. You ever hear of it? Well, Grey and this woman Snyder killed her husband for the insurance money. Walter Lippmann went to that trial one day and she brushed by him, what was her name? Lee Snyder.*

*Her name was actually Ruth Snyder.

Walter said it seemed very odd to be inhaling the perfume or being brushed by the dress of a woman he knew was going to be electrocuted. So the Snyder-Grey case provided the basis. The big influence in *how* I wrote *The Postman Always Rings Twice* was this strange guy, Vincent Lawrence, who had more effect on my writing than anyone else. He had a device which he thought was so important—the "love rack" he called it. I have never yet, as I sit here, figured out how this goddamn rack was spelled . . . whether it was *wrack*, or *rack*, or what dictionary connection could be found between the word and his concept. What he meant by the "love rack" was the poetic situation whereby the audience felt the love between the characters. He called this the "one, the two, and the three." Someone, I think it was Phil Goodman, the producer and another great influence, who once reminded him that this one, two, and three was nothing more than Aristotle's beginning, middle, and end. OK, Goody, Lawrence said, who the hell was Aristotle, and who did he lick? I always thought that was the perfect philistinism.

INTERVIEWER

How did it work?

CAIN

Lawrence would explain what he meant with an illustration, say a picture like *Susan Lenox*, where Garbo was an ill-abused Swedish farm girl who jumped into a wagon and brought the whip down over the horses and went galloping away and ended up in front of this farmhouse that Clark Gable, who was an engineer, had rented. And he takes her in. He's very honorable with her, doesn't do anything, gives her a place to sleep, puts her horses away and feeds them . . . He didn't have any horses himself, but he did have two dozen ears of corn to feed hers. Well, the next day he takes the day off and the two of them go fishing. He's still very honorable, and she's very self-conscious and standoffish. She reels in a fish (they used a live fish—must have had it in a bucket). She says, I'll cook him for your supper. And with that she gave herself away; his arms went around her. This fish, this live fish, was what Lawrence meant by a "love rack"; the audience suddenly felt what the characters felt. Before Lawrence got to Hollywood, they had simpler effects, created by what was called the mixmaster system. You know, *he'd* look at *her* through the forest window, looking over the lilies, and this was thought to be the way to do it; then they'd go down to the amusement park together and go through the what do you call it? Shoot de chute?

Tunnel of love.

CAIN

The tunnel of love, and all the rest of it. It was what was called the montage, and at the end of the montage they were supposed to be in love. Lawrence just wouldn't have this. He said this love rack had to be honest, it had to be real poetry. He revolutionized picture-writing in Hollywood; he hadn't been out there long before they all accepted his goddamn love rack.

The other important influence at this time was Bob Riskin, who had been detailed by Harry Cohn, the President of Columbia, to talk to me and find out whether I ticked. Riskin, whose wife was Fay Wray—the girl who did the screech in the original *King Kong*—was the ace writer at Columbia; he did all the Frank Capra pictures, like *It Happened One Night*. A tremendously successful guy. He said to me, You have the strangest mind. The problem is, the algebra must be right. He said, You seem to think that there's some way you can transform this equation, and transform it, and transform it, until you arrive at the perfect plot. It's not like that. The algebra has to be right, but it has to be *your* story. I made algebra of it all right, but it was my story, too, especially with the lingo in the mouth of a hobo with good grammar, like they have in California.

INTERVIEWER

The Postman Always Rings Twice wasn't actually your first attempt at writing a novel, was it?

CAIN

No. In 1922 when I was still on *The Baltimore Sun*, I took the winter off to go down and work in the mines. I tried to write the great American novel, and wrote three of them, none of them any good. I had to come slinking back to work admitting that the great American novel hadn't been written. Actually, the strange thing is that novels aren't written by young guys. I was saying that before. You have to wait for your mind to catch up with whatever it is it's working on; then you can write a novel. I knew Sinclair Lewis fairly well. Until he was in his late thirties he was just a "fictioneer" for *The Saturday Evening Post*. He wrote things like "Turn to the Right" and *Free Air*, mostly just dedicated to the Automobile Age. At that time he was always riding around in a car, having his picture taken at the wheel with that wife he had, I forget her name. But then when he was thirty-eight years old he got the idea for *Main Street*, and after that it was a new kettle of fish and a new writer. I learned from him, and also from the most prolific novelist I think this country ever had. Does the name William Gilbert Patten mean anything to you? His pen name was Burt L. Standish. Certainly you've heard of Frank Merriwell, "Dime Store" Merriwell.

The books about Merriwell came out on top of each other. Anyway, I wrote Standish up for *The Saturday Evening Post*. I've got to make a confession to you—I couldn't, as a boy, read a Frank Merriwell story. When I wrote him up, I tried and tried to read a Frank Merriwell, and I'll be goddamned if I've ever read one through yet. They were so utterly naive, and so horribly written. But I learned from Standish, learned from his mistakes. And I admired the discipline that turned out all those books. You know, in all Frank Merriwell's perfection, he had a fault. Once when I was talking about how perfect Frank Merriwell was, Sinclair Lewis corrected me. No, no, Jim, he said, Frank had a weakness—he gambled, had to deal with it all the time. Just then Phil Goodman asked Lewis, Red, how much would Babbitt have made this year?

Oh, I don't know, said Lewis in his falsetto, I think this year about ten thousand a year.

Oh, much more than that.

No, says Lewis, don't forget that George (Babbitt) had a failing. He couldn't keep his mouth shut, so he never got taken in on anything big.

Well, there are two writers who fall into the category of what Mark Twain called a "trained novelist." Each apparently developed his own characters on the basis of a weakness. I have no consciousness of ever developing a character that way, of developing any character any particular way. Perhaps it's something I should be concerned about, but I'm not.

INTERVIEWER

So do you work from a story or a situation?

CAIN

I don't think I can answer that. I doubt if any writer could answer that. I don't know what I work from.

INTERVIEWER

But there are devices one can use to set up a story, aren't there? Such as the love rack, or the algebraic analysis of a story.

CAIN

Devices, yes. Like the old switcheroo. I used quite a few in my book called *Past All Dishonor*. It's about Virginia City in the Civil War days of the big whorehouses. It's about a boy who fell for a girl who worked in a house. Every guy in town could have her for ten bucks except him, and the reason was that she half-loved him. This was a very nice situation, and I was able to do something with it. I was able to top it, and that's always what you try to do when you have a situation: You pull it, you switch it, you top it, which is the old Hollywood formula for a running gag. In *Past All Dishonor* I had this guy kill the rich man she was going to marry—that was what all the Virginia City whores could look forward to, some rich miner that would marry them in spite of their "dishonor" (that's why San Francisco genealogy is such an unpopular subject). So he shot the guy she was going to marry. Here's where I switched it: he then had to enlist quickly in the Union Army, though he himself was a Confederate. He did it to save his own life because he knew this guy's friends would plug him, and also the woman that owned the whorehouse where the girl worked was going to plug him, too, because this rich guy was going to buy the whorehouse so *she* could retire. So, he enlisted in the Union Army to save his own goddamn life.

Well, she's outside, waiting outside the barracks. He goes out there expecting the gun, she's going to get him; he knows he's going to have to face the music. And this is where I switched it again: she says, You killed him for me. She's an ambitious girl, but to her the most exciting thing in her life is that he would kill a man for her. For the first time in her life, she's in love. So he deserts the Union Army, and they go traipsing off into the mountains. They plan this robbery very carefully. They rob the safe on a train, which he cracks open and it just spews out jewels and money. They take all this off on their two horses and a mule, leading them up over the snow. They're heading to Nevada, to escape into Mexico. He's got the girl and more money than either of them ever dreamed of, and jewels and everything. Up there in the hills they hear dogs barking. They can't be sure they're not being followed, so he goes out and camps by a rock to look, with his gun. It's been established in the book how he became an expert gunman, and how he learned to wheel and shoot, all in one motion, to do it quick. I think I quoted the saying that a gun is like breath to a drowning man—it has to be drawn in haste. He pretty well decides that the dogs are after a deer, not after him. And then he hears a twig crack behind him, and he wheels and shoots.

INTERVIEWER

And it's the woman.

CAIN

And all that stuff, every jewel was there, she has on her. Quite a switcheroo. I said to my little wife, Florence, It just had to be in the snow, where she could just sink down . . . and Florence said, Because you had cleansed her with that bullet. The snow was symbolic, she said, it was perfect. Well, now I've gone and admired my own book.

INTERVIEWER

What about your novel *The Butterfly*?

CAIN

That was never made into a film either, and it would be even better for the screen than *Past All Dishonor*, especially these days. That one was about a guy who fell for his own daughter and began laying her. He falls for her so hard! You see, I had this material left over from when I was going to write that first novel about the coal fields down in West Virginia. The one I told you about. I'm a member of the United Mine Workers. I worked in the coal mines. By the way, it was Thornton Wilder who got involved in that book and suggested I work on it again.

INTERVIEWER

What was the origin of *Double Indemnity*?

CAIN

I wrote that under terrible pressure. I had been East to deal with an alimony contract problem I had. I had made a lot of money suddenly; I wanted to buy out from under it. But it took every dime I had. When I got back to Hollywood I needed money but quick. I can remember how the idea started. One day at the lunch table of the *New York World* Arthur Krock was talking about an early experience in his career, something that happened on the *Louisville Courier-Journal*. One night the copyboy came up with the news that the *Journal* was selling for a dollar apiece down in the street. The bulldog edition. Why? There was a lingerie ad in there. The copy said, If These Sizes Are Too Big, Take a Tuck in Them. That's not what came out in the paper. Arthur said, You spend your whole life guarding against this sort of thing. Well, three weeks later the same thing happens on Arthur's paper. He's hopping! You guard and guard and then this happens. Well he found out that a printer did it on purpose; he hauled the printer in and said, I know you did it but you won't get out of here unless you fess up about it, because I don't want anybody on this paper to think he can get away with something like this. So the guy said, You're right, I did it, I did it. OK. When Arthur told me the story I thought about certain traits in human nature. Then out in Hollywood I was trying to think of an idea for a story quick and it flits through my mind: Suppose instead of a publisher this had been an insurance agent whose job it was to guard against that one guy who would gyp the company out of money by getting a policy on a barn he intended to burn down and suppose he collaborated with him rather than guarding against him. Wondering about that was how the story came about.

INTERVIEWER

Was *Double Indemnity* sold to the movies right away?

CAIN

It was published as one of a trilogy of shorter novels, *Three of a Kind* they called it. Two of the stories had already been sold to the pictures by Swanson, my agent, but *Double Indemnity* had not been. So Swanson got some page proofs stitched up and distributed them around. Billy Wilder couldn't find his secretary one day. Around four o'clock in the afternoon he came out of his office to look for her, and she still wasn't there, so he asked the relief girl, Well, where is she? Every time I come out here she isn't here.

Well I don't know, Mr. Wilder, but I think she's still in the ladies' room reading that book.

What book?

Some story Mr. Swanson left here, she said.

At which moment the girl came in with the story pressed against her bosom. Wilder took it home to see why the girl couldn't put it down. Next day he wanted to do it as a picture.

INTERVIEWER

Did you ever go and see the film? What did you think of it?

CAIN

I don't go. There are some foods some people just don't like. I just don't like movies. People tell me, Don't you *care* what they've done to your book? I tell them, they haven't done anything to my book. It's right there on the shelf. They paid me and that's the end of it.

INTERVIEWER

Which of your own books would you say stand up best?

CAIN

The book that stands up for me is the one that sold the most copies; that's the only test for me and that one was *The Postman Always Rings Twice*. It didn't sell as many in the first edition as *The Butterfly* did. But there's the silver kangaroo over there on the shelf that Pocket Books gave me when *The Postman* passed the million-copy mark. That must have been thirty years ago. The thing still goes on, and how many editions, how many copies it's sold, I haven't the faintest idea. Certainly it's done the best in English, but it's been translated into eighteen languages.

INTERVIEWER

How did you react to Albert Camus's praise of your writing?

CAIN

He wrote something about me—more or less admitting that he had patterned one of his books on mine, and that he revered me as a great American writer. But I never read Camus. In some ways I'm ignorant. In other ways I'm not. At fiction I'm not. But I read very little of it. I'm afraid to because I might like some guy's book too well! Another thing: when you write fiction, the other guy's book just tortures you—you're always rewriting it for him. You don't read it just as a reader; you read it as a guy in the business. Better not read it at all. I've read a great deal of American history.

INTERVIEWER

Have you read the two writers who have so often been identified with you—Dashiell Hammett and Raymond Chandler?

CAIN

I read a few pages of Dashiell Hammett, that's all. And Chandler. Well, I tried. That book about a bald, old man with two nympho daughters. That's all right. I kept reading. Then it turned out the old man raises orchids. That's *too* good. When it's too good, you do it over again. Too good is too easy. If it's too easy you have to worry. If you're not lying awake at night worrying about it, the reader isn't going to, either. I always know that when I get a good night's sleep, the next day I'm not going to get any work done. Writing a novel is like working on foreign policy. There are problems to be solved. It's not all inspirational.

INTERVIEWER

Like Camus and a few other writers you treat crime from the point of the people to whom it has personal implications . . . rather than from the point of view of the detective. What is your own view of violence?

CAIN

Oh, yes. This girl came to interview me the other day. She must have spent the whole trip thinking up the question: how do I see myself as part of the literature of violence? I take no interest in violence. There's more violence in *Macbeth* and *Hamlet* than in my books. I don't write whodunits. You can't end a story with the cops getting the killer. I don't think the law is a very interesting nemesis. I write love stories. The dynamics of a love story are almost abstract. The better your abstraction, the more it comes to life when you do it—the excitement of the idea lurking there. Algebra. Suspense comes from making sure your algebra is right. Time is the only critic. If your algebra is right, if the progression is logical, but still surprising, it keeps.

How related is style to your objectives? You are so well-known for your "hard-boiled" manner of writing . . .

CAIN
Let's talk about this so-called style. I don't know what they're talking about—"tough," "hard-boiled." I tried to write as people talk. That was one of the first arguments I ever had with my father—my father was all hell for people talking as they *should* talk. I, the incipient novelist, even as a boy, was fascinated by the way people *do* talk. The first man I ever sat at the feet of who enchanted me not only by what he told me but by *how* he talked, was Ike Newton, who put in the brick walk over at Washington College, right after my father became president. My father decided we needed a new brick walk down the side of the campus instead of the boardwalk they had. Every year when they burned off the grass in the spring, the boardwalk would kind of catch fire and there'd be charred ends of the boards. Well, this bothered my father. If he'd known more about American history, that kind of American history (he knew plenty about American history but not that kind), he'd have known that boardwalks had figured very prominently in our history, like in Virginia City: the boardwalk there was an institution. But he had Ike Newton put in a brick walk and I would sit out there while he worked, listening to him. He was a stocky man, rather nicely put together. He had a hammer with a screwdriver in the end of it that he'd tap the bricks with. Well, Ike Newton put the bricks in, gauging them with his eye, and doing a beautiful thing, and as he worked he talked. The way he'd use language! I'd go home and talk about it, to my mother's utter horror, and to my father's horror, too, because he was such a shot on the way people *should* talk. My childhood was nothing but one long lesson: not *preventative* but *preventive*; not *sort of a* but *a sort of*; not *those kind* but *that kind* or *those kinds*. Jesus Christ, on and on and on.

INTERVIEWER

Since language is obviously such an important part of your own writing, do you feel the motion pictures were able to transplant and communicate the Cain story and style?

CAIN

When they were making *Double Indemnity* in Hollywood, Billy Wilder complained that Raymond Chandler was throwing away my nice, terse dialogue; he got some student actors in from the Paramount school, coached them up, to let Chandler hear what it would be like if he would only put exactly what was in the book in his screenplay. To Wilder's utter astonishment, it sounded like holy hell. Chandler explained to Wilder what the trouble was—that Cain's dialogue is written to the eye. That ragged right-hand margin that is so exciting and wonderful to look at can't be recited by actors. Chandler said, Now that we've got that out of the way, let's dialogue it with the same spirit Cain has in the book but not the identical words. Wilder still didn't believe him. They got me over there, purportedly to discuss something else, but the real reason was that Wilder hoped I would contradict Chandler, and somehow explain what had evaporated when the kids tried to do my lines. But, of course, I bore Chandler out, reminding Wilder I could write spoken stuff well enough, but on the page there just wasn't any room for talky climaxes. Chandler, who was an older man, was a bit irked by Wilder's omniscience, and he was pleased I backed him up.

INTERVIEWER

Did you ever hear praise about your books, or the movies made from them, that you felt appreciated their intention?

CAIN

Carey Wilson, the producer of *Postman*—big shot on the Metro lot—liked my work. Why he liked me I never found out. But he once said, What I like about your books—they're about dumb people that I know and that I bump into in the parking lot. I can believe them and you put them into interesting situations. After all, how the hell could I care about a hobo and a waitress out there in that place you put them in your first book. For Chrissakes, I couldn't put the goddamn thing down for two hours!

Issue 73, 1978

Rebecca West

The Art of Fiction

There is no hard place of human experience that Dame Rebecca West has not scaled in her work. When she first appeared in London as a working writer, in 1912, on the suffragette newspaper *The Freewoman*, she dazzled her audience by the precocious ambition of her voice and its barbed brilliance. None of this ever faded, and the areas of seeking became ever wider. H. G. Wells wrote to her toward the end of their painful relationship: "I love your clear open hard-hitting generous mind first of all and still I love it most of all, because it is the most of you."

Rebecca West was born Cicily Isabel Fairfield in London, in December of 1892. She changed her name to that of the heroine of Ibsen's play *Rosmersholm*, who is characterized by a burning passionate will. As "Rebecca West" she began in journalism and literary criticism, and continued to write throughout the traumatic years when she was alone bringing up her only child, Anthony Panther West, born to her and H. G. Wells in 1914. She published her first book in 1916 and her first novel, *The Return of the Soldier*, in 1918, an intense and poetic story of a veteran's loss of memory which draws with confidence on Freudian theories of the personality. She wrote novels throughout the twenties (*The Judge*, 1922; *Harriet Hume, A London Fantasy*, 1929), and in 1928 collected her criticism in *The Strange Necessity*. The subject of the title essay is the touchstone of West's philosophy: the unquenchable and healing need of human beings for art and literature. More essays followed in *Ending in Earnest*:

Once more it had died and been reborn.

Its rebirth, I calculated rapidly, was likely to be followed by an agonising existence. I knew at once, as everybody must who had any knowledge of international affairs, what foreign powers had combined to kill this man. It appeared to me then, as I lay in bed in the nursing-home, inevitable that war must follow; and indeed it must have done, had not the Yugoslavian Government exercised an iron control over its population then and thereafter, and abstained from the smallest provocative action against its enemies. On that forbearance, which is indeed one of the most extraordinary feats of statesmanship performed in post-war Europe, I could not be expected to rely. So I saw myself widowed and childless, which was another instance of the archaic outlook of the back of the mind, for in the next war we women will have hardly any reason to fear bereavement, as bombardment unpreceded by declaration of war will send us and our loved ones to the next world in the breathless unity of scrambled eggs. That thought did not then occur to me, so I rang for my nurse, and when she came I cried to her, "Get me a telephone quickly! I must speak to my husband at once. A most terrible thing has happened. The King of Yugoslavia has been assassinated." "Oh, dear!" she replied. "Did you know him?" "No," I said. "Then why," she said, "do you think it is so terrible?"

Her words made me realise that the word 'idiot' comes from a Greek root meaning a private person. She was certainly intelligent in her work and was probably so in her personal life, but her unawareness of the bonds that linked her to strangers made her follow her fate in a darkness deep as that cast by malformed cells in the brain. It might be argued that she was happier so; but that is true only in the most limited sense. She would not be happy long. A population which does not know that the assassination of the King of Yugoslavia might precipitate a European war is a perpetual temptation to its governors; it will believe any lies, it can be seduced into supporting unnecessary wars and peace treaties that favour class interests. But it might be

A manuscript page from Rebecca West's *Black Lamb and Grey Falcon*.

A Literary Log (1931), in which, notably, she acclaimed the genius of D. H. Lawrence. Two years later she published her biographical masterwork, *St. Augustine.*

In the late thirties she traveled widely with her husband, Henry Maxwell Andrews, in the Balkans, and from these experiences she built her formidable analysis of European conflict leading up to the Second World War, *Black Lamb and Grey Falcon* (1940). The marked political and historical character of this work, with its emphasis on firsthand observation, led naturally to the postwar books, *The Meaning of Treason* (1947) and *A Train of Powder* (1955). Her account of the Nuremberg trials is a matchless investigation of the natures of Nazism and of freedom. However unrelenting her dissection of the personalities and the clashes of betrayal and loyalty, Rebecca West never loses in these works an extraordinary capacity for empathy with all the people involved—the accused, the witnesses, the judges or the lawyers, the authorities.

In *Black Lamb and Grey Falcon* she wrote: "There is nothing rarer than a man who can be trusted never to throw away happiness." Her loosely autobiographical novel, *The Fountain Overflows* (1956), and her political thriller *The Birds Fall Down* (1966) are testimony to West's curiosity, energy, and grip on what she has termed the "will to live."

In her hallway hangs a drawing of her done by Wyndham Lewis in the thirties, "before the ruin," as she puts it. In fact, in person, there is no ruin, not of her brilliant, penetrating brown eyes, the energy of her voice, and her attention to all things. She was wearing a bright and patterned caftan when we first met, a loose blouse over trousers the second time. Cataracts mean she has two pairs of spectacles, on chains like necklaces; arthritis has made a stick necessary. Her hair is white and short; she wears beautiful rings. Her voice has kept some of the vowel sounds of the Edwardian period, and some of its turns of phrase: "I can't see someone or something" meaning "I can't tolerate." She says words of foreign derivation, like *memoirs*, with the accent of the parent language. We sat in her sitting room, a room filled with drawings and paintings with a wide bay window looking out on

some of London's tall trees. Their leaves, which were turning when
we met, almost brushed against the windowpanes.

—*Marina Warner, 1981*

INTERVIEWER

In your novel *The Fountain Overflows*, you describe the poverty of
the educated class very beautifully. Was that your background?

REBECCA WEST

Oh, yes. I'll tell you what the position was. We had lots of pleasant
furniture that had belonged to my father's family, none that had belonged to my mother's family, because they didn't die—the whole
family all went on to their eighties, nineties—but we had furniture,
and we had masses of books, and we had a very good piano my
mother played on. We were poor because my father's father died
when he and his three brothers were schoolboys. Their mother was a
member of the Plymouth Brethren and a religious fanatic with a conscience that should have been held down and, you know, been eu-
nuchized or castrated. She refused to keep on, to accept any longer,
an annuity, which she was given by the royal family. And nobody
knows why she was given it, and she found out the reason and she
didn't approve of it, and she refused it, and they were poor forever after. The maddening thing was nobody ever knew why she said to
Queen Victoria, I cannot accept this allowance. It was hard on my father, who was in the army, because you needed money to be an officer. He was a ballistics expert. He did quite well in various things.

INTERVIEWER

He was a professional soldier?

WEST

No. Not all his life. He left the army after he got his captaincy. He
went out to America and he ran a mine and wrote a certain amount,
mostly on political science. He wrote well. He had a great mechanical

mind and he drew very well. He did all sorts of things, and he'd had a fairly good training at Woolwich, a military academy. We were the children of his second marriage and he could no longer make much money. He went out to Africa and just got ill there. He came back and died in Liverpool when I was twelve or thirteen.

INTERVIEWER

Was he a remote and admirable figure, as the father is in *The Fountain Overflows*?

WEST

Oh, he wasn't so cracked as the father and he didn't sell furniture that didn't belong to him and all that sort of thing. That was rather a remembrance of another strange character.

INTERVIEWER

You've written very movingly, in several of your books, on how cruel natural death is, how it is the greatest hardship, as opposed to some of the more violent deaths that you've also written about. Was it a very traumatic experience for you, as a child, when you lost your father?

WEST

Oh, yes, it was terrible . . . The whole of life was extremely uncomfortable for us at that time. We had really got into terrible financial straits, not through anybody's fault. My mother had had to work very hard, and though she was a very good pianist, she was out of the running by then, and when she realized that my father was old and wasn't going to be able to go on with things, she very nobly went and learned typewriting. Do you know people are always writing in the papers and saying that typists started in the last war, but they've been going on since the eighties and the nineties and 1900. Well, my mother did some typing for American evangelists called Torry and Alexander and she took over their music. They toured in England and my mother whacked the "Glory Song," a famous hymn—you still hear it whistled in the streets—out on the grand piano on the platform. It was a very noble thing to do. She wasn't well and she wasn't

young, and then we came up to Scotland. My sister was studying
medicine. My other sister had a scholarship at Cheltenham, which
was rather useless to her; she was very brilliant indeed, and amusing
as well.

INTERVIEWER

Which sister was that?

WEST

That's Winifred, who was more or less like Mary in *The Fountain
Overflows*. Then there was myself, who had to go and try to get schol-
arships, which I usually did, at the local school. My mother ran a typing business and I assisted her, which was amusing and which gave
me a quickness of eye, which has been quite useful. She used to type
manuscripts, particularly for the music faculty in Edinburgh. There
was a German professor she'd known all her life. He used to send
along pieces and I remember still with horror and amusement an
enormous German book of his on program music with sentences like
"If the hearer turns his attention to the flutes and the piccolos, surely
there will come to his mind the dawn rising over the bronze horses of
Venice." There is a lot of rather good idiom of writing I can summon
up, if necessary, about music in the post-Wagnerian period, which
was very, very lush.

INTERVIEWER

Were you brought up to play yourself?

WEST

I played, but not well. From an early age—but it was not detected
for many, many years—I've had difficulty about hearing. Finally, I lost
my hearing almost entirely in this ear. I got pneumonia in it, which I
think is rather chic. Then I thought I'd got my hearing back slowly,
but really I'd learned to lip-read and, it's an extraordinary thing,
young people—if they lose their hearing young—learn lip-reading unconsciously, lots of them. It's quite common. I did that without
knowing—when I got double cataracts, I suddenly found my hearing

going and I said, Goodness, I've gone deaf at the same time as my eyes are going wrong. But my aurist, who's a very nice man, said, No, you haven't. Your lip-reading power is breaking down, which was very disappointing, but, on the other hand, I was amazed at the ingenuity of the human animal. It did strike me as an extraordinary thing.

INTERVIEWER

In your home, was the atmosphere for women very emancipated because you were left alone?

WEST

Oh, yes. We were left alone. We had an uncle, who was very preoccupied. He was principal of the Royal Academy of Music, Sir Alexander MacKenzie, and he didn't really think anything of any woman but his wife. He was very thoughtless about his own daughter, who was an actress who acted very well in the early Chekhov plays. He treated her very inconsiderately and made her come back and nurse her mother and leave her husband in Paris, and the husband, after six years, lost heart and went off with someone else. We were very feminist altogether, and it was a very inspiring thing. Who is that man, David Mitchell, who writes silly hysterical books about Christabel Pankhurst? What is he? Who is he?

INTERVIEWER

He's now writing a book about the Jesuits.

WEST

The Jesuits? How does he know about the Jesuits?

INTERVIEWER

You thought his book on Christabel was hysterical, did you?

WEST

Absolute rubbish and nonsense. He writes about how she went to Paris and how she didn't go down to the cafés and meet the young revolutionaries. But how on earth was she to find out where they were? Because, you see, the Bolshevik generation was not yet identifiable. How would she find out any of the people, who hadn't really made their mark? It was an obscure time in the history of revolution. It was a time when very remarkable people were coming up, but they weren't visible yet. She did know the people like Henri de Rochefort very well. Mitchell also says she took a flat and had a housekeeper, who was also a very good cook, and didn't that show great luxury? Well, if he'd asked anybody, he would have found that, in those days, you couldn't take a furnished flat or house in Paris, nor, so far as I know, in most parts of France, unless you took a servant, who was left by the owner. All the furnished houses I ever had in France, modest as they were, had somebody that I had to take with the house.

INTERVIEWER

But you yourself broke with the suffragette movement.

WEST

I was too young and unimportant for that to mean much. I admired them enormously, but all that business about venereal disease, which was supposed to be round every corner, seemed to me excessive. I wasn't in a position to judge, but it did seem a bit silly. [Christabel Pankhurst headed a chastity campaign for women.]

INTERVIEWER

Christabel, in her later phase, became the equivalent of a misogynist. She became very, what would the word be, misanthropic against men only, didn't she?

WEST

It wasn't quite that. She fell curiously into a sort of transatlantic form of mysticism, where there is a sort of repudiation of sex. Do you ever read anything about Thomas Lake Harris? He was an American mystic. Curious thing—you repudiated sex but you had a "counterpart," and you usually could get a counterpart by getting into bed with somebody else, with whom your relations were sup-

posed to be chaste, but when you lay in his arms, you were really lying in the counterpart's arms, and—isn't it a convenient arrangement? That was one sort of pattern of American mysticism and
dottyism. Christabel got caught up with that vagueness—though not
with counterparts. If you read Harris's sermons—somebody took
them down and I had a look at them—they were all very queer like
that, disguised sexuality, but I wouldn't say the worse for that.

INTERVIEWER

You have written that there is a great difference between a male
sensibility and a female sensibility, and you have a marvelous phrase
for it in *Black Lamb and Grey Falcon*.

WEST

Idiots and lunatics. It's a perfectly good division. [The Greek root
of *idiot* means "private person"; men "see the world as if by moon-
light, which shows the outlines of every object but not the details in-
dicative of their nature."] It seems to me in any assembly where you get
people, who are male and female, in a crisis, the women are apt to get
up and, with a big wave of the hand, say, It's all very well talking about
the defenses of the country, but there are thirty-six thousand houses in
whatever (wherever they're living) that have no bathrooms. Surely it's
more important to have clean children for the future. Silly stuff, when
the enemy's at the gate. But men are just as silly. Even when there are no
enemies at the gate, they won't attend to the bathrooms, because they
say defense is more important. It's mental deficiency in both cases.

INTERVIEWER

But do you think it's innate or do you think it's produced by culture?

WEST

Oh, I really can't tell you that. It's awfully hard. You can't imagine
what maleness and femaleness would be if you got back to them in
pure laboratory state, can you? I suspect the political imbecility is
very great on both sides.

I've never gone anywhere where the men have come up to my infantile expectations. I always have gone through life constantly being surprised by the extreme, marvelous qualities of a small minority of men. But I can't see the rest of them. They seem awful rubbish.

INTERVIEWER

In many of the political things that you've written, it would be impossible to tell that you were a woman, except that here and there you sometimes produce a comparison to do with a child or something, which may betray a certain feminine stance, but, in fact, you have overcome completely this division between idiot and lunatic. You're not an "idiot" at all. You don't think only of the personal angle.

WEST

I think that probably comes of isolation, that I grew up just as I was without much interference from social images except at my school.

INTERVIEWER

What were they at school?

WEST

We had large classes, which was an ineffable benefit, because the teachers really hadn't time to muck about with our characters. You see, the people who wanted to learn, sat and learned, and the people who didn't, didn't learn, but there was no time, you know, for bringing out the best in us, thank God. I had some magnificent teachers, actually, a Miss MacDonald, who taught me Latin irregular verbs.

INTERVIEWER

Did you have a classical training?

WEST

No, no. I had no Greek. They didn't teach any Greek for the reason that our school took on from a very early school, at which they had followed Madame de Maintenon's school at St. Cyr, where the children were taught Latin but not Greek. Why do you think I wasn't taught Greek? Because Madame de Maintenon thought girls shouldn't learn Greek in case they fell into the toils of the heretical Eastern Orthodox Church, which is rather funny, considering we were all good girls at Edinburgh. Very curious bit of history, that.

INTERVIEWER

And this tradition reached as far as Scotland?

WEST

Well, you see, the man who was the begetter of our school had been to St. Cyr, and he just took the whole thing on.

INTERVIEWER

What did your mother expect you to be? What images did she set up for you?

WEST

There was a great idea that I should be an actress because a woman called Rosina Fillipi had seen me act in a play and she thought I was terribly good as a comedian, as a sort of low-comedy character, and she said, If you come to the Royal Academy of Dramatic Art, I will look after you and you can get a job. I'm the only person I ever heard of who wanted to go on the stage not because I was stagestruck but it just seemed to be the thing to do. I loved the theater. I still love it, but I had no stagestruck feeling. I felt how nice if people would give me a part. I went to the Royal Academy of Art, where there was a man called Kenneth Barnes who ran it, who had got his job because he was the brother of the Vanbrughs—Irene and Violet Vanbrugh, if that means anything to you. He couldn't understand what Rosina Fillipi had seen in me and he made me very uncomfortable. I didn't stay out the course.

INTERVIEWER

But you chose the name of a dramatic character—Rebecca West.

Yes. Not really for any profound reason. It was just to get a pseudonym.

It really wasn't profound? You don't think unconsciously it was?

People have always been putting me down in any role that was convenient but it would not, I think, naturally have been my own idea. I've aroused hostility in an extraordinary lot of people. I've never known why. I don't think I'm formidable.

I think that your hallmark is that you have always disliked people who wanted approval. You like the heterodox.

I should like to be approved of, oh, yes. I blench. I hate being disapproved of. I've had rather a lot of it.

And yet, in your writing, there is quite a strong strain of impatience with people who do things because society approves of it.

Oh, yes. I think I see what you mean. Oh, that's Scotch, I think, yes, Scotch, because—oh, yes, and it's also a bit of my mother and my father. My father was educated by Elysée and Eli Reclus, two famous French brothers, early geographers; my cracked grandmother, the religious maniac who refused the family fortune, had hired them because they were refugees in England; she thought that, as young Frenchmen in England, they must be Protestants who had escaped from the wicked Catholics' persecution. They were actually anarchists and they'd escaped, run away from France, because they'd seized the town hall—I can't remember which town it was—in the course of an émeute against Louis-Napoléon. They were very sweet. They said, when they found out the mistake, Oh, well, we must be careful about teaching the children. They taught them awfully well. My father was a very, very well-educated man, and so were all his brothers.

INTERVIEWER

What did you read at home as a child? Who were the early formative influences?

WEST

Oh, pretty well everything. We read a terrific lot of Shakespeare, which my mother knew by heart and so did my father—and a lot of George Borrow. Funny thing to read, but—really early Victorian England was quite familiar to me because of that. Oh, lots—I can't think. My mother and my sister, Winifred, who was much the cleverest of us, she read frightfully good poetry. She taught me a lot of poetry, which I've all forgotten now, but you know, if I see the first line, I can go on.

INTERVIEWER

Would you acknowledge Conrad or anyone else as an influence on you?

WEST

Well, I longed, when I was young, to write as well as Mark Twain. It's beautiful stuff and I always liked him. If I wanted to write anything that attacked anybody, I used to have a look at his attack on Christian Science, which is beautifully written. He was a man of very great shrewdness. The earliest article on the Nazis, on Nazism, a sort of first foretaste, a prophetic view of the war, was an article by Mark Twain in *Harper's* in, I should think, the nineties. He went to listen to the Parliament in Vienna and he describes an awful row and what the point of view of Luger, the Lord Mayor, was, and the man called George Schwartz, I think, who started the first Nazi paper, and what it must all lead to. It's beautifully done.

It's the very first notice that I've ever found of the Austrian Nazi Party, that started it all.

INTERVIEWER

What was your first conscious encounter with fascism?

WEST

A lot of boys, who stopped my sister and myself and took her hockey stick away from her. The thing was they weren't doing it as robbery but it was fun and good fellowship, and they were the boys together. That was the first. They were just street children. We had a brick wall and an alley behind it and we used to come up half the alley, if we were going into the house of some neighbors, and there these boys caught us in the alley and they took it away; but we fought them and screamed and shouted and got back the hockey stick.

INTERVIEWER

That was when?

WEST

That must have been—I was born in 1892—about 1903, or, no, earlier than that, just in this century perhaps.

INTERVIEWER

Yes, so, before the First World War, you saw the seeds of fascism.

WEST

No, no. I just saw violence. There was the race thing and sacred Germanism and all that, but the enemy before the First World War you can't really compare with fascism. It was the imperialism of Germany and the supremacy of the army, but that isn't exactly fascism. I think you could say, there was more fascism, but of an intellectualized kind, in France. The crux of the Dreyfus case was that it didn't matter whether Dreyfus was guilty or not, you mustn't spoil the image of the army. That was more or less fascist.

INTERVIEWER

But do you feel, with your strong sense of justice and of pity, that our wars have remained as terrible, or do you feel that we have learned?

WEST

I don't know what *you've* learned. I'll tell you I think the Second World War was much more comfortable because in the First World War the position of women was so terrible, because there you were, not in danger. Men were going out and getting killed for you and you'd much prefer they weren't. My father was always very tender about armies, having been a soldier. The awful feeling for a small professional army was that they were recruited from poor people who went out and got killed. That was, do you know, very disagreeable. There was a genuine humanitarian feeling of guilt about that in the first war. It was very curious, you see. There I sat on my balcony in Leigh-on-Sea and heard guns going in France. It was a most peculiar war. It was really better, in the Second World War, when the people at home got bombed. I found it a relief. You were taking your chance and you might be killed and you weren't in that pampered sort of unnatural state. I find the whole idea of a professional army very disgusting still. Lacking a normal life, they turn into scoundrels. As Wellington said, they're despised for being scoundrels and it's not their fault and they die like flies and have the worst discomforts.

INTERVIEWER

And yet a conspired army, as fought in Vietnam—you laugh?

WEST

Well, I can't help thinking that the whole of the Vietnam War was the blackest comedy that ever was, because it showed the way you can't teach humanity anything. We'd all learned in the rest of the world that you can't now go round and put out your hand and, across seas, exercise power; but the poor Americans had not learned that and they tried to do it. The remoteness of America from German attack had made them feel confident. They didn't really believe that anything could reach out and kill them. Americans are quite unconscious now that we look on them as just as much beaten as we are. They're quite unconscious of that. They always have talked of Vietnam as if by getting out they were surrendering the prospect of victory, as if they were being noble by renouncing the possibility of victory. But they couldn't have had a victory. They couldn't possibly have won.

INTERVIEWER

But when you say they're beaten as we are, in what way do you mean we are beaten?

WEST

Only as regards world power. We can't put our hands out and order things to happen a long way away. Oh, I think we're also beaten in other ways—in industry. I think the war between the public and the unions is very difficult and I don't see where its solution lies.

INTERVIEWER

Have you ever seen a society about which you really felt here is society that works for the benefit of its citizens without harming others?

WEST

No, I think the earth itself is slightly resistant to routine. You might come to a place that was favorable, because of a discovery of minerals that could be mined more easily, you know, "place mines," as they call the ones on the surface, and you'd think that was very nice and they would get on with it. Then round the corner you'd find there was a dispute about water rights. Humanity wasn't obviously a made-to-order thing. It's a continual struggle, isn't it?

INTERVIEWER

Have you ever been tempted at all to any religious belief?

WEST

Oh, yes. It all seems so damned silly and incomprehensible, there might as well be a silly and incomprehensible solution, don't you think? I'd be quite prepared for anything to happen, but not very respectfully, I think.

INTERVIEWER

I think you might stand up to God.

WEST

No, not exactly that, but I don't think there would be a God who would really demand it. If there is a God, I don't think He would demand that anybody bow down or stand up to Him. I have often a suspicion God is still trying to work things out and hasn't finished.

INTERVIEWER

Were your parents at all believing?

WEST

My mother was, in a sort of musical way, and I think my father accepted it as part of the structure, but didn't do anything. We always went to church and enjoyed it. I don't feel the slightest resistance to the Church except when it's a bad landlord or something like that. I don't see why people feel any *écrasez l'infâme*. I know much *infâme*-ier things than religion, much more worthy of being *écrasez*-ed.

INTERVIEWER

What can you remember as being a moment of great happiness?

WEST

Extremely few. I had a very unhappy time with H. G. Wells, because I was a victim of a sort of sadistic situation. Partly people disapproved of H. G. so much less than they did of me, and they were very horrible to me, and it was very hard. It was particularly hard later, people being horrid to me because I was living with H. G., when I was trying as hard as I could to leave him. It was really absurd, and now I think it's rather funny, but it wasn't funny at the time. Then I had a short time of happiness on my own and a time of happiness with my marriage [Rebecca West married Henry Andrews in 1930], but then my husband got ill, very ill. He had meningitis, this thing that's always struck at people near me, when he was young and then he got cerebral arteriosclerosis, and after years it came down on him. He was in a very unhappy state of illness for a good many years before he died, but we had a great many good years together. I was very happy.

INTERVIEWER

Have any of the men you've known helped you?

WEST

The men near you always hinder you because they always want you to do the traditional female things and they take a lot of time. My mother helped me to work because she always talked to me as if I were grown-up.

INTERVIEWER

Do you feel men did not want to help you as a writer?

WEST

Oh, yes! So many men hate you. When my husband was dying I had some very strange dialogues. People were very rude just because they'd heard I was a woman writer. That kind of rudeness is as bad as ever.

INTERVIEWER

Would it have been easier to have been a man?

WEST

It certainly would have been.

INTERVIEWER

Are there any advantages at all in being a woman and a writer?

WEST

None whatsoever. You could have a good time as a woman, but you'd have a much better time as a man. If in the course of some process, people turn up a card with a man's name on it and then a card with a woman's, they feel much softer toward the man, even though he might be a convicted criminal. They'd treat the man's card with greater tenderness.

INTERVIEWER

You don't think there's been an improvement?

WEST

Not very much.

INTERVIEWER

Everyone is still very curious about your love affair with H. G. Wells.

WEST

Why, I can't see why. It was a very long time ago, and it wasn't interesting. Why would I have brought it to an end if it had been interesting? It wasn't.

INTERVIEWER

What did your husband, Henry Andrews, do?

WEST

He was unfortunately put into a bank. He should have been an art historian. He got out of the bank in the end because he was too ill. He did a bit in the war where he was in the Ministry of Economic Warfare and very good. He was a delightfully funny man. He said very funny things, and he was very scholarly and he was very generous and he was very kind. There were all sorts of pleasant things about him.

INTERVIEWER

You could talk to him.

WEST

We talked a very great deal, but it's extraordinary the really tragic and dreadful things there are in marriage that are funny. I've never known anybody to write about this. My husband would insist on going and driving a car, and he'd never been a good driver. Like all bad drivers, he thought he was the best driver in the world and he couldn't drive at all at the end and it was terrible. I'm one of the few women who have been driven on the left side of a bus queue, on the *near* side of the pavement. It was awful. Well, that really made my life poisoned for years. All the time I never thought I would live to the end of the year. I thought he would be sure to kill me here or there. And he meant no harm.

INTERVIEWER

You weren't able to tell him this?

WEST

I told him and he wouldn't believe me. Two doctors said to me it could be so bad for his ego values, if he was not allowed to drive a car. Doctors tend to be chumps. I have had two or three marvelous doctors. I have a marvelous doctor now, who's very nice, very funny and very clever, but some of my worst enemies have been doctors, I can assure you.

INTERVIEWER

You have actually been quite ill yourself, haven't you?

WEST

Well, I had an attack of TB when I was a schoolgirl. Everybody did in those days. It simply meant that you got a shot of TB in your youth and you didn't get it later on. It was rather dramatic. What was awful was that I got it at the same time as my great friend Flora Duncan, who was at school with me and whom I liked enormously; she died of it years afterwards in the most dreary way. She went with her aunt to stay in a hotel from which she was coming to lunch with me—this was just after I was married—and she pulled down the window and the bit where her left lung had gone thin started to hemorrhage; and she was dead in a few hours. They couldn't stop the hemorrhage. It has sometimes inconvenienced me, but as I've lived to be eighty-eight, I can't say I've really suffered very much from it. At the time it gave me a lot of time to read.

INTERVIEWER

When you look back on all the books that you've written, is there one that you like best?

WEST

Oh, no. They don't seem to me as good as they might be. But I really write to find out what I know about something and what is to be known about something. And I'm more or less experimental. I wish I could have written very much more but, to be absolutely frank, for twenty-five years, you see, I've had this disastrous personal trouble. You don't easily get over it if someone near to you is constantly attacking you in public. Do you know Anthony [West]?

INTERVIEWER

I've met him once. He's writing about Joan of Arc, he told me.

WEST

What on earth about Joan of Arc?

INTERVIEWER

He believes that she was a princess, a bastard princess.

WEST

Why? What an extraordinary idea.

INTERVIEWER

A lot of people do.

WEST

What! This is new to me. Who might she be?

INTERVIEWER

She's meant to be the result of an incestuous adulterous match, the queen and the queen's brother-in-law, Louis d'Orléans.

WEST

I wish he'd turn his mind to other problems than bastardy. Alas. He's writing about six books, he told me. But I wonder why this. Whose theory is this? I never heard of it.

INTERVIEWER

Oh, it's a very old one. It was produced in 1810 by Pierre Caze in a play. Instead of accepting that Joan of Arc was exciting for spiritual reasons, you say she was exciting because she was a royal princess—which is a practical solution.

WEST

Nonsense. Have you seen Princess Anne? Can you imagine, if she appeared and said, "Save England," or whatever, that it would work? What a wonderful idea.

INTERVIEWER

What are you working on now?

WEST

I've been looking at old photographs—Rangoon in the last century. Goodness, some are absolutely beautiful. It's funny how photographs were better in the past than they are now.

INTERVIEWER

Why are you looking at Rangoon?

WEST

In what I'm writing now, I'm describing my husband's mother's life. She went out to Rangoon and lived there in vast, great big rooms each the size of a gymnasium, and full of cluttered little tables.

INTERVIEWER

She was the wife of an official, was she?

WEST

No, she was the wife of a man who had a job in Wallace Export-Import. They exported Burmese teak and they imported machinery. I've got masses of photographs I have to give to the Institute of Machinery but I never get round to it, showing the machines, as they came in. They had the largest army of elephants ever. There are beautiful photographs in this book of things like a lot of elephants crossing a wide river in a sort of floating island. She was a lady of very mixed ancestry, my husband's mother, and after Rangoon, she came back to Hamburg. Her mother was a Miss Chapman, who was related to the Chapman family that T. E. Lawrence belonged to. They lived in Lancashire, and then she married a local alien, a member of the hereditary Teutonic Knights of Lithuania. She had various children in Lithuania, and then her daughter came to live in Hamburg and married Lewis Andrews, who was working in this firm in Rangoon, and ultimately became my mother-in-law.

INTERVIEWER

What are you writing about her?

WEST

It comes into my memoirs. Poor widow. She took her son [Henry Andrews] out with her to Hamburg and kept him too long. It was 1914 and the war came. Eventually she was sent back to England, but

he was sent into a camp. He was there all through the war, in Ruh-
leben [the civilian POW camp at Spandau]. It was very sad. It did
spoil his life, really. He was nineteen. It was very tough. But these
young creatures were highly educated; he wrote quite clever letters to
Romain Rolland.

INTERVIEWER

How far have you got with your memoirs?

WEST

I've nearly got my father and mother to the end of their respective
careers. It's been supernatural, which is always encouraging. Do you
know, my mother was always saying that the scenery in Australia was
so extraordinarily beautiful, and my father did some very nice pictures of Australian landscapes. Suddenly, a man started sending me
picture books of Australia. He said, I've always liked your books, and
I wanted to send these to you. So extraordinarily dead-on; pictures of
what Australia was like when my parents were there in the last century.

INTERVIEWER

Are you taking only a section of your life in your memoirs?

WEST

Well, I hope to cover most of it, but still, I've only just begun it really and I must really get on with it. I haven't read anybody's memoirs
for ages except Coulton's [medieval historian, author of *Five Centuries of Religion*], which I liked very much. He wrote a life called
Fourscore Years. Hated Catholics. When did you read him?

INTERVIEWER

I read him on the Virgin Mary.

WEST

You know, I don't really appreciate the Virgin Mary. She always
looks so dull. I particularly hate Raphael, Raphael's Madonnas. They
are awful, aren't they?

Are you working on anything else?

WEST

I'm doing a book for Weidenfeld on the 1900s, but it's not a long book. I'm not approaching the 1900s chronologically. I've started by doing a lot with the paintings of Sargent, and with some beautiful photographs. But that period in America has been done and done and done, and it's hard to be fresh. They've really dealt with nostalgia too fiercely. I begin with the death of Gladstone in 1898, and more I cannot tell you.

INTERVIEWER

You have lots of paintings. Have you written about them?

WEST

To a certain extent, yes. My husband bought the ones over there, but these I bought. It was lovely that I could buy them when they were cheap. They didn't cost me very much, even the Bonnard, and I think that's the best picture that Dufy ever painted. I have a passion, too, for Carol Weight, the man who painted this one, because I think he paints the contours of the land so beautifully. And that's by Vuillard, the woman over there, Madame Marchand. She committed suicide in the war, alas. She was a Polish Jewess, a friend of Colette's and a lot of other people.

INTERVIEWER

You have a high opinion of Colette, don't you?

WEST

Yes. I didn't like her very much as a person and I think she was repetitive and I hate all her knowing nudges about men, but I think she was a good writer on the whole and she was very good on landscape. She did a wonderful book called *Trio*. She was really more egotistical than you could possibly imagine, and she was outside a lot of experiences in a most curious way. I was taken to see her in Paris with a man who was a judge at Nuremberg. She didn't pick it up at all.

INTERVIEWER

You were in Paris again recently, I believe?

WEST

To film *The Birds Fall Down*, yes, for the BBC. It was quite fun. It was uncomfortable in many ways and I was so horrified by the cheap food in Paris. It was so bad. Terribly bad. The film turned out to be visually very beautiful. Sometimes it seemed to me a little slow. Some of the dresses are lovely.

INTERVIEWER

Have you had other books adapted?

WEST

No, people always buy them and then find they can't do them, so that I've gained financially but otherwise hardly ever. A man called Van Druten, who's forgotten now, did *The Return of the Soldier* as a play and it wasn't really good, though some of his plays were. I can't remember who acted it, or indeed anything about it.

INTERVIEWER

You've never written for the stage yourself?

WEST

I've had so little time to write. Also, theatrical people can't be bothered with me. I wrote a play in the twenties, which I think had lovely stuff in it, *Goodbye Nicholas*, and fourteen copies were lost by managers, fourteen, that's really true, and I just gave up. One of them, who lost three, was a man called Barry Jackson, who was at the Birmingham Repertory Theatre; after we'd had a terrific apologies and that kind of thing, about a year later he met me in the bar of some theater and said, Rebecca, why have you never written a play? They are like that.

INTERVIEWER

What was the play about?

WEST

Oh, it was about Kruger, the financier, who committed suicide. It just showed you how they did the fraud and what they thought about it. It was sound enough, but nobody was interested in it at all. Then I lent it to an old friend of mine. I'm sorry to say he used a lot of it, without acknowledgment, in a play of his, an American man.

INTERVIEWER

Who was that?

WEST

I won't tell you, but it was very naughty. But never mind. His play died a death too. I would like to write old-fashioned plays like de Musset's. I think they're lovely. I think de Musset's essay on Rachel and Malibran is one of the loveliest things in the world. It's lovely about acting and romanticism. It's beautifully written and it's quite wonderful.

INTERVIEWER

Rachel is quite important to you, because you wrote a beautiful thing in your lecture on McLuhan about her.

WEST

Oh, not *my* beauty, not *my* beauty, it's Valéry's, who wrote the beautiful thing and who loved Rachel. Isn't it a beautiful thing? The ear of the lover took down what his beloved Rachel was saying and commemorated the secret of it. It's really wonderful. It's about as nice a form of immortality as anyone could have, isn't it? I fell on the essay, when I was quite young, and then I read it again because Malibran [Maria-Felicia García, d. 1836] was the sister of Madame Viardot [Pauline García, d. 1910] who is, you know, the lady who is supposed to have been the mistress—but I think the duties were light—of Turgenev. Turgenev lived in the house of Madame Viardot nearly all his life, and she brought up his illegitimate daughter. She was an opera singer but she had a dreadful time getting jobs at the opera because she and her husband were anti-Bonapartist and the Bonapartists had command of the opera. She was a great girl, and it's a very terrible thing—all her life she wrote compositions but nobody has ever played them. She was terribly busy. There's a description of her as "*too* busy" in the letters of Brahms and Clara Schumann. The Garcías were people who had two odd genetic streaks—one was for longevity, the other was for music. The first García bumped his family all over the Americas and all over Europe as a musical troupe. There were several in the family; the brother taught at the Royal Academy of Music in London, where my uncle was principal, and he used to give children's parties. I remember going to a children's party and being kissed by the old gentleman who was the brother of Malibran. He lived to be a hundred and one. I think his descendants transplanted themselves to somewhere in the north of England. The life of the family has all sorts of odd things embedded in it. You know how in du Maurier's books, how in *Trilby* she vocalized to the music of Chopin's Nocturnes and people say that's so absurd. But Viardot did it and it apparently came off and Chopin himself liked it.

INTERVIEWER

Did you used to go to concerts a lot?

WEST

Yes, I used to and I used to listen on the radio. I can't do even the radio any longer. It doesn't seem to *respond*, as the Americans say.

INTERVIEWER

You said once that all your intelligence is in your hands.

WEST

Yes, a lot, I think. Isn't yours? My memory is certainly in my hands. I can remember things only if I have a pencil and I can write with it and I can play with it.

INTERVIEWER

You use a pencil, do you, when you write?

WEST

When anything important has to be written, yes. I think your hand concentrates for you. I don't know why it should be so.

INTERVIEWER

You never typed?

WEST

I did, but not now. I can't see in front and behind a typewriter now with cataract-operated eyes. If you have the spectacles for the front thing, you can't see the back, and I can't do with bifocals. I just get like a distracted hen. I can't do it. Hens must wear bifocals, if one looks closely. It explains it all. It's so difficult dealing with ribbons too. I can only write by hand now. I used to do a rough draft longhand and then another on the typewriter. I'm a very quick typist. When I had mumps I was shut up in a bedroom, because both my sisters had to sit examinations. When I came out, I could type.

INTERVIEWER

Do you do many drafts?

WEST

I fiddle away a lot at them. Particularly if it's a fairly elaborate thing. I've never been able to do just one draft. That seems a wonderful thing. Do you know anyone who can?

INTERVIEWER

I think D. H. Lawrence did.

WEST

You could often tell.

INTERVIEWER

How many hours a day do you write?

WEST

I don't manage much. When I write uninterrupted, I *can* write all day, straight through.

INTERVIEWER

Did you find any of your books especially easy to write?

WEST

No. It's a nauseating process. They're none of them easy.

INTERVIEWER

Have you ever abandoned a book before it was finished?

WEST

I've abandoned work because I've not had time. I've had a worrisome family thinking up monkey tricks to prevent me finishing books, and I had a terrible time when I was young and in the country, because I had no money, and no reference books, and I couldn't get up to London and to the London Library, where I had a subscription.

INTERVIEWER

There is a great diversity in your work. Did you find it difficult to combine criticism and journalism and history and fiction?

WEST

I did, really. My life has been dictated to and broken up by forces beyond my control. I couldn't control the two wars! The second war had a lot of personal consequences for me, both before and after. But I had enough money at that time, because I had a large herd of cows and a milk contract. I had to take some part in looking after the cows, but the dear things worked for me industriously. At one time I had to write articles because I had to put up a lot of money for family reasons. Everyone has to pay for their families every now and then.

INTERVIEWER

Who are the writers you admire? You commented recently that Tolstoy was most overrated.

WEST

I'm a heretic about Tolstoy. I really don't see *War and Peace* as a great novel because it seems constantly to be trying to prove that nobody who was in the war knew what was going on. Well, I don't know whoever thought they would—that if you put somebody down in the wildest sort of mess they understand what's happening. The point's very much better done, I think, by Joseph de Maistre. He wrote a very interesting essay in the late eighteenth century, saying how more and more people would not be able to know what was happening to them in wartime because it was all too complicated. He was in a very complicated state himself because he came from Aspramonte, which is a village on a hill near Nice. The people of Aspramonte were of the original Mediterranean population. They wore long hair all through the centuries, the conservative hippies. He was descended from a family who went round getting mulberry leaves for the silkworms. He got into the service of the king of Sardinia. He was sent as an ambassador to St. Petersburg. He wrote *Les Soirées de St.-Pétersbourg*, which is marvelous descriptive writing. He did a very good thing about hanging. He was for it, but his essay demonstrates the painfulness of ever considering whether you do hang people or not. I don't know how he became a diplomat for the king of Sardinia. I'm very often curious about people in history; they turn up in the oddest places. They strayed like goats in a road, but from class to class.

INTERVIEWER

Do you admire E. M. Forster?

WEST

No. I think the Indian one [*A Passage to India*] is very funny because it's all about people making a fuss about nothing, which isn't really enough. I can never understand how people read Proust at the same time. But they did. You can read Proust all the time. There is a book of that period that I do like very much, and that is *They Went* by Norman Douglas. It's about the king of a legendary country. I've read it several times and I've always found it beautiful.

INTERVIEWER

Are you interested in T. S. Eliot's writing?

WEST

Goodness! T. S. Eliot, whom I didn't like a bit? He was a poseur. He was married to this woman who was very pretty. My husband and I were asked to see them, and my husband roamed around the flat and there were endless photographs of T. S. Eliot and bits of his poetry done in embroidery by pious American ladies, and only one picture of his wife, and that was when she was getting married. Henry pointed it out to me and said, I don't think I like that man.

INTERVIEWER

What about the work of Somerset Maugham, whom you also knew?

WEST

He couldn't write for toffee, bless his heart. He wrote conventional short stories, much inferior to the work of other people. But they were much better than his plays, which were too frightful. He was an extremely interesting man, though, not a bit clever or cold or cynical.

I know of many affectionate things he did. He had a great capacity for falling in love with the wrong people. His taste seemed to give way under him so extraordinarily sometimes. He fascinated me by his appearance; he was so neatly made, like a swordstick that fits just so. Occasionally his conversation was beautifully funny and quite unmalicious. I object strongly to pictures of Maugham as if he were a second-rate Hollywood producer in the lavish age. His house was very pleasant and quiet and agreeable.

INTERVIEWER

Some critics think that sex is still written about with great awkwardness. Why is this?

WEST

I would have thought that was completely true of Kafka, who couldn't write about sex or value its place in life. I think there's an awful lot of nonsense in Lawrence when he writes about Mexican sacrifices and sexual violence. Their only relevance was to the Mexicans' lack of protein, as in the South Sea Islands. Funny, that's a wonderful thing. I don't know why more people don't write about it—how the whole of life must have been different when four-footed animals came in. They had just a few deer before, but not enough to go round, and so they prevented the deer from becoming extinct by making them sacred to the kings. It's much more interesting to write about that than about sex, which most of your audience knows about.

INTERVIEWER

Have you ever worked closely with a publisher who has suggested ideas to you?

WEST

No. I write books to find out about things. I wrote *Saint Augustine* because, believe it or not, there was no complete life in English at the time.

Have you never had a close relationship with an editor, who has helped you after the books were written?

No. I never met anybody with whom I could have discussed books before or after. One doesn't have people on one's wavelength as completely as that. And I very rarely found *The New Yorker* editors any good.

They have a tremendous reputation.

I don't know why.

When you read, do you just follow your imagination completely?

Well, I've had eighty-five years to read in.

I wondered whether you made book lists?

Yes, I do, but I'm often disappointed. I do think modern novels are boring on the whole. Somebody told me I ought to read a wonderful thing about how a family of children buried Mum in a cellar under concrete and she began to smell. But that's the sole point of the story. Mum just smells. That's all that happens. It is not enough.

INTERVIEWER

This is a new Ian McEwan, isn't it? I thought you, in your book on Augustine, made a marvelous comment that applies to him and to some of the other fashionable novelists now. You say that Augustinianism is "the ring-fence, in which the modern mind is still prisoner." I think that Ian McEwan is very Augustinian in his sense of unmovable evil in human life.

WEST

Yes, but he doesn't really do very much with it, does he? This thing just presents you with the hairs along people's groins and the smell, and very little else.

INTERVIEWER

Do you feel this relates to your feeling about the will to die in people, that this kind of very black outlook on the human body and human emotions is part of the suicidal streak that you've written about in both individuals and in society?

WEST

Oh, I suppose it is. It's very far-fetched, isn't it? One rarely recognizes the smell of Mum under the concrete, does one? I don't know. I cannot see the abysmal silliness of a lot of novels. Did you read a book called *The Honey Tree*? By Janice Elliott. If you didn't read it, it's no use talking about it. It's all about people who take a house and fornicate all over it, and they all have children, and their swollen bodies are a great source of satisfaction to Mrs. Elliott, and paternity does all sorts of things to men that I doubt, don't you?

INTERVIEWER

Perhaps. I believe you admire A. L. Barker.

WEST

Enormously, but I'm the only person who does, so far as I can make out. I think she's the best novelist now writing, not always, but I think *The Middling* is a magnificent novel. And *A Source of Embar-rassment*, about the woman who knew she was going to die. This last book, *The Heavy Feather*, is so good I can't believe it, and nobody likes it. And they are wrong. I am exaggerating, of course. Lots of people do admire her, but not enough.

INTERVIEWER

What are the particular qualities that you think she has that others at the moment haven't?

WEST

She really tells you what people do, the extraordinary things that people think, how extraordinary circumstances are, and how unex-pected the effect of various incidents. There's a terribly good thing in *The Heavy Feather*, where a woman goes home and there's a rail-way accident. The train is just jarred and the poor woman is sitting with a suitcase over her head. The suitcase falls on top of the woman sitting opposite her and kills her. This woman has been saying how happy she is and how all her children love her and how ideal her life is. Then the other, when she gets home, finds she's taken the woman's suitcase instead of her own, and it's got the address and she goes to take back the suitcase and try and get her own from the husband, who turns out to be Hindustani. The woman was white, and he's living there with a Hindustani girl and they're both terrified because they have been waiting for this white woman, who had no children and wasn't adored and was utterly miserable. The people come off the page to tell you what this would be like. You feel, Now I understand this better. And she also has in the book very good het-erosexuals and very good homosexuals—with the different quality quite marked.

INTERVIEWER

Yes. Would you place her as high as the women writers that you have said overcome the problem of being female in their writing? I am thinking of Madame de Sévigné, Madame de La Fayette, Jane Austen, Willa Cather, Virginia Woolf, Colette.

WEST

Oh, she's almost better than anybody, I think. She's much better than Iris Murdoch, I think. But then Iris Murdoch I like enormously except when she begins to clown and be funny, because I don't think she ever is very funny. She writes curious books on goodness. Have you read her philosophic works? I can't make head or tail of them. They're better written than anything else she writes. They are so strange. She says that one has to study what goodness is by looking at good people. She says that the trouble with good people is that, if they're men, usually very little is known about them because they're so obscure, and, as for women, goodness is rarely found in women except in the inarticulate mothers of large families, which is just such an idiotic remark, you can't believe it. Is she pulling one's leg? One hopes so. But even so, why?

INTERVIEWER

Do you have a high opinion of Ivy Compton-Burnett?

WEST

She had her own stereotype, and wrote too many books exactly like each other in form. But it was a damn good form. At the time of a rising in South Africa, when it seemed that the colored races were going to burst forth and one was afraid that the white suburbs were being set on fire, I managed to get in happy nights reading the novels of Ivy Compton-Burnett. But it was very funny that people believed in her story of herself. She was a nanny, and you had only to meet her to see it; all her stories are nanny stories, about how awful the family is. She was very, very clever. You'd have to be very tasteless not to see she had something unique to give her age . . .

INTERVIEWER

How do you feel about Doris Lessing?

WEST

I wish I knew her. I think she's a marvelous writer. There's a peculiar book about European refugees in Africa, but it fascinates. It's beautifully done, the play side of philosophy. They were talking about all their ideas and it was as if the children were trying to go into a shop and buy things not with coins but with butterscotch or toffee apples. It's very curious. Yes, she's the only person who absolutely gets the mood of today right, I think. An absolutely wonderful writer. She wrote a picaresque novel, *The Children of Violence*, I thought was very fine. Who got the Booker Prize? Does anybody know? [Iris Murdoch won it for *The Sea, The Sea*, after this meeting.]

INTERVIEWER

Do you follow prizes?

WEST

Not very much. I was on the Booker Prize Committee twice. It almost drove me mad. I think they give people prizes too late. This is a sad thought. They've been heard of as failures and they have become conditioned to failure, so it is rather wide of the point. It's nice for them, though.

INTERVIEWER

Do you feel that public taste has declined as expressed in things like prizes?

WEST

People in England read books. I have read Mr. McEwan, and I read new books all the time, whether I review them or not, but you see, most people in America are reading the same books over and over again. They read Scott Fitzgerald and Hemingway and James Joyce and Nabokov, and they haven't moved on anywhere for years.

INTERVIEWER

John Gross says in his book on the English man of letters that we are now as far from Joyce as Joyce was from George Eliot, but in terms of the progress of literature, we haven't moved at all.

WEST

Yes. It's curious. People have no desire to read anything new. It is bad that English is taught in universities. It's bad over here, where it's sometimes not badly taught, but over there, where it's horribly badly taught, it simply stops the thing in its tracks.

INTERVIEWER

Because people always look back on the past?

WEST

They don't even look onto the past. They look onto the certified past. There really were beautiful writers in America like G. W. Cable, who wrote about the South in the middle of the last century. It's very rich, rather Balzacian sort of stuff about the South, New Orleans and so on. But nobody reads him now.

INTERVIEWER

Why do you think English is so badly taught in America?

WEST

It's an absurd error to put modern English literature in the curriculum. You should read contemporary literature for pleasure or not read it at all. You shouldn't be taught to monkey with it. It's ghastly to think of all the little girls who are taught to read *To the Lighthouse*. It's not really substantial food for the young because there's such a strong feeling that Virginia Woolf was doing a set piece and it didn't really matter very much. She was putting on an act. Shakespeare didn't put on an act. But *Orlando* is a lovely original splash, a beautiful piece of fancy. Leonard Woolf had a tiresome mind. When you read his books about Malaya, and then the books of the cadets who went out there, he's so petty, and they have such an enthusiasm and such tolerance for the murderous habits of the natives. But he was certainly good to Virginia. I couldn't forgive Vanessa Bell for her awful muddy decorations and those awful pictures of Charlotte Brontë. And I hated Duncan Grant's pictures too. The best thing that was ever said about Bloomsbury was said by a lovely butler of mine. At dinner one evening, they began to talk of Faulkner's book in which someone uses a corncob for the purposes of rape. They were being terribly subtle, and doing this and that gesture over the table. The butler came into my son Anthony's room and asked, Do you know where they keep the Faulkners? It seems they're very saucy. Virginia Woolf's criticism was much better than criticism others were writing then.

INTERVIEWER

Among critics, do you admire Cyril Connolly? Or Malcolm Muggeridge?

WEST

Connolly? What an extraordinary thing to ask! He was a very good editor of *Horizon*, but he wasn't an interesting person. As for writing, he was fond of it, as you might say. But he didn't know much about it, did he? I've got no opinion of Muggeridge. He's very nice and friendly. Whatever have I read of his in the past? I can never think Christ is grateful for being alluded to as if He were a lost cause.

INTERVIEWER

Did you want to write about trials?

WEST

Not at all. I had done it once or twice, when I was very hard up, when I was young, just to get some money, and so I learned how to do them, and then I used to sit and listen to William Joyce [Lord Haw-Haw, hanged 1945] when he was broadcasting. Then I arranged to go to his trial because I was interested in him. A man called Theobald Matthew, who was director of public prosecutions, though not a prosecuting sort of person, said, I wish you'd report a lot of these trials because otherwise they will go unnoticed because there is so little newsprint. He said, Really, if you will consider it as war work, it would be extremely valuable. So I did that for one book [*The New Meaning of Treason*, 1947] and then I did it for another [*A Train of Powder*, 1955]. Most of the people in intelligence didn't agree with my views. I don't know whether it had any effect on them at all. Someone asked me recently how did I think intelligence had found out John Vassal? [British spy, jailed in 1963]. It seemed to me such a silly question. He had it tattooed on his forehead. I never know how people don't find out spies.

INTERVIEWER

Are you interested in espionage still?

WEST

I won't say I'm interested in spies, but they do turn up in my life in quite funny ways. There was a man called Sidney Reilly, who was a famous spy, a double agent. My mother-in-law was very upset because my husband married me instead of the daughter of a civil servant. My husband's mother thought she was a nice Catholic girl, who'd be so nice for my husband, and it always tickled me because it gradually emerged that this girl was the mistress of this *very* famous and very disreputable spy. It was a wonderful thing to have in your pocket against your mother-in-law. My mother-in-law was an enormous, huge woman, and extremely pathetic. She had had her life broken up so often. By the First World War, and then the Second. Between the wars she was perfectly happy going to tea at those old-fashioned tea places they had—Rumpelmayer's. But her other son was very ill and he went out to Australia and he had a weak lung, and she went to see him and she got caught by the war there. If you like Rumpelmayer's, you wouldn't want to be in Australia for six years.

INTERVIEWER

Do you enjoy reviewing for the *Sunday Telegraph*?

Yes, I do. I do. I would feel awfully cut off if I didn't review; I think it's such a good discipline. It makes you really open your mind to the book. Probably you wouldn't, if you just read it.

INTERVIEWER

Oh, yes. It concentrates one, yes. I thought your review of Christopher Isherwood's *Christopher and His Kind* was dazzling. You demolished him.

WEST

I was so horrified by the way he treated the little German pansy. Also I thought it must have been so disgusting for the people in the village on the Greek island. I know Greeks love money, but I think a lot of money would have to pass before you'd be reconciled to Isherwood making such a noise.

INTERVIEWER

When I read your review, I was completely convinced by your argument, that it was an extraordinary sort of obliviousness that comes from class privilege.

WEST

Well, I didn't want to make a butt of him. Do you know, a bookseller's assistant said to him, What do you think of Rebecca West's review of your book? and he is alleged to have said such a lovely thing: I shall think of some way of turning it to my advantage. You can't think how bad reviewing was when I first started to review, so dull and so dreadful. Nobody good but Lady Robert Cecil, one of the Salisbury family.

INTERVIEWER

But your reviews were absolutely sparkling. I love the essay you wrote about *The Uncles*.

WEST

Oh, Bennett was horrible about it. He was a horrible, mean-spirited, hateful man. I hated Arnold Bennett.

INTERVIEWER

But you were very nice about him.

WEST

Well, I thought so, and I think he was sometimes a very good writer. I do think *The Old Wives' Tale* is very good, don't you? He was a horrible man.

INTERVIEWER

Was he in a position to make things difficult for you then?

WEST

Yes. He was not nice. He lived with these two women, the French-woman to whom he was married and also the woman who was with him when he died. He was always telling other people how tiresome these women were. It was all very, as people say, unchivalrous.

INTERVIEWER

English writing hasn't really produced the kind of giants it produced in the twenties. The stagnation of English writing since then is extraordinary. Joyce, Virginia Woolf, Wells, Shaw—all these people were writing and who have we got to compare now?

WEST

I find Tom Stoppard just as amusing as I ever found Shaw. Very amusing, both as a playwright and as himself. But I'm not now an admirer of Shaw. It was a poor mind, I think. I liked his wife so much better. He *was* conceited, but in an odd way. Usually, you know, it's people shouting to keep their spirits up, but he really did think he was better than most people. I thought that book on Yeats's postbag was so good, letters that people wrote to Yeats. Did you read that? It's absolutely delightful. It's got delightful things like a very nicely phrased letter from a farmer, saying that he understands Yeats writes about supernatural matters and can he recommend a reliable witch? You know, charming things like that.

INTERVIEWER

Did you meet Yeats?

WEST

Yes. He wasn't a bit impressive and he wasn't my sort of person at all. He boomed at you like a foghorn. He was there one time when Philip Guedalla and two or three of us were all very young, and were talking nonsense about murderers in Shakespeare and whether a third murderer ever became a first murderer by working hard or were they, sort of, hereditary slots? Were they like Japanese specialists and one did one kind of murder, another did another? It was really awfully funny. Philip was very funny to be with. Then we started talking about something on the Western Isles but Yeats wouldn't join in, until we fussed round and were nice to him. But we were all wrong; what he liked was solemnity and, if you were big enough, heavy enough, and strong enough, he loved you. He loved great big women. He would have been mad about Vanessa Redgrave.

INTERVIEWER

Is your Irish birth important to you?

WEST

Frightfully, yes. I loved my family. I have a great affiliation to relations of mine called Denny. The present man is an architect, Sir Anthony Denny. He's exactly like Holbein's drawing of his ancestor, Anthony Denny, which I think is a great testimonial. Anthony Denny lives up in the Cotswolds, and he and his wife are most glamorous people in a very quiet way. They have two charming sons, one of them paints very well, and they adopted a child, a Vietnamese child. Tony went out to see his brother, who had fever there, and he was walking along a quay and one of the refugee babies, who was sitting about, suddenly ran up to him and clasped him round the knees and looked up in his face. So he just said, I'll have this one—and took him home. It was a most lovely reason. The Dennys did nice things like that. And then my father used to speak about this cousin in Ireland, in the west of Ireland, called Dickie Shoot. Dickie Shoot beggared himself by helping people.

INTERVIEWER

I always think it's astonishing how much literature Protestant Ireland has produced.

WEST

I don't think they're very poetical people or sensitive people really, but what a lot of literature they've produced compared with the Scotch, who I think have really deeper emotions. It's most peculiar.

INTERVIEWER

Shaw. Wilde. Whatever one thinks of their quality, there they are. Samuel Beckett. All from Protestant Irish stock.

WEST

You know, an Irish priest said a most beautiful thing to me the other day, and I absolutely loved it. He looked at those books and said—a very old man he is, he's older than I am, he must be over ninety—and he said to me, What are you doing with all your books when you're dead? You must have planned for them. I said, I'm giving those Oxford dictionaries to the grandson of Oscar Wilde, Merlin Holland. And he said, Oh, how beautiful that makes it all. It's rather as if it hadn't happened. I said, What do you mean? He said, Well, your family lives in Fitzwilliam Square and Wilde's people lived in Merrion Square and it's such a natural thing to do for a family in Fitzwilliam Square to give their Oxford dictionary to the son of a family living in Merrion Square. Almost as if it hadn't happened. He couldn't have added a word to it. I love Merlin. I went to see him out in Beirut with his mother, which was rather a trial. She's Australian in a big way but you know, it was so extraordinary, the glimpse I had of her. He was very fond of a ballet dancer, and we went out to lunch. We went up to her house, and after dinner Mrs. Holland, who is plump and sixty-something, got up and she turned on one of the records, *Swan Lake*, and danced to it, as she'd learned to, and she was quite beautiful. Obviously she should have been a dancer.

INTERVIEWER

Do you think it has become easier for women to follow their vocations?

WEST

I don't know. It's very hard. I've always found I've had too many family duties to enable me to write enough. I would have written much better and I would have written much more. Oh, men, whatever they may say, don't really have any barrier between them and their craft, and certainly I had.

INTERVIEWER

What inspired you later to write your great book on Yugoslavia? Was it the contact with the people?

WEST

What I was interested in really was wandering about with Henry. I wanted to write a book on Finland, which is a wonderful case of a small nation with empires here and there, so I learned Finnish and I read a Finnish novel. It was all about people riding bicycles. But then, when I went to Yugoslavia, I saw it was much more exciting with Austria and Russia and Turkey, and so I wrote that. I really did enjoy it terribly, loved it. I loved writing about Saint Augustine too. I like writing about heretics, anyway.

INTERVIEWER

You consider Augustine a heretic, do you?

WEST

Oh, no, he wasn't a heretic. Most of his life he wasn't at all a nice man, but that's quite a different thing. I like to think about people like the Donatists, who were really suffering agonies of one kind and another because the Roman Empire was splitting up and it was especially uncomfortable to be in Roman Africa. But they didn't know anything about economics, and did know about theology. Theology had taught them that if you suffered, it was usually because you'd offended God—so they invented an offense against God, which was that unworthy priests were celebrating the Sacraments. So that satisfied them and then they went round the country, looting and getting the food and the property they wanted because they said that they were punishing heretics. I think it's wonderful that in the past people overlooked things that now seem to us quite obvious, and thought they were doing things for the reasons they weren't, and tried to remedy them by actions. Perhaps there's some quite simple thing we'll think of someday, which will make us much happier.

Issue 79, 1981

Elizabeth Bishop

The Art of Poetry

T he interview took place at Lewis Wharf, Boston, on the afternoon of June 28, 1978, three days before Miss Bishop and two
friends were to leave for North Haven, a Maine island in Penobscot
Bay where she summered. Her living room, on the fourth floor of
Lewis Wharf, had a spectacular view of Boston Harbor; when I arrived, she immediately took me out on the balcony to point out such
Boston landmarks as Old North Church in the distance, mentioning
that Old Ironsides was moored nearby.

Her living room was spacious and attractive, with wide-planked
polished floors, a beamed ceiling, two old brick walls, and one wall of
books. Besides some comfortable modern furniture, the room in-
cluded a jacaranda rocker and other old pieces from Brazil, two paintings by Loren MacIver, a giant horse conch from Key West and a
Franklin stove with firewood in a donkey pannier, also from Brazil.
The most conspicuous piece was a large carved figurehead of an unknown beast, openmouthed, with horns and blue eyes, which hung
on one wall below the ceiling.

Her study, a smaller room down the hall, was in a state of disorder.
Literary magazines, books, and papers were piled everywhere. Photographs of Marianne Moore, Robert Lowell, and other friends hung
on the walls; one of Dom Pedro, the last emperor of Brazil, she especially liked to show to her Brazilian visitors. "Most have no idea who
he is," she said. "This is after he abdicated and shortly before he

A manuscript page from Elizabeth Bishop's "Sonnet."

died—he looked very sad." Her desk was tucked in a far corner by the only window, also with a north view of the harbor.

At sixty-seven, Miss Bishop was striking, her short, swept-back white hair setting off an unforgettably noble face. She was wearing a black tunic shirt, gold watch and earrings, gray slacks, and flat brown Japanese sandals that made her appear shorter than her actual height: five feet, four inches. Although she looked well and was in high spirits, she complained of having had a recent hay fever attack and declined to have her photograph taken with the wry comment, "Photographers, insurance salesmen, and funeral directors are the worst forms of life."

Seven or eight months later, after reading a profile I had written for *The Vassar Quarterly* (which had been based on this interview) and worrying that she sounded like "the soul of frivolity," she wrote me: "I once admired an interview with Fred Astaire in which he refused to discuss 'the dance,' his partners, or his 'career' and stuck determinedly to *golf*—so I hope that some readers will realize I do think about art once in a while even if babbling along like a very shallow brook . . ."

Though Miss Bishop did have the opportunity of correcting those portions of this interview incorporated in *The Vassar Quarterly* article, she never saw it in this form.

—*Elizabeth Spires, 1981*

INTERVIEWER

Your living room seems to be a wonderful combination of the old and new. Is there a story behind any of the pieces, especially that figurehead? It's quite imposing.

ELIZABETH BISHOP

I lived in an extremely modern house in Brazil. It was very beautiful, and when I finally moved I brought back things I liked best. So it's just a kind of mixture. I really like modern things, but while I was there I acquired so many other things I couldn't bear to give them up.

This figurehead is from the São Francisco River. Some are more beautiful; this is a very ugly one.

Is it supposed to ward off evil spirits?

Yes, I think so. They were used for about fifty years on one section, two or three hundred miles, of the river. It's nothing compared to the Amazon but it's the next biggest river in Brazil. This figurehead is primitive folk art. I think I even know who made it. There was a black man who carved twenty or thirty, and it's exactly his style. Some of them are made of much more beautiful wood. There's a famous one called the Red Horse made of jacaranda. It's beautiful, a great thing like this one, a horse with its mouth open, but for some reason they all just disappeared. I made a weeklong trip on that river in 1967 and didn't see one. The riverboat, a stern wheeler, had been built in 1880—something for the Mississippi, and you can't believe how tiny it was. We splashed along slowly for days and days . . . a very funny trip.

Did you spend so much of your life traveling because you were looking for a perfect place?

No, I don't think so. I really haven't traveled that much. It just happened that although I wasn't rich I had a very small income from my father, who died when I was eight months old, and it was enough when I got out of college to go places on. And I traveled extremely cheaply. I could get along in Brazil for some years but now I couldn't possibly live on it. But the biographical sketch in the first anthology I was in said, Oh, she's been to Morocco, Spain, et cetera, and this has been repeated for years even though I haven't been back to any of these places. But I never traveled the way students travel now. Compared to my students, who seem to go to Nepal every Easter vacation, I haven't been anywhere at all.

INTERVIEWER

Well, it always sounds as if you're very adventurous.

BISHOP

I want to do the Upper Amazon. Maybe I will. You start from Peru and go down—

INTERVIEWER

Do you write when you're actually traveling?

BISHOP

Yes, sometimes. It depends. I usually take notes but not always. And I keep a kind of diary. The two trips I've made that I liked best were the Amazon trip and one to the Galapagos Islands three or four years ago . . . I'd like very much to go back to Italy again because I haven't seen nearly enough of it. And Sicily. Venice is wonderful. Florence is rather strenuous, I think. I was last there in '64 with my Brazilian friend. We rented a car and did northern Italy for five or six weeks. We didn't go to Rome. I *must* go back. There are so many things I haven't seen yet. I like painting probably better than I like poetry. And I haven't been back to Paris for years. I don't like the prices!

INTERVIEWER

You mentioned earlier that you're leaving for North Haven in several days. Will this be a working vacation?

BISHOP

This summer I want to do a lot of work because I really haven't done anything for ages and there are a couple of things I'd like to finish before I die. Two or three poems and two long stories. Maybe three. I sometimes feel that I shouldn't keep going back to this place that I found just by chance through an ad in the Harvard *Crimson*. I should probably go to see some more art, cathedrals, and so on. But I'm so crazy about it that I keep going back. You can see the water, a great expanse of water and fields from the house. Islands are beautiful. Some of them come right up, granite, and then dark firs. North Haven isn't like that exactly, but it's very beautiful. The island is sparsely inhabited and a lot of the people who have homes there are fearfully rich. Probably if it weren't for these people the island would be deserted the way a great many Maine islands are, because the village is very tiny. But the inhabitants almost all work—they're lobstermen but they work as caretakers . . . The electricity there is rather sketchy. Two summers ago it was one hour on, one hour off. There I was with *two* electric typewriters and I couldn't keep working. There was a cartoon in the grocery store—it's eighteen miles from the mainland—a man in a hardware store saying, "I want an extension cord eighteen miles long!" Last year they did plug into the mainland—they put in cables. But once in a while the power still goes off.

INTERVIEWER

So you compose on the typewriter?

BISHOP

I can write prose on a typewriter. Not poetry. Nobody can read my writing so I write letters on it. And I've finally trained myself so I can write prose on it and then correct a great deal. But for poetry I use a pen. About halfway through sometimes I'll type out a few lines to see how they look.

William Carlos Williams wrote entirely on the typewriter. Robert Lowell printed—he never learned to write. He printed everything.

INTERVIEWER

You've never been as prolific as many of your contemporaries. Do you start a lot of poems and finish very few?

BISHOP

Yes. Alas, yes. I begin lots of things and then I give up on them. The last few years I haven't written as much because of teaching. I'm hoping that now that I'm free and have a Guggenheim I'll do a lot more.

INTERVIEWER

INTERVIEWER

How long did it take you to finish "The Moose"?

BISHOP

That was funny. I started that *years* ago—twenty years ago, at least—I had a stack of notes, the first two or three stanzas, and the last.

INTERVIEWER

It's such a dreamy poem. It seems to move the way a bus moves.

BISHOP

It was all true. The bus trip took place before I went to Brazil. I went up to visit my aunt. Actually, I was on the wrong bus. I went to the right place but it wasn't the express I was supposed to get. It went roundabout and it was all exactly the way I described it, except that I say "seven relatives." Well, they weren't really relatives, they were various stepsons and so on, but that's the only thing that isn't quite true. I wanted to finish it because I liked it, but I could never seem to get the middle part, to get from one place to the other. And then when I was still living in Cambridge I was asked to give the Phi Beta Kappa poem at Harvard. I was rather pleased and I remembered that I had another unfinished poem. It's about whales and it was written a long time ago too. I'm afraid I'll never publish it because it looks as if I were just trying to be up-to-date now that whales are a "cause."

INTERVIEWER

But it's finished now?

BISHOP

I think I could finish it very easily. I'm going to take it to Maine with me. I think I'll date it or nobody will believe I started it so long ago. At the time, though, I couldn't find the one about whales—this was in '73 or '74, I think—so I dug out "The Moose" and thought, Maybe I can finish it, and I did. The day of the ceremony for Phi Beta Kappa (which I'd never made in college) we were all sitting on the platform at Sanders Theater. And the man who had asked me to give the poem leaned across the president and said to me, whispering, What is the name of your poem? I said, "The Moose," M-o-o-s-e, and he got up and introduced me and said, Miss Bishop will now read a poem called "The *Moos*." Well, I choked and my hat was too big. And later the newspaper account read, "Miss Bishop read a poem called 'The Moose' and the tassle of her mortarboard swung back and forth over her face like a windshield wiper"!

The Glee Club was behind us and they sang rather badly, I thought, everybody thought. A friend of mine who couldn't come to this occasion but worked in one of the Harvard houses and knew some of the boys in the Glee Club asked one of them when they came back in their red jackets, Well, how was it? He said, Oh, it was all right but we didn't sing well—which was true—and then he said, A woman read a poem. My friend said, How was it? And he said, Well, as poems go, it wasn't bad!

INTERVIEWER

Have you ever had any poems that were gifts? Poems that seemed to write themselves?

BISHOP

Oh, yes. Once in a while it happens. I wanted to write a villanelle all my life but I never could. I'd start them but for some reason I never could finish them. And one day I couldn't believe it—it was like writing a letter.* There was one rhyme I couldn't get that ended in e-n-t and a friend of mine, the poet Frank Bidart, came to see me and I said, Frank, give me a rhyme. He gave me a word offhand and I put it in. But neither he nor I can remember which word it was. But that kind of thing doesn't happen very often. Maybe some poets always write that way. I don't know.

*The poem is "One Art," in *Geography III*.

INTERVIEWER

Didn't you used to give Marianne Moore rhymes?

BISHOP

Yes, when she was doing the La Fontaine translations. She'd call me up and read me something when I was in New York—I was in Brazil most of that time—and say she needed a rhyme. She said that she admired rhymes and meters very much. It was hard to tell whether she was pulling your leg or not sometimes. She was Celtic enough to be somewhat mysterious about these things.

INTERVIEWER

Critics often talk about your more recent poems being less formal, more "open," so to speak. They point out that *Geography III* has more of "you" in it, a wide emotional range. Do you agree with these perceptions?

BISHOP

This is what critics say. I've never written the things I'd like to write that I've admired all my life. Maybe one never does. Critics say the most incredible things!

INTERVIEWER

I've been reading a critical book about you that Anne Stevenson wrote. She said that in your poems nature was neutral.

BISHOP

Yes, I remember the word *neutral*. I wasn't quite sure what she meant by that.

INTERVIEWER

I thought she might have meant that if nature is neutral there isn't any guiding spirit or force.

BISHOP

Somebody famous—I can't think who it was—somebody extremely famous was asked if he had one question to ask the Sphinx and get an answer, what would it be? And he said, Is nature for us or against us? Well, I've never really thought about it one way or the other. I like the country, the seashore especially, and if I could drive, I'd probably be living in the country. Unfortunately, I've never learned to drive. I bought two cars. At least. I had an MG I adored for some years in Brazil. We lived on top of a mountain peak, and it took an hour to get somewhere where I could practice. And nobody really had time to take an afternoon off and give me driving lessons. So I never got my license. And I *never* would have driven in Rio, anyway. But if you can't drive, you can't live in the country.

INTERVIEWER

Do you have the painting here that your uncle did? The one "about the size of an old-style dollar bill" that you wrote about in "Poem"?

BISHOP

Oh, sure. Do you want to see it? It's not good enough to hang. Actually, he was my great-uncle. I never met him.

INTERVIEWER

The cows in this really are just one or two brushstrokes!

BISHOP

I exaggerated a little bit. There's a detail in the poem that isn't in the painting. I can't remember what it is now. My uncle did another painting when he was fourteen or fifteen years old that I wrote about in an early poem ["Large Bad Picture"]. An aunt who lived in Montreal had both of these and they used to hang in her front hall. I was dying to get them and I went there once and tried to buy them, but she wouldn't sell them to me. She was rather stingy. She died some years ago. I don't know who has the large one now.

When you were showing me your study, I noticed a shadow box hanging in the hall. Is it by Joseph Cornell?

BISHOP

No, I did that one. That's one of my little works. It's about infant mortality in Brazil. It's called *Anjinhos*, which means "little angels." That's what they call the babies and small children who die.

INTERVIEWER

What's the significance of the various objects?

BISHOP

I found the child's sandal on a beach wading east of Rio one Christmas and I finally decided to do something with it. The pacifier was bright red rubber. They sell them in big bottles and jars in drugstores in Brazil. I decided it couldn't be red, so I dyed it black with india ink. A nephew of my Brazilian friend, a very smart young man, came to call while I was doing this. He brought two American rock-and-roll musicians and we talked and talked and talked, and I never thought to explain in all the time they were there what I was doing. When they left, I thought, My God, they must think I'm a witch or something!

INTERVIEWER

What about the little bowls and skillets filled with rice?

BISHOP

Oh, they're just things children would be playing with. And of course rice and black beans are what Brazilians eat every day.

Cornell is superb. I first saw the *Medici Slot Machine* when I was in college. Oh, I loved it. To think one could have *bought* some of those things then. He was very strange. He got crushes on opera singers and ballet dancers. When I looked at his show in New York two years ago I nearly fainted, because one of my favorite books is a book he liked and used. It's a little book by an English scientist who wrote for children about soap bubbles [*Soap Bubbles*: *Their Colours and the Forces which Mold Them*, by Sir C. V. Boys, 1889].

His sister began writing me after she read Octavio Paz's poem for Cornell that I translated. (She doesn't read Spanish.) She sent me a German-French grammar that apparently he meant to do something with and never did. A lot of the pages were folded over and they're all made into star patterns with red ink around them . . . He lived in what was called Elysian Park. That's an awfully strange address to have.

INTERVIEWER

Until recently you were one of the few American poets who didn't make their living teaching or giving readings. What made you decide to start doing both?

BISHOP

I never wanted to teach in my life. I finally did because I wanted to leave Brazil and I needed the money. Since 1970 I've just been *swamped* with people sending me poems. They start to when they know you're in the country. I used to get them in Brazil, but not so much. They got lost in the mail quite often. I don't believe in teaching poetry at all, but that's what they want one to do. You see so many poems every week, you just lose all sense of judgment.

As for readings, I gave a reading in 1947 at Wellesley College two months after my first book appeared. And I was *sick* for days ahead of time. Oh, it was absurd. And then I did one in Washington in '49 and I was sick again and nobody could hear me. And then I didn't give any for twenty-six years. I don't mind reading now. I've gotten over my shyness a little bit. I think teaching helps. I've noticed that teachers aren't shy. They're rather aggressive. They get to be, finally.

INTERVIEWER

Did you ever take a writing course as a student?

BISHOP

When I went to Vassar I took sixteenth-century, seventeenth-century and eighteenth-century literature, and then a course in the novel. The kind of courses where you have to do a lot of reading. I don't think I believe in writing courses at all. There weren't any when I was there. There was a poetry-writing course in the evening, but not for credit. A couple of my friends went to it, but I never did.

The word *creative* drives me crazy. I don't like to regard it as therapy. I was in the hospital several years ago and somebody gave me Kenneth Koch's book *Rose, Where Did You Get That Red?* And it's true, children sometimes write wonderful things, paint wonderful pictures, but I think they should be *dis*couraged. From everything I've read and heard, the number of students in English departments taking literature courses has been falling off enormously. But at the same time the number of people who want to get in the writing classes seems to get bigger and bigger. There are usually two or three being given at Harvard every year. I'd get forty applicants for ten or twelve places. Fifty. It got bigger and bigger. I don't know if they do this to offset practical concerns, or what.

INTERVIEWER

I think people want to be able to say they do something creative like throw pots or write poems.

BISHOP

I just came back in March from reading in North Carolina and Arkansas, and I swear if I see any more handcrafts I'll go mad! I think we should go right straight back to the machine. You can only use so many leather belts, after all. I'm sorry. Maybe you do some of these things.

INTERVIEWER

Do many strangers send you poems?

BISHOP

Yes. It's very hard to know what to do. Sometimes I answer. I had a fan letter the other day, and it was adorable. It was in this childish handwriting. His name was Jimmy Sparks and he was in the sixth grade. He said his class was putting together a booklet of poems and he liked my poems very much—he mentioned three—because they rhymed and because they were about nature. His letter was so cute I did send him a postcard. I think he was supposed to ask me to send a handwritten poem or photograph—schools do this all the time—but he didn't say anything like that, and I'm sure he forgot his mission.

INTERVIEWER

What three poems did he like? "The Sandpiper"?

BISHOP

Yes, and the one about the mirror and the moon, "Insomnia," which Marianne Moore said was a cheap love poem.

INTERVIEWER

The one that ends, ". . . and you love me"?

BISHOP

Yes. I never liked that. I almost left it out. But last year it was put to music by Elliott Carter along with five other poems of mine* and it sounded much better as a song. Yes, Marianne was very opposed to that one.

INTERVIEWER

Maybe she didn't like the last line.

BISHOP

I don't think she ever believed in talking about the emotions much.

---

*"Anaphora," "The Sandpiper," "Argument," "O Breath," and "View of the Capitol from The Library of Congress."

INTERVIEWER

Getting back to teaching, did you devise formal assignments when you taught at Harvard? For example, to write a villanelle?

BISHOP

Yes, I made out a whole list of weekly assignments that I gave the class; but every two or three weeks was a free assignment and they could hand in what they wanted. Some classes were so prolific that I'd declare a moratorium. I'd say, Please, nobody write a poem for two weeks!

INTERVIEWER

Do you think you can generalize that beginning writers write better in forms than not?

BISHOP

I don't know. We did a sestina—we started one in class by drawing words out of a hat—and I wish I'd never suggested it because it seemed to have *swept* Harvard. Later, in the applications for my class, I'd get dozens of sestinas. The students seemed to think it was my favorite form—which it isn't.

INTERVIEWER

I once tried a sestina about a woman who watches soap operas all day.

BISHOP

Did you watch them in college?

INTERVIEWER

No.

BISHOP

Well, it seemed to be a fad at Harvard. Two or three years ago I taught a course in prose and discovered my students were watching the soap operas every morning and afternoon. I don't know when they studied. So I watched two or three just to see what was going on. They were *boring*. And the advertising! One student wrote a story about an old man who was getting ready to have an old lady to dinner (except she was really a ghost), and he polished a plate till he could see his face in it. It was quite well done, so I read some of it aloud, and said, But look, this is impossible. You can never see your face in a plate. The whole class, in unison, said, Joy! I said, What? What are you talking about? Well, it seems there's an ad for Joy soap liquid in which a woman holds up a plate and sees—you know the one? Even so, you can't! I found this very disturbing. TV was *real* and no one had observed that it wasn't. Like when Aristotle was right and no one pointed out, for centuries, that women *don't* have fewer teeth than men.

I had a friend bring me a small TV, black and white, when I was living in Brazil. We gave it to the maid almost immediately because we watched it only when there were things like political speeches, or a revolution coming on. But she loved it. She slept with it in her bed! I think it meant so much to her because she couldn't read. There was a soap opera that year called *The Right to Life*. It changed the whole schedule of Rio society's hours because it was on from eight to nine. The usual dinner hour's eight, so either you had to eat dinner before so that the maid could watch *The Right to Life* or eat much later, when it was over. We ate dinner about ten o'clock finally so that Joanna could watch this thing. I finally decided I had to see it too. It became a chic thing to do and everybody was talking about it. It was absolutely ghastly! They got the programs from Mexico and dubbed them in Portuguese. They were very corny and always very lurid. Corpses lying in coffins, miracles, nuns, even incest.

I had friends in Belo Horizonte, and the mother and their cook and a grandchild would watch the soap operas, the *novelas*, they're called, every night. The cook would get so excited she'd talk to the screen: No! No! Don't do that! You know he's a bad man, Doña So-and-so! They'd get so excited, they'd cry. And I knew of two old ladies, sisters, who got a TV. They'd knit and knit and watch it and cry and one of them would get up and say, Excuse me, I have to go to the bathroom—to the television!

INTERVIEWER

You were living in Brazil, weren't you, when you won the Pulitzer Prize in 1956?

BISHOP

Yes, it was pretty funny. We lived on top of a mountain peak—really way up in the air. I was alone in the house with Maria, the cook. A friend had gone to market. The telephone rang. It was a newsman from the American embassy and he asked me who it was in English, and of course it was very rare to hear someone speak in English. He said, Do you know you've won the Pulitzer Prize? Well, I thought it was a joke. I said, Oh, come on. And he said, Don't you hear me? The telephone connection was very bad and he was shrieking. And I said, Oh, it can't be. But he said it wasn't a joke. I couldn't make an impression on Maria with this news, but I felt I had to share it, so I hurried down the mountain a half mile or so to the next house, but no one was at home. I thought I should do something to celebrate, have a glass of wine or something. But all I could find in that house, a friend's, were some cookies from America, some awful chocolate cookies—Oreos, I think—so I ended up eating two of those. And that's how I celebrated winning the Pulitzer Prize.

The next day there was a picture in the afternoon paper—they take such things very seriously in Brazil—and the day after that my Brazilian friend went to market again. There was a big covered market with stalls for every kind of comestible, and there was one vegetable man we always went to. He said, Wasn't that Doña Elizabetchy's picture in the paper yesterday? She said, Yes, it was—she won a prize. And he said, You know, it's amazing! Last week Señora (Somebody) took a chance on a bicycle and *she* won! My customers are so lucky!

Isn't that marvelous?!

INTERVIEWER

I'd like to talk a little bit about your stories, especially "In the Village," which I've always admired. Do you see any connection, other than the obvious one of shared subject matter, between your stories and poems? In "method of attack," for example?

BISHOP

They're very closely related. I suspect that some of the stories I've written are actually prose poems and not very good stories. I have four about Nova Scotia. One came out last year in the *Southern Review*. I'm working on a long one now that I hope to finish this summer . . . "In the Village" was funny. I had made notes for various bits of it and was given too much cortisone—I have very bad asthma from time to time—and you don't need any sleep. You feel wonderful while it's going on, but to get off it is awful. So I couldn't sleep much and I sat up all night in the tropical heat. The story came from a combination of cortisone, I think, and the gin and tonic I drank in the middle of the night. I wrote it in two nights.

INTERVIEWER

That's incredible! It's a long, long story.

BISHOP

Extraordinary. I wish I could do it again but I'll never take cortisone again, if I can possibly avoid it.

INTERVIEWER

I'm always interested in how different poets go about writing about their childhood.

BISHOP

Everybody does. You can't help it, I suppose. You are fearfully observant then. You notice all kinds of things, but there's no way of putting them all together. My memories of some of those days are so much clearer than things that happened in 1950, say. I don't think one should make a cult of writing about childhood, however. I've always tried to avoid it. I find I have written some, I must say. I went to an analyst for a couple of years off and on in the forties, a very nice woman who was especially interested in writers, writers and blacks. She said it was amazing that I would remember things that happened to me when I was two. It's very rare, but apparently writers often do.

INTERVIEWER

Do you know what your earliest memory is?

BISHOP

I think I remember learning to walk. My mother was away and my grandmother was trying to encourage me to walk. It was in Canada and she had lots of plants in the window the way all ladies do there. I can remember this blur of plants and my grandmother holding out her arms. I must have toddled. It seems to me it's a memory. It's very hazy. I told my grandmother years and years later and she said, Yes, you did learn to walk while your mother was visiting someone. But you walk when you're one, don't you?

I remember my mother taking me for a ride on the swan boats here in Boston. I think I was three then. It was before we went back to Canada. Mother was dressed all in black—widows were in those days. She had a box of mixed peanuts and raisins. There were real swans floating around. I don't think they have them anymore. A swan came up and she fed it and it bit her finger. Maybe she just told me this, but I believed it because she showed me her black kid glove and said, See. The finger was split. Well, I was thrilled to death! Robert Lowell put those swan boats in two or three of the *Lord Weary's Castle* poems.

INTERVIEWER

Your childhood was difficult, and yet in many of your stories and poems about that time there's a tremendously lyrical quality as well as a great sense of loss and tragedy.

BISHOP

My father died, my mother went crazy when I was four or five years old. My relatives, I think they all felt so sorry for this child that they tried to do their very best. And I think they did. I lived with my grandparents in Nova Scotia. Then I lived with the ones in Worcester, Massachusetts, very briefly, and got terribly sick. This was when I was six and seven. Then I lived with my mother's older sister in Boston. I used to go to Nova Scotia for the summer. When I was twelve or thirteen I was improved enough to go to summer camp at Wellfleet until I went away to school when I was fifteen or sixteen. My aunt was devoted to me and she was awfully nice. She was married and had no children. But my relationship with my relatives—I was always a sort of a guest, and I think I've always felt like that.

INTERVIEWER

Was your adolescence a calmer time?

BISHOP

I was very romantic. I once walked from Nauset Light—I don't think it exists anymore—which is the beginning of the elbow [of Cape Cod], to the tip, Provincetown, all alone. It took me a night and a day. I went swimming from time to time but at that time the beach was absolutely deserted. There wasn't anything on the back shore, no buildings.

INTERVIEWER

How old would you have been?

BISHOP

Seventeen or eighteen. That's why I'd never go back—because I can't bear to think of the way it is now . . . I haven't been to Nantucket since—well, I hate to say. My senior year at college I went there for Christmas with my then boyfriend. Nobody knew we were there. It was this wonderful, romantic trip. We went the day after Christmas and stayed for about a week. It was terribly cold but beautiful. We took long walks on the moors. We stayed at a very nice inn and we thought that probably the landlady would throw us out (we were very young and this kind of thing wasn't so common then). We had a bottle of sherry or something innocent like that. On New Year's Eve about ten o'clock there was a knock on the door. It was our landlady with a tray of hot grogs! She came in and we had the loveliest time. She knew the people who ran the museum and they opened it for us. There are a couple of wonderful museums there.

INTERVIEWER

I heard a story that you once spent a night in a tree at Vassar outside Cushing dormitory. Is it true?

BISHOP

Yes, it was me, me and a friend whose name I can't remember. We really were crazy and those trees were wonderful to climb. I used to be a great tree climber. Oh, we probably gave up about three in the morning. How did that ever get around? I can't imagine! We stopped being friends afterwards. Well, actually she had invited two boys from West Point for the weekend and I found myself *stuck* with this youth all in [*her hands draw an imagined cape and uniform in the air*]—the dullest boy! I didn't know what to say! I nearly went mad. I think I sort of dropped the friend at that point . . . I lived in a great big corner room on the top floor of Cushing and I apparently had registered a little late because I had a roommate whom I had never wanted to have. A strange girl named Constance. I remember her entire side of the room was furnished in Scottie dogs—pillows, pictures, engravings, and photographs. And mine was rather bare. Except that I probably wasn't a good roommate either, because I had a theory at that time that one should write down all one's dreams. That that was the way to write poetry. So I kept a notebook of my dreams and thought if you ate a lot of awful cheese at bedtime you'd have interesting dreams. I went to Vassar with a pot about this big—it did have a cover!—of Roquefort cheese that I kept in the bottom of my bookcase . . . I think everyone's given to eccentricities at that age. I've heard that at Oxford Auden slept with a revolver under his pillow.

INTERVIEWER

As a young woman, did you have a sense of yourself as a writer?

BISHOP

No, it all just happens without your thinking about it. I never meant to go to Brazil. I never meant doing any of these things. I'm afraid in my life everything has just *happened*.

INTERVIEWER

You like to think there are reasons—

BISHOP

Yes, that people plan ahead, but I'm afraid I really didn't.

INTERVIEWER

But you'd always been interested in writing?

BISHOP

I'd written since I was a child, but when I went to Vassar I was going to be a composer. I'd studied music at Walnut Hill and had a rather good teacher. I'd had a year of counterpoint and I also played the piano. At Vassar you had to perform in public once a month. Well, this terrified me. I really was sick. So I played once and then I gave up the piano because I couldn't bear it. I don't think I'd mind now, but I can't play the piano anymore. Then the next year I switched to English.

It was a very literary class. Mary McCarthy was a year ahead of me. Eleanor Clark was in my class. And Muriel Rukeyser, for freshman year. We started a magazine you may have heard of, *Con Spirito*. I think I was a junior then. There were six or seven of us—Mary, Eleanor Clark and her older sister, my friends Margaret Miller and Frani Blough, and a couple of others. It was during Prohibition and we used to go downtown to a speakeasy and drink wine out of teacups. That was our big vice. Ghastly stuff! Most of us had submitted things to the *Vassar Review* and they'd been turned down. It was very old-fashioned then. We were all rather put out because *we* thought we were good. So we thought, Well, we'll start our own magazine. We thought it would be nice to have it anonymous, which it was. After its third issue the *Vassar Review* came around and a couple of our editors became editors on it and then they published things by us. But we had a wonderful time doing it while it lasted.

INTERVIEWER

I read in another interview you gave that you had enrolled or were ready to enroll after college in Cornell Medical School.

BISHOP

I think I had all the forms. This was the year after I had graduated from Vassar. But then I discovered I would have to take German and I'd already given up on German once, I thought it was so difficult. And I would have had to take another year of chemistry. I'd already published a few things and I think Marianne [Moore] discouraged me, and I didn't go. I just went off to Europe instead.

INTERVIEWER

Did the Depression have much reality for college students in the thirties?

BISHOP

Everybody was frantic trying to get jobs. All the intellectuals were communist except me. I'm always very perverse so I went in for T. S. Eliot and Anglo-Catholicism. But the spirit was pretty radical. It's funny. The girl who was the biggest radical—she was a year ahead of me—has been married for years and years to one of the heads of Time-Life. I've forgotten his name. He's very famous and couldn't be more conservative. He writes shocking editorials. I can still see her standing outside the library with a tambourine collecting money for this cause and that cause.

INTERVIEWER

Wanting to be a composer, a doctor, or a writer—how do you account for it?

BISHOP

Oh, I was interested in all those things. I'd like to be a painter most, I think. I never really sat down and said to myself, *I'm going to be a poet.* Never in my life. I'm still surprised that people think I am . . . I started publishing things in my senior year, I think, and I remember my first check for thirty-five dollars and that was rather an exciting moment. It was from something called *The Magazine*, published in California. They took a poem, they took a story—oh, I wish those poems had never been published! They're terrible! I did show the check to my roommate. I was on the newspaper, *The Miscellany*—and I really was, I don't know, mysterious. On the newspaper board they used to sit around and talk about how they could get published and so on and so on. I'd just hold my tongue. I was embarrassed by it. And still am. There's nothing more embarrassing than being a poet, really.

INTERVIEWER

It's especially difficult to tell people you're meeting for the first time that that's what you do.

BISHOP

Just last week a friend and I went to visit a wonderful lady I know in Quebec. She's seventy-four or seventy-five. And she didn't say this to me but she said to my friend, Alice, I'd like to ask my neighbor who has the big house next door to dinner, and she's so nice, but she'd be bound to ask Elizabeth what she does and if Elizabeth said she wrote poetry, the poor woman wouldn't say another word all evening! This is awful, you know, and I think no matter how modest you think you feel or how minor you think you are, there must be an awful core of ego somewhere for you to set yourself up to write poetry. I've never *felt* it, but it must be there.

INTERVIEWER

In your letter to me, you sounded rather wary of interviewers. Do you feel you've been misrepresented in interviews? For example, that your refusal to appear in all-women poetry anthologies has been misunderstood as a kind of disapproval of the feminist movement.

BISHOP

I've always considered myself a strong feminist. Recently I was interviewed by a reporter from the *Chicago Tribune*. After I talked to the girl for a few minutes, I realized that she wanted to play me off as an "old fashioned" against Erica Jong, and Adrienne [Rich], whom I like, and other violently feminist people. Which isn't true at all. I finally asked her if she'd ever read any of my poems. Well, it seemed she'd read *one* poem. I didn't see how she could interview me if she didn't know anything about me at all, and I told her so. She was nice enough to print a separate piece in the *Chicago Tribune* apart from the longer article on the others. I had said that I didn't believe in propaganda in poetry. That it rarely worked. What she had me saying was "Miss Bishop does not believe that poetry should convey the poet's personal philosophy." Which made me sound like a complete dumbbell! Where she got that, I don't know. This is why one gets nervous about interviews.

INTERVIEWER

Do you generally agree with anthologists' choices? Do you have any poems that are personal favorites? Ones you'd like to see anthologized that aren't?

BISHOP

I'd rather have—well, anything except "The Fish"! I've declared a moratorium on that. Anthologists repeat each other so finally a few years ago I said nobody could reprint "The Fish" unless they reprinted three others because I got so sick of it.

One or two more questions. You went to Yaddo several times early in your career. Did you find the atmosphere at an artist's colony helpful to your writing?

BISHOP

I went to Yaddo twice, once in the summer for two weeks, and for several months the winter before I went to Brazil. Mrs. Ames was very much in evidence then. I didn't like it in the summer because of the incessant coming and going, but the winter was rather different. There were only six of us, and just by luck we all liked each other and had a very good time. I wrote one poem, I think, in that whole stretch. The first time I liked the horse races, I'm afraid. In the summer—I think this still goes on—you can walk through the Whitney estate to the tracks. A friend and I used to walk there early in the morning and sit at the track and have coffee and blueberry muffins while they exercised the horses. I loved that. We went to a sale of yearlings in August and that was beautiful. The sale was in a big tent. The grooms had brass dustpans and brooms with brass handles and they'd go around after the little colts and sweep up the manure. That's what I remember best about Yaddo.

INTERVIEWER

It was around the time that you went to Yaddo, wasn't it, that you were consultant in poetry to The Library of Congress? Was that year in Washington more productive than your Yaddo experience?

BISHOP

I've suffered because I've been so shy all my life. A few years later I might have enjoyed it more but at the time I didn't like it much. I hated Washington. There were so many government buildings that looked like Moscow. There was a very nice secretary, Phyllis Armstrong, who got me through. I think she did most of the work. I'd write something and she'd say, Oh, no, that isn't official, so then she'd take it and rewrite it in gobbledygook. We used to bet on the horses—

Phyllis always bet the daily double. She and I would sit there reading the *Racing Form* and poets would come to call and Phyllis and I would be talking about our bets!

All the "survivors" of that job—a lot of them are dead—were invited to read there recently. There were thirteen of us, unfortunately.

INTERVIEWER

A friend of mine tried to get into that reading and she said it was jammed.

BISHOP

It was *mobbed!* And I don't know why. It couldn't have been a duller, more awful occasion. I think we were supposedly limited to ten minutes. I *stuck* to it. But there's no stopping somebody like James Dickey. Stafford was good. I'd never heard him and never met him. He read one very short poem that really brought tears to my eyes, he read it so beautifully.

I'm not very fond of poetry readings. I'd much rather read the book. I know I'm wrong. I've only been to a few poetry readings I could *bear*. Of course, you're too young to have gone through the Dylan Thomas craze . . .

When it was somebody like Cal Lowell or Marianne Moore, it's as if they were my children. I'd get terribly upset. I went to hear Marianne several times and finally I just couldn't go because I'd sit there with tears running down my face. I don't know, it's sort of embarrassing. You're so afraid they'll do something wrong.

Cal thought that the most important thing about readings was the remarks poets made in between the poems. The first time I heard him read was years ago at the New School for Social Research in a small, gray auditorium. It was with Allen Tate and Louise Bogan. Cal was very much younger than anybody else and had published just two books. He read a long, endless poem—I've forgotten its title*— about a Canadian nun in New Brunswick. I've forgotten what the

---

*"Mother Marine Therese" in *The Mills of the Kavanaughs*.

point of the poem is, but it's very, very long and it's quite beautiful, particularly in the beginning. Well, he started, and he read very badly. He kind of droned and everybody was trying to get it. He had gotten about two thirds of the way through when somebody yelled, Fire! There was a small fire in the lobby, nothing much, that was put out in about five minutes and everybody went back to their seats. Poor Cal said, I think I'd better begin over again, so he read the whole thing all over again! But his reading got much, much better in later years.

INTERVIEWER

He couldn't have done any better than the record the Poetry Center recently put out. It's wonderful. And very funny.

BISHOP

I haven't the courage to hear it.

Issue 80, 1981

Robert Stone

The Art of Fiction

R obert Stone lives in a small frame house on the Connecticut coast. Inside, a long white living room with curving walls suggests Oriental calm, and a pocket kitchen like a ship's galley offers the comic sight of tame ducks feeding on the water just below. The hesitant phrases of the Modern Jazz Quartet chime from a battered stereo flanked by bookshelves filled with fiction, philosophy, and church history. Over a built-in sofa hangs an unframed poster for *Who'll Stop The Rain?* the film Stone coauthored from his second novel, *Dog Soldiers*. Stone and his wife, Janice, moved into this house in the fall of 1981; they have a son and daughter, grown and gone.

The novelist works in an attic room crowded with cardboard boxes and manuscripts and decorated with several brightly colored samples of Spanish religious art. At one end of the long room, a wide window affords a view of a gray October sea; another looks down on the gravel parking lot of a clam bar. Stone writes at a table only a little larger than the word processor it supports. When his office phone rings, it may be an editor on the line begging him to cover a story, a director seeking to interest him in a new part (in the summer of 1982, Stone played Kent in a professional production of *King Lear* in California), or an interviewer plaguing him with yet another question that he will answer with care and unfailing courtesy.

Although the Stones have lived in many parts of the country, and for four years in London, changes of locale have rarely altered the writer's routine: "I get up very early, drink a pot of tea, and go for as

Ten miles to the south, the road on which they drove turned inland, crossed the mountains on the spine of Baja, and ran for thirty miles within sight of the Sea of Cortez. At the final curve of its eastward loop, a dirt track led from the highway toward the shore, ending at a well appointed fishing resort called Benson's Marina. At Benson's there was a large comfortable ranchhouse in the Sonoran style, a few fast powerboats rigged for big game fishing and a small air strip. Benson ran a pair of light aircraft for long distance transportation and fish spotting.

Early on during production, Lu Anne had been told about Benson's by Frank Carnehan; she and Lionel had hired Benson's son to fly them to San Lucas for a long weekend. The flight had produced much corporate anxiety after the fact because the film's insurance coverage did not apply to impromptu charter flights in unauthorized carriers. Charlie Freitag had been cross and Axelrod had been upbraided.

In the early hours of the morning, their car turned into Benson's and pulled up beside his dock. Walker had slept; a light cokey sleep, full of theatrical nightmares that had his sons in them.

Lu Anne walked straight to the lighted pier and stood next to the fuel pumps, looking out across the gulf. Walker climbed from the car and asked the driver to park it out of the way. In the shadow of the boat house, he had some more cocaine. The drug made him feel jittery and cold in the stiff ocean wind. Lu Anne had Lowndes' bottle of scotch in her tote bag, so he had a drink from it.

A Robert Stone manuscript page, from his novel *Children of Light*.

long as I can." Stone says he stops only when he has left himself a clear starting point for the following day. For weeks on end he will take few days off if his work is going well. "My imagination will still be functioning," he says with a laugh, "twelve hours after my brain is dead."

He lives more quietly now than in his years in the California counterculture as one of Ken Kesey's "Merry Pranksters"; his free time is given over to milder pleasures, such as the exploration by canoe of the salt lagoon behind his house. But even this quiet coast has its threat: The past summer, Stone told me, a large shark was spotted in the lagoon, just off the docks, importing a frisson of fear into the neighborhood.

Stone is in his late forties, a trim man whose thinning hair and well-barbered beard frame a ruddy, pensive face yet to be done justice by his book jacket photos. His voice, branded by years of Scotch and smoke, was deep and serene as we began our two days of talk.

—*William Crawford Woods, 1985*

INTERVIEWER

Was there one book that started you writing?

ROBERT STONE

It was a rereading of *The Great Gatsby* that made me think about writing a novel. I was living on St. Mark's Place in New York; it was a different world in those days. I was in my twenties. I decided I knew a few meanings; I understood patterns in life. I figured, I can't sell this understanding, or smoke it, so I will write a novel. I then started to write *A Hall of Mirrors*. It must have taken me six years, a dreadful amount of time. I really began work on the novel during my Stegner Fellowship at Stanford, which brought me out to California just about the time that everything was going slightly crazy. So I spent a lot of my time, when I should have been writing, experiencing death and transfiguration and rebirth on LSD in Palo Alto. It wasn't an atmosphere that was conducive to getting a whole lot of work done.

INTERVIEWER

You once described writing your first novel as a process that paralleled your life.

STONE

A Hall of Mirrors was something I shattered my youth against. All my youth went into it. I put everything I knew into that book. It was written through years of dramatic change, not only for me, but for the country. It covers the sixties from the Kennedy assassination through the civil rights movement to the beginning of acid, the hippies, the war . . .

INTERVIEWER

Does that mean you changed your conception of the book as you were writing it, that you tried to respond to those changes?

STONE

Yes. And to things that were happening with me. One way or another, it all went into the book. And of course it all went very slowly because once my Stegner Fellowship was over, my wife, Janice, and I had to take turns working. I'd work for twenty weeks and then be on unemployment for twenty weeks, and so on. So it took me a long, long time to finish it.

INTERVIEWER

You mention responding to national as well as personal change. Do you consciously try to write about America?

STONE

Yes, I do. That is my subject. America and Americans.

INTERVIEWER

You have been cited as a writer who addresses larger social issues. Do you start with those in mind, or do you simply start out with the characters and because you have political concerns these issues naturally come out?

It is very natural. You construct characters and set them going in their own interior landscape, and what they find to talk about and what confronts them are, of course, things that concern you most.

Is writing easy for you? Does it flow smoothly?

It's goddamn hard. Nobody really cares whether you do it or not. You have to make yourself do it. I'm very lazy and I suffer as a result. Of course, when it's going well there's nothing in the world like it. But it's also very lonely. If you do something you're really pleased with, you're in the crazy position of being exhilarated all by yourself. I remember finishing one section of *Dog Soldiers*—the end of Hicks's walk—in the basement of a college library, working at night, while the rest of the place was closed down, and I staggered out in tears, talking to myself, and ran into a security guard. It's hard to come down from a high in your work— it's one of the reasons writers drink. The exhilaration of your work turns into the daily depression of the aftermath. But if you heal that with a lot of Scotch you're not fit for duty the next day. When I was younger I was able to use hangovers, but now I have to go to bed early.

You really think of yourself as lazy?

Well, my books aren't lazy books, but I have a lazy way of working. I do a very rough first draft, and then a second, and sometimes I have to do a third because I didn't take the trouble to really organize the first. And I take breaks between drafts. And I do altogether too much traveling.

INTERVIEWER

You have gone for relatively long periods of time between books. Seven years between *A Hall of Mirrors* and *Dog Soldiers*, and then another seven before *A Flag for Sunrise*. Are you writing all that time?

STONE

It seems to me that I am. I was working all those years on *A Flag for Sunrise*. I could probably have gotten six books out of my three if I'd wanted to do smaller themes. Twice as many books and they would have been half as good. Six so-so books. I don't need that. I like big novels; I really admire the grand slam.

INTERVIEWER

Do you have any special requirements, conditions necessary for your working environment?

STONE

Well, of course, I find ways to delay the day as much as possible, but there are no particular rituals connected with that for me, like having a special coffee cup or sharpening six pencils. I do need physical order, because I'm addressing the insubstantiality of structures—that's where the blank page starts. No top, no bottom, no sides. I find it hard to sit still. I pace a lot. I've got to have a pen in my hand when I'm not actually typing.

INTERVIEWER

You mostly type?

STONE

Yes, until something becomes elusive. Then I write in longhand in order to be precise. On a typewriter or word processor you can rush something that shouldn't be rushed—you can lose nuance, richness, lucidity. The pen compels lucidity.

INTERVIEWER

Do you read work aloud to yourself?

STONE

No. My inner ear is very accurate. I know what the writing sounds like.

INTERVIEWER

Your prose is very rich in sensual detail—imagery intensified by the cadence of the sentence.

STONE

I use the white space. I'm interested in precise meaning and in re-verberation, in associative levels. What you're trying to do when you write is to crowd the reader out of his own space and occupy it with yours, in a good cause. You're trying to take over his sensibility and deliver an experience that moves from mere information.

INTERVIEWER

I see that. But one of the things I respond to most in your writing is the tremendous particularity, your way of relating language to reality. It seems to me that there's a danger, if language takes the reader too far into cosmic preoccupations, of losing that immediacy.

STONE

The object is to make a connection between your characters and the contour of things as they are. The danger is of becoming preten-tious. And yet it's necessary that a given dramatized scene have a rich-ness of reference. Take a basic philosophical question, why is there something rather than nothing? Two people in love, two people in a battle to the death, refer to that question. To say so directly is prepos-terous; you have to get there along the path of your art. How do you relate events to that basic question? You choose words that open up deeper and deeper levels of existence by sustaining a sound that perfectly serves the narrative and that at the same time relates through a series of associations to the larger questions.

INTERVIEWER

That would account for the shifting levels of your rhetoric, which plays the colloquial against high ornamentation. The effect is a constant tone of irony.

STONE

Irony is my friend and brother. "Minding true things by what their mockeries be." There's only one subject for fiction or poetry or even a joke—*how it is.* In all the arts, the payoff is always the same— recognition. If it works, you say that's real, that's truth, that's life, that's the way things are. "There it is."

INTERVIEWER

The classic aphorism of the Vietnam War.

STONE

Exactly.

INTERVIEWER

I understand one article you filed from Vietnam was about a Saigon rock festival. That certainly puts two worlds of the time together.

STONE

That was a funny scene. Stoned rear-echelon GIs and a Vietnamese band that was a phonocopy of the Grateful Dead. Meanwhile, a light plane kept circling overhead streaming a Christian banner attacking rock as the devil's music. There was an oncoming monsoon and the banner kept threatening to foul the guy's propeller. Finally he fell out of sight and everybody waited for the crash, which didn't come. I remember one very stoned GI saying to another, There it is.

INTERVIEWER

You were a correspondent in Vietnam in 1971.

STONE

Well, I was there less than two months, but every day was different. It was the kind of place where anything could have happened. There's nothing that couldn't have happened there. If you encountered choirs of seraphim up the river or if somebody said he'd just seen a vision of St. George on Hill 51, you'd just say, There it is . . . I was in Saigon a lot of the time. I did get deeper into I Corps, and I was in Cam Rahn Bay. But in Saigon I picked up with a guy who was involved in the dope trade there and in a very short time I had found out more than I really wanted to know. It was very frightening. I should also say that this period, 1971, was a time when, in the line, there was not a lot of combat involving American troops. There was rocketing up around Phu Bai, there were some bombs going off in Saigon, but nobody was quite sure who was responsible for them. American troops were not heavily engaged. It was the time of Vietnamization. The talks were going on in Paris, and American troops were being kept out of the line to keep the casualty rates down.

INTERVIEWER

Was Vietnam your first experience of war?

STONE

No, I first saw war when I was in the navy, in the Mediterranean, in 1956. I saw the French air attack on Port Said—jets from the carrier *Lafayette* coming in right on top of our radar mast and shelling. Those multicolored tracers in the night that I saw again in Vietnam I saw with something like nostalgia. But it was quite horrible. You could look through the glasses and see donkeys and people flying through the air, chewed up by 7.62s and rockets. It was a slaughter of civilians. But it always is.

INTERVIEWER

Are you interested in observing future wars, or have you had enough?

STONE

I don't know. There was a wonderful expression soldiers had in the American Civil War that captures the strangeness of combat, the charm—they called it "going to see the elephant." There are times when I feel that once you've seen war, you want to see it again.

INTERVIEWER

It seems to me that your work is in the tradition of twentieth-century fiction that takes war as its principal metaphor for our lives. Would you say that war is the most complete description of our situation?

STONE

It's literally true that the world is seen by the superpowers as a grid of specific targets. We're all on military maps. There happens to be no action in those zones at present, but they're there. And then there are the wars we fight with ourselves in our own cities. It is the simple truth that, wherever you are, there is an armed enemy present, not far away.

INTERVIEWER

I'd like to ask a little about your evolution as a writer.

STONE

My early life was very strange. I was a solitary; radio fashioned my imagination. Radio narrative always has to embody a full account of both action and scene. I began to do that myself. When I was seven or eight, I'd walk through Central Park like Sam Spade, describing aloud what I was doing, becoming both the actor and the writer setting him into the scene. That was where I developed an inner ear.

INTERVIEWER

So you grew up in New York?

STONE

For the most part we were in New York, my mother and I. It was just the two of us. My mother was, I now realize, schizophrenic, and sometimes she was better than at other times. She lost a job as a school-teacher in New York for medical reasons; she had a very small pension, and when she was very ill, there was really no place for me to go. Except this place that was—well, it functioned partly as a day school. My mother was in and out of hospitals. I was in an orphanage run by the Marist brothers from the age of six until just before I was ten.

INTERVIEWER

I wonder how her schizophrenia influenced your imagination.

STONE

I wonder that too. I am not really sure. One thing I know is that I usually can recognize schizophrenics when I see them. There is a certain way of speaking. I am talking about functioning schizophrenics, professional people; there are a lot of them around. It is very hard to talk about it in the abstract. In California, years ago, I had a doctor who would tell me these rather askew anecdotes that didn't seem to have any point. What it reminded me of was my mother's disconnection. Their associative patterns seemed to be similar. I finally realized what his problem was. He was about halfway into another kind of reality, but at the same time he was a doctor, functioning as a GP.

INTERVIEWER

Lu Anne, the heroine of *Children of Light*, is schizophrenic.

STONE

Lu Anne's condition is based on what I have experienced with people. There are people who have delusional systems they are really quite aware of and treat as nemeses. That is Lu Anne's condition; she has a lot of insight into her own delusional systems. Actually, many people have that, and I have been waiting a long time to write about it. It seems to be part of how I see things. I think that is partly because of my mother, whom I liked very much but who was very difficult for me to understand. When she was my contact person for reality, for information about the world, I got some confusing signals.

INTERVIEWER

Have you ever written about your childhood?

STONE

I don't write about my childhood or New York; I have hardly any references to it at all. In a way, that's because I always used my imagination as a kind of alternative life when I wanted to be in another place than the one I was in. I just didn't want to write about that stuff. I wanted to enjoy myself. I wasn't ready to write about it; perhaps I'm not ready to write about it yet.

INTERVIEWER

Did you read in the navy?

STONE

Yes. Everybody on a ship reads, whether it's comic books or Westerns or the Bible or whatever. They always read a lot. I was reading *Moby-Dick*, which sounds terribly precious, but I thought if you can't read *Moby-Dick* in the roaring forties you'll never read *Moby-Dick*. So I brought it along. I also read *Ulysses* on the same trip. I seem to have imprinted the ocean in a very strong way because I end up with all these marine images that just seem so readily at hand for me.

INTERVIEWER

Many people think of you as having a considerable grasp on the major shift in American culture from the Beats in the fifties to the sixties' counterculture.

STONE

I was in the right place at the right time to see that. It started out with Jack Kerouac's *On the Road* while I was still in the navy. My mother recommended the book to me. I am probably the only person who had *On the Road* recommended to him by his mother. It is very hard to go back and think about what *On the Road* was saying to me. I pick it up now and all I can see is Neal Cassady. I got to know him. It was a wonderful rendering of him, but I don't see much else in it. Now it just reminds me of somebody writing on speed. That may be uncharitable, but frankly I find it very sentimental. As I say, I am not sure what it was that moved me. I suppose there was that tradition of the American road. I can almost remember what that was like. Thinking about the great continent out there and the city intersections, that myth of the roadside traveler. It reminded me of how every once in a while my mother and I would take off on some migration to where things were going to be better, like Chicago or wherever. We went all the way to New Mexico. I can't remember what we were in quest of. We were in quest of something though. We usually ended up on welfare, then trying to get out of wherever we were. One time we went to Chicago and ended up in a Salvation Army shelter on the North Side because we ran out of money. We stayed for as long as the Salvation Army would keep us, and then somehow my mother scraped together money to get us back to New York. When we got back, we spent two nights sleeping on a roof. It was wild, you know. It was useful. On the one hand, it gave me a fear of chaos, and on the other hand, it was a romance with the world and bus stations and things like that.

INTERVIEWER

You didn't finish college, did you?

STONE

No, I started at New York University and hung on for about a year, but I couldn't stay with it. I was working at the *Daily News* at night and trying to go to classes in the daytime and I just couldn't do it, so I dropped out. In Greenwich Village, a lot of stuff was happening then. Janice worked in the Figaro and she also worked at the Seven Arts on Forty-third and Ninth Avenue. The Seven Arts, of course, was where Kerouac and Allen Ginsberg and Ray Bremser and all those other guys with droopy expressions were regulars. I kind of hung out smoking lots of cigarettes, looking very cool, listening to Coltrane. Janice and I were both at NYU until I quit. She had another job as a guidette in the RCA Building. We both got out about one o'clock—I from the *Daily News*. She took off her guidette uniform and put on her black stockings and was a waitress in the Seven Arts where I'd go to hang out.

INTERVIEWER

Were you writing poetry at that time?

STONE

Yes, I was writing it, and reading, and hanging out, though I didn't have too much time to hang out. I had to assume a languid posture in a hurry because I had to be up early in the morning. I really felt that hanging out was the price I had to pay, whether I wrote anything or not; these were the people who were more like me or what I wanted to be. One had the sense in those days that it was a relatively small thing, not mass bohemia like you had in the sixties. There was a lot of marijuana and you could really go to jail for years; we all thought it was very decadent and terrific of us. There was an espresso place on Sixth Street between First and Second Avenues run by a guy named Baron, who was a follower of Ayn Rand—he had a dollar sign outside his café. Baron sold peyote buttons. It was very hard to eat peyote; you had to put it in a Waring blender and do all sorts of things to get enough down. I remember being on peyote and seeing a wrestling match for the *Daily News* in Madison Square Garden; seeing this on peyote may have changed my life. Once I got my Stegner and got out to California, I happened to collide with Ken Kesey; he lived just a couple of streets away. That whole scene was just ready to take off. And I thought I knew all about peyote and drugs and such. It didn't bother me to experiment. Kesey had a job as an orderly in the Veteran's Hospital and he was involved in the first experiments that were being conducted in psychedelic drugs. He was a volunteer and so was his friend Vic Lovell, who is a psychologist now. They were doing all these crazy drugs on an experimental basis. Some of them worked, some of them did not. I can remember really off-the-wall things called IT-290s; they didn't even have names they were so arcane. Whatever IT-290 was, I remember walking through the woods and suddenly encountering this huge locomotive, a green locomotive with gold trim, a very detailed hallucination that I remember particularly well. I still have a lot of friends out there, people who I went through that stuff with.

INTERVIEWER

Were your friends important to your work at that point?

STONE

The whole scene probably set me back a year or two, but my friends were certainly important in my life. California in the early sixties was really quite wonderful. It seemed so civilized and so easy-going; really it was fun when the strangest thing around was us, and we were pretty harmless.

INTERVIEWER

A Hall of Mirrors is a cohesive book, considering the conditions under which it was written and the long span of time.

STONE

It was necessary that it be cohesive. I was looking for a vision of America, for a statement about the American condition. I was after a book that would be as ambitious as possible. I wanted to be an American Gogol if I could, I wanted to write *Dead Souls*. All of the characters represent ideas about America, about an America in a period of extraordinary, vivid transition.

INTERVIEWER

In a way, it seems to me that the novel is a kind of counterpart to *On the Road*.

STONE

On the Road twenty years after. In a way. Yes.

INTERVIEWER

Certainly Ray Hicks in *Dog Soldiers* has some biographical touches drawn from the same Neal Cassady who appeared as Dean

Moriarty in *On the Road*. Did you know Kerouac when you were hanging out with Kesey—"on the bus"?

STONE

I didn't know him well. And I didn't travel on the bus. I saw the bus off and greeted the bus when it arrived on Riverside Drive. We went to a party where Kerouac and Ginsberg and Orlovsky and those guys were, and Kerouac was at his drunken worst. He was also very jealous of Neal, who had shifted his allegiance to Kesey. But Neal was pretty exhausted too. I saw some films taken on the bus— Neal looked like he was tired from trying to keep up with the limitless energy of all those kids. Anyway . . . Kerouac at that party was drunk and pissed off, a situation I understand very well. The first thing I ever said to him was, Hey, Jack, have you got a cigarette? And he said, I ain't gonna give you no fucking cigarette, man, there's a drugstore on the corner, you can go down there and buy a fucking pack of cigarettes, don't ask me for cigarettes. That's my Kerouac story.

INTERVIEWER

That's a sad story. The passing of the torch. Is Tom Wolfe's book on Kesey, *The Electric Kool-Aid Acid Test*, a pretty good picture of that whole scene?

STONE

It's amazingly good. It also forces a coherence on that scene that it didn't necessarily have. I mean, that stuff was all so ephemeral, there was no philosophical core to it, particularly; it was all just goofiness.

INTERVIEWER

Well, the Wolfe book on Kesey does convey—or impose—the notion of religious quest.

STONE

It's hard to stay away from religion when you mess with acid.

Neal Cassady as a figure on that scene does more than form a historical link between the Beat Generation and the counterculture. He also carries on the image of the affectless sociopath as a major American cultural type, a figure of particular interest to you in your fiction.

STONE
Well, Cassady was a benign version of that figure. Gary Gilmore may be closer to what I mean, a vicious drifter of the kind America seems to produce in greater quantity than does any other country, probably because there is no moral center to our middle class. This society is so fractured. It never really had that period of high bourgeois cultural development that most European countries had. The American underclass has never had the tradition and stability of a European peasantry so it could never develop feudal loyalties. Instead we get these institutionalized personalities whose arrested emotions oblige them to mimic mood, feeling, love. This is the origin of their violence.

INTERVIEWER
Such people will always constitute the night side of a counterculture. Charles Manson. Gilmore. Figures like Kesey and Kerouac draw forth its princes and saints.

STONE
I think cultural undergrounds develop in the void left by the abdication of the official culture. During the sixties, so many august institutions seemed to have no self-confidence. The universities, corporations, the very fabric of the state. Everything you pushed just seemed to fall over. Everything was up for grabs. For me, the counterculture was like a party that spilled out into the world until one had the odd feeling in society that one was walking around looking at the results of a party that had ended a few years before—a big experiment. But there was no program, everybody wanted different things. I think Kesey wanted a cultural revolution, the nature of which was uncertain; he was just making it up as he went along. Other people were

into political reform. Others thought the drugs would fix it all. Peace
and love and dope.

INTERVIEWER

There's a lot of dope, and an epic amount of drinking in your
books—

STONE

I can't stop them from doing it. I just can't. It's getting ridiculous.
I get laughed at for the volume of chemicals that gets consumed, the
amount of dope and booze. And now this guy's doing it again in my
new book.

INTERVIEWER

Whom do you consider your literary forebears?

STONE

My "forebears" are unsurprising. The great masters, the late Victo-
rians; more Hemingway and Fitzgerald than Faulkner. I like Céline
and Nathanael West and Dos Passos. I can't really begin to characterize
my own style beyond saying that it closely reflects my thinking, my
world view. But in my first novel, I felt pretty free—I was all over the lot.
And I did try as forcefully as I could to invent a voice. It's filled with influences and echoes, but it's mine, as nearly as I can make it so. I began
A Hall of Mirrors as a realistic novel, but my life changed and the world
changed and when I thought about it I realized that "realism" was a fal-
lacy. It's simply not tenable. You have to write a poem about what
you're describing. You can't render, can't dissect. Zola was deluded.

INTERVIEWER

Those remarks suggest an affinity with writers like John Barth and
William Gass and Donald Barthelme. But I don't really see you in that
camp.

STONE

My difference with those writers is that they take realism too seriously and so have to react against it. I don't feel the necessity of reacting against it. I don't believe in it to start with. Realism as a theory of literature is meaningless. I can start with it as a mode precisely because I don't believe in it. I *know* it's all a world of words—what else could it be? I had the curious luck to be raised by a schizophrenic, which gives one a tremendous advantage in understanding the relationship of language to reality. I had to develop a model of reality in the face of being conditioned to a schizophrenic world. I had to sort out causality for myself. My mother's world was pure magic. And because I had no father I eventually went into a sort of orphanage when my mother could no longer cope. So at the age of six I went into an institution, which taught me to be a listener. I had to deal with all the ways people were coming on to me, had to listen to all their trips and sort them out. Realism wasn't an issue because there wasn't any. I always had a vaguely dreamlike sense of things. There was no strong distinction for me between objective and imaginative worlds.

INTERVIEWER

Life was failing to provide you with coherent narrative.

STONE

That's right. Life wasn't providing narrative so I had to. I had very little personal mythology of my own.

INTERVIEWER

All this suggests some intricate connections among living and writing and acting. Many of your characters seem preoccupied with the shifting roles in their lives—who am I here?

STONE

Yes. And my becoming a writer was my answer to that question. It was an absolute necessity. I had to create somebody significant or I would have been swept away. I've been known to say, not altogether facetiously, that life is a means of extracting fiction. If I start out with the claim that I tell stories to serve life, it's easy enough to reverse the terms.

INTERVIEWER

The characters in your books are often writers, but of forms other than fiction. Can you speak a bit about your own work in other forms?

STONE

I intend to write a play. I'd direct a film if the chance came my way. But with those forms too many other people get their hands on your work. The joy of fiction is its autonomy. You take the risks, you take the rap.

INTERVIEWER

Has your work as a screenwriter taught you anything about writing novels?

STONE

No. My screenplays have had no influence on my fiction. But many writers of my generation, which was spared television in its youth, grew up with their sense of narrative influenced by the structure of film. And you can go back much earlier to see that. Joyce, for example. Interestingly, Dickens seems to have anticipated the shape of the movies—look at the first few pages of *Great Expectations*.

INTERVIEWER

When you think of the writers of your generation, do you find a special constellation of contemporaries where you locate yourself?

STONE

Not really. I think more of generations of readers—for me, people who had some intense experience of the sixties. That's a generation I address. I share their concerns, their history. I get a certain amount of mail that reflects that. But there are no writers I'm aware of who are doing the same sort of thing I'm doing because I take seriously questions that the culture has largely obviated. In a sense, I'm a theologian. And so far as I know I'm the only one.

Does this connect in a way to what you've called the fractured state of American letters?

You have famous writers, but there's no center. There are the best-seller writers, who are anonymous, almost industrial figures. You have writers who write primarily for other writers. And you have writers with their separate and different constituencies. But American fiction is not in a state of high health. This has something to do with the economic exigencies of publishing, of course. There's a lot of pressure on the noncommercial novel, on what publishers call marginal fiction. Fewer first novels are published, fewer books of any real quality that don't seem immediately bankable. This has to show itself in a kind of reduced, duller national literature, at least for the near future.

As far as best-selling fiction is concerned—

The best-seller list has always for the most part been the work of hacks, but in the past there seems to have been more space for serious writers. The pressure that's squeezing them out is dangerous and worrying. At the same time there are all these academic writing programs turning out the new second lieutenants of literature, and some of them somehow do manage to get published.

All of your books offer the same general structure—multiple characters, introduced at disparate points woven slowly together until the principals collide. How is that done in the writing? Is one figure followed nearly to the end, or is each scene treated in what will be its final sequence?

STONE

The latter. To run all those lines out one at a time would quickly turn stale. You have to be able to surprise yourself. In *Dog Soldiers*, for example, I didn't know Hicks was going to shoot Dieter until the day I wrote it. I just began writing their dialogue until it became inevitable. I was always attracted to the idea of bringing different elements together. One of my favorite radio programs was *Tell Me a Story*, in which people were presented with three things to weave into one.

INTERVIEWER

As material emerges, do you control it with an outline? Charts, notebooks, things like that?

STONE

The only thing I do is make a short list that indicates sequence, very loosely. And then I sometimes jumble the stuff once I've got it written.

INTERVIEWER

You juxtapose sequences in ways you hadn't planned on?

STONE

Yes. Literally juggle them. But I don't use charts or notes.

INTERVIEWER

You don't plot through to a conclusion?

STONE

I know the beginning and usually the end. My problem is the middle—the second act, so to speak.

INTERVIEWER

At what point in the process of a book is your consciousness of technique strongest, as opposed to times when the sheer energy of invention carries you along?

STONE

There are always certain metaphorical events that have to carry special weight. My stress on technique will be strongest when I encounter them. But there's no point at which the pleasure of invention justifies you in self-indulgence. You can never give yourself a break, you always have to make the hardest decisions. That means, for example, writing a brilliant passage and then throwing it away if there's no use for it in terms of the total design. It means scorning to find a clever way around problems that must be grappled with. There are times you have to take the chance that you may derail the structure of your book.

INTERVIEWER

Can you give an example?

STONE

Well, the meeting of the revolutionaries in *A Flag for Sunrise* broke some rules of structure. They invaded the order of the book—for good reason—and then were never seen again. That scene was tough, I had to rewrite it a lot. The scene of Naftali's suicide—I must have rewritten that eight times. And cut it to the bone. In the book, it's only a fourth as long as it was in earlier drafts. All kinds of great lines—they had to go. It took forever. I couldn't get it right for the longest time. And when I reread it in the finished book, I thought it was awful. I was desolate. But Janice persuaded me that the scene was good. I always feel desolate when I finish a book. I thought that *A Flag for Sunrise* had some good scenes, but it troubled me overall. I fell into a great depression.

INTERVIEWER

Has there ever been a negative criticism of your work that you found useful?

STONE

Well, I've seen negative positions I could respect. But I don't know that I learned anything from them. Negative criticism of my work tends to be very vitriolic.

INTERVIEWER

The religious element in your work often asserts itself in classic existential form—for example, Hicks's ideal of ideas embodied in action, or Holliwell's remark in *A Flag for Sunrise*, "There's always a place for God—there's some question as to whether he's in it." This seems a near reflection of Heidegger's assertion that he is neither theistic nor atheistic but adrift in a world from which God is absent.

STONE

I feel a very deep connection to the existentialist tradition of God as an absence—not a meaningless void, but a negative presence we live in terms of. I do have the sense of a transcendent plane from which I'm barred and I want to play off of it. If it's there, I'll get one sound. If it's not, I'll get a different sound.

INTERVIEWER

Was the Catholic orphanage the start of your religious opinions?

STONE

Yes. I felt very rebellious. Every once in a while I would get very angry at the whole structure, although I guess I believed it. I was in that very difficult position you get in when you really believe in God, and at the same time you are very angry; God is this huge creature who we must know, love, and serve, though actually you feel like you want to kick the son of a bitch. The effect on me was I felt I was just doing things wrong.

INTERVIEWER

Do you have a fully articulated theory of fiction? In the sense, say, that Conrad framed his in the preface to *The Nigger of the Narcissus*?

STONE

"Fiction must justify itself in every line." Yes. I'm beginning to frame one—and along rather Conradian lines. Prose fiction must first of all perform the traditional functions of storytelling. We *need* stories. We can't identify ourselves without them. We're always telling ourselves stories about who we are: that's what history is, what the idea of a nation or an individual is. The purpose of fiction is to help us answer the question we must constantly be asking ourselves, who do we think we are and what do we think we're doing.

INTERVIEWER

This quest can, on the part of some of your characters, particularly the more blighted or thwarted, take very brutal forms. Think of Rheinhardt, in *A Hall of Mirrors*, who can't seem to make America deliver on the American dream.

STONE

What I'm always trying to do is define that process in American life that puts people in a state of anomie, of frustration. The national promise is so great that a tremendous bitterness is evoked by its elusiveness. That was Fitzgerald's subject, and it's mine. So many people go bonkers in this country—I mean, they're doing all the right things and they're still not getting off.

INTERVIEWER

Do you think those expectations will be changed by the economic fact that most Americans will probably live in somewhat more straitened circumstances for some years to come?

STONE

I'm not sure. I think even the poorest people, partly for purely commercial reasons, are still encouraged to think of themselves as candidates for participation in the big American payoff. And of course the nature of the payoff has changed—no more white picket fences. The mass media has taught everybody the glamour of crime. When you're a crook, you're on the side of the chaos; how can you lose? If you're the guy that walks home from the felt factory after twenty years on the job and gets blown away by a freak on angel dust for the pay in your pockets, you're a chump.

INTERVIEWER

This touches on a condition central to your work—what you've called everybody's "diminishing margin of protection." Thus in *Dog Soldiers* you replay Vietnam in Southern California. And in the other books people are always falling prey to some form of planned or random violence—

STONE

We live in a time of ongoing war and the threat of violence is very close to all of us. It's not an exotic thing. You have to be pretty lucky to get through a year without witnessing it.

INTERVIEWER

If a writer explores violence at length in his work, is there a sense in which he inevitably celebrates it?

STONE

I would call it a coming to terms. There is a catharsis. For me, it's a way of dealing with the violence in myself. I think it can do that for the reader as well. Violence *is* a preoccupation of mine. It occurs in my books perhaps disproportionately. But it's been my fortune to see rather a lot of it and to have to think about it. I try to curb my fears in what I write. There's a sense in which I use my characters as scapegoats to pay my dues for me, to ward with their flesh danger away from mine. You know, when some drama intrudes on your life your first impulse is to recount it—to turn disaster into anecdote or art. I deal with much that's negative and gruesome, but I don't write to dispirit people. I write to give them courage, to make them confront things as they are in a more courageous way.

INTERVIEWER

Let me return to Conrad, with whom you've claimed some affinity. I've seen it suggested that Freud and Conrad provide polar notions of reality and thus suggest a continuum along which we may locate ourselves. In Freud there's the faith that psychic reality is knowable once we strip away the skins of neurotic fiction that conceal it. In Conrad, we find reality numinous, and indeed composed of all our fictions about it.

STONE

Well, Freud created a mythology out of a nineteenth-century scientific optimism; he said that the glow in the haunted house was just phosphorescence from the swamp—a comforting high-bourgeois myth. Conrad was a man of the world and a skeptic who worked not on the basis of ideology but of common sense. He saw things as they are without wanting to reduce them to theory. In that respect he's closer to the temper of our own time and certainly closer to my own ideas about reality and about how to explore it in fiction.

INTERVIEWER

Conrad provided you with a powerful epigraph for *Dog Soldiers*. And Robert Lowell one for *A Hall of Mirrors*. There's no epigraph for *A Flag for Sunrise*.

STONE

It's in the book. The Emily Dickinson poem Justin quotes. "A wife—at daybreak—shall I be—"

INTERVIEWER

Of course. "Sunrise, hast thou a flag for me?" That throws a lot of the weight of the book on Sister Justin.

STONE

It gives many of her scenes the quality of metaphorical event I mentioned. It links religious themes with erotic encounter. But it also summarizes a larger idea, the question of what awaits us all on the morning after the battle, so to speak. What will be there to claim our allegiance—the red banner of revolution, or some emblem we can't recognize but that we've somehow created? And of course I intend an ironic reference to the American flag.

INTERVIEWER

Do you have your own ways, like Hicks, of "endeavoring to lead a spiritual life"? I mean, distinct from your work.

STONE

I attempt to. I'm always looking for a spiritual discipline I can live with. When I stopped being religious, being a Catholic, it was—as I did not realize at the time, but have come to since—devastating to me. It was a spiritual and moral devastation—shattering. And yet there was no trauma at the time; it seemed painless, it felt like ordinary maturation. But it left a great hunger.

INTERVIEWER

Is Catholicism still important to you?

STONE

Somebody has said that it's almost as hard to stop being a Catholic as it is to stop being a black. But I greatly admire the Protestant spirit, the Protestant heroes—Luther, Kierkegaard. And I admire the great skeptics—Erasmus and Montaigne, that cast of mind. It's very valuable. And, ironically, it's built into the kind of rigorous training in language and logic that I received.

INTERVIEWER

Catholic reason enabled you to cast off Catholic faith?

STONE

Well, it surely wasn't intended to. But I did learn the lucid analysis of rhetorical argument and thus became more immune to propaganda. And yet the skepticism that led me out of religious belief also leads me out of secular complacency.

INTERVIEWER

Aside from that childhood training in rhetoric, did you learn anything about writing in other academic programs? Anything useful or valuable about creative writing?

STONE

Not really. But a creative writing class can at least be good for morale. When I teach writing, I do things like take classes to bars and race tracks to listen to dialogue. But that kind of thing has limited usefulness. There's no body of technology to impart. But that doesn't mean classes can't help. The idea that young writers ought to be out slinging hash or covering the fights or whatever is bullshit. There's a point where a class can do a lot of good. You know, you throw the rock and you get the splash.

INTERVIEWER

Your own experience in a way represents a synthesis of available models for American novelists—some academic background and connection, and an active life in a varied world.

STONE

I think writers at present can pass fairly easily between these worlds. I have no academic credentials aside from my work, but I've been able to teach and I sometimes enjoy it.

INTERVIEWER

Do you have any interest in writers' conferences and colonies, that kind of thing?

STONE

I've been several times to a wonderful conference in Alaska that's filled with trappers and fishermen and people who spend a lot of time alone. Every year, on the winter solstice, they get together to talk books and writing and to party.

INTERVIEWER

You've been accorded from the beginning a handsome ration of prizes, awards, literary recognition of that kind. Has that had an effect on your work—given you an image you had to live in terms of?

STONE

I've kept my edge, stayed hungry, I think. I never sold so many copies that I got overfed. It's less things like prizes than the simple fact of your first publication that changes everything forever. The minute you appear in print you lose some freedom and innocence and accept a degree of responsibility.

INTERVIEWER

Are there things you'd like to attempt in fiction that you haven't done yet?

STONE

I'd like to write more comic stuff. I mean, there's always some humor in all the awfulness I write about, but sometimes I think of writing—well, I don't know that I could write a purely humorous book that wouldn't have some sort of ghastliness in it. It would have to be a weird kind of humor.

INTERVIEWER

Are there areas of weakness in your work so far that you can identify, things that dissatisfy you?

STONE

Ken Kesey once told me I use too many commas.

INTERVIEWER

Do you ever have writer's block?

STONE

I have a lot of depressed periods during which I'm incapable of working. But I'm not blocked by material or anything when I'm actually writing. I turn up more stuff I want to do than I have room or time to do it in.

INTERVIEWER

That must be in part because you don't stay in your study numbed by an inward gaze, but return repeatedly to the world of experience—to Central America, for example. It's that fact that gives your work its political dimension and lets your readers encounter realized characters in a recognizable world. Incidentally, I'm interested in a remark of yours I encountered somewhere to the effect that Central America is a "due bill coming up for payment."

STONE

No mystery there. That's been a sphere of influence we've exploited economically and dominated politically and militarily very much the way the French, with a bit more success, continue to dominate their former colonies in Africa. We've run that part of the world without a lot of respect for the people who live down there; we've looked down on them as racial inferiors. I have a copy of the *Navy Times* from around 1913 that carries an ad for Shinola shoe polish that says, "Whether you're going on the beach for a party or storming ashore to teach the greasers a lesson, you want to look sharp!" We saw these places as banana republics peopled by gooks who somehow were not quite real people. Nobody thought it compromised American virtue to kick their ass if they got out of line. It was, you know, the white man's burden. And we have to remember that when Kipling passed that duty on to the United States there was no cynicism or irony intended. I don't believe this country has simply been some horror story of racism and murder. But we have incurred a blood debt and it *is* coming up for payment. The end of empire comes for everybody and it's coming for us. So now we're faced with this area close to our southern sea frontier where people have it in for us and are only too eager to collaborate with our enemies. I mean, if there was an invasion of the United States and whoever it was wanted to have a Central American legion, they'd get plenty of volunteers.

INTERVIEWER

You've remarked in your own voice, as has Holliwell in *A Flag for Sunrise*, that we've exported what's worst in our culture, while what's best doesn't export. What is best? What have we got at home that keeps us going?

STONE

Idealism. A tradition of rectitude that genuinely does exist in American society and that sometimes has been translated into government. Enlightenment ideas written into the Constitution. Emerson and Thoreau. The whole tradition so wonderfully mythologized in John Ford's Westerns—the Boston schoolmarm seeking service on the frontier. We've tried to export that in the form of, say, missions to China, but it hasn't really worked because we were more a commercial than a military or cultural empire, so it was our appetites that we exported, along with the relevant parts of our popular culture. The French at least attempted to include their artistic traditions in their *mission civiliatrice*; they and the British, to a lesser extent, did have something to offer their colonials. All we wanted was to do business. The point is that so much that is best in America is a state of mind that you can't export.

INTERVIEWER

But, as you say, we do export shoddy aspects of our culture along with our commerce. Holliwell argues this in his speech in Compostella.

STONE

Low-level pop culture, yes. Because America has managed to create a working class with the leisure and money to command the resources of the society but without the taste to enhance those resources. From that derived the pop culture we've exported. Now that isn't evil but it is a form of pollution. It's why you get Central American Indians with transistor radios glued to their skulls. I don't mean to make a reactionary argument about the purity of the noble savage. But there is such a thing as authenticity. You'll recall that Holliwell's speech attacks American culture but also America's enemies. He sees, as I see, contradictions that simply have to be faced and that possibly cannot be solved. There's a shared Marxist and American attitude that where there's a problem there must be a solution. What about the problem that doesn't have a solution?

INTERVIEWER

There it is.

STONE

There it is. That aphorism may not be the least significant link between Central America and Vietnam.

INTERVIEWER

You've raised the specter that haunts all of your work—as an aspect of American culture that fuels Rheinhardt's spite in *A Hall of Mirrors*, as the heart of the darkness of *Dog Soldiers*, and as a dreadful nostalgia in *A Flag for Sunrise*. Do you think the war will persist as a background for your work for some time?

STONE

I'm constantly drawn back to it. I had to keep myself from doing that in my new book, *Children of Light*, which is about the personal lives of some fucked-up people, unhappy writers and actors in the movie business. But even here I try to refer those lives to the American condition, my usual subject. And the war, as you say, continues to haunt us.

Issue 98, 1985

Robert Gottlieb

The Art of Editing

Robert Gottlieb is a man of eclectic tastes, and it is difficult to make generalizations about the authors he has worked with or the hundreds of books he has edited. In his years at Simon & Schuster, where he became editor in chief, and as publisher and editor in chief of Knopf, he edited a number of big best-sellers, such as Jessica Mitford's *The American Way of Death*, Robert Crichton's *The Secret of Santa Vittoria*, Charles Portis's *True Grit*, Thomas Tryon's *The Other*, and Nora Ephron's *Heartburn*. He worked on several personal histories, such as Brooke Hayward's *Haywire*, Barbara Goldsmith's *Little Gloria . . . Happy at Last*, Jean Stein and George Plimpton's *Edie: An American Biography*, and the autobiographies of Diana Vreeland, Gloria Vanderbilt, and Irene Selznick. He has edited historians and biographers including Barbara Tuchman, Antonia Fraser, Robert K. Massie, and Antony Lukas; dance books by Margot Fonteyn, Mikhail Baryshnikov, Natalia Makarova, Paul Taylor, and Lincoln Kirstein; fiction writers such as John Cheever, Salman Rushdie, John Gardner, Len Deighton, Sybille Bedford, Sylvia Ashton-Warner, Ray Bradbury, Elia Kazan, Margaret Drabble, Richard Adams, V. S. Naipaul, and Edna O'Brien; Hollywood figures Lauren Bacall, Liv Ullmann, Sidney Poitier, and Myrna Loy; musicians John Lennon, Paul Simon, and Bob Dylan; and thinkers such as Bruno Bettelheim, B. F. Skinner, Janet Malcolm, and Carl Schorske. He has helped to shape some of the most influential books of the last fifty years, but nonetheless finds it difficult to understand why anyone would be interested in the nitpicky complaints, the fights over punctuation, the informal therapy, and the reading and re-reading of manuscripts that make up his professional life.

Gottlieb was born in New York City in 1931 and grew up in Manhattan. He read "Henry James, Jane Austen, George Eliot, Proust—the great moralists of the novel. Of course," he says, "I admired the Russians tremendously, but I didn't feel that I'd learned anything from them personally. I learned how to behave from *Emma*—not from *The Brothers Karamazov*." He graduated from Columbia in 1952, the year his first son was born. (He has since had two more children with his second wife, actress Maria Tucci.) He spent two years studying at Cambridge and then in 1955 got a job at Simon & Schuster as editorial assistant to Jack Goodman, the editor in chief.

Publishing was a very different business in the fifties. Many of the big houses were still owned by their founders—Bennett Cerf and Donald Klopfer owned Random House; Alfred Knopf owned Knopf; Dick Simon and Max Schuster were still at Simon & Schuster. As a result, publishers were frequently willing and able to lose money publishing books they liked, and tended to foster a sense that theirs were houses with missions more lofty than profit. "It is not a happy business now," says Gottlieb, "and it once was. It was smaller. The stakes were lower. It was a less sophisticated world."

In 1957, Jack Goodman unexpectedly died, and at about the same time, Simon & Schuster was sold back by the Marshall Field estate to two of its original owners, Max Schuster and Leon Shimkin. Schuster and Shimkin didn't get along, things became strained, and within a few months most of the senior staff had left the company. The owners neglected to hire anybody new, and so suddenly, as Gottlieb puts it, "the kids were running the store." Within a few years Gottlieb became managing editor, and a few years after that, editor in chief. Then, in 1968, he left Simon & Schuster to become editor in chief and publisher of Knopf.

Next to reading, Gottlieb's grand passion is ballet, and from the mid-seventies to the mid-eighties, while at Knopf, Gottlieb served on the New York City Ballet's board of directors, in which capacity he organized ballets from the company's repertoire into programs for each season and oversaw its advertising and subscription campaigns. (A third, lesser, passion of Gottlieb's is acquiring odd objects—including vintage plastic handbags, of which he has a notorious collection.)

In 1987, at the invitation of its new owner, S. I. Newhouse (who also owns Knopf), Gottlieb left Knopf to take over *The New Yorker*. The announcement of his appointment was received with undisguised hostility by the magazine's staff, who suspected Newhouse had ousted Gottlieb's predecessor, the venerated William Shawn, editor since 1952, against his will. Dozens of the magazine's staff members signed a petition requesting that Gottlieb refuse Newhouse's offer. He didn't. "I never took it personally," Gottlieb explains. "I knew that the same thing would have happened to anyone. I didn't even read the names of the people who signed the letter, many of whom were good friends of mine. I knew that I felt a lot of goodwill toward the magazine, and I assumed that it would prevail. And, indeed, once I got there, everyone was wonderful, couldn't have been nicer. I just got to work, and everybody got to work with me."

In 1992, Gottlieb agreed to retire from *The New Yorker* to make way for former *Vanity Fair* editor Tina Brown. (He says he told Newhouse when he was hired that he would be a curator rather than a revolutionary, and that if Newhouse wanted radical change he should find someone else.) Then sixty-one, Gottlieb decided he didn't want to begin running something else, and offered his services to Sonny Mehta, who had taken over Knopf when Gottlieb left. Since then, Gottlieb has been working gratis for Knopf (he received a large settlement from Newhouse when he left *The New Yorker*) on books like John le Carré's *The Night Manager*, Katharine Graham's autobiography, Mordecai Richler's forthcoming book on Israel, Arlene Croce's study of Balanchine, David Thomson's biographical dictionary of the cinema, Eve Arnold's retrospective and various *New Yorker* cartoon books.

My interviews with Gottlieb, who looks something like a taller and less rufous version of Woody Allen, took place in the living room of his townhouse on East Forty-eighth Street—two blocks from the Knopf offices on Fiftieth, and half a mile from *The New Yorker* on West Forty-third. His living room overlooks the Turtle Bay Gardens—

a rather formal private park that combines what would be the back-
yards of the houses on that block between Forty-eighth and Forty-
ninth Streets. From the window Gottlieb pointed out Katharine
Hepburn's house across the way (he was her editor at Knopf) and the
garden patio where Janet Malcolm had one of her famous lunches
with Jeffrey Masson.

The interviewees in this piece were suggested by Gottlieb himself.
Their comments and Gottlieb's responses were combined afterwards—
there was no direct conversation. Joseph Heller, Doris Lessing, John
le Carré, Cynthia Ozick, Michael Crichton, Chaim Potok, Toni Morrison, Robert Caro, and Mordecai Richler are all authors Gottlieb has
edited. Charles McGrath worked with Gottlieb at *The New Yorker*,
where McGrath is deputy editor. Lynn Nesbit is a literary agent who
has worked with Gottlieb on a number of books.

—Larissa MacFarquhar, 1994

JOSEPH HELLER

When I finally completed my second novel, *Something Happened*,
The New York Times interviewed me about having finished the book,
and I talked to them about Bob's value to me as an editor. The day the
interview ran, Bob called me and said he didn't think it was a good
idea to talk about editing and the contributions of editors, since the
public likes to think everything in the book comes right from the author. That's true, and so from that time on, I haven't.

ROBERT GOTTLIEB

Of course, if anybody says nice things about me in print it's pleasant. But the fact is, this glorification of editors, of which I have been
an extreme example, is not a wholesome thing. The editor's relationship to a book should be an invisible one. The last thing anyone reading *Jane Eyre* would want to know, for example, is that I had
convinced Charlotte Brontë that the first Mrs. Rochester should go
up in flames. The most famous case of editorial intervention in English literature has always bothered me—you know, that Dickens's
friend Bulwer-Lytton advised him to change the end of *Great Expec-*

tations: I don't want to know that! As a critic, of course, as a literary historian, I'm interested, but as a reader, I find it very disconcerting. Nobody should know what I told Joe Heller and how grateful he is, if he is. It's unkind to the reader and just out of place.

HELLER

Some of Bob's suggestions for *Catch-22* involved a lot of work. There was a chapter that came on page two hundred or three hundred of the manuscript—I believe it was the one with Colonel Cathcart; it was either that or the Major Major chapter—and he said he liked this chapter, and it was a shame we didn't get to it earlier. I agreed with him, and I cut about fifty or sixty pages from the opening just to get there more quickly.

GOTTLIEB

Joe Heller and I have always been on exactly the same wavelength editorially, and the most extraordinary proof of this came up when we were working on *Something Happened*. It's a deeply disturbing book about a very conflicted man—a man who is consumed with anxiety and all kinds of serious moral problems—and his name was Bill Slocum. Well, we went through the whole book, and divided it up into chapters and all the rest of it, and at the end of the process I said, Joe, this is going to sound crazy to you but this guy is not a Bill. He said, Oh really, what do you think he is? I said, He's a Bob. And Joe looked at me and said, He *was* a Bob, and I changed his name to Bill because I thought you would be offended if I made him a Bob. I said, Oh no, I don't think he's anything like me, it's just that this character is a Bob. So we changed it back. It was absolutely amazing. How did it happen? I don't know. I suppose our convoluted, neurotic, New York Jewish minds work the same way.

DORIS LESSING

What makes Bob a great editor, probably the best of his time, is that he has read everything, is soaked in the best that has been said and thought and brings this weight of experience into use when he judges the work of his authors. You may think that this kind of background should be taken for granted. Well, once upon a time one could assume that an editor in a serious publishing house had read, could make comparisons. But these days this is not what you find in publishing houses.

GOTTLIEB

A lot of things one doesn't usually think about can affect the reading experience. The way you structure the book, for example—whether you divide it into chapters or let it run uninterrupted, whether you give the chapters titles . . . Years ago I edited a wonderful novel that later became a successful movie, *Lilith*, by J. R. Salamanca. It was a powerful and affecting book, and the character who dominated it, who sparked it, was the character named Lilith, but she didn't turn up at all in the first sixty or eighty pages. I don't remember what the original title was, but I suggested to Jack that he change it to *Lilith*, because that way through all the opening pages of the book when Lilith hadn't yet appeared, the reader would be *expecting* her. So just by changing the title one created a tension that wouldn't have been there otherwise.

JOHN LE CARRÉ

Bob will tell me how he understands a story, and where he feels slightly disappointed, perhaps; where the satisfactions are not what he expected, or something of that kind—it remains very loose. He will say to me, I'm going to draw a wavy line down these pages; for me, they're too lyrical, too self-conscious, too over-the-top. And I will say, OK, for the moment I disagree because I'm in love with every word I've written, but I'll rake it over and lick my wounds, and we'll see what happens. Or he'll say something like, Actually you didn't need this beautiful passage of description here . . . in fact I think it's really a pain. As a rule, he has no quarrel with my characters, though he has always felt I am weaker on girls than on boys, and I think that's true. Occasionally I'll say I disagree, in which case we will leave the matter in suspense until I recognize that he is right. In no case have I ever regretted taking Bob's advice. In all the large things, he's always been right.

GOTTLIEB

For a while I was editing the two best writers of quality who were
writing spy novels, John le Carré and Len Deighton, and you couldn't
find a more perfect pair of opposites in the editorial process. Le
Carré is unbelievably sensitive to editorial suggestion because his ear
is so good and because his imagination is so fertile—he'll take the
slightest hint and come back with thirty extraordinary new pages.
Deighton, on the other hand—who is *totally* willing, *couldn't* be more
eager for suggestions—is one of those writers for whom, once a sentence is down on paper, it takes on a reality that no amount of good
will or effort can change. So you can say to him, Len, this is a terrific
story but there is a serious problem. He'll say, What is it? What is it?
And you say, Well, on page thirty-seven this character is killed, but on
page a hundred and eighteen he appears at a party. Oh my God, Len
says, this is terrible, but I'll fix it, don't worry. Then you get the manuscript back, and you turn to page thirty-seven, and he'll have
changed it to, He was *almost* killed.

LE CARRÉ

A Perfect Spy is the novel of mine that is closest to my heart. It is
also my most autobiographical novel, and it skates along the edge of a
great deal of childhood pain and stuff. It's always a queasy business
when a writer starts moaning about his childhood, so the only way I
could redeem the situation was by making the son much less pleasant
in many ways. Bob pointed out the places where he felt that the fiction
became so autobiographical that it became embarrassing—where he
felt that I had really spilled into private experience and had thrown
away the mask. He was terribly good at that. What we left on the cutting room floor still makes me blush.

CYNTHIA OZICK

Bob became my editor when David Segal, who had been my editor
and heart's friend at Knopf, died at the age of forty-two of a heart attack just before Christmas 1970. On that same day, or within a week,
Bob and Maria's little daughter Elizabeth was born. Bob called me

from the hospital right after her birth and said, Don't worry, you're not abandoned, your editor is gone, but I am here, and I will be your editor and publish you. Don't feel that you're deserted or lost. It was one of the most astounding acts of generosity I've encountered in my life. It occurred in the middle of birth, death, bewilderment, grief. Now, very often when I am writing, I have something like a bird sitting on my right shoulder, a watchful bird looking over my shoulder at what I am doing. I want that bird's approval—I have to get it. It is a very critical bird, who is in a way a burden, but also grants me *permission*. This bird is the mind of Bob Gottlieb. It is to him I present what I am working on when I am finished, and it is him I want to satisfy, and more than satisfy—gratify.

TONI MORRISON

I never write with Bob in mind; that would be very bad for me. He isn't the ideal reader for the product, but he is the ideal editor for it.

GOTTLIEB

The first thing writers want—and this sounds so basic, but you'd be surprised how unbasic it is in the publishing world—is a quick response. Once they've finished a new manuscript and put it in the mail, they exist in a state of suspended emotional and psychic animation until they hear from their editor, and it's cruelty to animals to keep them waiting. I'm lucky, because I happen to be a very quick reader, so I can almost always read a new manuscript overnight. Besides, when I receive a manuscript from a writer I've been working with I'm consumed by curiosity to know what he or she has written. But easy or not, one's first job is a swift and honest response—tempered, of course, by tact.

It took me some time, when I was a very young man, to grasp that a writer—even a mature, experienced one—could have made an emotional transference to me. But of course it makes sense: the editor gives or withholds approval, and even to a certain extent controls the purse strings. It's a relationship fraught with difficulty, because it can lead to infantilizing and then to resentment. Somehow, to be helpful, an editor has to embody authority yet not become possessive or controlling.

MICHAEL CRICHTON

Bob became my editor just after he had moved to Knopf from Simon & Schuster in 1968. Lynn Nesbit was my agent. She recommended Bob partly because she thought I'd like him and partly because he was an overnight person. I was being driven mad by the usual publishing business of waiting a month for manuscripts to be read, because in those days I was in medical school and medicine is so fast. To send a manuscript to New York and wait a month—well, you might as well wait for your next reincarnation.

When I sent Bob a draft of *The Andromeda Strain*—the first book I did for him—in 1968 he said he would publish it if I would agree to completely rewrite it. I gulped and said OK. He gave me his feelings about what had to happen on the phone, in about twenty minutes. He was very quick. Anyway, I rewrote it completely. He called me up and said, Well, this is good, now you only have to rewrite *half* of it. Again, he told me what needed to happen—for the book to begin in what was then the middle, and fill in the material from the beginning sometime later on.

Finally we had the manuscript in some kind of shape. I was just completely exhausted. He said to me, Dear boy, you've got this ending backwards. (He's married to an actress, and he has a very theatrical manner. He calls me "dear boy," like an English actor might do.) I don't remember *exactly* the way it was, but I had it so that one of the characters was supposed to turn on a nuclear device, and there was suspense about whether or not that would happen. Bob said, No, no, the switch has to turn *itself* on automatically, and the character has to turn it *off*. He was absolutely right. That was the first time I understood that when there is something wrong in writing, the chances are that there is either too much of it, too little of it, or that it is in some way *backwards*.

GOTTLIEB

When Michael wrote *The Andromeda Strain* he assumed he had to fill out the characters of all those scientists and make them real people, as in a conventional novel. But that wasn't where his interest lay, and so he had only done it at the surface level. Somehow it occurred to me that instead of trying to flesh the characters out further and make the novel more conventional, we ought to strip that stuff out completely and make it a documentary, only a fictional one.

CRICHTON

What Bob actually said to me was that he thought the manuscript should be factually persuasive, like a *New Yorker* piece. I thought that was a very interesting idea, but I couldn't see how to do it. I couldn't take his suggestion literally, because in those days the signature of *New Yorker* writers like Lillian Ross was that they were using fictional storytelling techniques in their nonfiction, and my problem was that I had to get *away* from fictional techniques. Finally, I began to think about what I would do if the story were real. Suppose this had actually happened and I were a reporter, what would my book look like? There was a book on my shelf at the time by Walter Sullivan called *We Are Not Alone*. I started thumbing through it, noticing the vocabulary, the cadences of nonfiction and how the structure of the sentences conveys a sense of reality that is not found in fiction.

As soon as I began to do that, it became clear to me that the author of a nonfiction account would not have the access to the characters' innermost thoughts in the way that you assume for fiction. So I began to take all that stuff out and make the book colder and more impersonal— but I didn't do it completely. Bob read it and said, Look, this book can either go this way or that way, and you'll have to decide what you want to do. Ultimately he thought I should just take all the novelistic passages out. He thought the characters shouldn't have any relationships with each other, and that all the dialogue should advance the plot.

He took a much more radical step than I would have dared. It was never again as it was with *The Andromeda Strain*, mostly because I think in the process of working on it Bob taught me a tremendous amount about editing. I never again sent him a manuscript in such a mess. A part of me became Bob, or acted like Bob, and as I was writing I would sit there and think, This is what he's going to say, and I'd go fix it. Before *The Andromeda Strain* I didn't really know the extent to which you could write a draft and *not* accept it but rather tear it all apart, move things around, rework them, and then put it all back together. I had never gone through that process in my previous writing, and Bob put me through it. Occasionally Bob has said to me, The new book doesn't work. Forget it. Which I have done. That has happened a few times. But it was in part a result of my method of working, which is to go off and tell nobody what I'm doing and write something; sometimes it would work and sometimes it wouldn't. I guess because of my youth it didn't seem so devastating. I just thought, Oh well, that didn't work, I'll go do something else. I don't work that way anymore—I'm too old.

Even now, when Bob first calls me back about a manuscript, I panic. But I'll tell you, I think every writer should have tattooed backwards on his forehead, like AMBULANCE on ambulances, the words *everybody needs an editor*.

GOTTLIEB

It's often the case that the most strained moments in books are the very beginning and the very end—the getting in and the getting out. The ending especially: it's awkward, as if the writer doesn't know when the book is over and nervously says it all again. Sometimes the most useful thing you can tell a writer is, Here's where the book ends—in these next two and a half pages you're just clearing your throat. When I first read Chaim Potok's *The Chosen*, to use an extreme example, I recognized that the book had come to an end, and that Chaim had written three hundred more pages. The material that was the motor of the book had worked itself out, and he had gone on to write the sequel. So I called up Chaim's agent and said, I love the book and would like to talk to him about it, but please explain to him it's only on the condition that he drop the last three hundred pages that I want to publish it; if he wants to leave it as it is, it's a different book. Chaim immediately saw the point, so there was no problem.

MORRISON

Endings I always know, because that's always what the book is about. The problem is getting there. I used to have these really awful beginnings—never really beginnings, they were *starts*—and Bob always caught them. He would say, This is not a beginning, the book is not grounded yet. I originally began *Sula*, for example, with what is now chapter two. Bob told me he felt the first words of the manuscript—"National Suicide Day"—were not the beginning of the book. So I spent a summer trying to write a beginning. And I did it to my satisfaction and, I think, to his.

OZICK

I will tell you two stories, one about somebody else and one about myself. The somebody else is a close friend, also edited by Bob, who when writing a novel tends to find herself writing episodes or short stories. He said to her, Maybe that's just how you write a novel: you have to write short stories, and then you put them together and that's the novel. I, on the other hand, have begun novels and then abandoned them and they have become short stories. He said to me just the opposite: Maybe this is how you write short stories. You have to think you're doing a novel, and then it turns out to be a short story.

MORRISON

Writing my first two books, *The Bluest Eye* and *Sula*, I had the anxiety of a new writer who needs to make sure every sentence is exactly the right one. Sometimes that produces a kind of precious, jeweled quality—a tightness, which I particularly wanted in *Sula*. Then after I finished *Sula* and was working on the third book, *Song of Solomon*, Bob said to me, You can loosen, open up. Your writing doesn't have to be so contained; it can be *wider*. I'm not sure these were his exact words, but I know that the consequence of the remarks was that I *did* relax and begin to open up to possibilities. It was because I was able to open up to those possibilities that I began to think things like, What would happen if indeed I followed this strange notion or image or picture I had in my mind of this woman who had no navel . . . whereas normally I would have dismissed such an idea as recklessness. It was as if he had said, Be reckless in your imagination.

GOTTLIEB

I remember the discussion with Toni as she was beginning *Song of Solomon*, because although we always did some marginal cosmetic work on her manuscripts, obviously a writer of her powers and discrimination doesn't need a lot of help with her prose. I think I served Toni best by encouraging her—helping to free her to be herself. The only other real help I gave to her was noneditorial: I encouraged her to stop editing and to write full-time, something I knew she wanted to do. As I remember it, I reassured her about her finances—but what I was really saying was, You're not an editor who does some writing, you're a *writer*—acknowledge it; there's nothing to be scared of. We always understood each other—two editors, two lovers of reading, and exactly the same age.

ROBERT CARO

When I first handed in the manuscript of *The Power Broker* it was over a million words. With the technology of that time there was a limited number of words you could fit between two covers and have what they call a manageable trade book—something like seven hundred thousand words, around thirteen-hundred pages. Bob didn't want to do the thing in volumes. He told me, I can get people interested in Robert Moses once, but not twice. So we had to cut three hundred thousand words. That's like cutting a five-hundred-page book out of a book. It's not easy. I would come into Knopf in the morning, day after day, and Bob was running the company, but he would shut the door of his office and we would work on the manuscript all day. Late in the afternoon when I left, there would be a line of people outside his office, waiting for him. I remember there was a point near the end when we thought we were done, but it turned out someone had miscounted. Bob called the next week and said, Bob, I have some bad news. We have to cut fifty thousand more words. It was a terrible thing.

GOTTLIEB

It took a year. *The Power Broker* was Caro's first book, and he had worked on it for eight years in isolation, just him and his wife. It was agony for him to cut it. It was painful for me, too, because I loved the material. I could have read twice as much, but I couldn't print twice as much.

CARO

In order to get enough money to finish *The Power Broker* I had signed a two-book contract with Knopf. After *The Power Broker* I was supposed to do a biography of Fiorello LaGuardia. But I realized after I had signed the contract that I didn't really want to do it. I had seen Robert Moses's life as a way to study how power works in the cities, and I wanted to study the same thing on a national level through the life of Lyndon Johnson, since I thought he understood power better than any other American president. I also wanted to do it in more than one volume, because there were things cut out of *The Power Broker* that I thought should not have been cut.

I expected a big fight over this, because back then nobody was doing multivolume biographies except academics. So I went in to see Bob about it. Before I had said anything, he said to me, Bob, I've been thinking about you and what you ought to do. I know you've been planning to do the LaGuardia book, but I think what you should really do is a biography of Lyndon Johnson. And he said, I think you should do it in several volumes. It was really quite startling.

GOTTLIEB

That's something an editor can do—come up with an idea for a book. I've done this with happy results a few times. Potok's *Wanderings*, for instance, was originally my idea. I thought, I am a Jew who knows nothing about Jewishness. I grew up in an atheist household; I never attended anything. I thought that Chaim could write a very popular and useful book that might instruct someone like me. Years later, I suggested Henry VIII's six wives to Antonia Fraser, and she pounced on it and did a superb job. The most important instance was when I convinced John Cheever to let me put together his collected stories. He kept saying, Why do you want to do this? These stories have all appeared in collections already. I told him it was going to be an immensely important book, and that he should let me read everything, make a selection and see if he liked it—which is what happened. Eventually, after his death, I was asked by his family to edit his journals, for both *The New Yorker* and Knopf. It was the hardest job I've ever done—it involved wrestling a hundred and twenty-five thousand words out of several million. The material was very dark, and most of all, with no author to work with, I was out there alone—with all the responsibility of presenting not only John's words, but his life. But it was also the most gratifying job I've ever done, and one of the very few times in my working life when I've felt I'd actually achieved something.

MORRISON

What I find most useful are the moments when Bob is disturbed by something in a book. He is a marvelous reader, and surrenders completely to a text, so when he finds something invalid or unpersuasive, or if something leaves him disoriented, I know it is important for me to go back to it. I pay a very rigorous attention especially to that level of comfort a reader needs in order to accept the kind of gestures of fantasy I include. I know and he knows I need to create a sense of absolute stability in order to be able to transport the reader into a realm that is not "realistic."

GOTTLIEB

You have to surrender to a book. If you do, when something in it seems to be going askew, you are wounded. The more you have surrendered to a book, the more jarring its errors appear. I read a manuscript very quickly, the moment I get it. I usually won't use a pencil the first time through because I'm just reading for impressions. When I reach the end, I'll call the writer and say, I think it's very fine (or whatever), but I think there are problems *here* and *here*. At that point I don't know *why* I think that—I just think it. Then I go back and read the manuscript again, more slowly, and I find and mark the places where I had negative reactions to try to figure out what's wrong. The second time through I think about solutions—maybe this needs expanding, maybe there's too much of *this* so it's blurring *that*.

Editing requires you to be always open, always responding. It is very important, for example, not to allow yourself to want the writer to write a certain kind of book. Sometimes that's hard. My favorite of Heller's books is *Something Happened*. When we are working on a manuscript, Joe is always telling me (rightly) that I want him to write *Something Happened* again, and that he could only write it once. Inevitably you will like some of a writer's books better than others. But when you're working on a manuscript, that can't matter. You have to be inside *that* book and do your best to make it as good as it can be. And if you can't approach it in that spirit, you shouldn't be working on it.

POTOK

Bob always zeroes in on those aspects of a manuscript I also have some questions about. He reads the entire book through, and then we talk about it. He is so tuned in to what I'm doing that we can talk in shorthand—someone listening to the conversation probably wouldn't be able to understand what was being said.

CHARLES McGRATH

Bob has an uncanny knack for putting his finger on that one sentence, or that one paragraph, that somewhere in the back of your mind you knew wasn't quite right but was close enough so that you decided to worry about it later. Then you forgot about it, or you convinced yourself that it was okay, because it was too much trouble to change. He always goes right to those places. It's an instinct. He and I share a belief that if you take care of all the tiny problems in a piece, all that small attention will somehow make a big difference. Sometimes I think that's just a touching faith of ours, and that, in fact, nobody ever notices whether, say, you use the same word twice in a paragraph. At other times, I'm convinced that the details are all that matter.

GOTTLIEB

Editing is simply the application of the common sense of any good reader. That's why, to be an editor, you have to be a reader. It's the number one qualification. Because you could have all the editorial tools, but if you're not a responsive reader you won't sense where the problems lie. I am a reader. My life is reading. In fact, I was about forty years old when I had an amazing revelation—this is going to sound dumb—it suddenly came to me that not every person in the world assumed, without thinking about it, that reading was the most important thing in life. I hadn't known that. I hadn't even known that *I* had thought it, it was so basic to me.

Oddly enough, I find that reading noneditorially is a very different experience for me. When I'm reading for pleasure I don't tend to think as an editor, even with books I've edited. I remember, for instance, that when the finished book of le Carré's *Tinker, Tailor, Soldier, Spy* came into the office I decided to reread it although it had only been three or four months since I'd read it in galleys. It was as if I were reading something I had never read before, because I was reading it simply for fun. Very rarely have I had the impulse to make changes in a book I'm just reading for pleasure or instruction. It's only bad translations that drive me to madness and make me reach for a pencil.

McGRATH

Bob is the best-read person I've ever met. I used to have a somewhat inflated notion of how well-read I was, but Bob makes me look like someone who's just got his first library card. It's because his ear is so well trained that he never falters in questions of tone.

LE CARRÉ

Bob is very brainy in academic terms, much more erudite, much brainier than I am. He's very cosmopolitan in some ways. He's got quite a European soul, although he is also the quintessential New Yorker. I think he was at Cambridge for a couple of years, so he relishes the notions of understatement and disguise and so on.

MORRISON

I can never tell Bob—in fact I've only recently begun to tell *any-body*—what I am doing *critically* in a book. If I think I am recasting language in a certain way, or manipulating history so that it becomes flesh—whatever I think is radical and interventionist and different about my work in terms of American literature in general—the lit-crit stuff—I never get into that with Bob. He isn't interested in it, and it wouldn't be useful for us to talk about it, because *enfin* a book has to work as a book for someone who just isn't going to pick up on all these clever things you think you're doing. Sometimes Bob will say he thinks I'm editorializing, and I can't remember a time when he hasn't been right about that. He sees those places where, particularly earlier on, you didn't know how to dramatize something, so you editorialized it. I always know what I will not alter under any circumstances. Sometimes I just say no, and Bob won't pursue it, because he knows that if I say no it means something quite different from "I don't want to." It's in the areas in which you did the best you could, but you weren't entirely pleased, or you weren't quite sure, that you need the third eye. Given a few more years I suppose I would identify the problem myself, but a good editor is a shortcut.

CRICHTON

In my experience of writing, you generally start out with some overall idea that you can see fairly clearly, as if you were standing on a dock and looking at a ship on the ocean. At first you can see the entire ship, but then as you begin work you're in the boiler room and you can't see the ship anymore. All you can see are the pipes and the grease and the fittings of the boiler room and, you have to *assume*, the ship's exterior. What you really want in an editor is someone who's still on the dock, who can say, Hi, I'm looking at your ship, and it's missing a bow, the front mast is crooked, and it looks to me as if your propellers are going to have to be fixed.

GOTTLIEB

For some writers a solution provided by an editor is of no use. When I worked with Margaret Atwood at *The New Yorker*, for instance, whether there was a plot problem or a punctuation problem, if the solution came from her it worked wonderfully. But if I offered one myself, it never took. Now another writer might say, It's no good your telling me this is the *wrong* word if you don't give me the *right* word.

Of course, I have also spent a great deal of my life working with writers who are simply bad. I have fixed more sentences than most people have read in their lives. I remember Michael Korda and I, years ago, used to write whole pages of other people's novels together. And sometimes problems are unsolvable. There are books that are never going to come fully to life, either because the idea was wrong, or it was the wrong idea for that writer, or the writer is just not good. Then the reviewers say, What this book needed was a good editor. But those are usually the books that have had the *most* editing.

CRICHTON

Once I called Bob because I'd read a book he had edited and had found it redundant. I called him up and said, Boy, that book wasn't very well edited. There was a *very* snarky silence because he did not take criticism well at *all*. There was this long silence. Then he said, Dear boy! I think you should consider, when you read a book that seems to you to be not well-enough edited, that perhaps it has already been *incredibly* edited. And of course that was probably true.

LE CARRÉ

Bob knows how much to tell me and how much to leave to me. I think that is really one of his crucial virtues. There are so many young editors I hear of who are practically trying to write the book for you. Bob is like a good movie director with an actor—he's just trying to get the best out of you.

CRICHTON

Bob always says he is an editor, not a writer. He has a way of not competing with you, which is very reassuring. If you hear criticism from Bob you never think, as you sometimes do with other people, Well, he's just jealous because he wants to be me. And that helps in terms of hearing things from him that you might not want to hear. It was from Bob that I learned to ask readers, Tell me how you reacted, not what you think ought to be done. Because very often people will jump to their sense of what needs to be fixed and bypass the initial reader's perception of what was lacking in his experience. Also, I'm usually better at fixing my own writing than they are.

GOTTLIEB

Your job as an editor is to figure out what the book needs, but the writer has to provide it. You can't be the one who says, Send him to Hong Kong at this point, let him have a love affair with a cocker spaniel. Rather, you say, This book needs something at this point: it needs opening up, it needs a direction, it needs excitement. When people say to me, Oh you're so creative, I try to explain that I'm *not* creative. I simply have certain other qualities that are necessary for my kind of work. It has liberated me, being happy being what I am. There are editors who will always feel guilty that they aren't writers. I can write perfectly well—anybody who's educated can write perfectly well. But I dislike writing: it's very, very hard, and I just don't like the activity. Whereas reading is like breathing.

MORRISON

I think we erroneously give pride of place to the act of writing rather than the act of reading. People think you just read because you can understand the language, but a certain kind of reading is a very high-level intellectual process. I have such reverence for that kind of sensitive reading—it is not just absorbing things and identifying what's wrong but a much deeper thing that I can see would be perfectly satisfying. Anyway, this separation is fairly recent: not long ago the great readers *were* the great writers, the great critics *were* the great novelists, the great poets *were* the great translators. People didn't make these big distinctions about which one was more thrilling than the other.

Writing for me is just a very sustained process of reading. The only difference is that writing a book might take three or four years, and *I'm* doing it. I never wrote a line until after I became an editor, and only then because I wanted to read something that I couldn't find. That was the first book I wrote.

OZICK

If Bob identifies a snag in a manuscript and neither one of us can immediately come up with a solution, he will always say to me, go figure it out, and then come back. His fixes are never, as often happens with other editors, editorial patches, impositions that don't match the language or the tone of the writer. The point about Bob Gottlieb is that he never imposes.

MORDECAI RICHLER

I cannot tolerate editors who go in for line-by-line criticism, or who cross out words and substitute words of their own, or who will cross out two pages and write over them *cut*. Bob has never been so officious.

GOTTLIEB

Many people have this vulgar idea that writers and editors are at each others' throats, that they are antagonistic. That is craziness. No editor should work with a book he doesn't like, because his job as an editor is to make something better of what it is. If you try to turn a book into something it isn't, you're doomed to disaster.

An editor has to be selfless, and yet has also to be strong-minded. If you don't know what you think, or if you're nervous about expressing your opinions, what good is that to a writer? I remember one book of John Cheever's I was working on, I felt there was a minor problem with the ending. At first I thought, Who am I to be telling John Cheever to change the end of his novel? And then I thought,

Well, I'm the editor he chose, and I can't, out of cowardice, withhold what I think. I'm not forcing him to do anything. I'm saying, This is what I think is wrong, and it's up to him to decide whether to take my advice or not. As it happened, he immediately got the point and found a solution.

CARO

I have a bad temper and, though Bob would deny it, so does he. While we were editing we were always jumping up and getting out of the room to cool off. Now he, of course, had the great advantage over me because when we were working at Knopf he could leave and go to somebody else's office and transact some business, but I had no place to go but the bathroom. I went to the bathroom a lot, as I remember. And oh, his tone! If you heard his tone! It gets me so angry I have to try to drown it out. I try not to hear the insulting things he's saying because, as I said, I have a very bad temper.

GOTTLIEB

Bob Caro and I are always shouting at each other and carrying on because for him each manuscript has been so much work, so much effort, so much obsessive concentration, that everything is of equal weight because everything is of total weight. Your job with a writer like that is to be able to say, You may have done an equally brilliant job on all of these things, but this has more weight than that, and you have to give some of that up. Sometimes in the heat of discussion, that can seem to a writer like an attack. And that's not helpful, though at times it can be therapeutic. If you are a good editor, your relationship with every writer is different. To some writers you say things you couldn't say to others, either because they'd be angry or because it would be too devastating to them. You can't have only one way of doing things; on some instinctual level you have to respond not just to the words of the writer but to the temperament of the writer. That may be hard for some editors; I haven't found it hard, perhaps because I like to please people. Joe Heller and I, for instance, have never had a bad moment because he is perfectly detached. When you're editing a manuscript with him the two of you can look at it as though you were two surgeons examining a body stretched out upon a table. You just cut it open, deal with the offending organs, and stitch it up again. Joe is completely objective, he has that kind of mind, even immediately after finishing a book.

We worked like dogs on *Catch-22*, and then just before it went to press I was reading it again, and I came to a chapter I'd always hated. I thought it was pretentious and literary. I said to Joe, You know, I've always hated this chapter, and he said, Well take it out. And out it went. He printed it many years later in *Esquire* as the lost chapter of *Catch-22*. That's Joe Heller. Now that doesn't mean he's better than Bob Caro. It means he has a completely different temperament in relation to his work. Joe is a pragmatist; Bob is a romantic.

Doris Lessing also has a very removed attitude to her writing. You can say to Doris exactly what you think without fear either of wounding her or overly influencing her. The day after she gave me the manuscript for *The Summer Before the Dark* we were walking in Queen Mary's rose garden in London; she asked me what I thought about the manuscript. I said I liked it very much and told her I was sure it was going to be her most successful book. She said, Now that's interesting, because it's by no means my *best* book. There are not many writers whose clarity and disinterestedness are such that they could say that about a book they had *just finished*.

LE CARRÉ

There are some writers who put in a first chapter and need lunch immediately. They need babysitting; they need to be able to call up at two A.M. and say they're about to slit their wrists and so on. I don't want to see my publishers, editors, or anybody until I've produced my baby. If I have frightful headaches about how to make my story work or how to end it or something like that, I will never communicate them until I resolve the thing somehow. So my first use of Bob, if you will, is for his spontaneous response to something he knows nothing about. Then I'm dealing with the Bob Gottlieb who might have picked the novel up in a bookshop.

GOTTLIEB

Some writers need you to read their book as they're writing it. I worked with one writer who wanted to call me up every day and read me what she had written. I discouraged her.

MORRISON

Some authors really want their books to be loved and want themselves to be loved, but I don't want that. I don't want my hand held, I don't want to be stroked, I don't want to be patronized, I don't want any of those things. And I never got any of that from Bob. As a result, our editing sessions are vital, they are hard, and they are *tremendous* fun.

CARO

The most important thing I ever heard Bob say was at Knopf one time when we were standing in the hallway outside his office and some other editor came along and, in that jocular way editors have, he said, So, when is this book going to be delivered? Bob said, *Don't ever ask him that.* I've never forgotten it. All through our relationship we've had a tacit understanding that the words *delivery date* are never to be mentioned.

CRICHTON

From time to time ours was an irritable relationship. Sometimes in later years I would send Bob drafts that were not cleaned up enough, and he would be a little short about the fact that he was being shown something that was not ready. He would never address it directly. He would never say, Why are you sending me this, you haven't worked on it enough. There would just be this *feeling*.

Bob is very skillful at motivation. He really knows how to make you work. He would call me up and say, Dear boy! I have read your manuscript, and here is what you have to do. And he was not above saying, I don't know if you can do it this way, I don't know if you're up to it—which of course would drive me into a fury of effort. It was *very* effective. And it was only years later that I thought, You know, I think he probably said that on purpose.

GOTTLIEB

I certainly didn't say anything like that to Michael on purpose. I do what I think I have to do and respond to people as I respond to them. I intensely dislike manipulating people, just as I resent being manipulated.

As an editor I have to be tactful, of course (which I wasn't very good at when I was young). But goodwill has to be natural. You can't fake it. It just doesn't work that way.

LE CARRÉ

Negotiations were always tight with Bob. He was celebrated for not believing in huge advances, and it didn't matter that three other houses were offering literally twice what he was offering. He felt that for half the money, you got the best. Most publishers, when you arrive in New York with your (as you hope) best-selling manuscript, send flowers to your suite, arrange for a limo, maybe, at the airport, and then let you go and put on the nosebag at some great restaurant. The whole idea is to make you feel great. With Bob you did best to arrive in jeans and sneakers, and then you lay on your tummy side-by-side with him on the floor of his office and sandwiches were brought up.

After I finished one book, I think it was *A Perfect Spy*, my agent called me and said, Okay, we've got x-zillion yen and whatnot, and I said, *And lunch*. My agent said, What? I said, *And lunch*. When I get to New York I want to be taken, by Bob, to a decent restaurant for once and not eat one of those lousy tuna sandwiches lying on my tummy in his room. Bob called me that evening and said, I think we have a deal; and is that true about lunch? And I said, Yup, Bob, that's the break point in the deal. Very well, he said. Not a lot of laughter. So I arrived in New York, and there was Bob, a rare sight in a suit, and we went to a restaurant he had found out about. He ate *extremely* frugally, and drank nothing, and watched me with venomous eyes as I made my way through the menu.

GOTTLIEB

Yes, boys must have their fun! The thing is, when I was a kid in publishing in the fifties, the way business was done, the way you met people, was at lunches. So when I had been at Simon & Schuster a year they said, You should have an expense account. I said, That's very nice, but I don't know anybody to take out to lunch. So they said, Well, we'd better give you an agent. The agent they gave me was a young man named Georges Borchardt. They gave me Georges because I read French, and at the time Georges was handling only French books. So Georges and I had many, many lunches on my expense account, and we're close friends to this day. But after a while, of course, I met more people until I got to the point where having lunch with them all the time seemed to be yielding diminishing returns—you're out for two hours, two and a half hours, you overeat, you've wasted all that time, it's disgusting. So when I went to Knopf I said, This is it, I won't do lunch anymore. The best thing that ever came from my spartan eating habits was that I first met my great pal Nora Ephron when the *Times Book Review* commissioned her to do some fatuous piece on how and where editors lunched.

CARO

Bob and I would have big fights over colons and semicolons. Semicolons are not quite as forceful as colons. And dashes are very important to me—I establish my rhythm with them. We could spend a long time fighting over an adjective. We had such fights that sometimes he would bring in another editor as a buffer. When Bob is editing something he's very careful that the rhythm stays the same, which is very hard to do. I had huge fights with William Shawn when he excerpted *The Power Broker* for *The New Yorker*. One time my editor there, William Whitworth, who's now at *The Atlantic*, put Shawn on the line, and Shawn said, But we've hardly changed it at all, we haven't changed any of the words. I said, But you ran three paragraphs together—paragraphs *matter* to me, they're part of my rhythm. You're combining sentences, making periods into semicolons, semicolons into commas—that *is* changing my writing. Those fights were not nice fights; they were bitter, angry fights. Now there's never anything like that with Bob.

I've always believed that for a nonfiction work to endure, its prose has to be at just as high a level as that of a good novel, and Bob believes that too. When we're working together, what matters—and it is *all* that matters—is what is on the page.

MCGRATH

There's always a tension between a writer's idiosyncratic way of presenting himself and the house style, but magazines need house style. If you don't have some kind of consistent way of doing things, it looks as if you've lost your mind.

GOTTLIEB

This is in fact the great difference between being a book editor and being a magazine editor, as I discovered in my years at *The New Yorker*. In book publishing, the editor and the author have the same goal: to make the book as good as it can be and to sell as many copies as possible. In a magazine, it's a different matter. Of course a magazine editor wants the writing to be as good as possible, but he wants it to be as good as possible *for the magazine*, while the writer wants to preserve his piece's integrity. At a magazine, the writer can always withdraw his piece, but basically the editor is in charge. In book publishing, editors are the servants of the writers, and if we don't serve writers well, they leave us.

Another difference is that a book publishing house is much less bound up with the personality of its editor in chief. A good house is a collection of highly individual editors with very individual tastes, all of whom contribute different things to the list. A magazine, on the other hand, is in a sense an *emanation* of its chief editor—of his impulses and views and, to use a disgusting word, *vision*. The editors I worked with at *The New Yorker* were not essentially procuring editors—they were working editors. Only The Editor had the authority to buy a piece.

Magazines have to be run that way, because a magazine has to be itself. A magazine's subscribers and advertisers and owner have a right to get every week or month whatever it is they've been led to expect they're going to get. If someone becomes an *Economist* advertiser because he likes *The Economist*, and then one day opens an issue and sees his ad in a magazine that looks more like *Playboy*, he's not going to be happy. And vice versa. A publishing house has much more leeway, because its constituency isn't fixed. Nobody out there is buying a hundred fifty Knopf books a year. Someone might buy *In the Kitchen with Rosie* or Cormac McCarthy or *Miss Piggy's Guide to Life* or *The Audubon Guide to Wildflowers of the East* or *How We Die*, but he won't buy all of them. This also means that as a book publisher you are far less conscious of people looking over your shoulder—if your house comes out with a profit, no one's going to complain that this year's list looks different from last year's. Then again, I have never worked in an unsuccessful publishing house. I suppose that if your books are crummy and you're losing money every year, you'll feel the Loch Ness monster on your tail.

MCGRATH

People have accused *New Yorker* style of being comma-ridden, but Bob had no trouble with it. In fact Bob sometimes wanted commas where even Miss Gould, our great copy editor, didn't see the need for them, which was quite astonishing to some of us. Bob is concerned above all with making the meaning and intention of a sentence crystal clear. He can become quite ingenious, almost paranoid, thinking of ways that a reader might possibly misconstrue something.

He is a Tartar, too, about participial clauses. He will often take a relative clause—a *that* clause or a *which* clause—and make it into a participial phrase or a gerund phrase. And he has a great nose for cant and pretension and highfalutin crap of any sort. He goes at it like a terrier. It's as if he can smell it.

GOTTLIEB

I have idiosyncrasies in punctuation, like everybody else. Because one of the formative writers of my life was Henry James, it's all too easy for me to pepper a text with dashes. Many people don't like dashes. With le Carré, I'm always putting commas in, and he's always taking them out, but we know that about each other. He'll say, Look, if you absolutely need this one, have it. And I'll say, Well, I would have liked it, but I guess I can live without it. We accommodate each other. When I was a young firebrand it never occurred to me that I might be wrong, or that I wasn't going to have my way, or that it wasn't my job to impose my views. I could get into twenty-minute shouting matches over semicolons, because every semicolon was a matter of life or death. As you grow older you realize that there are bad lines in *King Lear* and it has survived.

McGRATH

There was a certain type of writing we used to laugh about a lot. We called it "cry of the loon" writing—that kind of overblown nature prose. Bob has a deadly instinct for when that stuff has gone ripe. He has a fine ear for English as it's spoken, and a lot of his work as an editor is taking stilted, artificial language and pushing it in the direction of the vernacular. How words sound on a page (if that's not an oxymoron) is what Bob listens for.

GOTTLIEB

There are certain locutions I become obsessed with. I hate the overuse of the word *continued*—he *continued* to eat his soup, instead of he *went on eating* his soup. That is something I must have changed ten thousand times in five years at *The New Yorker*. Impoverished vocabulary disturbs me. I used to joke with my colleagues about V.E.— verb enrichment. I hate it when a writer uses the word *walk* thirty times in two pages, for example. At *The New Yorker* changing things like that was difficult because the editors there had been trained that an editor does not *improve* writing, he makes it *correct*. I was a book editor, though, and my job has always been to help writers make books better.

I often argue with Bob Caro about his use of certain words—*loom*, for example, because it's such an inflated verb. One of Bob's great talents is creating a scene, and that's wonderful, but when you're a biographer or a historian, whose basic concern is accuracy, you must be very wary of overloading the language to make dramatic points. Caro likes to dramatize, and he tends to see people as larger than life. As I've often said to him, he's even done that to me; he's romanticized me as The Editor, as the one he can trust.

LE CARRÉ

Bob is a very fastidious man. Battle scenes, for example. I wrote *The Honourable Schoolboy* just after returning from Cambodia and Vietnam, where I had been hanging around with a journalist, so it had battlefield sequences and things. Bob tends to go very quiet when he reads that stuff and turns over the pages rather quickly. It's not a world he's ever had to venture into, thank God, and I think he just doesn't care for it very much. I would not see him as the best person to edit *The Naked and the Dead*, for example. Or James Jones. Still, Bob is amazingly catholic as an editor; that is to say, I know that if I'd written a golf book, Bob would have been very good about my golf book. He would not have tried to turn it into a prose poem about something different. I expect with his romantic novelists he doesn't fight with them about split infinitives; he doesn't worry too much about dangling clauses. He can live with bad books if they're *good* bad books.

McGRATH

Anyone can take a piece and tart it up, and in so doing layer another sensibility or another vocabulary on top of what's there, but Bob doesn't do that. He has a great ability to get inside a piece and instinctively understand the terms and the vocabulary of the writer, and make changes in those terms and that vocabulary. This is one of the hallmarks of great editing: when it is done right, you don't notice it.

GOTTLIEB

I happen to be a kind of word whore. I will read anything from Racine to a nurse romance, if it's a good nurse romance. Many people just aren't like that. Some of my closest friends cannot read anything that isn't substantial—they don't see the point. I don't, however, like a certain kind of very rich, ornate, literary writing. I feel as if I'm being choked, as if gravel is being poured down my throat. Books like *Under the Volcano*, for instance, are not for me.

LYNN NESBIT

I probably wouldn't send a postmodernist writer to Bob. Bob likes books with a strong sense of narrative. I think he would have admired Donald Barthelme or William Gass, but they wouldn't be *natural* writers for him to work with.

GOTTLIEB

Some marriages are not made in heaven. I inherited Gail Godwin from another editor who had published Godwin's early work at Harper's. Now, Gail was extremely sensitive, and she viewed herself as a highly successful commercial writer, whereas I viewed her as a rather literary writer with a limited readership. She couldn't live that way, and eventually, although we worked together very cordially on several books, she moved to Viking. She had shown them a book she was working on, and they saw it the way she saw it—as a major commercial novel—and they paid her a lot of money, and indeed it became a big best-seller and made her famous and successful. I didn't read her that way, and I still feel that her earlier work, which was less commercial, is more interesting. But she wanted to develop in a different direction, and I'm sure she doesn't feel that she compromised in any way to do that. In other words, I was the wrong editor-publisher for her and she was wise to leave me.

One writer I worked with—I don't remember who it was—got absolutely nothing out of the one meeting we had. Some time afterwards he wrote an article for a magazine and, referring to this encounter (without using my name), he wrote something like: He told me to let it breathe. What does that mean? A completely useless, stupid remark. Now I knew exactly what I meant, and another writer would have known exactly what I meant, but the comment was useless to him. It wasn't a bad thing for me to say, nor was he being stupid or resistant—it was just that my ways of communicating were never going to work with him. It was not a proper marriage, and luckily we got a quick divorce.

LESSING

I don't remember any serious disagreements, but this does not mean Bob has liked everything I have written. He doesn't like *The Sentimental Agents*, for instance, which I do like.

GOTTLIEB

I did think *The Sentimental Agents* was rather schematic. It was an idea rather than fiction. It's part of Doris's space fiction series, and like all space fiction, or science fiction, it is underlain by a highly moralistic, utopian impulse. When that kind of thing works it's because the idea becomes clothed in specifics that are interesting, exciting, moving, whatever, and in most of the books in that series I think that did happen, but in this particular book I felt the ideas were bare.

RICHLER

Once when *Maclean's* magazine was running a profile on me they rang Bob and ran one of my quotes by him. Asked about my film work, I had told *Maclean's* I used other muscles. Yes, said Bob, his sphincter.

MORRISON

Bob once used an adjective about one of my books—*Beloved*—that I'd never, ever, ever heard him use before, about my book or anybody else's. He said *great*. It's funny, because everybody says *great* about anything. What's the weather like? It's great. How do you feel? Great. But I know that when Bob said it, in that context, he meant *that*. He didn't mean something else. He might say wonderful, when something was wonderfully done, but he never said *great*.

CARO

In all the hours of working on *The Power Broker* Bob never said one nice thing to me—never a single complimentary word, either about the book as a whole or about a single portion of the book. That was also true of my second book, *The Path to Power*. But then he got soft. When we finished the last page of the last book we worked on, *Means of Ascent*, he held up the manuscript for a moment and said, slowly, as if he didn't want to say it, Not bad. Those are the only two complimentary words he has ever said to me, to this day.

LESSING

Bob has been advising me and editing my work for thirty or more years. It is hard to remember details now. I have just been reading my diary for 1978, where it records that I spent some days making alterations he suggested. I remember cutting quite a bit out of *The Sirian Experiments*. I cut a bit out of *The Four-Gated City* at his suggestion, which perhaps was a mistake. Bob has made mistakes. But, nearly always, he is right. I don't think Bob would be surprised to hear that I would describe him as an authoritarian personality. Why should he? I've told him so. We are good enough friends for us both to put up with this kind of mutual criticism.

GOTTLIEB

Well, I describe *her* as authoritarian. So there you are. But this is actually more complicated than that, because my neurotic vision of myself is of a fly on the wall. I see myself as an observer, as someone who could not possibly affect any other human being, not even my children. Now, I'm an acute observer and an analyzed person, so I know perfectly well from the evidence of my eyes and ears that I have a strong personality and have no problem running large organizations, and I know that I've had a considerable effect on many people. I know I have a great deal of personal authority. But there's a disparity between what I know and what I feel. I've never quite understood why people do what I say. But then, I've never taken myself very seriously.

POTOK

There is a certainty, an ease, an assuredness that comes from Bob, and when you're a writer and you're constantly living in a world of panic and uncertainty, to have that in an editor is a valuable thing indeed.

MORRISON

Bob and I used to joke about our egos being so huge that they didn't exist—which is a way of saying that neither he nor I felt we were in competition with anybody. That's not a very nice thing to say about myself or him; but at the same time, it's important to remember that a large ego can be generous and enabling, because of its lack of envy. There was a way in which our confidence was wide-spirited.

NESBIT

People always say Bob has such an enormous ego, but I say that Bob takes this enormous ego and lends it to the writer, thereby reinforcing the writer's ego. Bob is very generous with his ego.

GOTTLIEB

When you're dealing with nonprofessional writers, you have to give them a tremendous amount of encouragement simply to convince them that they can write at all. Lauren Bacall is a perfect example. I knew she could write her own book, and I knew that she would never be satisfied if she had a ghostwriter, but she didn't know how to do it, so finally we set up a system. She would come into the office every day and write in longhand on yellow pads, and every night little elves would type up what she had written during the day. She kept saying, Is it all right? and I would say, Yes, yes, it's fine. You write it, I'll edit it. And it *was* fine. Of course, it needed standard editorial work, but it was her book, it came right out of her. Betty Bacall is a bright Jewish girl from New York—she wasn't going to write a bad book.

I did Liv Ullmann's book too. She had already written it in Norwegian and had it translated, and she wanted someone to edit it in English. The first time I met her it was winter, and she came into the office wearing a big fur coat. I took her coat, we had a long talk, and after about forty-five minutes I said, Come on, I'll walk you around the office and introduce you to some of the people you'll be working with. She said all right, and she stood up and started putting on her coat. I said, Why are you putting on your coat, it's boiling in these offices, and she said, I'm putting on my coat because I'm so fat I don't want anyone to see me. Now, I'm married to an actress, and this triggered something in me, and I completely forgot that I had just met her forty-five minutes ago. I said, Wait a minute. Number one, it's very hot in here. Number two, you do *not* look fat, you look great. And number three, you're not putting on your coat. This is just what I would have said to my wife, Maria. And she said, Oh, fine, and took off her coat. Because she's an actress—she needed the director to tell her she looked great and she needed reassurance. Yet she had written a very fine book on her own.

OZICK

Whenever I have a problem, Bob always says to me, Well, *Maria* . . . and then goes on to tell me how he had *exactly* this sort of problem with *Maria*, and here is the way *Maria* handled it. He is so skilled at this that I've never been able to tell whether Maria has always had exactly my problems or whether she has become a kind of pedagogical—or even mythological—device. It depends, of course, on what kind of human being he is, but an editor is often a father figure, a mother figure, a kind of ministerial figure . . . a *teacher* is really what I mean—someone who stands in authority over you and has something to tell you. I've had certain stumbling-block problems in my life, as others have, and every few years I would go and see Bob on some editorial occasion, and I would tell him where I was stumped and how I was stumbling. He would talk to me about whatever it was and generally give me enough perspective in an hour or an hour and a half that I left his office feeling restored and able to put my hands back on the ropes. I never thought that at *The New Yorker* he would have time to do Cynthia-therapy, but he did.

HELLER

Bob and I think of each other as close friends, but ten years might go by before we talk to each other or drop each other a note. In between my novels—and my novels come at long intervals—we've barely communicated.

CARO

We have, basically, no social relationship whatsoever. When the Book-of-the-Month Club bought the first volume of the Lyndon Johnson trilogy they had a lunch for me. Al Silverman, who was then the president, started the conversation saying, Well, you two must see so much of each other . . . There was an embarassing silence—at that point Bob and I hadn't seen each other socially for years.

CRICHTON

There is absolutely no question that I see Bob paternally. Absolutely no question. There is a lot of jealousy involved in your relationship with your editor. You don't want to walk into the office and see another writer chatting with Bob—you'd want to kill them. So you learn to schedule your appointments so you can see Daddy all by yourself. I remember at one point I wanted a larger advance and Bob didn't want to give it to me. He asked Lynn Nesbit, my agent, Why does Michael want such a big advance? And she said, Well, Bob, I think he wants to buy a house. Bob said, Well what does he need such a big house for, and she said, Bob, he's married now and has a child. There was a way in which, as with a parent, I was always this young kid to him, and it never really changed. So maybe there was some countertransference too.

LE CARRÉ

Young writers taken on by publishing houses these days seem to be treated with a great deal more sanity than used to be the case. American publishing went through a phase: just as American acting was haunted by the Brando example, so American publishing was haunted by the Fitzgerald example. For decades it was regarded as almost mandatory that a writer be drunk half the day, that he have an appallingly untidy sex life, be manic-depressive, need a doctor. . . . I have the impression that publishers don't do all that wet-nursing in the way that they used to. You're much more on your own, and that may not be a bad thing. I don't think writers need all that sympathy. They need to be told when their books are bad. The excessively sycophantic phase of American publishing has been forced off the stream because it's simply not cost-effective anymore.

LESSING

There have been two pressures that have eroded excellence in publishing. One is its increasing commercialization, the other is politics. We now have a generation of people whose literary education has consisted not of being soaked in excellence, but of judging novels and stories by their theme or by the color or political stance of their authors. Now it is common to meet editors who will talk about a second-rate book as if it were the best. My guess is that they probably started off with high standards—that is, if they weren't political—but the commercial pressures slowly brought them low.

LE CARRÉ

It is necessary to remember that the great middle-European tradition of publishing and editing, which was largely that of Jewish intellectuals, moved almost in toto to the United States and didn't stop much in England. The excellence of the editorial process at Knopf, with or without Bob, is still streets ahead of anything at a British counterpart. The British style, with the exception of a few houses, is pretty much to print what they've bought, these days, misspellings and all. I'm not trying to make some spiteful point, it's just a fact of life. I think American publishing is pretty resilient, despite its anxieties, and it does produce very clever people. The trouble is that the tempo of it all—the speed with which books go on and off the market and shoot to the top of the best-seller list, only to be unheard of three months later—produces a much faster and more careless approach to the product itself. That is true. But that has its advantages too, I expect.

McGRATH

These days most people at the heads of magazines and publishing houses don't do the nitpicky stuff that Bob does. They don't have time. Perhaps they hope the little stuff will get done by someone else, or perhaps they secretly believe that even if it isn't done they can get away with it. There has been a great change in the notion of what editing means. Increasingly, editing means going to lunch. It means editing with a credit card, not with a pencil.

NESBIT

There's so much concern for the bottom line these days. Of course, it's not that twenty-five years ago everyone was publishing such wonderful literary things and didn't care about finances; but now that the publishing houses have become larger, and books sell many more copies than they used to, writers want bigger advances, the pressures are greater. I think that's one of the reasons that, when Bob left Knopf, he was glad to be out.

LE CARRÉ

You have to give a little thought, in human terms, to what Bob's doing at the moment. It's an extraordinary situation, where the guy was captain of the ship all those years, and now goes back as a humble member of the crew, working as a line editor, without any executive powers at all. Bob had three ambitions in his life. They involved the New York City Ballet, Knopf, and *The New Yorker*. And he achieved them all. There's a Jewish prayer that says, May we never realize our dreams; but Bob did realize his dreams, and it ended with *The New Yorker*. And at sixty-one he decided that what he really liked doing was what he had done at the beginning of his publishing life, which was editing.

MORRISON

I was an editor myself for a long while, and I have great difficulty explaining what was so gratifying about it. I suppose editing is almost maternal at times: you see yourself as being able to deliver something nurturing and corrective, and the benefit and the pleasure is in seeing the nurturing and the corrective show without your fingerprints. If it has your fingerprints on it, it's no good. It's like knowing you've been successful with your children when they don't need you.

GOTTLIEB

What is it that impels this act of editing? I know that in my case it's not merely about words. Whatever I look at, whatever I encounter, I want it to be good—whether it's what you're wearing, or how the restaurant has laid the table, or what's going on on stage, or what the president said last night, or how two people are talking to each other at a bus stop. I don't want to interfere with it or control it, exactly—I want it to *work*, I want it to be happy, I want it to come out right. If I hadn't gone into publishing, I might have been a psychoanalyst; I might have been, I think, a rabbi, if I'd been at all religious. My impulse to make things good, and to make good things better, is almost ungovernable. I suppose it's lucky I found a wholesome outlet for it.

This is going to sound ungrateful, but I've had more recognition than anybody should have for doing a job that isn't running the United Nations, and I used to ask myself, Why have I done so well? I really didn't understand it. I used to feel I was a fraud because I had had so much success and done so little to deserve it. And then I realized, you don't have to be a genius to be an editor. You don't have to have a great inspirational talent to be a publisher. You just have to be capable, hard-working, energetic, sensible, and full of goodwill. Those shouldn't be rare qualities, and they don't deserve a lot of credit, because you're either born with them or you're not. It's luck. And that's why you can be as good an editor your first day on the job as on your last; you're not developing some unique and profound gift.

But publishing has changed in many ways, and one of them is that these days many editors don't edit. There are editors now who basically make deals; they have assistant editors or associate editors who do the actual editing for them. When I was growing up in the business, editors, even if they were heads of publishing houses, tended to edit what they brought in, or they had someone who worked with them who could help them. Now it's much more splintered, and the business of publishing has become far more complicated and fierce and febrile.

On the other hand, one has to remember that the time I look back on as the golden age was seen by people like Alfred Knopf as the age of the slobs, as opposed to prewar publishing, which was the *true* golden age. At a certain point you have to face the fact that you've turned into an old fart—that you can't tell whether the zeitgeist has actually changed for the worse or whether you've simply fallen behind and aren't in touch anymore.

Issue 132, 1994

Richard Price

The Art of Fiction

R ichard Price has proven that there can indeed be a third act in
the career of an American writer. After a distinguished debut as
a novelist, with *The Wanderers*, and a subsequent literary faltering
that led to his recasting himself as a screenwriter of studio-produced
movies, Price returned in recent years to fiction with *Clockers*, a mon-
umental work that is both a murder mystery and a descendant of literary naturalism.

In fact, at the time of this interview, as Price was finishing a spate
of screenplays, script-doctoring assignments, and embarking on a
new novel, this member of the first generation of writers who grew up
as much with television as with books seemed poised to shuttle back
and forth between the composition of capacious and highly regarded
novels and what is often seen by writers as the devouring maw of the
motion-picture industry.

Price's fiction has always been cinematic. *The Wanderers*, a novel
about an eponymous gang he wrote while in the Columbia University writing program, was an evocation and exaggeration of his childhood in the Bronx housing projects and was made into a film soon
after publication. That novel was followed in quick, almost annual,
succession by *Bloodbrothers*, also adapted for the screen, *Ladies'
Man*, and *The Breaks*, this last harkening back to his college experience at Cornell.

While contending with a cocaine addiction, having produced two
unfinished novels and feeling that he had cannibalized his own life as

I'm GONNA WANT YOU TO WALK ME THROUGH the scene you think you CAN DO THAT?

We're gonna go back to Armstrong now ~~then what we can do~~ " he said pulling ~~into~~ out onto JFK Boulevard, the reflectors tape clothing had strobing the ~~tortoress~~ street corners. ~~approxrss~~

"NO.. I dont WANT ~~the~~ ~~GO~~ shes not there.. ~~THAT..~~

"Most likely not, Jab.."

"What do you think of my dream ?" ~~she said asked into flatly,~~ ~~almost like a demand~~

"What do I think?" Andre talking associating dreams more with ~~some old fortunes~~ stories than with analysis " IS IT

"Do you ~~think~~ ~~of~~ true?" ~~you can think that Brenda..~~ ~~you got to be painting abright?~~ "Brenda you got ~~to~~ ~~the~~ positive attitude.." ~~HAVE A~~

"I ~~went~~ go look for the car." she blurted, abruptly twisted around as if someone might be hiding in the rear seat.

Andre had seen that sunnel-lipped anxiety in victims before, PRISONER that adrenalized helplessness, people ~~dealing with~~ a clock that had no hands

" no I ~~can~~ cant do that right now, because if we run up on ~~the guy~~ it? I cant get involved in a apprehension with you setting next to me.."

A manuscript page from *Freedomland*, a novel by Richard Price.

a subject matter, Price accepted a screenwriting assignment that, though never made into a film, became a kind of calling card. Since then his prolific screen credits include *The Color of Money* (a 1986 sequel to Robert Rossen's 1961 film *The Hustler* that was directed by Martin Scorsese), "Life Lessons," Martin Scorsese's half-hour segment for *New York Stories* (1989), *Sea of Love* (1989, a quasi-adaptation of his novel *Ladies' Man*), *Night and the City* (a 1992 remake of the Jules Dassin film), *Kiss of Death* (a remake of the 1947 noir), *Mad Dog and Glory*, and the forthcoming *Ransom*.

In researching his movies and finding that worlds beyond his own experience could feed his imagination, Price discovered that "talent travels" and determined to return to the novel. After immersing himself in the diverse lives of Jersey City housing projects, a nightmare version of the terrain of his childhood, he wrote *Clockers*, which takes its name from lower-echelon crack dealers. In many ways that novel is an answer to the challenge Tom Wolfe laid down in his essay "The Billion-Footed Beast" for writers to enlarge the scope of the novel through engagement in the larger social issues. *Clockers* was widely recognized as a dispatch from the asphalt combat zone of the American underclass, but Price, having stalled earlier as a novelist, seems prouder of its artfulness.

On meeting Price, one is struck first by his extreme verbal intensity. His earlier career ambition to be a labor lawyer is easy to imagine. Although one might not notice, even after a number of meetings, that Price's right hand is imperfect—a result of complications during his birth—his physical self-consciousness is apparent and he goes to some effort in managing new acquaintances to avoid shaking hands.

The first two sessions of this interview were conducted in the summer of 1993 at a loft on lower Broadway in New York where Price lived with his wife, Judy Hudson, a talented painter, and their two daughters, a home he would soon be moving from. We conversed in the kitchen area of the open central space. The walls were hung with paintings by Hudson and her contemporaries—Bachelor, Linhares, Taafe.

Price has since moved to a new home, where the third session of this interview took place. He now lives in a brownstone near Gramercy Park, which still bears many effects from a previous owner, a member of FDR's brain trust, who decorated it with Art Deco details, including a bathroom featuring huge double bathtubs and a deep-sea motif. In the living room hangs one of the better examples of Julian Schnabel's work—a gift for Price's consulting on the script of that artist's forthcoming biopic of Jean Michel Basquiat.

The whole suggests a place decorated with the grace and tasteful eye of downtown artists into whose lives a great deal of money has recently flowed. During the interview, signs of the couple's young daughters were in evidence; twice they buzzed on an intercom to demand, not without charm, the family's video-account rental number. Friends of the couple had remarked that Judy Hudson was the secret to Price; attractive, accessible and funny, she seemed surprisingly uncomplicated for an artist.

Price's office, the first he has had in the place he lives, is dominated at one end by a large desk where he writes, at the other by a fireplace blocked with the poster of the movie Clockers. A large Chinese box. A many-drawered chest, like an old typesetter's case. A Jonathan Borofsky print. A Phillip Guston print. A Sugimoto photo of a theater screen, with a proscenium decorated by Botticelli's *Venus on a Half Shell*. Leaning against a wall is an Oscar-nomination certificate for his screenplay of *The Color of Money*. Price says, "You're supposed to hang that in the bathroom where everyone who comes to your home will be forced to stare at it and see how, since you keep it there, you don't take it very seriously."

One senses that the writer is proud of the domesticity he has achieved, but that he is not particularly attached to the material objects of the world he and his family have created. At the center of the room is a coffee table surrounded by a couch and chairs—on its surface as if arranged for inspection, are three stacks of Day-Glo orange notebooks, the startling color of a traffic cop's safety vest. Placed before the notebooks, front and center, is a typescript, shy of a hundred pages. As Price sits down to talk, he glances intently for a moment at the novel in progress perhaps to reassure himself that it is still there.

—*James Linville, 1996*

INTERVIEWER

What started you writing?

RICHARD PRICE

Well, my grandfather wrote poetry. He came from Russia. He worked in a factory, but he had also worked in Yiddish theater on the Lower East Side of New York as a stagehand. He read all the great Russian novelists and he yearned to say something. He would sit in his living-room chair and make declarations in this heavy European accent like, When the black man finally realizes what was done to him in this country . . . I don't wanna *be* here. Or, If the bride isn't a virgin, at some point in the marriage there's gonna *be* a fight, things will be said . . . and there's gonna be *no* way to fix the words.

I mean I didn't even know what a virgin *was* but I felt awed by the tone of finality, of *pronouncement*. He wrote little stories, prose poems in Yiddish; my father translated them into English and they'd be published in a YMHA journal in Brooklyn. I remember a story about a dying wife, a husband's bedside vigil, a glittering candle. The candle finally goes out the minute the wife draws her last breath. He was kind of like the O. Henry Miller of Minsk. I was seven, eight years old and I was fascinated by the idea of seeing my grandfather's name and work on a printed page. Later, in college, I always went for the writing classes. I'd get up at these open readings at coffeehouses, read these long beat/hippy things and get a good reaction from people. It was like being high. Back then, I would take a story, break it up arbitrarily, and call it a poem. I had no idea where to break anything. Rhythm, meter, I didn't know any of this stuff. I just had a way with words and I also had a very strong visceral reaction to the applause that I would get.

INTERVIEWER
Were books an influence?

PRICE

The books that made me want to be a writer were books like Hubert Selby's *Last Exit to Brooklyn*, where I recognized people who were somewhat meaner and more desperate than the people I grew up with, but who were much closer to my own experience than anything I'd ever read before. I mean, I didn't *have* a red pony. I didn't grow up in nineteenth-century London. With *Last Exit to Brooklyn*, I realized that my own life and world were valid grounds for literature, and that if I wrote about the things that I knew it was honorable—that old corny thing: I searched the world over for treasures, not realizing there were diamonds in my own backyard.

INTERVIEWER

How old were you when you read *Last Exit*?

PRICE

I was sixteen or seventeen. I was a major screwup in school, but I always read. Libraries. Paperbacks. I read *City of Night* and all the Evergreen and Grove Press stuff. I read a lot of horror stuff. I read Steinbeck. Although my experience wasn't Okie, rural, there was something in the simplicity of his prose that was very seductive. It made me feel that I didn't have to construct sentences like a nineteenth-century Englishman to be a writer.

INTERVIEWER

You intended to go to law school, but you ended up a writer . . .

PRICE

I always wanted to be a writer, but coming from a working-class background it was hard to feel I had that right. If you're the first generation of your family to go to college, the pressure on graduation is to go for financial security. The whole point of going to college is to get a *job*. You have it drilled into your head—job, money, security. Wanting to be an artist doesn't jibe with any of those three. If you go back to these people who have "slaved and sacrificed" to send you to school, who are the authority figures in your life, and you tell them that you want to be a writer, a dancer, a poet, a singer, an actor, and to do so you're going to wait tables, drive a cab, sort mail, with your Cornell University degree, they look at you like you're slitting their throats. They just don't have it in their life experience to be support-ive of a choice like that.

Because I came from that kind of background, it was a scary deci-sion not to go to law school. Maybe one reason *The Wanderers* got the attention it did was that nobody coming from my background with such an intimate knowledge of white housing-project life was writing about it. The smartest minds of my generation in the projects became doctors, lawyers, engineers, businessmen; they went the route that would fulfill the economic mandate.

INTERVIEWER

Had you ever met a writer before you decided to be one?

PRICE

At Cornell the class of 1958 or 1959 was amazing—with Richard Farina, Ronald Sukenick, Thomas Pynchon, Joanna Russ, Steve Katz, all of whom are working writers now in various degrees of ac-claim or obscurity. When I was at Cornell from 1967 to 1971 two or three of them came back to teach. It was the first time I sat in a room with a teacher who wasn't as old as my father. Here was a guy wearing a vest over a T-shirt. He had boots on, and his hair was longer than mine. A novelist! I couldn't take my eyes off him. I felt, Ah, to be a writer! I could be like this teacher and have that long, gray hair . . . boots up on the table and cursing in class! It made me dizzy just to look at the guy. I don't remember a thing he said to me, except that he usually made encouraging noises: You're good. You're okay, keep writing, blah, blah . . . He gave us this reading list that ranged from Céline to Walter Abish to Mallarmé and Rimbaud, names I'd never even heard of. The books looked so groovy, so cool, and so hip. I bought every one of them. I walked around with Alfred Jarry and Henri Michaux under my arm, but I didn't understand what they were trying to do, to *say*. I had no context for any of them. The only one I could get through on the list was Henry Miller. One writing teacher gave us his own novel and, frankly, I couldn't understand that either.

INTERVIEWER

What kinds of things did you write for him?

PRICE

I had a talent for making ten-page word soufflés that were sort of tasty. In the late sixties anything went. Everybody was an artist in the late sixties. Sort of like punk music in the seventies.

INTERVIEWER

You once mentioned some pancake poems.

PRICE

Some crazy Hungarian guy wrote those. He'd write them on round paper, bring them to class, read them, pour syrup on them and then eat them. The sixties. I will be eternally grateful to Richard Brautigan for *Rommell Drives on Deep into Egypt* and *A Confederate General from Big Sur*. I'd look at this stuff: Jesus . . . If this could get published, I can get published . . .

INTERVIEWER

Could you tell me how you work?

PRICE

It's important to me to have a place to work outside of where I live. So I have always found myself an office. I go off to work as if I had a clock to punch; at the end of the day I come home as if I had just gotten off the commuter train. I need to impose a structure on myself. Otherwise I can go three or four days without looking at a piece of paper. I try to keep it as close to a nine-to-five job as I'm able, probably closer to ten to four. I spend the first hour reading the *Daily News*, answering phone calls, lining up paper clips, doing anything but working. Toward the end of the end of the morning, I realize I have no choice but to finally get to work. Sometimes I'll be transported by the work; sometimes it just won't come. The most painful part of the day is getting to the moment when I see I have no choice but to do it.

INTERVIEWER

During that typical ten-to-four writing day how much time are you actually creating something new?

PRICE

About half of the time. Typically, what I'll do is write a page, reread it, edit it, write half a page more, and then I'll go back to the very first thing I wrote that morning. It's like the nursery rhyme "The House That Jack Built," where you go back to the first line of the poem and go all the way through, adding a line each time, and then back to the first. So, I don't know whether I'm editing, reediting, or writing something new, but it's kind of a creeping, incremental style of writing. I always sort of half-know where I'm going.

INTERVIEWER

How much revising did you do for *Clockers*?

PRICE

About a year and a half's worth. I had an endless, interminable draft, well over one thousand pages, with no ending in sight. I gave it to John Sterling, my editor, and with him I went back and started on page one and attacked the manuscript for a number of things: consistency of tone, a narrowed point of view, filling in all the holes in the plot. I tried to weed out excessive writing and cut down on the personality of the narrative voice. We wound up going back to page one three times and working our way through to page one thousand-plus—eighteen months of rewriting. Sterling would say, You have too many speakers, too many points of view, and your narrative voice is too florid. There are still some big-time problems with consistency of tone. Let's start on page one again. It was like wrestling a zeppelin.

That must have been time-consuming for an editor.

Very. Earlier, writing the first draft, I went through a process with him in which every day for a solid year I read to him over the phone everything I wrote. It seems I needed to do that . . . to hear "good dog." His goal in humoring me like this was to get me to the end so he could have a manuscript to work with. For him it must have been like talking to a head-job or a child, coaxing and comforting, saying, Ooh, that's good. Wow. Oh, you're such a good writer. Very good. What page are we on? How many pages do you think you have left? What time is it? March?

No criticisms?

Every once in a while he couldn't help it. He'd see I was taking a dogleg somewhere into the woods. But basically he understood that his role on the phone was almost that of a psychiatric nurse.

You were just fortunate in finding the right editor for *Clockers*.

We sort of grew into this relationship. Before I wrote a word of *Clockers* I had arranged to tell the story aloud to a number of publishers. Whoever was interested could bid against the others. I didn't trust my prose at that moment in time, because I had been writing movie scripts for eight years. I said, At this point I can talk so much better than I can write. Let me just talk. If it's inadequate, don't bid. I was confident enough in my story that if they could hear it, they would have the faith to go with it. If not, fine. Worse comes to worst, I would actually have to start writing something. But I wanted a setup where I knew someone was literally waiting for pages, because what I feared in going back to fiction was the isolation: the phone not ringing, no hugger-mugger, no emergency meetings, no "Clint has an idea . . ." I wanted someone waiting, someone keeping the light burning in the window. As it was, we had about nine publishing houses bidding. John Sterling of Houghton Mifflin was the last guy to hear the story. Every time I'd tell the story I'd tell it a little differently. I would always ad-lib a bit. I'd hear myself say something that I'd never said before and I'd think, Whoa, I'd better write that down. I was continually working out the story verbally in front of people. I keep hearing these days that nobody edits anymore, that editors are basically in-house expediters, but I've been lucky, always getting these guys who like to get into the trenches and duke it out over everything from punctuation to psychological consistency. I've since started a new novel and I went with Sterling from Houghton Mifflin to Broadway Books . . . like the story of Ruth, "Whither thou goest . . ."

INTERVIEWER

How'd you learn to do this—walking into a publisher's office and telling them a story?

PRICE

It's from the studios. The way you get work with them is by being a salesman, by walking into an office where people have the power to commission projects and saying, Have I got a story for you! Then you try to tell them the story as succinctly and as seductively as possible so they can envision the movie and the stars they might snag. It never occurred to me that you don't do this with a publisher.

INTERVIEWER

Do you act out the characters' parts or just describe the characters?

PRICE

Well, I'm not going to sit in front of some publisher and do black dialect or New Jersey—cop dialect. I'd quote to them an imagined exchange that symbolized the type of dynamic that I wanted to write about. "This is what this guy said and this was the reaction." In a way, I would act it out. Given the fact that I wasn't giving anything on paper to these people, I wanted them to know that while it's one thing to have an idea for a story, you've also got to get across that you know your stuff.

Let me tell you how *Clockers* got me back to fiction. First, I had had my own painful experience with cocaine, although I had been clean for about eight years by the time I started on the novel. In 1986 to 1987, crack hit the newspapers. You couldn't pick up a newspaper and *not* find the word *crack* in every article, including the weather report and the sports page. It seemed crack was this new nihilistic monster that was going to destroy us, the ultimate thing that was going to lead to the undoing of civilization. My own drug experience was such that I fell apart on your typical middle-class sniffing cocaine. But after I straightened out, this demon, this *crack* came along, ten times more potent, addictive and debilitating. It seized my imagination because, although I was clean, I was still having nightmares. This new thing seemed like kryptonite and to make amends for being a coke-jerk all those years, I began teaching in a rehab center in the Bronx. My students were adolescent crack addicts or crack dealers—many of them from broken homes, homes in which some of the parents had criminal histories, homes in which there were intravenous drug problems, sexual abuse, physical abuse, suicide attempts. Some of these kids going home to a house where, if the father was there and not in Rikers, he was chopping up lines on the table. And there *I* was, educated, mainstream, in my early thirties, financially solvent, professionally established, having almost fallen through the earth on pedestrian coke-sniffing, looking out at a room full of adolescents with nightmare backgrounds who had fallen prey to the same drug that almost killed me, but who were taking it in a form *ten* times more pernicious, and they were saying to me that they they smoked crack in order to *cope*? That made me crazy. So *Clockers* came about through the teaching experience, the crack epidemic, my not too ancient memories of drugs, and (last but not least) returning to the world of housing projects from which I came.

The first time I went back was with the police when I was doing research for *Sea of Love*. We went to these projects looking for a witness to a homicide, and that night I looked around and even though I'd spent the first eighteen years of my life in buildings like these, I felt like I had landed on a distant planet. They had turned into such tiger pits. The only things that looked familiar to me were the bricks. I felt this disorientation; it made me feel like, I know this, but I don't know this. Actually, I don't know *anything*. And I was seized by the desire to understand what happened to the projects. I felt compelled to return to the world I came from to find out what happened.

INTERVIEWER

What year was this?

PRICE

About 1985. I had stopped doing drugs in 1982. The funny thing is, once you stop doing drugs, you don't see it anymore because you're not around the people who have it. You don't even have to do that by design. It's sort of like when you're single everybody you know is single, when you get married everybody you know is married and when you have a baby everybody you know has a baby. You move into the circle of what your status and commitment are at that moment. I hadn't been around drugs for years; I literally hadn't seen any. The first time I saw it again was about a year and a half into the book when one of the guys I was running with brought out a kilo of coke, like a loaf of bread, and this giant wok and began chopping rocks with a bowie knife, mixing it with Italian baby laxative, what they call "stepping on it." Well, the last thing I wanted was to be high right then. A guy with a bowie knife chopping up his kilo? I'm not going to get strung out around here. Anyway, the urge was no longer there.

Did you ever try writing under the influence of cocaine?

I'm not Thomas de Quincey or Coleridge. I'm not William Bur-
roughs. I don't feel anything creative for me can come out of writing
under the influence of a drug. One danger is that cocaine gives you
the illusion of being creative; you get into this vicious circle of feeling
so inspired by this chemical in your system that you do write. Then
you come down and the next day you look at what you wrote and get
depressed. What you see before you is yesterday's rush transformed
into burbly bullshit, at which point you start to panic because now
you're *really* behind your deadline or whatever and you better get
cracking, but you're too depleted, physically and mentally, and therefore what you realize is, in order to jump-start yourself, maybe just a
wee hair of the dog would be in order, so you go out and score again.

And here comes another day's worth of deluded flop-sweat trying
to pass for art. I mean, you might be able to squeeze out a dazzling
paragraph or two, but it's the law of diminishing returns. In the end,
the coke will overwhelm the work. I got to the point where I had to do
a line to write a line. You might do coke in order to write, but by the
end you're writing in order to do coke.

I've never written anything good on coke. I mean, I've written
good paragraphs and good pages, but if I were to write a story for one
hundred days on coke, I might write one hundred good pages, but
they wouldn't be pages that belonged together—a hundred pages for
a hundred different books. Unfortunately, with a novel they're all supposed to be for the same story. Nobody can write well using cocaine.
It's the worst drug of all for an artist.

Take marijuana: when you're stoned you know you're stoned and
you stop smoking. When you're shooting heroin, you don't keep
shooting. You don't think, Maybe I should shoot some more. You're
nodding. You stop. You put down the needle. When you're drinking,
you can't drink endlessly. You're going to vomit or you're going to
pass out. You stop. Cocaine is the only drug that you can take and

take, and nothing stops you except running out of the stuff. And when you're blasted you don't realize that you've got garbage for brains.

One of Elmore Leonard's characters came across with the awful realization that addiction not only destroys your body and brain, but also dominates your consciousness. Twenty-four hours a day an addict is thinking about where they are in relation to their drug. They are thinking about how high they are. They're thinking about the fact that they're not high. They're thinking about scoring. They're thinking about cleaning up. They're thinking about cutting back, about getting better stuff. Endlessly thinking. Twenty-four, seven, three hundred and sixty-five. It simply dominates your thoughts around the clock.

INTERVIEWER

To get off it . . .

PRICE

It got to the point where I wanted to do something about it. I quit through self-disgust.

INTERVIEWER

Did you find a substitute?

PRICE

Baseball cards—1955, 1956, 1957.

INTERVIEWER

What's the prize of the collection?

PRICE

A first year Mickey Mantle, which should be worth thousands of dollars, except somebody sat on it. So now I just use it to scrape crumbs off the table.

INTERVIEWER

To get back to *Clockers*. Did the story evolve as you wrote it?

PRICE

The more I hung out doing research, the more the story changed, the more specific and the more intimate it became, and also the more daunting and endless. You're hanging out with drug dealers; the world of the drug dealers impinges on the world of poverty-in-general; the world of poverty-in-general impinges on the world of welfare, which impinges on criminal justice, which impinges on social work, which impinges on the world of education. So everything I learned naturally led to something else.

Also, seeing the world through cops' eyes, all you see are situations among people in which police are required, and that is wild on a day-in, day-out basis, that's addictive. You have a backstage pass to the greatest show on earth. As one cop said, One thing about God, he had to have been a genius to invent this job. But it wasn't like I was pulling a Margaret Mead number here. I'd known guys like these ever since I was a kid. So I was out there day and night, compiling, compiling, compiling. I couldn't stop. I felt like a degenerate gambler who gambles until he craps out. I felt if I went out with these guys just one more time, something *so* phenomenal was going to happen, something so epiphanic . . . and I got hooked on hanging out waiting for this tomorrow that I was afraid of missing.

At one point, I had a stack of notebooks two feet high of overheard things, sights, descriptions, sounds. Six months after Houghton Miflin had bought the book, I was still coming in with anecdotes, snatches of conversation, war stories. The novel was taking shape, shaping *me*, but I hadn't written a word. So, for my fortieth birthday my editor took me to lunch and he hit me with this hideous question: Well, this is all good and well. This stuff is amazing. This is going to be a phenomenal book. Let me just ask you . . . What's the first sentence?

I was simply afraid. Actual writing is no fun for me. Going out and hanging out and getting impressions out there on the streets, that's fun. I was running with everybody. I was like one of those guys who jumps off the stage into the audience and gets passed around. I got myself passed around for three years. So you've got all these good lines in a notebook, but then what? I think it was Norman Mailer who said that the fact that something really happened is the defense of the bad novelist. At some point I got so hooked on research that after a while it seemed out of the question to make things up. Ultimately, everything in *Clockers* was pure fiction, but in the beginning I had to learn enough about the texture of *truth* out there in order to have the confidence to make up lies, responsible lies.

INTERVIEWER

Incidentally, why do you think these people spoke to you?

PRICE

First of all, I was completely honest with everybody. Nobody really has an audience for their life. If you're a drug dealer or a cop or a woman on welfare with four kids, and suddenly here I come, a writer, saying, Look, I want to write a book. What you do and how you make it through the day is mysterious to me. I would like to learn how you make it from dawn to dusk and then back to dawn. People want to talk. People have a lot to get off their chests: You want to know how I survive in my life? Well, somebody should write a *book*; let me tell you. I was a guest in the house of their life. People took me in. I made no judgments.

INTERVIEWER

Did you ever get into a dangerous situation?

PRICE

Sometimes I'd go out with the cops and it would get kind of hairy, not because they were doing a "well, tonight we raid Mr. Big," but they'd get their load on and stuff would happen. I could never be left alone. I had to run when they ran. It can be pretty scary to get lost in a building. You're with the cops. Everybody *hates* the cops. Once there was a drug dealer, Earl, who had seen me in the company of the cops when they were stripping him down, harassing him, breaking his balls. Then the next night I come around to his turf with another drug dealer at three o'clock in the morning to be introduced to him, this big four-hundred pound Bluto. Since Earl had seen me with the cops, I needed the second drug dealer to front for me and explain to Earl that I was not a cop. I was a *writer*, somebody who wanted to hang out with drug dealers *and* the cops. The front guy says, Yeah, I'll take care of it. I'll take care of it. First thing, he leaves me in the car. He jumps out of the car and he gets into kind of a shadow-boxing, slap-boxing fistfight with Earl, their way of saying hello to each other: How you doing you fat motherfucker? Hey, when's the last time you saw your dick? They're cursing each other out like this when some girl comes up and my escort—the guy who's supposed to be explaining why I hang with cops—leaves Earl and goes off around the corner to dry hump her, and they're like *whup, whup, whup*, up against the wall when Earl, this big four-hundred pounder, comes over and looks at me in the car. He goes, Oh, shit, there's that cop! Willie! You brought a motherfucking cop! All the guys come running, reaching for their pieces, gold chains jangling.

Wait a minute! I say, No! I'm a *writer*! I held out my books and started speed-rapping my way out of God knows what kind of payback. But, I was very lucky. A couple of good war stories were the worst that happened.

INTERVIEWER

When you're writing a book do you tend to avoid reading other books?

PRICE

I'm very protective of myself. I once made the mistake of reading *Sophie's Choice* while I was trying to write *The Breaks*. It was like trying to sing while somebody else is singing another song in the background. I just got completely off course, not that I had much of a course to begin with. So, when I'm writing a book all I read is genre stuff; I'm very careful not to read anything too good, that's going to make me anxious. When I was writing *Clockers* I would not read anything about urban experience. A nonfiction book on exactly the same subject might have been a source of information for me, but I wouldn't have been able to stand the anxiety of not having covered an area that its author found essential.

INTERVIEWER

Do you show your work to other writers?

PRICE

Not anymore. In the beginning I was so enraptured by everything I wrote, I thought I was the cat's pajamas. I just couldn't wait to read my stuff to people. I'd read to a fire hydrant. And if the reaction was negative, I would just shrug it off. These people are wrong. The end. I had three novels out before I was thirty and I just felt like everything I did was great. I wasn't interested in what I didn't know. It's when you're older that you realize how ignorant you are. The older I get, the more insecure I feel about my work, although I do think it's better. I'm glad for whatever my early work got me, but it's painful to reread.

INTERVIEWER

Your first book was *The Wanderers*.

PRICE

I wrote *The Wanderers* when I was still in school. The book started out basically as assignments for my creative-writing classes at Columbia. Being published almost felt like the prize for handing in the best term paper. I didn't even know I was working on a book. I was just writing: It's time to write another one of these stories about these guys, the Wanderers. In class I read what turned out to be the first story of *The Wanderers*, and everybody hated it. Then Dan Halpern, who had started the literary magazine *Antaeus* and was a student in class with me, said, Well, I like it. I'd like to publish it. Can I have it? I'd never been published. It took a year for it to come out. Meanwhile, I had gone off to Stanford on a fellowship in their creative-writing program. Out there in Palo Alto, I felt so isolated from my past life that a great need came over me to crystallize my memories of the Bronx, my adolescence, the textures of a life to which I knew I'd never return. So my need to write about these *mooks* kicked into high gear—it was all tied into homesickness and disorientation. I was writing in the same manner and for the same reason that someone would whistle a tune as they navigated a dark and creepy forest.

When it was published in *Antaeus*, an editor at Houghton Mifflin wrote me a letter saying, I'd like to see more stuff like this if you have it. By the time I got that letter I had ten stories, about two-hundred pages. Houghton Mifflin bought the book for like four thousand bucks. My editor straightened out the grammar. I didn't even know I was doing what I was doing. I was twenty-four when it was published.

INTERVIEWER

You make it sound effortless.

PRICE

If I had known what I was doing, truly known what I was doing, I might not have been able to do it. Sometimes, things come easy. You're oblivious to the statistics, the big picture. No book since has been that easy for me.

The first book is always the most fun, because when you write your first book you're just a writer. Then you get published. Then you become an author, and once you're an author the whole thing changes. You have a track record. You have a public. A certain literary persona. You can become very self-conscious and start to compete with yourself. No fun at all.

INTERVIEWER

How did your novel *Ladies' Man* come about?

PRICE

Ladies' Man came out of an assignment from *Penthouse*. They wanted a series of three articles about public places in which you can go and either participate in or observe actual sex: massage parlors, backroom gay bars, Plato's Retreat-type places, even singles bars. At the time I had never been to any of these places, not even a singles bar. So I went to a singles retreat in the Catskills—just the most desultory, horrific, depressing place. Fourteen guys and three women. Pocked handball courts. Dead birds in the swimming pool.

Then an old friend of mine who is gay took me to the back rooms of bars like The Anvil, The Toilet, The Ramp, The Strap, The Stirrup, The Eagle's Nest, and God knows what. I started writing about this stuff and I couldn't stop. It was so freaky, such a sense of anarchy, anything goes. It's like you go crazy. You don't need amyl nitrite; just being in there is like a giant popper. My first reaction in those leather bars was, Christ, I hope nobody makes eye contact with me. Then, after about forty-five minutes, I found myself wondering, How come nobody's making eye contact with me? Am I that ugly? And it hit me that under all the cruising and anonymity of the backroom bars, there existed the same undercurrent of desire and neediness that I experienced at the singles weekend in the Catskills. Well, obviously there were a lot more people getting their rocks off in the backrooms, but . . .

So I realized I wanted to write a story about a guy who goes to a place like The Eagle's Nest, then the Catskills place, singles bars, massage parlors. Like *Lost Weekend*, but about sex, not alcohol. So I bought back the articles from *Penthouse* because I wanted to use the material for a book. That's how *Ladies' Man* began.

INTERVIEWER

Writing became more difficult later?

PRICE

The hardest book for me ever to write, and the least satisfying, was *The Breaks*. I was writing in a blind panic because I couldn't think of anything to write about. I had published three books, one every other year. All of a sudden I ran out of autobiography and I started spinning my wheels. I began two books I never finished and never sent out because they were empty. You can write because you have something you want to work with, or you can write because you're desperate to keep your name out there. If you write because the subject intrigues you and challenges you and makes your life as a writer engaging, and then you get to a place where you realize that, at this moment in time, you don't have anything to write about, you're going to stop. But if you're writing because you haven't been published and your star is dimming, then you write regardless. And if you have enough talent you'll deliver readable page after readable page after readable page, but all of it will add up to nothing because you're just treading water.

In *Ladies' Man* I had the whole book outlined. It was an easy structure: seven days. In seven days I wanted the guy to go here, here, here, and here. I plotted out his week. It just fell into my lap. Afterwards, I thought, If that took me three weeks, maybe the next one will take me a week. This is great. Then, after that I'll write a book a day. I'll be like Georges Simenon, seventy-four books a year! No such luck.

The first draft of *Ladies' Man* took me three weeks. It was the opposite of the Judeo-Christian work ethic—the harder you work the greater the reward. Sometimes what's easiest is the best simply because you're in complete sync and harmony with what you're writing about. That's why it was easy.

INTERVIEWER

Did you start writing the screenplays because you wanted to support a family or because of frustration as a novelist?

PRICE

I started to write screenplays because as a novelist I felt the well was dry. It had been for a while. I'd had a lot of offers to do screenplays over the years, so . . . let's see what happens. I knew if I stayed with the novel I was just going to kill myself. I was going to fall off a cliff.

INTERVIEWER

How much did the Hollywood people know about you?

PRICE

My first two books were made into movies, neither of which I worked on—*The Wanderers* and *Bloodbrothers*. I had offers because the people out there could see that my novels were very cinematic. I had grown up on TV and movies as much as on books, and it showed— a visual and aural momentum that lent itself very easily to film.

Actually, I didn't literally go out there. I stayed in New York. I came up with an idea about a mailman who wins the lottery and how it changes his life—"Wingo." It was never made but it was pretty good and it got around. Your first script, even if it's good, probably won't get made, but it's the best calling card you can have short of having a movie.

After that, Martin Scorsese was looking for a writer. I met with him for three hours and went off and wrote *Night and the City*. It was too Scorsesian for Scorsese to do, but he saw that I could write; he asked me to get involved with *The Color of Money* and I got nominated for an Oscar. First time out at the box. Never happened again though . . . In any event, once one of your scripts is made into a movie, well, it's sort of like being a baseball manager. There are only thirty of you; and even if you're terrible, by virtue of the fact that you have managed a pro team, there will always be a job for you more or less. Once you get something on film and it attracts any kind of notice, it's never that hard again.

INTERVIEWER

Do you find the lack of control you have as a screenwriter frustrating?

PRICE

It's enough to drive you to write novels. Almost. This is the immutable law of the business: the only screenplays that aren't tampered with are the ones that aren't made. Making a movie is an ensemble act. Writers are not authors out there. And scripts are not books. They're blueprints. You work with others or you're gone.

INTERVIEWER

You wouldn't want to direct your own screenplays?

PRICE

It is sort of a natural law that if you have any kind of significant success as a screenwriter, the next thing to do (according to Darwin or someone) is to parlay that into some kind of deal where you'll end up directing. Why would anybody want to stay a screenwriter, constantly handing your stuff over to other people to execute? On the other hand, I don't know anything about directing, but what I've seen I don't like. It takes over your entire life, physically, mentally, emotionally. If I weren't a novelist and if I hadn't written *Clockers*, I probably would've taken a stab at being a director, simply out of despair. Sometimes the fear of the unknown is not as great as the fear of things staying the way they are.

INTERVIEWER

Do you want to keep writing both novels and screenplays?

PRICE

Every screenwriter loves to trash screenwriting. It's like shooting fish in a barrel. They trash the calculatedness, the cynicism, the idiocy, the pandering. But if they're really honest, they'll also admit they love the action, the interaction. Depending on whom you're working with, screenwriting is fun up to a point. And movies have such an impact on people. Thomas Kenealy once told me about a time he was with the guerrillas in Eritrea during the civil war in Ethiopia. They were sitting on the cusp of the desert under the moon. They all had their muskets; they were about to attack some place. Wanting to chill out before they mobilized, they watched *The Color of Money* on video. So every once in a while the hugeness of Hollywood gets to you—the number of people who see a movie compared to the number of people who read a book. So as a screenwriter you keep hoping against hope—just because they screwed me the last time doesn't mean they're going to screw me this time. Well, of course they will. They're just going to screw you in a way you haven't been screwed before.

The first draft is the most creative, the most like real writing because it's just you and the story. The minute they get a hold of that first draft it ceases to be fun because it's all about making everybody happy. Raymond Chandler said that the danger of Hollywood for a writer is that you learn to put everything you've got into your first draft and then you steel yourself not to care what happens because you know you're going to be powerless after that. If you do that time and time again, the heart goes out of you.

Do you work on the set?

Depends on the director. There are some directors who like to have a writer on a leash, sitting at their feet in case something comes up. There are other directors who feel that a writer on the set is an anxiety trigger. Actors live in a constant state of insecurity, a constant fear of "am I going to show my ass out there?" When they see a writer it makes them think about what they are going to say and if it could be better. So a lot of directors would like to keep the writer off the set for that reason. Then there are directors who don't want the writer freaking out because his script is being used only as a blueprint, which is what a script should be. Things are going to come up and the script is going to change in order to make the actor happier. He doesn't want to say what you wrote, he's got his own take. Yes, it might not be as well-said or well-written as what you had, but what you gain in sort of cutting the quality of the writing a bit is a better performance because the actor feels more in control of what he's doing. Everything's a compromise. The art of movies is the art of collaboration. I always trash how stupid screenwriting is, but the more I do, the more I realize it's really about the art of push-me pull-you, of creative negotiation. It's not about writing. Movies are not scripts; they're living pictures. There's an amazing difference between what works on paper and what works in the flesh. Sometimes what can look like breathless dialogue on the page sounds like "creative writing" in the mouth of an actor. It doesn't make a difference how good the actor is, it's just not human speech. When you read books in which the dialogue seems dead-on and exquisitely truthful to the character you'd be amazed at how artificial those lines would sound if actually spoken by actors. It's remarkable how little can be too much. And sometimes you get better movies off more patchy scripts, because the actor has to reach deeper to make the connection. Whereas, if I write it out, dictate what the actor is supposed to be feeling, telling him to make this gesture, to say it with *this* tone of voice, to take *this* exact amount of time between words, actors can read it and think, Beautiful, this guy did it all for me. Then they just go through the motions. And oftentimes the end result won't be as good as that other movie they were in where the script was fairly crappy, but the actor had to bring more to the party. It's exasperating, but that's the reality of it. You don't hold the page up to the camera and follow the bouncing ball. It's got to make it into the flesh and then all sorts of things happen.

INTERVIEWER

What place does the novel have in the world? Why do you keep writing them?

PRICE

Because the novel is *me* . . . what *I* have to say. When people come up and say, Oh! You wrote *Sea of Love*? That was my favorite movie, I feel like they're talking to somebody standing between me and them. I don't feel like I own it. I ask myself, What kind of writer am I that I write something and then I don't want to take ownership of the final product? It's nauseating. I don't mean nauseating in a condemnatory way, I mean that you actually get a feeling of vertigo and nausea about who you are.

INTERVIEWER

Is that why you decided to do *Clockers* next? To get back to the novel?

PRICE

First of all, I got an awful lot of confidence back as a writer because my screenplays were well-regarded. But at the same time I never wanted to be a screenwriter, first and foremost because a screenwriter is not a real writer. You're not an architect; you're a draftsman. I wanted to be a real writer again . . . when I felt like I had something I wanted to write about. Out of my research for *Sea of Love* I found myself in places and with people that moved me as a writer and made me want to write in a way that I hadn't felt for over ten years. And I knew that I had to have control over this material, not some studio. I didn't want to have to buckle under to someone's marketing strategy, be dependent on a director's interpretation, on editing decisions, advertising campaigns, PG ratings. All of a sudden, I found myself in the middle of something. It took a decade to get there. I didn't even know where I was. I just knew I was in the right place. I didn't even have the story. But it was a combination of *where* I was and *what* I was at that point in time.

INTERVIEWER

Can writing be taught?

PRICE

You can't teach talent anymore than you can teach somebody to be an athlete. But maybe you help the writer find their story, and that's ninety-nine percent of it. Oftentimes, it's a matter of lining up the archer with the target. I had a student in one of my classes. He was writing all this stuff about these black guys in the South Bronx who were on angel dust . . . the most amoral thrill-killers. They were evil, evil. But it was all so over-the-top to the point of being silly. He didn't know what he was talking about. I didn't know this stuff either, but I knew enough to know that this wasn't it.

I said to the kid, Why are you writing this? Are you from the Bronx? He says, No. From New Jersey.

Are you a former angel-dust sniffer? Do you run with a gang? He says, No. My father's a fireman out in Toms River.

Oh, so he's a black fireman in suburban New Jersey? Christ! Why don't you write about that? I mean, nobody writes about black guys in the suburbs. I said, Why are you writing this other stuff?

He said to me, Well, I figure people are expecting me to write this stuff.

What if they do? First of all, they don't. Second, even if they did, which is stupid, why should I read you? What do you know that I don't know?

He turned out to be one of these kids in the early eighties who was bombing trains with graffiti—one of these guys who was part of the whole train-signing subculture, you know, *Turk 182*. He wrote a story, over a hundred pages long, about what it was like to be one of these guys—fifteen pages alone on how to steal aerosol cans from hardware stores. He could describe the smell of spray paint mixing with that rush of tunnel air when someone jerked open the connecting door on a moving train that you were "decorating." He wrote about the Atlantic Avenue station in Brooklyn where all the graffiti-signers would hang out, their informal clubhouse, how they all kept scrapbooks of each other's tags. Who would know that stuff except somebody who really knew? And it was great. The guy was bringing in the news. Now, whether it's art or not depends on how good he is. But he went from this painful chicken scratch of five-page bullshit about angel-dust killers to writing stuff that smacked of authenticity and intimacy.

That is the job of the writing teacher: what do you think you should be writing about? At Yale I had the same problem. They'd write ten pages of well-worded this or that, but where's the story? I finally came up with an assignment. I hate giving assignments. I hated getting them and I hate giving them. But—the last of the good assignments—I made them all find a photograph of their family taken at least one year before the writer was born. I said, All right. Write me a story that starts the minute these people break this pose. Where did they go? What did they do? We all have stories about our family, most of them are apocryphal, but whether you love or hate your family, they're yours and these are your stories. On the other hand, Tom McGuane once said, I've done a lot of horrible things in my life but I never taught creative writing.

INTERVIEWER

What about your work since *Clockers*?

PRICE

I got into writing a script for *Clockers* because it was sold to Universal for Martin Scorsese. I had done three movies with him. Even did a Michael Jackson video with him. So, I spent a year writing a script based on *Clockers*, which is sort of like going from being the parent to the babysitter, because now this story is theirs—they bought it, and I'm just a hired pen. It's like you gave birth, sold the child and then were hired on as the kid's caretaker. And the new parents can give you the boot if they don't like your work. So I was writing for Scorsese, DeNiro was involved too, but ultimately those guys decided to do *Casino* instead.

So Spike Lee jumped in and said, I read your book, I read all the drafts, and with all due respect I like to write my own stuff. So he took over as the screenwriter. It was a very strange experience. When a movie is made from your own raw material, you come into the movie theater with so much psychic luggage. Everybody else is there just watching a movie, whereas you see what you first wrote as fiction, transformed into script, then changed by Spike, then changed again by the actors, the editing, et cetera. You're sitting watching a simple dialogue exchange and you trip out down memory lane and the next thing you know twenty minutes have gone by and you have no idea what's been happening on the screen since that little dialogue exchange made you wander off. It's like driving along a highway drifting off, and when you come back to driving consciousness twenty miles have gone by. Who's been driving while you were gone? In a way I can never watch the movie, because everything I'd see would take me out of the movie and back to the script, back to Spike's script, back to the novel, back to the experience that provoked the novel. I could never follow the damn thing, because my mind would keep taking me away. The funny thing is, what I liked best in the movie was the stuff I had nothing to do with—that wasn't in the book—where Spike had to go back and shoot transitional stuff; I had no idea what he was doing. There I felt most like a moviegoer.

INTERVIEWER

Is the process for getting the idea for a novel very different from the process for a screenplay?

PRICE

My screenplay ideas were given to me, or taken from something I've done, or something that's very "surface" for me, like *Mad Dog and Glory*. In Jamaica, I saw a dynamic between two people—one of them a woman from Miami, the other a Jamaican busboy working in a hotel, Lance, with whom I became friendly when I bought some of his ganja. Lance found out that I had a car. He said, Oh, man. I'll take you into the jungle tomorrow. We'll go visit my grandparents in Sav-La-Mar. To have a car is a treat down there. He said, We'll take a *ride*. I said OK. He showed up with this blonde, lanky, gum-chewing woman from Miami named Jody Goldfarb. Jody was about six inches taller than him, and I couldn't figure out what they were doing together, except that maybe she's a tourist who likes to get down with the natives. I spent all day with them driving around the jungle. They weren't even talking to each other . . . not hostile, but awkward. I had no idea what their relationship was. Then by chance she wound up on my flight back to Miami. I said, Oh, is that guy your boyfriend?

She says, No, but my friend Lou from Miami came down to the hotel about a month ago. He got in trouble swimming, and Lance jumped in and saved him. When Lou got back to Miami he said to me, How'd you like a trip to Jamaica? I'd like you to be this guy's friend. I owe him one. If you do something for me, I'll remember it. She says, The next thing I knew I was standing behind the hotel near the employees' quonset huts in a bikini wearing a sash that said, Thanks, Lou. She was a human thank-you present. God knows who "Lou from Miami" was, but it didn't sound good.

That story stayed with me for ten years, but it was not something I'd really wanted to go into depth with in a novel. The ideas I have for screenplays are ideas I can hold in my hand without anything dribbling out onto the floor. Things that come to me as novels I don't even know how to describe, because they have no beginning, no end, and I'm not even sure where the center is. What comes to me as a screenplay is usually something I can describe in a paragraph.

INTERVIEWER

Is that in the nature of the movie business or of film story?

PRICE

It's the nature of studio business in Hollywood. People there want something new but familiar; they don't like you to deviate too much from what they've seen before. What they've seen before has a fiscal track record. If you're going to invest fifty million dollars in a movie, you would like to know who the parents are. If you're buying a race-horse, you'd like the bloodlines to include Citation and Whirlaway, not Maude and Mr. Ed. If you tried to pitch *The Crying Game* to a Hollywood studio, you'd have to say, Well, it's out of *Malcolm X* and sired by *Tootsie*. But if you just say to them, Look, this is a very small story. It's sort of political. It's sort of a thriller. It's sort of a love story. It takes place in England. It's very small-time people. One of them's a transvestite, the other a terrorist. And, it's *quite* unusual. They'd say, Great. Go tell it to Miramax.

INTERVIEWER

What did you learn from screenplays that you think might have helped you write *Clockers*?

PRICE

What I learned in screenplays is that I don't have to write about myself all the time. I had a number of assignments for which I had to write about people that were completely outside my sphere, but I learned that if I simply hung out and absorbed their world a bit, I was able to create characters that were compelling and somewhat faithful to their sources. I didn't learn to do that as a novelist. I did it as a screenwriter and that gave me the confidence to take on *Clockers* and all these characters who were not of my personal experience.

INTERVIEWER

Is it easy to go from the novel to screenwriting?

PRICE

The danger of going from screenplays to books, books to screen-plays is the danger of movie-addiction. Screenplays are for me like dope: I'm gonna quit. I swear. Right after this last script. Excuses, excuses: I need the money. This one's a surefire go. How can I not work with this actor. How can I say no to this director. Three scripts later I'm still writing scripts. That's what happened to me. I went back after *Clockers* and wrote three movies, including *Clockers*, *Kiss of Death*—with Nicolas Cage and David Caruso—and *Ransom* with Mel Gibson.

But now I'm finished with all of that. I'm at work on a new book. I've gone back to the same fictional place as *Clockers*. When I did *Clockers* I went in and saw the urban world in a microcosm in Jersey City and I came out with this huge book. But I also felt I had taken a teaspoon from the ocean, that I could go back to that place and explore various aspects of the urban world for the rest of my life and not make a dent. It's in no way a sequel to *Clockers*. It's about politics and the media. So I'm hanging out again.

INTERVIEWER

I want to apologize for asking a personal question, but would you tell me about your hand?

PRICE

My hand? Well, I was born with a mild case of cerebral palsy. It's no big thing on a day-to-day basis; mostly people get uncomfortable when they have to shake hands with me. What the hell . . . of course, I'd like to be a weight lifter, but I can't.

INTERVIEWER

You'd like to be a weight lifter?

PRICE

Anybody who has something wrong with them physically is kind of obsessed with their appearance, so I'm always dabbling with weight lifting. My left hand's twice as strong as my right hand, so I never get anywhere with it, but . . .

INTERVIEWER

I don't want to get too abstruse here, but do you consider there's any connection between all this and your becoming a writer?

PRICE

If you've got something obviously awry in your appearance people treat you differently, like you're a special case. It never stopped me from playing sports. I played handball for my high-school team. You have to be ambidextrous to be a good handball player. I developed a backhand to compensate. It was no big deal. But, then there would be all this drama. The gym teacher would see me playing with that fouled-up hand and he'd call me over with tears in his eyes and he'd say, Son, you can always play on my team.

It's not like you walk around thinking about it all day. But as you grow up with this sense of yourself being singular, in some way you get hooked on the singularity of yourself. To be an artist is to be singular. I think, in some people, before the desire to write there is the desire to be special. That's not exactly healthy, and there's nothing relevant to creativity in that. Maybe I was just trying to maintain that sort of special thing by writing.

My grandmother, who was a big influence on my life, would take me under her wing because there was something wrong with my hand. She was a very unhappy person herself, very heavy, about five feet tall. Really overweight. Like two hundred pounds or more. It was her against the world and she saw me as her ally. I think she tended to see herself as a freak. There was something wrong with my hand, so we were fellow freaks . . . although she never said that to me. To go to her house on a Saturday was like getting parole for a day. I didn't understand how unhappy and isolated she was, but she'd be all filled with this melodrama about everything. We'd sit and look out her Bronx kitchen window and watch the East 172nd Street follies. She'd see a black man who lived across the street and she'd say, Oh, this one is a gentleman, married to this white piece of trash. She goes with anything in pants. She has him wrapped around her little finger. Do you know how much of a gentleman this man is? If he goes into his building lobby to go into the elevator and he sees a white woman there who's gonna get spooked by him because he's a black man, do you know what he does? He steps *out* of the lobby so she can go up the elevator herself. Now, *this* is a gentleman. But that whore he's married to . . . ?

Then there'd be some other guy: Oh, this son-of-a-bitch, he's a junkie. Every time he sticks a needle in his arm it's like sticking a needle in his mother's heart. She comes to me, she says, Mrs. Rosenbaum, what can I do! What can I do! Richard, what am I going to tell her?

It was this constant rat-tat-tat. I'm six and I'm with the fattest, biggest ball of love to me. This is my grandmother. Then we'd go all day to monster movies. She'd be talking back to the screen the whole time.

INTERVIEWER

Monster movies?

PRICE

In a neighborhood you wouldn't go into with a tank. We'd watch *The Attack of the Praying Mantis*, along with *The Crawling Eye* and *The Creature From Green Hell*. She'd be the only person over fourteen in the whole theater. Not only that, the only person over one hundred and fifty pounds. She'd pack up these big, big vinyl, sort of, beach bags. She'd make sandwiches, thermoses of coffee, and chocolate milk, and bring plums and nectarines. If there was a turkey carcass, she'd wrap it in silver foil so we could pick on the bones. We'd go into the movies with all this. We were ready for anything. And when we came out of the theater we'd have those little light dots in front of our eyes because we'd gone in at noon and we'd be coming out at five o'clock. Coming out, she'd walk all hunched over. She was only in her fifties, but she was so arthritic and rheumatic and heavy. We'd walk all the way back home, about one block every twenty minutes with that nonstop commentary about everybody who crossed our path. She lived on the third floor of a walk-up, so that took another hour, one step at a time. Then we get up there, and even after the triple horror feature we'd watch *Zacherly's Shock Theater*, pro wrestling, Roller Derby—everything—drama, stories, tragedies, drama, drama.

One time she took me to a wrestling arena in the early fifties in the height of summer. She had me on her lap and when one of the villains walked by she jabbed him with a hatpin. She was what was known as a Hatpin Mary. So, for the next match, when Nature Boy Buddy Rogers, this peroxide pompadoured villain, who wore a leopard-skin Tarzan getup, came strutting down the aisle, people were looking at my grandmother and they started chanting, Stick him! Stick him! He heard the chant and stood right over us, daring her. She was paralyzed, so he took her hand with the hatpin, a woman who probably felt very unloved by the world, bowed down and kissed it, said, "Madam." And then he continued walking toward the ring. At which point my grandmother dropped me, just dropped me on the floor. I remember ten, fifteen years later, when I would watch wrestling with my grandmother, every once in a while she'd say, I wonder how Nature Boy Buddy Rogers is doing. He's such a nice guy.

INTERVIEWER

Did your mom know about this going on?

PRICE

I guess. My grandmother's house was heaven for me. When I started writing in earnest I just thought back to the time with her, all those Saturdays, all those movies, all that commentary on the world under her window, then I started thinking about my friends, about other aspects of my childhood; the out-of-whack passions, crushes, terrors, and I began writing this sort of magic realism bullshit aka stories about the Bronx.

As I always told my students, We all grow up with ten great stories about our families, our childhoods . . . they probably have nothing to do with the truth of things, but they're yours. You know them. And you love them. So use them. And that's what I did. That's what I reached for, to become a writer.

Now, at this point in my life I've paid all my bills, I've fulfilled all my screenwriting obligations, I'm financially flush, for the next year I have nothing to do but work on this novel without distraction. So, I'm looking at all my notes, at my nice clean desk, my stack of unwrapped ready-to-go legal pads, and all I can think of is that saying "if God hates your guts he grants you your deepest wish."

Issue 138, 1996

Billy Wilder

The Art of Screenwriting

Billy Wilder, one of American cinema's premiere writer-directors, has always maintained that movies are "authored," and has always felt that much of a film's direction ideally should take place in the writing. Like many of the medium's great filmmakers, Wilder began his career as a writer, yet he is unique in the extent of his involvement in the development of the material he has directed. Indeed, he has cowritten all twenty-four of his films.

Samuel "Billy" Wilder was born June 22, 1906, in Sucha Beskidzka, in the Austro-Hungarian Empire. After years as a reporter—highlighted by a single day during which he interviewed Richard Straus, Arthur Schnitzler, Alfred Adler, and Sigmund Freud—Wilder gravitated to Berlin. There he worked as a crime reporter, drama critic, and (so he claims) gigolo, before he began to produce scenarios for the booming German film industry, finally writing over two hundred, including the notable precursor of neorealism, *People on Sunday* (1929). Wilder, driven by Hitler's ascendancy, left Berlin; his mother, grandmother, and stepfather, who stayed in Vienna, perished later in the Holocaust. He arrived in Hollywood, with only a temporary visa and almost no English, to share a room and a can of soup a day with the actor Peter Lorre. Later he upgraded his quarters to a vestibule near the woman's restroom at the Chateau Marmont on Sunset Boulevard.

Wilder began his American career at a moment when studios had begun to let some screenwriters direct their own scripts—or, as one film executive said, let the lunatics take over the asylum—a phenomenon that sparked the careers of a number of remarkable writer-directors (Preston Sturges, John Huston, Joseph Mankiewicz). At the time, Ernst Lubitsch, an émigré from the earlier, silent, period, was head of production at Paramount, where Wilder first flourished, the only time a filmmaker has been in charge of a major studio.

As a contract writer at Paramount, Wilder cowrote a number of films with Charles Brackett, among them *Ball of Fire*, directed by Howard Hawks, *Bluebeard's Eighth Wife* and *Ninotchka*, both directed by Lubitsch. Although he credits the experience of working with Lubitsch for teaching him much of what he knew about film, Wilder grew increasingly exasperated by the misinterpretation of his work by lesser filmmakers. He resolved to become a director himself.

Wilder's films show an extraordinary range, from film noir to screwball comedy. Although he claims that as a director he aspired to an unobtrusive style of shooting, all his films, nonetheless are marked by a singular vision—elegant dramatization of character through action, distinctive dialogue, and a sour/sweet, or even misanthropic, view of humanity—qualities that stem, for the most part, from the writing. Wilder's credits as a director and cowriter include *Double Indemnity*, *Sunset Boulevard*, *Sabrina*, *Ace in the Hole*, *Stalag 17*, *The Lost Weekend*, *Some Like It Hot*, and *The Apartment*. Four films directed and cowritten by Wilder have been selected by the National Film Registry of the Library of Congress for recognition and preservation. Only director John Ford, with five, has more.

The office where he goes every weekday is a simple suite on the second floor of a low-rise office building. On the wall across from his desk, in gilt letters eight inches high is the question HOW WOULD LUBITSCH DO IT? A day bed, like an analyst's couch, is set against one wall. The opposite wall is decorated with personal photos, including a number of him with some of cinema's other great writer-directors—John Huston, Akira Kurosawa, and Federico Fellini. Wilder points out a Polaroid collage depicting a paper-strewn desk—"David Hockney's portrait of my office"—and then, with mercurial amusement, a number of his own creations: a goofy series of plaster casts of a bust

of Nefertiti, each painted and decorated with the distinctive features
of a number of cultural figures—a Groucho Nefertiti, an Einstein Nefertiti, a Little Tramp Nefertiti. Wilder mentions with some pride the
"one-man show" of these figurines that had been presented at a
gallery nearby.

Asked about his noted art collection, Wilder says, "I didn't get rich
as a director, I got rich selling art. Thirty-four million dollars to be
exact, when it went on sale at Christie's." When asked for tips on collecting he says, "Sure, don't collect. Buy what you like, hold onto it,
enjoy it." Later he would offer a number of other get-rich tips: "Back
some pornographic films and then, as a hedge to balance your invest-
ment should family values rise, buy stock in Disney." Also, "Bet con-
sistently against the Los Angeles Rams."

A restless man, taller than expected, Wilder wears large black-
framed glasses, and conducts himself with the air of a benevolent,
even exuberant, dictator. When firmly settled in a large chair behind
his desk, he says, "Now, you wanted to ask me a question."

—*James Linville, 1996*

INTERVIEWER

You're known as a writer and director for your sharp eye. Could
that have anything to do with your sense of yourself as an outsider?

BILLY WILDER

Everything was new to me when I arrived in America, so I looked
closely. I had arrived in the country on a six-month visitor's visa, and
I had great difficulty obtaining an immigration visa that would allow
me to stay on. Also, the status of my English was rather poor. I
couldn't rearrange the furniture in my mouth—the tonsils, the curved
palate. I've never lost my accent. Ernst Lubitsch, who came in 1922,
had a much heavier accent than mine, as did Otto Preminger. Children can get the pronunciation in a few weeks, but English is a tough
language because there are so many letters in words that are totally
useless. *Though* and *through*. And *tough*!

Coming to the American movie industry at a time when many distinguished German directors were working, did you feel part of a special group?

There were some excellent German directors, led by Mr. Lubitsch, but I simply met him and shook his hand; he had no interest in me when I arrived. In fact, he was very reluctant to give jobs to Germans; it was only four years later that he hired me. I had written some pictures in Germany, usually working alone. But when I came here I had to have a collaborator on account of my unsteady English and my knowledge of only about three hundred words. Later I found that if I had a good collaborator it was very pleasant to talk to somebody and not come into an empty office. The head of the writers' department at Paramount had the good idea to pair me with Charles Brackett, a distinguished man from the East, who had gone to Harvard Law School and was about fifteen years older than I. I liked working with him. He was a very good man. He was a member of the Algonquin round table. He had been the movie critic or theater critic on *The New Yorker* in the beginning, the twenties.

One day, Brackett and I were called in to see Lubitsch. He told us he was thinking vaguely about doing an adaptation of a French play about a millionaire—a very straightforward law-abiding guy, who would never have an affair with a woman unless he was married to her. So he married seven times!

That would be Gary Cooper. Claudette Colbert was to be the woman who was in love with him, who'd insist "I'll marry you, but only to be the final wife." As the meeting was being adjourned, I said, I have a meet-cute for your story. (A "meet-cute" was a staple of romantic comedies back then, where boy meets girl in a particular way, and sparks fly.) Let's say your millionaire is an American who is very stingy. He goes to a department store in Nice on the French Riviera where he wants to buy a pajama top, but just the top, because he never wears the pants. She has come to the same counter to buy pajamas for her father, who as it happens only wears the pants. That broke the ice, and we were put to work on that picture, which became *Bluebeard's Eighth Wife*.

Lubitsch, of course, would always find a way to make something better. He put another twist on that meeting. Brackett and I were at Lubitsch's house working, when during a break he emerged from the bathroom and said, What if when Gary Cooper comes in to the store to buy the pajama top, the salesman gets the floor manager, and Cooper again explains he only wants to buy the top. The floor manager says, Absolutely not, but when he sees Cooper will not be stopped, the floor manager says, Maybe I could talk to the store manager. The store manager says, That's unheard of! but ends up calling the department store's owner, whom he disturbs in bed. We see the owner in a close shot go to get the phone. He says, It's an outrage! And as the owner goes back to his bed you see that he doesn't wear pajama pants either.

INTERVIEWER

When you first met Lubitsch over lunch, did you think of that meet-cute on the spot?

WILDER

No, I already had that. I had been hoping to use it for something, and when he told us the story of the picture I saw how it might fit. I had dozens of meet-cutes. Whenever I thought of one I'd put it in a little notebook. Back then they were de rigeur, a staple of screwball comedies. Every comedy writer was working on his meet-cutes; but of course we don't do that anymore. Later, I did a version of the meet-cute for *The Apartment*, where Jack Lemmon and Shirley MacLaine, who when they see each other every day have this little routine together. And in *Sabrina*, where she reappears and the younger Larrabee, William Holden, doesn't recognize her—him not recognizing her becomes a kind of meet-cute. When Sydney Pollack was remaking that movie, I told him they should make the Larrabee family's company a bankrupt company, and Sabrina's competition for the younger Larrabee the daughter of a Japanese prospective-buyer.

You have a gold-framed legend on the wall across from your desk. How Would Lubitsch do it?

WILDER
When I would write a romantic comedy along the Lubitschian line, if I got stopped in the middle of a scene, I'd think, How would Lubitsch do it?

INTERVIEWER
Well, how did he do it?

WILDER
One example I can give you of Lubitsch's thinking was in *Ninotchka*, a romantic comedy that Brackett and I wrote for him. Ninotchka was to be a really straight Leninist, a strong and immovable Russian commissar, and we were wondering how we could dramatize that she, without wanting to, was falling in love. How could we do it? Charles Brackett and I wrote twenty pages, thirty pages, forty pages! All very laboriously.

Lubitsch didn't like what we'd done, didn't like it at all. So he called us in to have another conference at his house. We talked about it, but of course we were still, well . . . blocked. In any case, Lubitsch excused himself to go to the bathroom, and when he came back into the living room he announced, Boys, I've got it.

It's funny, but we noticed that whenever he came up with an idea, I mean a really *great* idea, it was after he came out of the can. I started to suspect that he had a little ghostwriter in the bowl of the toilet there.

I've got the answer, he said. It's the hat.

The hat? No, what do you mean the hat?

He explained that when Ninotchka arrives in Paris the porter is about to carry her things from the train. She asks, Why would you want to carry these? Aren't you ashamed? He says, It depends on the tip. She says, You should be ashamed. It's undignified for a man to carry someone else's things. I'll carry them myself.

At the Ritz Hotel, where the three other commissars are staying, there's a long corridor of windows showing various objects. Just windows, no store. She passes one window with three crazy hats. She stops in front of it and says, "That is ludicrous. How can a civilization of people that put things like that on their head survive?" Later she plans to see the sights of Paris—the Louvre, the Alexandre III Bridge, the Place de la Concorde. Instead she'll visit the electricity works, the factories, gathering practical things they can put to use back in Moscow. On the way out of the hotel she passes that window again with the three crazy hats.

Now the story starts to develop between Ninotchka, or Garbo, and Melvyn Douglas, all sorts of little things that add up, but we haven't seen the change yet. She opens the window of her hotel room overlooking the Place Vendôme. It's beautiful, and she smiles. The three commissars come to her room. They're finally prepared to get down to work. But she says, "No, no, no, it's too beautiful to work. We have the rules, but they have the weather. Why don't you go to the races. It's Sunday. It's beautiful in Longchamps," and she gives them money to gamble.

As they leave for the track at Longchamps, she locks the door to the suite, then the door to the room. She goes back into the bedroom, opens a drawer, and out of the drawer she takes the craziest of the hats! She picks it up, puts it on, looks at herself in the mirror. That's it. Not a word. Nothing. But she has fallen into the trap of capitalism, and we know where we're going from there . . . all from a half page of description and one line of dialogue. "Beautiful weather. Why don't you go have yourselves a wonderful day?"

INTERVIEWER

He returned from the bathroom with all this?

WILDER

Yes, and it was like that whenever we were stuck. I guess now I feel he didn't go often enough.

You've indicated where Lubitsch got his ideas. Where do you get yours?

WILDER

I don't know. I just get them. Some of them in the toilet, I'm afraid. I have a black book here with all sorts of entries. A little bit of dialogue I've overheard. An idea for a character. A bit of background. Some boy-meets-girl scenarios.

While I was working with Mr. Lemmon for the first time on *Some Like It Hot*, I thought to myself, This guy's got a little bit of genius. I would love to make another picture with him, but I don't have a story. So I looked in my little black book and I came across a note about David Lean's movie *Brief Encounter*, that story about a married woman who lives in the country, comes to London, and meets a man. They have an affair in his friend's apartment. What I had written was, What about the friend who has to crawl back into that warm bed?

I had made that note ten years earlier, I couldn't touch it because of censorship, but suddenly there it was—*The Apartment*—all suggested by this note and by the qualities of an actor with whom I wanted to make my next picture. It was ideal for Lemmon, the combination of sweet and sour. I liked it when someone called that picture a dirty fairy tale.

INTERVIEWER

Sunset Boulevard?

WILDER

For a long time I wanted to do a comedy about Hollywood. God forgive me, I wanted to have Mae West and Marlon Brando. Look what became of that idea! Instead it became a tragedy of a silent-picture actress, still rich, but fallen down into the abyss after talkies. "I am big. It's the pictures that got small." I had that line early on.

Someplace else I had the idea for a writer who is down on his luck. It didn't quite fall into place until we got Gloria Swanson.

We had gone to Pola Negri first. We called her on the phone, and there was too much Polish accent. You see why some of these people didn't make the transition to sound. We went to Pickfair and visited Mary Pickford. Brackett began to tell her the story, because he was the more serious one. I stopped him: No, don't do it. I waved him off. She was going to be insulted if we told her she was to play a woman who begins a love affair with a man half her age. I said to her, We're very sorry, but it's no use. The story gets very vulgar.

Gloria Swanson had been a big star, in command of an entire studio. She worked with DeMille. Once she was dressed, her hair done to perfection, they placed her on a sedan and two strong men would carry her onto the set so no curl would be displaced. But later she did a couple of sound pictures that were terrible. When I gave her the script, she said, I *must* do this, and she turned out to be an absolute angel.

I used stars wherever I could in *Sunset Boulevard*. I used Cecil B. DeMille to play the big important studio director. I used Erich von Stroheim to play the director who directed the first pictures with Swanson, which he in fact did. I thought, Now, if there is a bridge game at the house of a silent star, and if I am to show that our hero, the writer, has been degraded to being the butler who cleans ashtrays, who would be there? I got Harry B. Warner, who played Jesus in DeMille's biblical pictures, Anna Q. Nilsson, and Buster Keaton, who was an excellent bridge player, a tournament player. The picture industry was only fifty or sixty years old, so some of the original people were still around. Because old Hollywood was dead, these people weren't exactly busy. They had the time, got some money, a little recognition. They were delighted to do it.

INTERVIEWER

Did you ever feel disappointed with your results, that the picture you had imagined or even written hadn't turned out?

WILDER

Sure, I've made blunders, for God's sake. Sometimes you lay an egg, and people will say, It was too early. Audiences weren't ready for it. Bullshit. If it's good, it's good. If it's bad, it's bad.

The tragedy of the picture maker, as opposed to the playwright, is that for the playwright the play debuts in Bedford, Massachusetts, and then you take it to Pittsburgh. If it stinks you bury it. If you examine the credits of Moss Hart or George Kaufman, no one ever brings up the play that bombed in the provinces and was buried after four shows.

With a picture that doesn't work, no matter how stupid and how bad, they're still going to try to squeeze every single penny out of it. You go home one night and turn on the TV and suddenly, there on television, staring back at you, on prime time, that lousy picture, that *thing*, is back! We don't bury our dead; we keep them around smelling badly.

INTERVIEWER

Is there one you have in mind?

WILDER

Don't make me. I may lose my breakfast.

Now, I do have to admit I was disappointed by the lack of success of some pictures I thought were good, such as *Ace in the Hole*. I liked the movie very much but it did not generate any "must-see" mood in audiences.

On the other hand, sometimes you'll have a rough time, and the film will turn out all right. On *Sabrina* I had a very rough time with Humphrey Bogart. It was the first time he'd worked with Paramount. Every evening after shooting, people would have a drink in my office, and a couple of times I forgot to invite him. He was very angry and never forgave me.

Sometimes when you finish a picture you just don't know whether it's good or bad. When Frank Capra was shooting Claudette Colbert in *It Happened One Night*, after the last shot she said, Will that be all Mr. Capra?

We're all done.

All right. Now why don't you go and fuck yourself. She thought the picture was shit, but she won the Academy Award for it.

So you're never quite sure how your work will be received or the course your career will take. We knew we'd gotten a strong reaction at the first big preview of *Sunset Boulevard*. After the screening, Barbara Stanwyck went up and kissed the hem of Gloria Swanson's robe, or dress, or whatever she was wearing that night. Gloria had given such an incredible performance. Then in the big Paramount screening room, Louis B. Mayer said loudly, We need to kick Wilder out of America if he's going to bite the hand that feeds him. He was with his contingent from MGM, the king then, but in front of all his department heads, I told him just what he could do. I walked out just as the reception was starting.

Although the movie was a great success, it was about Hollywood, exaggerated and dramatized, and it really hit a nerve. So on the way down the steps I had to pass all those people from MGM, the class studio . . . all those people who thought this picture would soil the taste of Hollywood.

After *Sunset Boulevard*, Brackett and I parted friends. Twelve years together, but the split had been coming. It's like a box of matches: you pick up the match and strike it against the box, and there's always fire, but then one day there is just one small corner of that abrasive paper left for you to strike the match on. It was not there anymore. The match wasn't striking. One of us said, Look, whatever I have to give and whatever you have to offer, it's just not enough. We can end on the good note of *Sunset Boulevard*. A picture that was revolutionary for its day.

INTERVIEWER

How do collaborators work together?

WILDER

Brackett and I used to share two offices together with a secretary in between. When we were writing he always laid down on the couch in my office while I would walk around with a stick in my hand.

Why the stick?

I don't know. I just needed something to keep my hands busy and a pencil wasn't long enough. He always had the yellow legal tablet, and he wrote in longhand, then we'd hand it to the secretary. Brackett and I would discuss everything, the picture as a whole, the curtain situations—first act, second act and then the end of the picture—and the curtain lines. Then we would break it down and go to a specific scene and discuss the mood and so forth, then we'd figure out what bit of the story we'd tell in those ten pages of the scene.

Was it the same working with I. A. L. Diamond?

Pretty much the same as with Brackett. Discuss the story, break it down into scenes, and then I would dictate and he would type. Or he would sit there thinking, and I would write on a yellow tablet and show it to him.

How's this? I'd say.

No. No good, he'd say. Never in an insistent way, however.

Or he might suggest something to me, and I'd shake my head. He'd just take it, tear it up, and put it in the wastebasket, and we'd never come back to it.

We had a great deal of trust in each other. But sometimes with writing you just can't tell, especially if you're writing under pressure. Diamond and I were writing the final scene of *Some Like It Hot* the week before we shot it. We'd come to the situation where Lemmon tries to convince Joe B. Brown that he cannot marry him.

"Why?" Brown says.

"Because I smoke!"

"That's all right as far as I'm concerned."

Finally Lemmon rips his wig off and yells at him, "I'm a boy! Because I'm a boy!"

Diamond and I were in our room working together, waiting for the next line—Joe B. Brown's response, the final line, the curtain line of the film—to come to us. Then I heard Diamond say, "Nobody's perfect." I thought about it and I said, Well, let's put in "Nobody's perfect" for now. But only for the time being. We have a whole week to think about it. We thought about it all week. Neither of us could come up with anything better, so we shot that line, still not entirely satisfied. When we screened the movie, that line got one of the biggest laughs I've ever heard in the theater. But we just hadn't trusted it when we wrote it; we just didn't see it. "Nobody's perfect." The line had come too easily, just popped out.

INTERVIEWER

I understand your collaboration with Raymond Chandler was more difficult?

WILDER

Yes. Chandler had never been inside a studio. He was writing for one of the hard-boiled serial magazines, *The Black Mask*—the original pulp fiction—and he'd been stringing tennis rackets to make ends meet. Just before then, James M. Cain had written *The Postman Always Rings Twice*, and then a similar story, *Double Indemnity*, which was serialized in three or four installments in the late *Liberty* magazine.

Paramount bought *Double Indemnity*, and I was eager to work with Cain, but he was tied up working on a picture at Fox called *Western Union*. A producer-friend brought me some Chandler stories from *The Black Mask*. You could see the man had a wonderful eye. I remember two lines from those stories especially: "Nothing is emptier than an empty swimming pool." The other is when Marlowe goes to Pasadena in the middle of the summer and drops in on a very old man who is sitting in a greenhouse covered in three blankets. He says, "Out of his ears grew hair long enough to catch a moth." A great eye . . . but then you don't know if that will work in pictures because the details in writing have to be photographable.

I said to Joe Sistrom, Let's give him a try. Chandler came into the studio, and we gave him the Cain story *Double Indemnity* to read. He came back the next day: I read that story. It's absolute shit! He hated Cain because of Cain's big success with *The Postman Always Rings Twice*.

He said, Well, I'll do it anyway. Give me a screenplay so I can familiarize myself with the format. This is Friday. Do you want it a week from Monday?

Holy shit, we said. We usually took five to six months on a script.

Don't worry, he said. He had no idea that I was not only the director but was supposed to write it with him.

He came back in ten days with eighty pages of absolute bullshit. He had some good phrases of dialogue, but they must have given him a script written by someone who wanted to be a director. He'd put in directions for fade-ins, dissolves, all kinds of camera moves to show he'd grasped the technique.

I sat him down and explained we'd have to work together. We always met at nine o'clock, and would quit at about four-thirty. I had to explain a lot to him as we went along, but he was very helpful to me. What we were doing together had real electricity. He was a very, very good writer—but not of scripts.

One morning, I'm sitting there in the office, ten o'clock and no Chandler. Eleven o'clock. At eleven-thirty, I called Joe Sistrom, the producer of *Double Indemnity*, and asked, What happened to Chandler?

I was going to call you. I just got a letter from him in which he resigns.

Apparently he had resigned because, while we were sitting in the office with the sun shining through, I had asked him to close the curtains and I had not said *please*. He accused me of having as many as three martinis at lunch. Furthermore, he wrote that he found it very disconcerting that Mr. Wilder gets two, three, sometimes even four calls from obviously young girls.

Naturally. I would take a phone call, three or four minutes, to say, Let's meet at that restaurant there, or, Let's go for a drink here. He was about twenty years older than I was, and his wife was older than him, elderly. And I was on the phone with *girls*! Sex was rampant then, but I was just looking out for myself. Later, in a biography he said all sorts of nasty things about me—that I was a Nazi, that I was uncooperative and rude, and God knows what. Maybe the antagonism even helped. He was a peculiar guy, but I was very glad to have worked with him.

INTERVIEWER

Why have so many novelists and playwrights from the East, people like F. Scott Fitzgerald and Dorothy Parker, had such a terrible time out here?

WILDER

Well, because they were hired for very big amounts of money. I remember those days in New York when one writer would say to the other, I'm broke. I'm going to go to Hollywood and steal another fifty thousand. Moreover, they didn't know what movie writing entailed. You have to know the rules before you break them, and they simply didn't school themselves. I'm not just talking about essayists or newspapermen; it was even the novelists. None of them took it seriously, and when they would be confronted by their superior, the producer or the director, who had a louder voice and the weight of the studio behind him, they were not particularly interested in taking advice. Their idea was, Well, crap, everybody in America has got a screenplay inside them—the policeman around the corner here, the waiter in Denver. *Everybody*. And his *sister*! I've seen ten movies. Now, if they would only let me do it my way . . . But it's not that easy. To begin to make even a mediocre film you have to learn the rules. You have to know about timing, about creating characters, a little about camera position, just enough to know if what you're suggesting is possible. They pooh-poohed it.

I remember Fitzgerald when he was working at Paramount and I was there working with Brackett. Brackett, who was from the East, had written novels and plays, and had been at Paramount for years. Brackett and I used to take breaks and go to a little coffee joint across the street from the studio. Oblath's! we used to say. The only place in the world you can get a greasy Tom Collins. Whenever we saw Scott Fitzgerald there, we'd talk with him, but he never once asked us anything about writing screenplays.

Pictures are something like plays. They share an architecture and a spirit. A good picture writer is a kind of poet, but a poet who plans his structure like a craftsman and is able to tell what's wrong with the third act. What a veteran screenwriter produces might not be good, but it would be technically correct; if he has a problem in the third act he certainly knows to look for the seed of the problem in the first act. Scott just didn't seem particularly interested in any of these matters.

INTERVIEWER

Faulkner seemed to have his difficulties too.

WILDER

I heard he was hired by MGM, was at the studio for three months, quit and went back home; MGM never figured it out and they kept sending the checks down to Mississippi. A friend of mine was hired by MGM to do a script and he inherited the office where Faulkner had been working. In the desk he found a yellow legal pad with three words on it: Boy. Girl. Policeman. But Faulkner did some work.

At some point he worked with Howard Hawks on *To Have and Have Not*, and he cowrote *The Land of the Pharaohs*. On that movie they went way over schedule with production and far past their estimated costs. On screen, there were thousands of slaves dragging enormous stones to build the pyramids. It was like an ant heap. When they finally finished the film and screened it for Jack Warner, Warner said to Hawks, Well, Howard, if all the people who are in the picture come to see it, we may break even.

But there were other writers out here who were clever and good and made a little fortune. The playwrights Ben Hecht and Charles MacArthur, for example. Hecht truly endeared himself to the people he worked with. A producer or director would be in a jam . . . the set built, the leads hired, the shooting begun, only to admit to themselves finally that the script they had was unusable. They would bring out Hecht, and he would lie in bed at Charles Lederer's house and on a yellow tablet produce a pile of sheets, a screenplay ready to go. They'd take that night's pages from Hecht's hands, forward them to Mr. Selznick, who'd fiddle with them, have the pages mimeographed and put in the actor's hands by morning. It was a crazy way to work, but Hecht took the work very seriously, though not as seriously as he would a play of his. They call that sort of thing script doctoring. If Hecht had wanted, he could have had credit on a hundred more pictures.

INTERVIEWER

Does the script you've written change as you direct it?

WILDER

As someone who directed scripts that I myself had cowritten, what I demanded from actors was very simple: learn your lines.

That reminds me. George Bernard Shaw was directing a production of his play *Pygmalion*, with a very well-known illustrious actor, Sir Something. The fellow came to rehearsal, a little bit drunk, and he began to invent a little. Shaw listened for a while and then yelled, Stop! For Christ's sake, why the hell didn't you learn the script?

Sir Something said, What on earth are you talking about? I know my lines.

Shaw screamed back at him, Yes, you know *your* lines, but you don't know *my* lines.

On a picture, I would ask the actors to know their lines. Sometimes they would study the part at night and might ask me to come by to discuss things. In the morning, we would sit in chairs around a long table off to the side and read the day's scene once more. It was wonderful to work with some actors. Jack Lemmon. If we were to start at nine, he'd be there at eight-fifteen with a mug of coffee and his pages from the night before. He'd say, Last night I was running lines with

Felicia—his wife—and had this wonderful idea. What do you think here? And he'd go on. It might be wonderful and we'd use it, or I might just look at him, and then he'd say, Well, I don't like it either. He worked hard and had many ideas, but he never was interfering.

Sometimes I'd have an actor so stubborn that I'd say, All right, let's do it two ways. We'd do it my way, and I'd say to my assistant, Print that. Then to the actor, All right, now your way. We'd do it his way with no celluloid in the camera.

INTERVIEWER

What was it like working as a writer for a studio?

WILDER

When I was a writer at Paramount, the studio had a swarm of writers under contract—a hundred and four! They worked in the Writers Building, the Writers Annex, and the Writers Annex Annex. All of us were writing! We were not getting big salaries but we were writing. It was fun. We made a little money. Some like Ben Hecht made a lot of money. All the writers were required to hand in eleven pages every Thursday. Why on Thursday? Who knows? Why eleven pages? Who knows? Over a thousand pages a week were being written.

It was all very tightly controlled. We even worked on Saturdays from nine until noon, knocking off half a day so we could watch USC or UCLA play football in the Coliseum. When the unions negotiated the workweek back to five days, the executives ran around screaming the studio was going to go broke.

There was one guy at the studio whom all the writers turned in their work to—a Yale man who was at *Life* when his classmates Henry Luce and Briton Haddon founded the magazine. Everyone at the start of the magazine had the option of getting something like seventy-five dollars a week or part of his salary in *Time* stock. Some buildings at Yale were built by people who went for the stock. Our guy at Paramount used to say proudly, I went for the cash.

INTERVIEWER

What happened to the thousand-plus pages a week that were being generated?

WILDER

Most of the writing just gathered dust. There were five or six producers, each specializing in different kinds of pictures. They would read the writing over the weekend and make comments.

INTERVIEWER

What were the producers' comments like?

WILDER

I was talking once with a writer who had worked at Columbia who showed me a script that had just been read by Samuel Briskin, one of the big men at that studio. I looked at the script. On every page, there was at the bottom just one word: *improve*.

INTERVIEWER

Like *The New Yorker* editor Harold Ross's imperative "make better."

WILDER

That would be one word too many for these producers. Just *improve*.

INTERVIEWER

What about the "Scheherazades" one hears about?

WILDER

They were the guys who would tell producers stories, or the plots of screenplays and books. There was one guy who never wrote a word but who came up with ideas. One of them was: San Francisco. 1906 earthquake. Nelson Eddy. Jeanette McDonald.

Great! Terrific! Cheers from the producers. A film came out of that sentence.

Do you know how Nelson Eddy ended up with his name? He was Eddie Nelson. He just reversed it. Don't laugh! Eddie Nelson is nothing. Nelson Eddy was a star.

The studio era was of course very different from today. There were many different fiefdoms scattered around town, each producing its own sort of picture. The Paramount people would not converse with the MGM people, wouldn't even see each other. The MGM people especially would not consort for dinner or even lunch with the people from Fox.

One night before I was to begin *One, Two, Three* I had dinner at the home of Mr. and Mrs. William Goetz, who always had wonderful food. I was seated next to Mrs. Edie Goetz, Louis Mayer's younger daughter, and she asked what sort of picture I was going to make. I told her it was set in Berlin and we'd be shooting in Germany.

Who plays the lead?

Jimmy Cagney. As it happens, it was his last picture except for that cameo in *Ragtime*.

She said, Who?

Jimmy Cagney. You know, the little gangster who for years was in all those Warner Brothers . . .

Oh! Daddy didn't allow us to watch Warner Brothers pictures. She had no idea who he was.

Back then, each studio had a certain look. You could walk in in the middle of a picture and tell what studio it was. Warner Brothers were mostly gangster movies. For a while Universal did a lot of horror pictures. MGM you knew because everything was white. Mr. Cedric Gibbons, the head of production design, wanted everything white silk no matter where it was set. If MGM had produced Mr. Scorsese's *Mean Streets*, Cedric Gibbons would have designed all of Little Italy in white.

INTERVIEWER

Film really is considered a director's medium, isn't it?

WILDER

Film's thought of as a director's medium because the director creates the end product that appears on the screen. It's that stupid auteur theory again, that the director is the author of the film. But what does the director shoot—the telephone book? Writers became much more important when sound came in, but they've had to put up a valiant fight to get the credit they deserve.

Recently, the Writers' Guild has negotiated with the studios to move the writer's credit to a place just before the director's, a more prominent position, bumping aside the producers. The producers are screaming! You look at an ad in the papers and they are littered with the names of producers: A So-and-So and So-and-So Production, Produced by Another Four Names! Executive Producer Somebody Else. Things are slowly changing. But even so the position of a writer working with a studio is not secure, certainly nothing like a writer working in the theater in New York. There a playwright sits in his seat in the empty parquet during rehearsals, right alongside the director, and together they try to make the production flow. If there is a problem, they have a little talk. The director says to the writer, Is it all right if the guy who says, Good morning. How are you? instead enters without saying anything? And the playwright says, No! "Good morning. How are you?" stays. And it stays.

Nobody consults the movie writer. In production, they just go wildly ahead. If the star has another picture coming up, and they need to finish the picture by Monday, they'll just tear out ten pages. To make it work somehow, they add a few stupid lines.

In the studio era, screenwriters were always on the losing end in battles with the director or the studio. Just to show you the impotence of the screenwriter then, I'll tell you a story from before I became a director. Brackett and I were writing a picture called *Hold Back the Dawn*. Back then, no writer was allowed on the set. If the actors and the director weren't interpreting the script correctly, if they didn't have the accent on the right word when they were delivering a gag, if they didn't know where the humor was, a writer might very well pipe up. A director would feel that the writer was creating a disruption.

For *Hold Back the Dawn*, we had written a story about a man trying to immigrate into the U.S. without the proper papers. Charles Boyer, who played the lead, is at rope's end, destitute, stranded in a filthy hotel—the Esperanza—across the border, near Mexicali or Calexico. He is lying in this lousy bed, holding a walking stick, when he sees a cockroach walk up the wall and onto a mirror hanging on the wall. Boyer sticks the end of the walking stick in front of the cockroach and says, "Wait a minute, you. Where are you going? Where are your papers? You haven't got them? Then you can't enter." The cockroach tries to walk around the stick, and the Boyer character keeps stopping it.

One day Brackett and I were having lunch across the street from Paramount. We were in the middle of writing the third act of the picture. As we left our table to walk out, we saw Boyer, the star, seated at a table, his little French lunch spread out before him, his napkin tucked in just so, a bottle of red wine open on the table. We stopped by and said, Charles, how are you?

Oh, fine. Thank you.

Although we were still working on the script, Mitchell Leisen had already begun to direct the production. I said, And what are you shooting today, Charles?

We're shooting this scene where I'm in bed and . . .

Oh! The scene with the cockroach! That's a wonderful scene.

Yes, well, we didn't use the cockroach.

Didn't use the cockroach? Oh, Charles, why not?

Because the scene is idiotic. I have told Mr. Leisen so, and he agreed with me. How do you suppose a man can talk to some *thing* that cannot answer you? Then Boyer looked out the window. That was all. End of discussion. As we walked back to the studio to continue to write the third act, I said to Brackett, That son of a bitch. If he doesn't talk to the cockroach, he doesn't talk to *anybody*! We gave him as few lines as possible . . . wrote him right out of the third act.

INTERVIEWER

Was that one of the reasons you became a director, the difficulty of protecting the writing?

WILDER

That was certainly one of the reasons. I don't come from the theater or any dramatic school like the Strasberg school, and I didn't particularly have ambitions to be a director, to be a despot of the
soundstage. I just wanted to protect the script. It's not that I had a vision or theory I wanted to express as a director; I had no signature or
style, except for what I learned from when I was working with Lubitsch and from analyzing his pictures—to do things as elegantly and
as simply as possible.

INTERVIEWER

If you'd always had more respectful directors, such as Lubitsch,
would you have become a director?

WILDER

Absolutely not. Lubitsch would have directed my scripts considerably better and more clearly than I. Lubitsch or Ford or Cukor. They
were very good directors, but one wasn't always assured of working
with directors like that.

INTERVIEWER

I see Federico Fellini on your wall of photos.

WILDER

He also was a writer who became a director. I like *La Strada*, the
first one with his wife, a lot. And I loved *La Dolce Vita*.

Up above that picture is a photo of myself, Mr. Akira Kurosawa,
and Mr. John Huston. Like Mr. Fellini and me, they too were writers
who became directors. That picture was taken at the presentation of
the Academy Award for best picture some years back.

The plan for the presentation was for three writer-directors to
hand out the award—John Huston, Akira Kurosawa, and myself.
Huston was in a wheelchair and on oxygen for his emphysema. He
had terrible breathing problems. But we were going to make him get
up to join us on stage. They had the presentation carefully orches-

trated so they could have Huston at the podium first, and then he would have forty-five seconds before he would have to get back to his wheelchair and put the oxygen mask on.

Jane Fonda arrived with the envelope and handed it to Mr. Huston. Huston was to open the envelope and give it to Kurosawa. Kurosawa was to fish the piece of paper with the name of the winner out of the envelope and hand it to me, then I was to read the winner's name. Kurosawa was not very agile, it turned out, and when he reached his fingers into the envelope, he fumbled and couldn't grab hold of the piece of paper with the winner's name on it. All the while I was sweating it out; three hundred million people around the world were watching and waiting. Mr. Huston only had about ten seconds before he'd need more oxygen.

While Mr. Kurosawa was fumbling with the piece of paper, I almost said something that would have finished me. I almost said to him, Pearl Harbor you could find! Fortunately, he produced the slip of paper, and I didn't say it. I read the name of the winner aloud. I forget now which picture won—*Gandhi* or *Out of Africa*. Mr. Huston moved immediately toward the wings, and backstage to the oxygen.

Mr. Huston made a wonderful picture that year, *Prizzi's Honor*, that was also up for the Best Picture Award. If he had won, we would have had to give him more oxygen to recover before he could come back and accept. I voted for *Prizzi's Honor*. I voted for Mr. Huston.

Issue 138, 1996

Jack Gilbert

The Art of Poetry

O n the rare occasions when Jack Gilbert gives public readings—
whether in New York, Pittsburgh, or San Francisco—it is not
unusual for men and women in the audience to tell him how his poems have saved their lives. At these gatherings, one may also hear wild
stories about Gilbert: he was a junkie, he was homeless, he was married numerous times. In reality, he has never been addicted to drugs,
has been impoverished but never homeless, and was married only
once. The fascination with Gilbert is a response, above all, to the
power of his poetry, but it also reflects the mystique of a life lived utterly without regard for the conventions of literary fortune and fame.

Gilbert was born in Pittsburgh in 1925. He failed out of high
school and worked as an exterminator and door-to-door salesman before being admitted, thanks to a clerical error, to the University of
Pittsburgh. There he met the poet Gerald Stern, his exact contemporary. Gilbert started writing poetry, he says, because Stern did. After
college he traveled to Paris and worked briefly at the *Herald Tribune*
before spending several years in Italy, where he met Gianna Gelmetti,
the first great love of his life. But Gelmetti's family, recognizing that
Gilbert would never provide her with much financial or domestic security, persuaded him to end the relationship and he returned to
America—first to San Francisco and then to New York—where his career as a poet began.

In 1962 Gilbert's first book, *Views of Jeopardy*, won the Yale
Younger Poets Prize and was considered for the Pulitzer Prize along-

THE GREAT DEBATE

WHO WOULD WANT TO BE
THINKING DAY AND NIGHT?
THE YOUNG MAN ASKED.
EATING HIS CHICKEN AWKWARDLY
IN THE BEAUTIFUL COOL SHADE.
ME, I SAID, BEFORE I COULD
PREVENT IT. STOP MYSELF
AND HEARD HOW THAT SOUNDED.
BUT KNEW WHAT WOULD HAPPEN
IF I ADDED TO ~~ANOTHER REMARK~~ QUALIFIED IT ~~SOMEONE~~
ME, I SAID AGAIN. BUT HE
WAS ALREADY TALKING ABOUT
HOW HIS DOCTOR CURED HIS KNEE
WITH MAGIC.
(AND HOW STUPID AMERICANS ~~ARE~~

~~JULY~~ JUNE 16, 1979

THE GREAT DEBATE

Who would want to be thinking day and night?
the young man ~~asked~~ said, eating his chicken ~~awkwardly~~
in the beautiful cool shade. Me, I said
before I could stop myself. Heard how ~~that~~ it sounded
but knew what would happen if I qualified it.
Me, I said again, but he was already talking
about how a doctor had cured his knee with magic.

Two manuscript drafts of an unpublished Jack Gilbert poem.

side collections by Robert Frost and William Carlos Williams. *The New York Times* called Gilbert "inescapably gifted," Theodore Roethke and Stanley Kunitz praised his candor and control, and Stephen Spender hailed his work as "witty, serious, and skillful." He was photographed for *Glamour* and *Vogue*, and was widely feted by the literary establishment. Although he continued to write, he did not publish again for almost twenty years.

In 1966 Gilbert left the country with his companion, the poet Linda Gregg. They lived in Greece, on the islands of Paros and Santorini, and for a brief period in Denmark and England. "All Jack ever wanted to know was that he was awake—that the trees in bloom were almond trees—and to walk down the road to get breakfast," Gregg, who remains close to Gilbert, says. "He never cared if he was poor or had to sleep on a park bench." After five years overseas, the couple returned to San Francisco, where they separated. Gilbert soon met and married Michiko Nogami, a sculptor twenty-one years younger than him. They settled in Japan and Gilbert taught at Rikkyo University until 1975, when he was appointed chief lecturer on American literature for the U.S. State Department and he embarked with Nogami on a fifteen-country tour. In 1982, at the insistence of his friend and editor Gordon Lish, Gilbert published a second book, *Monolithos*. That same year, Nogami died of cancer. She was thirty-six. Gilbert published a series of poems dedicated to her in a memorial chapbook, *Kochan*, and then, again, went silent—this time for a decade, during which he lived intermittently in Northampton, Massachusetts; San Francisco; and Florida.

The speaker in the poems of Gilbert's third collection, *The Great Fires: Poems, 1982–1992*, often asks to be given a second chance: "Let me fall / in love one last time, I beg them. / Teach me mortality, frighten me / into the present. Help me to find / the heft of these days." *The Great Fires* received many accolades and earned Gilbert a Lannan Literary Award. He did not publish again until last year, when *The New Yorker* presented eight of his poems over seven months in the run-up to the publication of his fourth book, *Refusing Heaven*. "Jack rises up like an eel," says Alice Quinn, *The New Yorker*'s poetry editor. "He dictates how and when the world sees his poems." In the new book, Gilbert's work expresses a deep satisfaction in the ephemeral nature of life: "We look up at the stars and they are / not there. We see memory / of when they were, once upon a time. / And that too is more than enough."

Gilbert now lives a modest, solitary life in Northampton, where he rents a room in the home of a friend, Henry Lyman. It is a cedar-shingled house that looks out over a winding river and a vast meadow—an idyllic spot that Gilbert says brings him great comfort. This interview took place there in two sessions, in January and in July of this year. Gilbert, who is eighty, appeared frail—his hair white and windswept—but his eyes were startlingly bright. On both occasions, we had the same lunch that he and Lyman have almost every day: bruschetta with smoked salmon. Gilbert's voice was high-pitched and he was hesitant to talk about himself. Instead he wanted to know where I was from, what I'd studied, what I wanted from life and from him. When the subject turned back to his work, he admitted that he hopes his poems give people a sense of possibilities.

—*Sarah Fay, 2005*

INTERVIEWER

You once said that you were the only person you knew who left Pittsburgh a true romantic—one who woke up happy, though aware of his mortality, every day.

JACK GILBERT

It's true—it wasn't easy in Pittsburgh. But I'm sure there were others.

INTERVIEWER

Did you ever think you would live this long?

GILBERT

I once dreamed that I'd live to be sixty. In those days that was how old you could live to be. But many of my ancestors lived to a hundred. I have this mechanism, this body, which has been so kind to me. I've never been in a hospital, except once—I fell.

There's a poem about that, "All the Way from There to Here."

GILBERT

I was supposed to die. I fell head down from ninety feet. When I didn't die right away, they let me go home. I insisted because it was Christmas. If I was going to die, I wanted to die under the Christmas tree with Linda. I still didn't die. But I couldn't support my own torso because I'd broken my spine and chest. Linda and I wanted to go to Europe, so I had them build something that was like an exoskeleton. After saying good-bye to the doctors, I walked toward the door with Linda and when I got halfway there the doctor in charge said, Oh, one thing. If you feel a little bit of tingling in your fingers, that will mean that the paralysis has started. That never happened. So I've been blessed.

INTERVIEWER

What were you doing ninety feet up?

GILBERT

Showing off. I was with Linda and her father didn't approve at all. I mean, he was resentful that I was bedding his daughter without any official rights. On Christmas Day we went up on his mountain to find a tree that would suit Linda. We were walking along and he was be-having himself. We kept walking until we came to these trees. He was crazy about nature. He said, You know, if you cut off the top of that tree—if you could cut just the top—the tree wouldn't die, and it would make it a more attractive tree without that spindly, weak top.

Being the bad guy with his lovely daughter, I immediately took the rope and saw and started climbing. I didn't know anything about it. I knew a lot about apple trees because I'd spent time in an orchard. But not a forest. I was way up there. I climbed to the top, but I'm no fool—I tied myself to the trunk. I thought I would tug on the treetop until it snapped, except in the middle of doing this there was a big gust of wind that snapped the thing, and it fell on me and was pushing me down. I was all right at first because I had tied myself in, except after a while—they couldn't get to me quickly enough—my thighs started to give way. I was heroic about it, but my thighs gave way, and the rope too. I plummeted down, shearing off the branches. I was going so fast that the speed just butchered the tree. Luckily I landed on dirt.

INTERVIEWER

How was it that you knew about apple trees?

GILBERT

I spent two summers on my grandparents' farm. And when I was thirteen, we lived in a huge house on the outskirts of Pittsburgh. I don't know if my father stole it—this was during the Depression. During the day, my mother and father went into town, leaving my siblings and me all alone in this magnificent house, three stories high and no one there but us. We played on the roof, in the laundry chutes. It was extraordinarily dangerous. It was lovely, legendary. We owned that little world. In the back of the house were two orchards, one filled with peaches, the other with apples. We were always in the apple trees—frequently falling down.

INTERVIEWER

Do you think you would have become a poet if you'd stayed in Pittsburgh?

GILBERT

Why not? I was kind of a strange boy to be in Pittsburgh. I spent so much time reading. Even if I started a book that was boring, it was almost impossible for me not to finish it. I couldn't get the story out of my head until I knew what happened. I had such curiosity. And you might not think it, but the power of Pittsburgh, the grandeur, those three great rivers, was magnificent. Even working in the steel mills. You can't work in a steel mill and think small. Giant converters hundreds of feet high. Every night, the sky looked enormous. It was a torrent of flames—of fire. The place that Pittsburgh used to be had such scale. My father never brought home three pounds of potatoes. He always came home with crates of things. Everything was grand, heroic. Everything seemed to be gigantic in Pittsburgh—the people, the history. Sinuousness. Power. Substance. Meaningfulness.

INTERVIEWER

Can you name some of your early influences?

GILBERT

Almost any book in the library—knights saving ladies, cowboys trying to kill the bad guy. I just devoured books; each new story opened a new vista.

INTERVIEWER

Were you surprised when your first book, *Views of Jeopardy*, won the Yale Younger Poets Prize and was considered for the Pulitzer?

GILBERT

Sure. It was an accident.

INTERVIEWER

Is it true that they couldn't find you to tell you that you'd won?

GILBERT

It was more of an accident than that. I had gone to Italy and fallen in love—for the first time—with an extraordinarily beautiful woman, but her sister convinced me that I should give her up. She said, You're never going to hold a job. You're not going to be able to support Gianna. She should have babies. Gianna was made to have babies. And it was true.

But that was an awful thing for me to do; I should have talked it over with Gianna.

Anyhow, I was gathering all of my things to leave Italy. Gianna's brother-in-law—Cleve Moffet, a writer—had an application for some kind of competition. He talked about it but decided he wasn't going to do anything with it. When he got up to go to lunch he picked up the form and threw it in my lap saying, You should do it. I forgot about it until I was leaving to go back to America. The application must have gotten mixed in with the stuff I was packing. When I got to New York and was throwing things away, I must have found it and sent it in. I don't know. I forgot about it.

Later, I was living in the East Village and this one night there was pounding on the door and there was Cleve standing in the hall. He was agitated and said, They're looking all over for you. I asked who, and he explained that somebody wanted to give me the Yale prize. I didn't know what to do, how to express it. I took him out with my two friends and we had milkshakes.

The next day I roamed about trying to find a way to feel about what had happened. I finally lay down under the Brooklyn Bridge to try to feel something. I lay there all afternoon, and then I called the people at Yale.

INTERVIEWER

The journal *Genesis West*—or its editor Gordon Lish—devoted its fall 1962 issue to you. Theodore Roethke, Stephen Spender, Muriel Rukeyser, Stanley Kunitz, and others sang your praises. You were only thirty-seven years old. Did that influence you and your work?

GILBERT

It was shockingly generous. It pleased me. Gordon Lish kindly pushed me. I was proud and grateful, but it didn't change my work much. I enjoyed those six months of being famous. Fame is a lot of fun, but it's not interesting. I loved being noticed and praised, even the banquets. But they didn't have anything that I wanted. After about six months, I found it boring. There were so many things to do, to live. I didn't want to be praised all of the time—I liked the idea but I didn't invest much in it.

INTERVIEWER

You went abroad soon afterwards—to Greece on a Guggenheim Fellowship. Did success influence your decision to go? Were you running away from something?

GILBERT

It wasn't that. I didn't want to stay in New York and go to dinners. I was also puzzled by the fact that so many of the established poets didn't like each other. There's competition, naturally—and naturally you relate to someone who can promote you. That's not awful; that's the way the world works. It's just not the way I work. But don't get me wrong, what they're doing—these meetings where they give each other prizes—I think it's wonderful.

INTERVIEWER

Really?

GILBERT

Yes. The people who are famous have earned it; they've earned it to an extraordinary degree. They've given their lives to it, they're professionals, they work hard, and they raise families. And they're very smart, they stay at their desks all the time—they send out everything. They teach, which is not easy. What they do is important, but there's no way that I would use my life for that.

INTERVIEWER

So you lived abroad.

GILBERT

Many times.

INTERVIEWER

For much of your life. You lived in Japan, Italy, Greece, Denmark, England . . .

GILBERT

Lots more.

INTERVIEWER

Do you think it's important for American writers to live abroad?

GILBERT

At least at some point—so you have something to compare to what you think is normal, and you encounter things you aren't used to. One of the great dangers is familiarity.

INTERVIEWER

Is that a danger overseas too? Last summer you went back to Greece.

GILBERT

Linda wanted to finish a book she had been writing; she asked me to go with her. So we went to Paros. Unfortunately, we found the Greece we knew was no longer there. Our Greece was wonderfully bucolic. Very quiet, peaceful, slow, friendly—farmers plowing, a couple of men in small boats, almost no electronics. A civilization that lasted four hundred years is gone now. Gone the way Paris is gone, the way Italy is gone. All gone. Everything that I dreamed of is gone. It was such a blessing to get over there when it still was. All of the things that I loved were on the brink of disappearing without my knowing it. You can't go to Paris anymore; it's not there. Greece and Japan aren't there anymore. The places I've loved no longer exist.

INTERVIEWER

What's there instead?

GILBERT

Mechanisms mostly. Europe is now rich, busy, and modern.

INTERVIEWER

When you were abroad, did you consider yourself an expatriate?

GILBERT

No. You have to understand I didn't visit places; I lived places. It makes all the difference in the world.

INTERVIEWER

Was it a solitary existence?

GILBERT

Well, of course at times it was lonely, but I don't think it bothered me much. I've been very lucky. A large part of my life I've been with someone—girlfriends, male friends. They're very, very important to me. I've been blessed by knowing and being with them.

INTERVIEWER

How did your foreign settings—those places—figure into your poems?

GILBERT

It's more how those places resonate in me. Rather than writing a poem about those places, they create something I write about.

INTERVIEWER

Did being removed from the literary community benefit you?

GILBERT

Sure.

INTERVIEWER

What did you like most about it?

GILBERT

Paying attention to being alive. This is hard—when I try to explain, it sounds false. But I don't know any other way to say it. I'm so grateful. There's nothing I've wanted that I haven't had. Michiko dying, I regret terribly, and losing Linda's love, I regret equally. And not doing some of the things I wanted to do. But I still feel grateful. It's almost unfair to have been as happy as I've been. I didn't earn it; I had a lot of luck. But I was also very, very stubborn. I was determined to get what I wanted as a life.

Do you think that your idea of happiness differs from most people's idea of happiness?

GILBERT

Sure. I'm vain enough to think that I've made a successful life. I've had everything I've ever wanted. You can't beat that.

INTERVIEWER

When you lived overseas, did you get up every day and write?

GILBERT

If I was in an extraordinary place, I didn't want to take out my notebook and start writing down what the front of the pagoda looked like. I wanted to experience it before I wrote it down.

INTERVIEWER

What is the most exotic place you ever lived?

GILBERT

The jungle in Bali.

INTERVIEWER

Why?

GILBERT

If you don't know, I can't tell you.

INTERVIEWER

When did you stop traveling?

GILBERT

I don't think I've stopped. Traveling became more difficult about a year ago, but Linda and I went to Greece again. And this year, we'll probably go someplace else.

A couple of decades ago, I finished going all the way around the world. And after that I suddenly realized I had lived all of my dreams. I had lots of them and I've fulfilled them all. Now it's time to live the adult dreams, if I can find them. The others were dreams from childhood—first love and such, which is wonderful. It's interesting to discover that we don't have adult dreams—pleasure and pride, but not really adult dreams.

Let me try to explain. I have a poem, "Trying to Have Something Left Over," in which I've been unfaithful to my wife and she knows it and she's mad. It's the last night and I'm going to say good-bye to Anna, the other woman. She's had a baby—not by me—and her husband has left her because he couldn't take all that muck of a baby being born. This is the last night I'll ever see her and I feel incredibly tender and grateful and loving toward her. And we're not in bed—previously we had a wild relationship. Anyway, here's the last night to say good-bye. She's cleaning house quietly and sadly, and I'm entertaining her boy, her baby, throwing him up in the air and catching him. It's a poem about that. Sad and tender. A truly adult dream. Profound tenderness.

That's what I like to write as poems. Not because it's sad, but because it matters. So much poetry that's written today doesn't need to be written. I don't understand the need for trickery or some new way of arranging words on a page. You're allowed to do that. You're allowed to write all kinds of poetry, but there's a whole world out there.

INTERVIEWER

What are some other adult dreams?

GILBERT

For a year and a half, I tried to figure that out. I had lived all of my youthful dreams, but I couldn't think of many adult ones. I finally realized that we don't have many dreams for adults because historically people have always died much younger than they do today. People died at forty-two. They died young. I think I've only found two other adult dreams.

What are they?

I'm not going to tell.

How did you start writing?

I started writing poetry because I finally got to go to college and I met Gerald Stern. We started hanging out together. I was interested in writing novels, but he was always talking about poetry—usually poetry, sometimes fiction. We were competitive with each other. So I decided I would write poetry for a semester and then go back to writing novels. I never went back. I mean, I've written prose. I've written several novels that no one has seen. Well, one was published.

My Mother Taught Me, an erotic novel, wasn't it?

It's about sexuality. You have to understand, people were writing sex books but no one was writing them well. I thought pornography should be as much of a genre as cowboy stories. But pornography is boring. Childish. Unhealthy. I thought, Why not have a novel of sexuality that's not paralyzed by the need for orgasm? So I wrote a good pornographic novel to show it could be done. An enjoyment rather than a momentary excitement. There were so many pornographic novels written; why weren't they effective? A momentary spasm. Some people will have an orgasm if you say a dirty word or say, What he did to her body was . . . But what if you approach it as a real novel? The idea of entertainment intrigued me at the time—so I wrote one.

INTERVIEWER

Did writing poetry come easily for you?

GILBERT

Yes. During that period it was mostly instinct. Stories were important to me. Novels were very important to me.

INTERVIEWER

Do you think reading novels taught you how to write poems?

GILBERT

I think the scope of novels—the sense of the lives of the characters in the books I read—came naturally to me.

INTERVIEWER

Did school influence you as a young writer?

GILBERT

No, I failed high school; I got into college by mistake. I failed freshman English eight times. I was interested in learning, but I wanted to understand too, which meant I was fighting with the teachers all the time. Everybody accepted the fact that I was smart but I wouldn't obey. I didn't believe what they said unless they could prove it.

INTERVIEWER

Was your defiance—your resistance—ultimately an advantage?

GILBERT

Yes and no. It takes much longer if you have to find it all and do it all for yourself. My mind was not available for the impress of teachers or other people's styles. The other arts were important to me. At one time I was working in photography with Ansel Adams. He offered to help me with my photographs if I would help him write his books, which was fine until we ran short of money and the woman I was with finally said she was tired of cooking pancakes.

How did you get involved with Ansel Adams?

GILBERT

I was teaching a class and some of his students got to know me. I wish I'd been able to continue working with him, but it was either him or the woman. I chose the woman. After that I went to Italy and everything went into my falling in love for the first time. I did some painting there and won a fourth prize. I wish I had continued with painting *and* photography—novels too. But I was excited.

INTERVIEWER

What was Ansel Adams like?

GILBERT

Very German.

INTERVIEWER

Have you ever looked to other writers for inspiration?

GILBERT

I liked many writers but never found a teacher.

INTERVIEWER

In your interview with Gordon Lish in *Genesis West*, you say that there are two kinds of poetry. On the one hand, there are poems that give delight; on the other, there are poems that do something else. What do you mean by "something else"?

GILBERT

I think serious poems should make something happen that's not correct or entertaining or clever. I want something that matters to my heart, and I don't mean "Linda left me." I don't want that. I'll write that poem, but that's not what I'm talking about. I'm talking about being in danger—as we all are—of dying. How can you spend your life on games or intricately accomplished things? And politics? Politics is fine. There's a place to care for the injustice of the world, but that's not what the poem is about. The poem is about the heart. Not the heart as in "I'm in love" or "my girl cheated on me"—I mean the conscious heart, the fact that we are the only things in the entire universe that know true consciousness. We're the only things—leaving religion out of it—we're the only things in the world that know spring is coming.

INTERVIEWER

How do you start a poem?

GILBERT

There's no one way. Sometimes I'm walking along the street and I find it there. Sometimes it's something I've been thinking about. Sometimes it's an apparition.

INTERVIEWER

How do you know when you've finished one?

GILBERT

If I'm writing well it comes to an end with an almost-audible click. When I started out I wouldn't write a poem until I knew the first line and the last line and what it was about and what would make it a success. I was a tyrant and I was good at it. But the most important day in my career as a writer was when Linda said, Did you ever think of listening to your poems? And my poetry changed. I didn't give up making precreated poetry, but you have to write a poem the way you ride a horse—you have to know what to do with it. You have to be in charge of a horse or it will eat all day—you'll never get back to the barn. But if you tell the horse how to be a horse, if you force it, the horse will probably break a leg. The horse and rider have to be together.

INTERVIEWER

Is that why your style is unadorned and not ornamental?

Oh, I like ornament at the right time, but I don't want a poem to be made out of decoration. If you like that kind of poetry, more power to you, but it doesn't interest me. When I read the poems that matter to me, it stuns me how much the presence of the heart—in all its forms—is endlessly available there. To experience ourselves in an important way just knocks me out. It puzzles me why people have given that up for cleverness. Some of them are ingenious, more ingenious than I am, but so many of them aren't any good at being alive.

You once likened it to a poet giving birth without ever getting pregnant.

Yes. A lot of poets don't have any poems to write. After their first book, what are they going to do? They can't keep saying their hearts are broken. They start to write poems about childhood. Then what do they do? Some of it is just academic poetry—they learn how to write the poem perfectly. But I don't think anybody should be criticized because their taste is different from mine. Such poems are extraordinarily deft. There's a lot of art in them. But I don't understand where the meat is. I don't know what I'm supposed to do with this kind of poetry. It won't change my life, so why should I read it? Why should I write it?

By the time some writers—particularly poets—are twenty-seven or twenty-eight they've often used up the germinal quality that is their writing, the thing that is their heart. Not for the great poets, but for many poets this is true. The inspiration starts to wane. Many have learned enough to cover that with devices or technique or they just go back and write the same stories about their childhood over and over. It's why so much poetry feels artificial.

Do you think this has anything to do with the fact that so many poets come out of M.F.A. programs and go right on to teach?

GILBERT

If I answer that I'll get into a rant, but I'll tell you—I think poetry was killed by money. When I started out, no poet in America could make a living in poetry except Ogden Nash. And he did it with light verse.

INTERVIEWER

Why?

GILBERT

Because people weren't interested in the poetry of that time. Poetry is an unnatural art, as my mother said to me one day. She had been reading some of my poems and said, Jack, why do you do this? What does it mean? And I told her. She said, Well, if that's what it meant, why did you have to go all the way around the barn to say so? It's true. So much of that elaborateness is not necessary. I really want to say something to someone that they will feel significantly inside themselves, and if I'm not doing that then I'm wasting our time.

INTERVIEWER

Have your poems ever adhered to strict form?

GILBERT

Sure. There's a poem of mine, a villanelle. Villanelles have a strict form, but not my versions. A poem sometimes has to have some imperfection. But if you put things in a poem just because you know they work, that doesn't help. If everything is balanced there's usually no energy in it. Good art almost always breaks the rules—subtly, sometimes radically. But of course if it's clever mush, it's a waste of time.

INTERVIEWER

You once wrote, "Poetry is a bit like cows who must be freshened if the farmer wants to keep getting milk."

GILBERT

Yes, every seven years.

INTERVIEWER

What do you mean by "freshened"?

GILBERT

You have to have achieved something inside. You can't make a poem out of something that's not there. And it won't be there unless you want it to be there. And if you don't want it to be there, you're in trouble. I'll stop there.

INTERVIEWER

No, go on.

GILBERT

Why do so many poets settle for so little? I don't understand why they're not greedy for what's inside them. The heart has the ability to experience so much—and we don't have much time.

INTERVIEWER

You taught in universities very rarely, only when you had to—just enough so that you could travel and write. Do you think writing poetry can be taught?

GILBERT

I can teach people how to *write* poetry, but I can't teach people how to *have* poetry, which is more than just technique. You have to feel it—to experience it, whether in a daze or brightly. Often you don't know what you have. I once worked on a poem for twelve years before I found it.

INTERVIEWER

Did you learn anything of value from teaching?

GILBERT

No.

INTERVIEWER

Were you a good teacher?

GILBERT

Excellent.

INTERVIEWER

This may sound silly, but what is poetry?

GILBERT

It's a challenge. It's boring—sometimes. It's maddening. It's impossible. It's a blessing. The craftsmanship, the difficulty of making a poem—rightly, adequately, newly. If nothing else, it's wonderful to be that close to magic.

INTERVIEWER

What, other than yourself, is the subject of your poems?

GILBERT

Those I love. Being. Living my life without being diverted into things that people so often get diverted into. Being alive is so extraordinary I don't know why people limit it to riches, pride, security—all of those things life is built on. People miss so much because they want money and comfort and pride, a house and a job to pay for the house. And they have to get a car. You can't see anything from a car. It's moving too fast. People take vacations. That's their reward—the vacation. Why not the life? Vacations are second-rate. People deprive themselves of so much of their lives—until it's too late. Though I understand that often you don't have a choice.

INTERVIEWER

Is there a community—of writers or of anyone—to which you feel you belong?

GILBERT

Not anymore. No.

INTERVIEWER

Was there ever? Have you ever felt that someplace was home?

GILBERT

San Francisco during the sixties maybe. I lived there for seven years, like a hippie without drugs. That was lovely.

INTERVIEWER

In the late 1950s you were in Jack Spicer's poetry workshop—what was that like?

GILBERT

You have to understand that Jack and I were very different. We knew each other well. We hung out the way everyone hung out in San Francisco at that time. We used to play chess a lot. He always lost. One day he was sitting there mumbling to himself and finally said, You cheat! What do you mean, I cheat? I said. How can you cheat at chess? You're not so stupid that I could take pieces off the board. And he said, You cheat. You're thinking. He was dead serious.

INTERVIEWER

You say it was lovely to belong in San Francisco in the sixties. It was also an intense literary scene. Did you ever feel that you were in anyone's shadow?

GILBERT

There were people I respected, but we weren't fighting. Today, you have to do something to distinguish yourself. Maybe because there's so much money in poetry now. We used to type our poems and then go around and nail them up. Nobody would give Allen Ginsberg any money for "Howl." It wasn't in the running.

INTERVIEWER

You knew Ginsberg. How did you meet?

GILBERT

We had an argument about meter. He was trying to explain anapests to one of the young poets in North Beach. I leaned over and told him he was wrong. He was fresh from New York and of course thought he knew everything. He was affronted. We started arguing. Finally, he admitted I was right and he took out a matchbook, scribbled his address on it, handed it to me, and said, Come and see me. I liked him.

When he came to town he wanted to write little quatrains. They were neat, but they weren't very good. We liked each other, but I kept laughing at him nicely. One day, he got on a bus and went across the Golden Gate Bridge to see me in Sausalito. The streets turned to lanes, and the lanes to gravel, and the gravel turned into a path and then just woods. Up and up. He finally reached the abandoned house where I was living. After we talked, he said he had something he wanted to show me. He got two pages out of his bag. I read them and then read them again. I looked at him and told him they were terrific. Those two pages eventually became "Howl."

INTERVIEWER

Some of the Beat writers used drink and drugs to spur their work. What about you?

GILBERT

I did smoke tobacco for about a week when I was thirteen. It was boring. I was never interested in chemicals making me excited or loving or happy. It's like with sexual stimulants—it would make me feel as if someone else were making love to the woman I was with. I want to be the person making love to her, not the chemical.

INTERVIEWER

It sounds like even in your San Francisco days you sustained a rather remote life away from others. Is solitude important for you?

GILBERT

I don't know how to answer that because I've always lived a life with a lot of quiet in it—either alone or with someone I'm in love with.

INTERVIEWER

Do you think that being reclusive has preserved your career?

GILBERT

Certainly to the point that it gave me some control over my vanity and helped me keep a grip on what really matters.

INTERVIEWER

You expose a lot of yourself in your poetry. Are your poems taken directly from your life?

GILBERT

Yes, why would I invent them?

INTERVIEWER

Do you ever feel uncomfortable about naming the women you've been with in your poems?

GILBERT

No, I'm so proud—even the ones that didn't work out, like Gianna.

INTERVIEWER

What was your life with Michiko like?

GILBERT

Pure. It was all the same piece of cloth—always gentle, always devilish. Always loving.

INTERVIEWER

What was your life with Linda like?

GILBERT

It had more substance to it. She was the most valuable person in my life. She's the most important person in the world to me.

INTERVIEWER

Did you and Linda ever collaborate?

GILBERT

We were intertwined. We read each other's poetry, appreciated each other's poetry, discarded each other's poetry. The presence of that spirit in my life—gentleness, beauty . . . Pretty soon I'm going to start singing.

INTERVIEWER

When you look back on your life, do you see it as divided between the three women you loved?

GILBERT

Yes and no. The highlights of my life have been the women I was in love with, but I've had a whole other life alone. I used to say that the only thing better than being alone was to be seriously in love.

INTERVIEWER

You don't get lonely.

GILBERT

No. I really don't like chitchat. Often when I went places with people I liked, they would chat the whole time. It's very human, but if there's going to be talk I want it to be interesting. I don't want to know that so-and-so spilled milk or how sad it is that she didn't get the dress she wanted. All of the things that people are shamed by or don't think they've succeeded in—I don't want to talk about that. I really like to meet people, to be with people, but I don't want to be chatting all the time. I like it when people talk about things.

INTERVIEWER

Is being childless good for a poet?

GILBERT

I could never have lived my life the way I have if I had children. There used to be a saying that every baby is a failed novel. I couldn't have roamed or taken so many chances or lived a life of deprivation. I couldn't have wasted great chunks of my life. But that would be a mistake for other people. Fine people. Smart people.

INTERVIEWER

Many writers talk about how difficult it is to write. Is poetry hard work?

GILBERT

They should try working in the steel mills in Pittsburgh. That's a very delicate kind of approach to the world—to be so frail that you can't stand having to write poetry. There are so many people who are really in trouble just making a living, who are really having a hard life. Besides, with poetry you're doing it for yourself. Other people are doing it because they have to feed the babies. But I do understand that it's hard to write, especially if you have a family.

INTERVIEWER

Which is most important to writing poetry, description or compression?

GILBERT

Neither. I would say presence, feeling, passion—not passion, but love. I usually say romantic love, but here I don't mean being thrilled. I mean the huge experience of loving another person and being loved by another person. But it's more than just liking someone or thinking they make you happy.

INTERVIEWER

In your poems, how important is the interplay between syntax and line breaks?

GILBERT

I don't think that way. I work by instinct and intelligence. By being smart, emotional, probing. By being sly, stubborn. By being lucky. Being serious. By being quietly passionate. By something almost like magic.

INTERVIEWER

To which of your poems are you most attached?

GILBERT

That's like asking to which of the women you've loved are you most attached—the best ones.

INTERVIEWER

Do you revise a great deal?

GILBERT

Yes.

INTERVIEWER

Do you throw away a lot of poems?

GILBERT

More than I would like.

INTERVIEWER

Was there a period of time when you didn't write?

GILBERT

No. But there was a long time when I didn't publish.

INTERVIEWER

Have you ever been tempted to publish more of your poems?

GILBERT

Sometimes. But I'm not interested in being famous.

INTERVIEWER

Do you have diaries, letters, and papers?

GILBERT

Yes. I have a room piled high with papers.

INTERVIEWER

Do you hope or dread that they'll be published someday?

GILBERT

I'm going to give them to Linda. She can do what she wants with them. I hope they can be sold, so that she can use the money.

INTERVIEWER

If you had to be remembered by just one book, which would you choose?

GILBERT

This current one, *Refusing Heaven*.

INTERVIEWER

Do you show your work to anyone as you go?

GILBERT

No. Well, occasionally I show it to the women I love and the men I'm friends with.

INTERVIEWER

How important is it for you to read your work to an audience?

GILBERT

Depends on the time in my life. I used to get excited when I gave a reading. Like any performer, I was vain—*very* vain. And proud, which is a different thing. I wanted to impress the audience. To feel the impact of the poems on an audience was intoxicating. I would feel drunk. I couldn't sleep. Like jazz musicians—after their performances they can't sleep. So they get together and play music. It's not just vanity. It's as if you've given birth to something you can't put down. It's partially about being pleased by my ability, but it's also like an artist merging with what he's done. That's more than just vanity. It's a kind of happiness—more than happiness.

A really good actor doesn't just get applause. He gets to the point where he has a power over his audience. He can make the woman in the red coat in the second row turn her head to the right. I don't know how to explain it, but you have control over your audience—not in a cheap way, in a wonderful way. That's what I used to feel. To give presence or being to an idea or an emotion or a perception or a desire—that was what was important for me. I didn't care about the audience. A chance to be alive, to experience the importance of being alive. Impressing someone or having people applaud—I still like it, but if it's not there I don't miss it.

INTERVIEWER

Do you think poetry should be performed?

GILBERT

No, God no. But it must be created so that you make something happen. You don't just fool the audience—make them love you or something like that. It's an art to make the audience experience what you're talking about.

INTERVIEWER

When you write, do you read your poems out loud?

GILBERT

Sometimes. If my instincts register that something is wrong with the rhythm then I work on it, but it's almost always unconscious.

The hard part for me is to find the poem—a poem that matters. To find what the poem knows that's special. I may think of writing about the same thing that everyone does, but I really like to write a poem that hasn't been written. And I don't mean its shape. I want to experience or discover ways of feeling that are fresh. I love it when I have perceived something fresh about being human and being happy.

Ezra Pound said "make it new." The great tragedy of that saying is he left out the essential word. It should be make it *importantly* new. So much of the time people are just aiming for novelty, surprise. I like to think that I've understood, that I've learned about something that matters—what the world should be, what life should be.

INTERVIEWER

Can you describe your life in Northampton in recent years?

GILBERT

Happiness. I'm in the midst of absolute beauty, quiet. A lot of being alone. I walk in the morning, then I listen to the news, then I eat something and start working.

INTERVIEWER

You've said before that you don't miss being young.

GILBERT

Oh, of course I miss being young.

INTERVIEWER

How is that different from not minding growing old?

GILBERT

Growing old is a mistake. It seems natural that we die and grow old. It's part of the bargain. You get to be young for a long time and then you start to get old. It's also a wonderful time, but it's a different kind of wonderful.

When I was young, I was very aware of death. I was determined not to die until I'd lived my life. So much so that I used to pray and make lists. I would say, I know you have to take me away. You have to kill me. But not yet. I'd make a sort of bargain—I accept that you will kill me, but don't let me die before I've fallen in love. And then the second prayer was, Don't let me die a virgin. I started making lists about what I wanted before I died. When I finally finished going around the world, I discovered that I'd lived every one of those lists.

INTERVIEWER

Are your writing habits the same today as they were when you were young?

GILBERT

I trust the poems more.

INTERVIEWER

When do you work best now?

GILBERT

In the morning. But for most of my life I wrote late at night. When you get old your brain doesn't function as well after noon.

INTERVIEWER

Do you keep to a work schedule?

GILBERT

No, I have an approximate rhythm, but I don't like the idea of anything creative being mechanical. That'll kill you. On the other hand, if I was not satisfied with how much I'd written in a year, then I would set out to write a hundred poems in a hundred days. I force myself to write poems even though I don't approve of it because it does keep something alive. So I guess I have a little bit of a pattern that I live by. For instance, the other day I woke up at one in the morning and worked until four in the afternoon. I do that a lot. I can do that because I don't have to accommodate anybody but me.

INTERVIEWER

So discipline is important to you?

GILBERT

Yes, because I'm lazy. If you have it in you, you want to create, but I won't force myself—because it's dangerous. People who are organized are in danger of making a process out of it and doing it by the numbers.

INTERVIEWER

Do you ever experience writer's block?

GILBERT

It depends if you consider laziness writer's block. I don't know. I've always been able to write at least satisfactory poems, ones that weren't mechanical.

INTERVIEWER

Do you feel you have any flaw as a writer?

GILBERT

I can't spell. I'm hopeless.

INTERVIEWER

What's your relationship with the contemporary literary community now?

GILBERT

I don't have one.

INTERVIEWER

Does that bother you?

GILBERT

No. Why? Why would it bother me? Those people are in business. They're hardworking.

INTERVIEWER

Don't you work hard?

GILBERT

Not in the same meaning of the word *hard*. I put in a lot of effort because it matters to me. Many of these people who teach would do anything not to teach. I don't have any obligations. I don't have a mortgage. These people are working hard at a great price.

INTERVIEWER

I'm struck by how rarely I see your poems in anthologies and how often I see the same poems by other poets over and over again. Do you think there's a disadvantage to spending most of your life abroad or outside of literary circles?

GILBERT

It's fatal, which is all right with me.

INTERVIEWER

Do you ever feel any professional antagonism toward other writers?

GILBERT

Them toward me or me toward them?

INTERVIEWER

You toward them.

GILBERT

No.

INTERVIEWER

Do you feel it from them toward you?

GILBERT

Sure. I contradict a lot of what they're doing. I don't go to the meetings and dinners. I don't hang out.

INTERVIEWER

Have you ever followed a particular religion?

GILBERT

Presbyterianism. Till I was about seven, I guess. My mother never went to church, but she was a believer. She loved God and believed God would be good to her. She sang when she cleaned the house on Sunday mornings.

INTERVIEWER

Do you consider yourself religious now?

GILBERT

I'd like to be. I think I'm very religious by temperament. I think it would be a great comfort to believe. But you don't have a choice. Either you believe or you don't. It's not a practical matter. Religion is a beautiful idea, but I don't have a choice.

INTERVIEWER

Where does your preoccupation with mythology and the gods come from?

GILBERT

Careless reading. I never read mythology or any fiction as if I were in a class. Myths give shape to what I feel about the world and my instinct about what I'm looking at. They inform what I think about the past.

INTERVIEWER

How has old age changed you? What's the main thing that it's altered in your life?

GILBERT

Romance. You can still play at it, but when you get into your sixties—even your fifties—romance seems a little bit silly. After people get to be thirty, generally speaking, they don't want excitement. The glands might flutter up every once in a while, but basically I think people want to be comfortable. To be sexual takes a lot of work. One of the difficulties, I think, is that when you look in the mirror it's hard to think of yourself as romantic.

INTERVIEWER

Toward the end of her life Elizabeth Bishop said that she wished she'd written more. Do you ever feel that way?

GILBERT

No, I still like writing poems. But I'm eighty. I think I should write something about getting old. It's never been explored appropriately.

INTERVIEWER

Have you ever thought of writing your memoirs?

GILBERT

Yes. Every once in a while someone asks to do it for me. Sometimes I'm interested because I've forgotten so much of the past and I like the idea of walking through my life. What's more, it's a profound experience to be with people from my past again. To be with my memories. Things that I thought I'd forgotten all of a sudden become visible, become present.

INTERVIEWER

Like a film?

GILBERT

Different than that. It's more like a feeling rising from the tops of my knees. Then I start remembering. It's complicated; a child seldom remembers anything before he's four years old. I just wonder how much I know, how much I've been through, that I no longer remember.

INTERVIEWER

Is there a particular time period in which you'd prefer to live?

GILBERT

To live with Michiko again. For a lot of reasons.

INTERVIEWER

Do you have any unfulfilled ambitions or regrets?

GILBERT

No.

INTERVIEWER

Is there a particular subject that you feel you haven't covered in your poems?

GILBERT

None that interests me.

INTERVIEWER

But you're still writing?

GILBERT

Yes.

INTERVIEWER

Does the United States—Northampton—feel like home to you now?

GILBERT

No, I don't have a home. Not anymore. When Linda's not teaching anymore we'll probably leave this lovely Massachusetts world for another fine world. To be happy. Very happy.

INTERVIEWER

Do you think poetry is relevant in our society anymore? Do you think it has a place?

GILBERT

Someone once asked Gandhi what he thought of Western civilization. And he's supposed to have said, "I think it would be a very good idea." That's the way I feel.

INTERVIEWER

Do you still wake happy but aware of your mortality?

GILBERT

Yes, though sometimes I have to have a cup of tea first.

Issue 175, 2005

Joan Didion

The Art of Nonfiction

T he last time this magazine spoke with Joan Didion, in August of 1977, she was living in California and had just published her third novel, *A Book of Common Prayer*. Didion was forty-two years old and well-known not only for her fiction but also for her work in magazines—reviews, reportage, and essays—some of which had been collected in *Slouching Towards Bethlehem* (1968). In addition, Didion and her husband, John Gregory Dunne (who was himself the subject of a *Paris Review* interview in 1996), had written a number of screenplays together, including *The Panic in Needle Park* (1971); an adaptation of her second novel, *Play It As It Lays* (1972); and *A Star Is Born* (1976). When Didion's first interview appeared in these pages in 1978, she was intent on exploring her gift for fiction and nonfiction. Since then, her breadth and craft as a writer have only grown deeper with each project.

Joan Didion was born in Sacramento, and both her parents, too, were native Californians. She studied English at Berkeley, and in 1956, after graduating, she won an essay contest sponsored by *Vogue* and moved to New York City to join the magazine's editorial staff. While at *Vogue*, she wrote fashion copy, as well as book and movie reviews. She also became a frequent contributor to the *National Review*, among other publications. In 1963, Didion published her first novel, *Run River*. The next year she married Dunne, and soon afterwards, they moved to Los Angeles. There, in 1965, they adopted their only child, Quintana Roo.

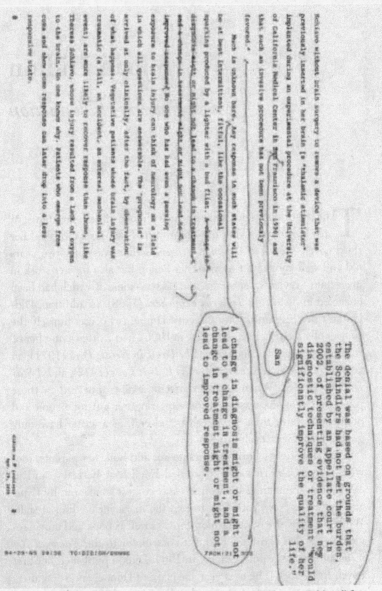

A manuscript page from Joan Didion's "The Case of Theresa Schiavo" for *The New York Review of Books*.

In 1973, Didion began writing for *The New York Review of Books*, where she has remained a regular contributor. While she has continued to write novels in recent decades—*Democracy* (1984) and *The Last Thing He Wanted* (1996)—she has increasingly explored different forms of nonfiction: critical essay, political reportage, memoir. In 1979, she published a second collection of her magazine work, *The White Album*, which was followed by *Salvador* (1983), *Miami* (1987), *After Henry* (1992), *Political Fictions* (2001), and *Where I Was From* (2003). In the spring of 2005, Didion was awarded a Gold Medal from the American Academy of Arts and Letters.

In December of 2003, shortly before their fortieth anniversary, Didion's husband died. Last fall, she published *The Year of Magical Thinking*, a book-length meditation on grief and memory. It became a best-seller, and won the National Book Award for nonfiction; Didion is now adapting the book for the stage as a monologue. Two months before the book's publication, Didion's thirty-nine-year-old daughter died after a long illness.

Our conversation took place over the course of two afternoons in the Manhattan apartment Didion shared with her husband. On the walls of the spacious flat, one could see many photographs of Didion, Dunne, and their daughter. Daylight flooded the book-filled parlor. "When we got the place, we assumed the sun went all through the apartment. It doesn't," Didion said, laughing. Her laughter was the additional punctuation to her precise speech.

—*Hilton Als, 2006*

INTERVIEWER

By now you've written at least as much nonfiction as you have fiction. How would you describe the difference between writing the one or the other?

JOAN DIDION

Writing fiction is for me a fraught business, an occasion of daily dread for at least the first half of the novel, and sometimes all the way through. The work process is totally different from writing nonfiction. You have to sit down every day and make it up. You have no notes—or sometimes you do, I made extensive notes for *A Book of Common Prayer*—but the notes give you only the background, not the novel itself. In nonfiction the notes give you the piece. Writing nonfiction is more like sculpture, a matter of shaping the research into the finished thing. Novels are like paintings, specifically watercolors. Every stroke you put down you have to go with. Of course you can rewrite, but the original strokes are still there in the texture of the thing.

INTERVIEWER

Do you do a lot of rewriting?

DIDION

When I'm working on a book, I constantly retype my own sentences. Every day I go back to page one and just retype what I have. It gets me into a rhythm. Once I get over maybe a hundred pages, I won't go back to page one, but I might go back to page fifty-five, or twenty, even. But then every once in a while I feel the need to go to page one again and start rewriting. At the end of the day, I mark up the pages I've done—pages or *page*—all the way back to page one. I mark them up so that I can retype them in the morning. It gets me past that blank terror.

INTERVIEWER

Did you do that sort of retyping for *The Year of Magical Thinking*?

DIDION

I did. It was especially important with this book because so much of it depended on echo. I wrote it in three months, but I marked it up every night.

INTERVIEWER

The book moves quickly. Did you think about how your readers would read it?

DIDION

Of course, you always think about how it will be read. I always aim for a reading in one sitting.

INTERVIEWER

At what point did you know that the notes you were writing in response to John's death would be a book for publication?

DIDION

John died December 30, 2003. Except for a few lines written a day or so after he died, I didn't begin making the notes that became the book until the following October. After a few days of making notes, I realized that I was thinking about how to structure a book, which was the point at which I realized that I was writing one. This realization in no way changed what I was writing.

INTERVIEWER

Was it difficult to finish the book? Or were you happy to have your life back—to live with a lower level of self-scrutiny?

DIDION

Yes. It was difficult to finish the book. I didn't want to let John go. I don't really have my life back yet, since Quintana died only on August 26.

INTERVIEWER

Since you write about yourself, interviewers tend to ask about your personal life; I want to ask you about writing and books. In the past you've written pieces on V. S. Naipaul, Graham Greene, Norman Mailer, and Ernest Hemingway—titanic, controversial iconoclasts whom you tend to defend. Were these the writers you grew up with and wanted to emulate?

DIDION

Hemingway was really early. I probably started reading him when I was just eleven or twelve. There was just something magnetic to me in the arrangement of those sentences. Because they were so simple—or rather they appeared to be so simple, but they weren't.

Something I was looking up the other day, that's been in the back of my mind, is a study done several years ago about young women's writing skills and the incidence of Alzheimer's. As it happens, the subjects were all nuns, because all of these women had been trained in a certain convent. They found that those who wrote simple sentences as young women later had a higher incidence of Alzheimer's, while those who wrote complicated sentences with several clauses had a lower incidence of Alzheimer's. The assumption—which I thought was probably erroneous—was that those who tended to write simple sentences as young women did not have strong memory skills.

INTERVIEWER

Though you wouldn't classify Hemingway's sentences as simple.

DIDION

No, they're deceptively simple because he always brings a change in.

INTERVIEWER

Did you think you could write that kind of sentence? Did you want to try?

DIDION

I didn't think that I could do them, but I thought that I could learn—because they felt so natural. I could see how they worked once I started typing them out. That was when I was about fifteen. I would just type those stories. It's a great way to get rhythms into your head.

INTERVIEWER

Did you read anyone else before Hemingway?

DIDION

No one who attracted me in that way. I had been reading a lot of plays. I had a misguided idea that I wanted to act. The form this took was not acting, however, but reading plays. Sacramento was not a place where you saw a lot of plays. I think the first play I ever saw was the Lunts in the touring company of *O Mistress Mine*. I don't think that that's what inspired me. The Theater Guild used to do plays on the radio, and I remember being very excited about listening to them. I remember memorizing speeches from *Death of a Salesman* and *Member of the Wedding* in the period right after the war.

INTERVIEWER

Which playwrights did you read?

DIDION

I remember at one point going through everything of Eugene O'Neill's. I was struck by the sheer theatricality of his plays. You could see how they worked. I read them all one summer. I had nosebleeds, and for some reason it took all summer to get the appointment to get my nose cauterized. So I just lay still on the porch all day and read Eugene O'Neill. That was all I did. And dab at my face with an ice cube.

INTERVIEWER

What you really seem to have responded to in these early influences was style—voice and form.

DIDION

Yes, but another writer I read in high school who just knocked me out was Theodore Dreiser. I read *An American Tragedy* all in one weekend and couldn't put it down—I locked myself in my room. Now that was antithetical to every other book I was reading at the time because Dreiser really had no style, but it was powerful.

And one book I totally missed when I first read it was *Moby-Dick*. I reread it when Quintana was assigned it in high school. It was clear that she wasn't going to get through it unless we did little talks about it at dinner. I had not gotten it at all when I read it at her age. I had missed that wild control of language. What I had thought discursive were really these great leaps. The book had just seemed a jumble; I didn't get the control in it.

INTERVIEWER

After high school you wanted to go Stanford. Why?

DIDION

It's pretty straightforward—all my friends were going to Stanford.

INTERVIEWER

But you went to Berkeley and majored in literature. What were you reading there?

DIDION

The people I did the most work on were Henry James and D. H. Lawrence, who I was not high on. He irritated me on almost every level.

INTERVIEWER

He didn't know anything about women at all.

DIDION

No, nothing. And the writing was so clotted and sentimental. It didn't work for me on any level.

INTERVIEWER

Was he writing too quickly, do you think?

DIDION

I don't know, I think he just had a clotted and sentimental mind.

You mentioned reading *Moby-Dick*. Do you do much rereading?

DIDION
I often reread *Victory*, which is maybe my favorite book in the world.

INTERVIEWER
Conrad? Really? Why?

DIDION
The story is told thirdhand. It's not a story the narrator even heard from someone who experienced it. The narrator seems to have heard it from people he runs into around the Malacca Strait. So there's this fantastic distancing of the narrative, except that when you're in the middle of it, it remains very immediate. It's incredibly skillful. I have never started a novel—I mean except the first, when I was starting a novel just to start a novel—I've never written one without rereading *Victory*. It opens up the possibilities of a novel. It makes it seem worth doing. In the same way, John and I always prepared for writing a movie by watching *The Third Man*. It's perfectly told.

INTERVIEWER
Conrad was also a huge inspiration for Naipaul, whose work you admire. What drew you to Naipaul?

DIDION
I read the nonfiction first. But the novel that really attracted me—and I still read the beginning of it now and then—is *Guerillas*. It has that bauxite factory in the opening pages, which just gives you the whole feel of that part of the world. That was a thrilling book to me. The nonfiction had the same effect on me as reading Elizabeth Hardwick—you get the sense that it's possible simply to go through life noticing things and writing them down and that this is OK, it's worth doing. That the seemingly insignificant things that most of us

spend our days noticing are really significant, have meaning, and tell us something. Naipaul is a great person to read before you have to do a piece. And Edmund Wilson, his essays for *The American Earthquake*. They have that everyday-traveler-in-the-world aspect, which is the opposite of an authoritative tone.

INTERVIEWER

Was it as a student at Berkeley that you began to feel that you were a writer?

DIDION

No, it began to feel almost impossible at Berkeley because we were constantly being impressed with the fact that everybody else had done it already and better. It was very daunting to me. I didn't think I could write. It took me a couple of years after I got out of Berkeley before I dared to start writing. That academic mind-set—which was kind of shallow in my case anyway—had begun to fade. Then I did write a novel over a long period of time, *Run River*. And after that it seemed feasible that maybe I could write another one.

INTERVIEWER

You had come to New York by then and were working at *Vogue*, while writing at night. Did you see writing that novel as a way of being back in California?

DIDION

Yes, it was a way of not being homesick. But I had a really hard time getting the next book going. I couldn't get past a few notes. It was *Play It As It Lays*, but it wasn't called that—I mean it didn't have a name and it wasn't what it is. For one, it was set in New York. Then, in June of 1964, John and I went to California and I started doing pieces for *The Saturday Evening Post*. We needed the money because neither one of us was working. And during the course of doing these pieces I was out in the world enough that an actual story for this so-called second novel presented itself, and then I started writing it.

What had you been missing about California? What were you not getting in New York?

Rivers. I was living on the East Side, and on the weekend I'd walk over to the Hudson and then I'd walk back to the East River. I kept thinking, All right, they are rivers, but they aren't California rivers. I really missed California rivers. Also the sun going down in the West. That's one of the big advantages to Columbia-Presbyterian hospital—you can see the sunset. There's always something missing about late afternoon to me on the East Coast. Late afternoon on the West Coast ends with the sky doing all its brilliant stuff. Here it just gets dark.

The other thing I missed was horizons. I missed that on the West Coast, too, if we weren't living at the beach, but I noticed at some point that practically every painting or lithograph I bought had a horizon in it. Because it's very soothing.

Why did you decide to come back east in 1988?

Part of it was that Quintana was in college here, at Barnard, and part of it was that John was between books and having a hard time getting started on a new one. He felt that it was making him stale to be in one place for a long time. We had been living in Brentwood for ten years, which was longer than we had ever lived in any one place. And I think he just thought it was time to move. I didn't particularly, but we left. Even before moving, we had a little apartment in New York. To justify having it, John felt that we had to spend some periods of time there, which was extremely inconvenient for me. The apartment in New York was not very comfortable, and on arrival you would always have to arrange to get the windows washed and get food in . . . It was cheaper when we stayed at the Carlyle.

INTERVIEWER

But when you finally moved to New York, was it a bad move?

DIDION

No, it was fine. It just took me about a year, maybe two years all told. The time spent looking for an apartment, selling the house in California, the actual move, having work done, remembering where I put things when I unpacked—it probably took two years out of my effective working life. Though I feel that it's been the right place to be after John died. I would not have wanted to be in a house in Brentwood Park after he died.

INTERVIEWER

Why not?

DIDION

For entirely logistical reasons. In New York I didn't need to drive to dinner. There wasn't likely to be a brush fire. I wasn't going to see a snake in the pool.

INTERVIEWER

You said that you started writing for *The Saturday Evening Post* because you and John were broke. Is that where the idea of working for movies came from—the need for cash?

DIDION

Yes it was. One of the things that had made us go to Los Angeles was we had a nutty idea that we could write for television. We had a bunch of meetings with television executives, and they would explain to us, for example, the principle of *Bonanza*. The principle of *Bonanza* was: break a leg at the Ponderosa. I looked blankly at the executive and he said, Somebody rides into town, and to make the story work, he's got to break a leg so he's around for two weeks. So we never wrote for *Bonanza*. We did, however, have one story idea picked up by *Chrysler Theatre*. We were paid a thousand dollars for it.

That was also why we started to write for the movies. We thought of it as a way to buy time. But nobody was asking us to write movies. John and his brother Nick and I took an option on *The Panic in Needle Park* and put it together ourselves. I had read the book by James Mills and it just immediately said *movie* to me. I think that the three of us each put in a thousand dollars, which was enormous at the time.

INTERVIEWER

How did you make it work as a collaboration? What were the mechanics?

DIDION

On that one, my memory is that I wrote the treatment, which was just voices. Though whenever I say I did something, or vice versa, the other person would go over it, run it through the typewriter. It was always a back-and-forth thing.

INTERVIEWER

Did you learn anything about writing from the movie work?

DIDION

Yes. I learned a lot of fictional technique. Before I'd written movies, I never could do big set-piece scenes with a lot of different speakers—when you've got twelve people around a dinner table talking at cross purposes. I had always been impressed by other people's ability to do that. Anthony Powell comes to mind. I think the first book I did those big scenes in was *A Book of Common Prayer*.

INTERVIEWER

But screenwriting is very different from prose narrative.

DIDION

It's *not* writing. You're making notes for the director—for the director more than the actors. Sidney Pollack once told us that every screenwriter should go to the Actor's Studio because there was no better way to learn what an actor needed. I'm guilty of not thinking enough about what actors need. I think instead about what the director needs.

INTERVIEWER

John wrote that Robert De Niro asked you to write a scene in *True Confessions* without a single word of dialogue—the opposite of your treatment for *The Panic in Needle Park*.

DIDION

Yeah, which is great. It's something that every writer understands, but if you turn in a scene like that to a producer, he's going to want to know where the words are.

INTERVIEWER

At the other end of the writing spectrum, there's *The New York Review of Books* and your editor there, Robert Silvers. In the seventies you wrote for him about Hollywood, Woody Allen, Naipaul, and Patty Hearst. All of those essays were, broadly speaking, book reviews. How did you make the shift to pure reporting for the *Review*?

DIDION

In 1982, John and I were going to San Salvador, and Bob expressed interest in having one or both of us write something about it. After we'd been there a few days, it became clear that I was going to do it rather than John, because John was working on a novel. Then when I started writing it, it got very long. I gave it to Bob, in its full length, and my idea was that he would figure out something to take from it. I didn't hear from him for a long time. So I wasn't expecting much, but then he called and said he was going to run the whole thing, in three parts.

INTERVIEWER

So he was able to find the through-line of the piece?

DIDION

The through-line in "Salvador" was always pretty clear: I went somewhere, this is what I saw. Very simple, like a travel piece. How Bob edited "Salvador" was by constantly nudging me toward updates on the situation and by pointing out weaker material. When I gave him the text, for example, it had a very weak ending, which was about meeting an American evangelical student on the flight home. In other words it was the travel piece carried to its logical and not very interesting conclusion. The way Bob led me away from this was to suggest not that I cut it (it's still there), but that I follow it—and so ground it—with a return to the political situation.

INTERVIEWER

How did you decide to write about Miami in 1987?

DIDION

Ever since the Kennedy assassination, I had wanted to do something that took place in that part of the world. I thought it was really interesting that so much of the news in America, especially if you read through the assassination hearings, was coming out of our political relations with the Caribbean and Central and South America. So when we got the little apartment in New York, I thought, Well that's something useful I can do out of New York: I can fly to Miami.

INTERVIEWER

Had you spent time down south before that?

DIDION

Yes, in 1970. I had been writing a column for *Life*, but neither *Life* nor I were happy with it. We weren't on the same page. I had a contract, so if I turned something in, they had to pay me. But it was soul-searing to turn things in that didn't run. So after about seven columns, I quit. It was agreed that I would do longer pieces. And I said that I was interested in driving around the Gulf Coast, and somehow that got translated into "The Mind of the White South." I had a theory that if I could understand the South, I would understand something about California, because a lot of the California settlers came from the Border South. So I wanted to look into that. It turned out that what I was actually interested in was the South as a gateway to the Caribbean. I should have known that at the time because my original plan had been to drive all over the Gulf Coast.

We began that trip in New Orleans and spent a week there. New Orleans was fantastic. Then we drove around the Mississippi Coast, and that was fantastic too, but in New Orleans, you get a strong sense of the Caribbean. I used a lot of that week in New Orleans in *Common Prayer*. It was the most interesting place I had been in a long time. It was a week in which everything everybody said was astonishing to me.

INTERVIEWER

Three years later you started writing for *The New York Review of Books*. Was that daunting? In your essay "Why I Write" you express trepidation about intellectual, or ostensibly intellectual, matters. What freed you up enough to do that work for Bob?

DIDION

His trust. Nothing else. I couldn't even have imagined it if he hadn't responded. He recognized that it was a learning experience for me. Domestic politics, for example, was something I simply knew nothing about. And I had no interest. But Bob kept pushing me in that direction. He is really good at ascertaining what might interest you at any given moment and then just throwing a bunch of stuff at you that might or might not be related, and letting you go with it.

When I went to the political conventions in 1988—it was the first time I'd ever been to a convention—he would fax down to the hotel the front pages of *The New York Times* and *The Washington Post*. Well, you know, if there's anything you can get at a convention it's a newspaper. But he just wanted to make sure.

And then he's meticulous once you turn in a piece, in terms of making you plug in all relevant information so that everything gets covered and defended before the letters come. He spent a lot of time, for example, making sure that I acknowledged all the issues in the

Terri Schiavo piece, which had the potential for eliciting strong reactions. He's the person I trust more than anybody.

Why do you think he pushed you to write about politics?

I think he had a sense that I would be outside it enough.

No insider reporting—you didn't know anyone.

I didn't even know their names!

But now your political writing has a very strong point of view—you take sides. Is that something that usually happens during the reporting process, or during the writing?

If I am sufficiently interested in a political situation to write a piece about it, I generally have a point of view, although I don't usually recognize it. Something about a situation will bother me, so I will write a piece to find out what it is that bothers me.

When you moved into writing about politics, you moved away from the more personal writing you'd been doing. Was that a deliberate departure?

Yes, I was bored. For one thing, that kind of writing is limiting. Another reason was that I was getting a very strong response from readers, which was depressing because there was no way for me to reach out and help them back. I didn't want to become Miss Lonelyhearts.

And the pieces on El Salvador were the first in which politics really drive the narrative.

DIDION
Actually it was a novel, *Common Prayer*. We had gone to a film festival in Cartagena and I got sick there, some kind of salmonella. We left Cartagena and went to Bogotà, and then we came back to Los Angeles and I was sick for about four months. I started doing a lot of reading about South America, where I'd never been. There's a passage by Christopher Isherwood in a book of his called *The Condor and the Cows*, in which he describes arriving in Venezuela and being astonished to think that it had been down there every day of his life. That was the way that I felt about South America. Then later I started reading a lot about Central America because it was becoming clear to me that my novel had to take place in a rather small country. So that was when I started thinking more politically.

INTERVIEWER
But it still didn't push you into an interest in domestic politics.

DIDION
I didn't get the connection. I don't know why I didn't get the connection, since I wasn't interested in the politics of these countries per se, but rather in how American foreign policy affected them. And the extent to which we are involved abroad is entirely driven by our own domestic politics. So I don't know why I didn't get that.

I started to get this in *Salvador*, but not fully until *Miami*. Our policy with Cuba and with exiles has been totally driven by domestic politics. It still is. But it was very hard for me to understand the process of domestic politics. I could get the overall picture, but the actual words people said were almost unintelligible to me.

INTERVIEWER
How did it become clearer?

I realized that the words didn't have any actual meaning, that they described a negotiation more than they described an idea. But then you begin to see that the lack of specificity is specific in itself, that it is an obscuring device.

Did it help you when you were working on *Salvador* and *Miami* to talk to the political figures you were writing about?

In those cases it did. Though I didn't talk to a lot of American politicians. I remember talking to the then-president of El Salvador, who was astounding. We were talking about a new land reform law and I explained that I couldn't quite understand what was being said about it. We were discussing a provision—Provision 207—that seemed to me to say that landowners could arrange their affairs so as to be unaffected by the reform.

He said, 207 always applied only to 1979. That is what no one understands. I asked, Did he mean that 207 applied only to 1979 because no landowner would work against his interests by allowing tenants on his land after 207 took effect? He said, Exactly, no one would rent out land under 207. They would have to be crazy to do that.

Well, that was forthright. There are very few politicians who would say *exactly*.

Was it helpful to talk with John about your experiences there?

It was useful to talk to him about politics because he viscerally understood politics. He grew up in an Irish Catholic family in Hartford, a town where politics was part of what you ate for breakfast. I mean, it didn't take *him* a long time to understand that nobody was saying anything.

INTERVIEWER

After *Salvador*, you wrote your next novel, *Democracy*. It seems informed by the reporting you were doing about America's relationship to the world.

DIDION

The fall of Saigon, though it takes place offstage, was the main thing on my mind. Saigon fell while I was teaching at Berkeley in 1975. I couldn't get those images out of my head, and that was the strongest impulse behind *Democracy*. When the book came out, some people wondered why it began with the bomb tests in the Pacific, but I think those bomb tests formed a straight line to pushing the helicopters off the aircraft carriers when we were abandoning Saigon. It was a very clear progression in my mind. Mainly, I wanted to show that you could write a romance and still have the fall of Saigon, or the Iran-Contra affair. It would be hard for me to stay with a novel if I didn't see a very strong personal story at the center of it.

Democracy is really a much more complete version of *Common Prayer*, with basically the same structure. There is a narrator who tries to understand the character who's being talked about and reconstruct the story. I had a very clear picture in my mind of both those women, but I couldn't tell the story without standing way far away. Charlotte, in *Common Prayer*, was somebody who had a very expensive dress with a seam that was coming out. There was a kind of fevered carelessness to her. *Democracy* started out as a comedy, a comic novel. And I think that there is a more even view of life in it. I had a terrible time with it. I don't know why, but it never got easy.

In Brentwood we had a big safe-deposit box to put manuscripts in if we left town during fire season. It was such a big box that we never bothered to clean it out. When we were moving, in 1988, and I had to go through the box, I found I don't know how many different versions of the first ninety pages of *Democracy*, with different dates on them, written over several years. I would write ninety pages and not be able to go any further. I couldn't make the switch. I don't know how that was solved. Many of those drafts began with Billy Dillon coming to Amagansett to tell Inez that her father had shot her sister. It was very hard to get from there to any place. It didn't work. It was too conventional a narrative. I never hit the spot where I could sail through. I never got to that point, even at the very end.

INTERVIEWER

Was that a first for you?

DIDION

It was a first for a novel. I really did not think I was going to finish it two nights before I finished it. And when I did finish it, I had a sense that I was just abandoning it, that I was just calling it. It was sort of like Vietnam itself—why don't we say just we've won and leave? I didn't have a real sense of completion about it.

INTERVIEWER

Your novels are greatly informed by the travel and reporting you do for your nonfiction. Do you ever do research specifically for the fiction?

DIDION

Common Prayer was researched. We had someone working for us, Tina Moore, who was a fantastic researcher. She would go to the UCLA library, and I would say, Bring me back anything on plantation life in Central America. And she would come back and say, This is really what you're looking for—you'll love this. And it would not be plantation life in Central America. It would be Ceylon, but it would be fantastic. She had an instinct for what was the same story, and what I was looking for. What I was looking for were rules for living in the tropics. I didn't know that, but that's what I found. In *Democracy* I was more familiar with all the places.

INTERVIEWER

The last novel you wrote was *The Last Thing He Wanted*. That came out in 1996. Had you been working on it for a long time?

DIDION

No. I started it in the early fall or late summer of 1995, and I finished it at Christmas. It was a novel I had been thinking about writing for a while. I wanted to write a novel about the Iran-Contra affair, and get in all that stuff that was being lost. Basically it's a novel about Miami. I wanted it to be very densely plotted. I noticed that conspiracy was central to understanding that part of the world; everybody was always being set up in some way. The plot was going to be so complicated that I was going to have to write it fast or I wouldn't be able to keep it all in my head. If I forgot one little detail it wouldn't work, and half the readers didn't understand what happened in the end. Many people thought that Elena tried to kill Treat Morrison. Why did she want to kill him? they would ask me. But she didn't. Someone else did, and set her up. Apparently I didn't make that clear.

I had begun to lose patience with the conventions of writing. Descriptions went first; in both fiction and nonfiction, I just got impatient with those long paragraphs of description. By which I do not mean—obviously—the single detail that gives you the scene. I'm talking about description as a substitute for thinking. I think you can see me losing my patience as early as *Democracy*. That was why that book was so hard to write.

INTERVIEWER

After *Democracy* and *Miami*, and before *The Last Thing He Wanted*, there was the nonfiction collection *After Henry*, which strikes me as a way of coming back to New York and trying to understand what the city was.

DIDION

It has that long piece "Sentimental Journeys," about the Central Park jogger, which began with that impulse. We had been in New York a year or two, and I realized that I was living here without engaging the city at all. I might as well have been living in another city, because I didn't understand it, I didn't get it. So I realized that I needed to do some reporting on it. Bob and I decided I would do a series of short reporting pieces on New York, and the first one would be about the jogger. But it wasn't really reporting. It was coming at a situation from a lot of angles. I got so involved in it that, by the time I finished the piece, it was too long. I turned it in and Bob had some comments—many, many comments, which caused it to be even longer because he thought it needed so much additional material, which he was right about. By the time I'd plugged it all in, I'd added another six to eight thousand words. When I finally had finished it, I thought, That's all I have to do about New York.

INTERVIEWER

Although it is about the city, "Sentimental Journeys" is really about race and class and money.

DIDION

It seemed to me that the case was treated with a lot of contempt by the people who were handling it.

INTERVIEWER

How so?

DIDION

The prosecution thought they had the press and popular sentiment on their side. The case became a way of expressing the city's rage at being broke and being in another recession and not having a general comfort level, the sense that there were people sleeping on the streets—which there were. We moved here six months after the '87 stock market crash. Over the next couple of years, its effect on Madison Avenue was staggering. You could not walk down Madison Avenue at eight in the evening without having to avoid stepping on people sleeping in every doorway. There was a German television crew here doing a piece on the jogger, and they wanted to shoot in Harlem, but it was late in the day and they were losing the light. They kept asking me what the closest place was where they could shoot and see poverty. I said, Try Seventy-second and Madison. You know where Polo is now? That building was empty and the padlocks were broken and you could see rats scuttling around inside. The landlord had emptied it—I presume because he wanted to get higher rents—and then everything had crashed. There was nothing there. That entire block was a mess.

INTERVIEWER

So from California you had turned your attention to the third world, and now you were able to recognize New York because of the work you had done in the third world.

DIDION

A lot of what I had seen as New York's sentimentality is derived from the stories the city tells itself to rationalize its class contradictions. I didn't realize that until I started doing the jogger piece. Everything started falling into place on that piece. Bob would send me clips about the trial, but on this one I was on my own, because only I knew where it was going.

INTERVIEWER

In some of your early essays on California, your subject matter was as distinctively your own as your writing style. In recent decades, though, it's not so much the story but your take on the story that makes your work distinctive.

DIDION

The shift came about as I became more confident that my own take was worth doing. In the beginning, I didn't want to do any stories that anyone else was doing. As time went by, I got more comfortable with that. For example, on the Central Park jogger piece I could not get into the courtroom because I didn't have a police pass. This forced me into another approach, which turned out to be a more interesting one. At least to me.

INTERVIEWER

Wasn't it around the same time that you were also doing the "Letter from Los Angeles" for Robert Gottlieb at *The New Yorker*?

DIDION

Yes. Though I wasn't doing more than two of those a year. I think they only ran six to eight thousand words, but the idea was to do several things in each letter. I had never done that before, where you just really discuss what people are talking about that week. It was easy to do. It was a totally different tone from the Review. I went over those *New Yorker* pieces when I collected them. I probably took out some of the *New Yorker*'s editing, which is just their way of making everything sound a certain way.

INTERVIEWER

Can you characterize your methods as a reporter?

DIDION

I can't ask anything. Once in a while if I'm forced into it I will conduct an interview, but it's usually pro forma, just to establish my credentials as somebody who's allowed to hang around for a while. It doesn't matter to me what people say to me in the interview because I don't trust it. Sometimes you do interviews where you get a lot. But you don't get them from public figures.

When I was conducting interviews for the piece on Lakewood, it was essential to do interviews because that was the whole point. But these were not public figures. On the one hand, we were discussing what I was ostensibly there doing a piece about, which was the Spur Posse, a group of local high school boys who had been arrested for various infractions. But on the other hand, we were talking, because it was the first thing on everyone's mind, about the defense industry going downhill, which was what the town was about. That was a case in which I did interviewing and listened.

INTERVIEWER

Did the book about California, *Where I Was From*, grow out of that piece, or had you already been thinking about a book?

DIDION

I had actually started a book about California in the seventies. I had written some of that first part, which is about my family, but I could never go anywhere with it for two reasons. One was that I still hadn't figured out California. The other was that I didn't want to figure out California because whatever I figured out would be different from the California my mother and father had told me about. I didn't want to engage that.

INTERVIEWER

You felt like you were still their child?

DIDION

I just didn't see any point in engaging it. By the time I did the book they were dead.

INTERVIEWER

You said earlier that after *The White Album* you were tired of personal writing and didn't want to become Miss Lonelyheart. You must be getting a larger personal response from readers than ever with *The Year of Magical Thinking*. Is that difficult?

DIDION

I have been getting a very strong emotional response to *Magical Thinking*. But it's not a crazy response; it's not demanding. It's people trying to make sense of a fairly universal experience that most people don't talk about. So this is a case in which I have found myself able to deal with the response directly.

INTERVIEWER

Do you ever think you might go back to the idea of doing little pieces about New York?

DIDION

I don't know. It is still a possibility, but my basic question about New York was answered for me: it's criminal.

INTERVIEWER

That was your question?

DIDION

Yes, it's criminal.

INTERVIEWER

Do you find it stimulating in some way to live here?

DIDION

I find it really comfortable. During the time we lived in California, which lasted twenty-four years, I didn't miss New York after the first year. And after the second year I started to think of New York as sentimental. There were periods when I didn't even come to New York at all. One time I realized that I had been to Hong Kong twice since I had last been to New York. Then we started spending more time in New York. Both John and I were really happy to have been here on 9/11. I can't think of any place else I would have rather been on 9/11, and in the immediate aftermath.

INTERVIEWER

You could have stayed in Sacramento forever as a novelist, but you started to move out into the worlds of Hollywood and politics.

DIDION

I was never a big fan of people who don't leave home. I don't know why. It just seems part of your duty in life.

INTERVIEWER

I'm reminded of Charlotte in *A Book of Common Prayer*. She has no conception of the outside world but she wants to be in it.

DIDION

Although a novel takes place in the larger world, there's always some drive in it that is entirely personal—even if you don't know it while you're doing it. I realized some years after *A Book of Common Prayer* was finished that it was about my anticipating Quintana's growing up. I wrote it around 1975, so she would have been nine, but I was already anticipating separation and actually working through that ahead of time. So novels are also about things you're afraid you can't deal with.

INTERVIEWER

Are you working on one now?

DIDION

No. I haven't felt that I wanted to bury myself for that intense a period.

INTERVIEWER

You want to be in the world a bit.

DIDION

Yeah. A little bit.

Issue 176, 2006

Contributors

Saul Bellow (1915–2005) was the author of fourteen novels and received the Nobel Prize for Literature in 1976. Bellow was born in Canada to Russian émigré parents. When he was nine, the family moved to Chicago, and he later attended the University of Chicago and Northwestern University. He published his first novel, *Dangling Man*, in 1944, but it was his third book, *The Adventures of Augie March* (1953), that won him major critical acclaim and a National Book Award—a prize he won twice more, for *Herzog* in 1965, and *Mr. Sammler's Planet* in 1970. He also won the Pulitzer Prize, for *Humboldt's Gift* (1975). His last book, *Ravelstein*, was published in 2000. *Gordon Lloyd Harper* is senior staff emeritus at the Institute of Cultural Affairs in Seattle, Washington.

Elizabeth Bishop (1911–79) was born in Worcester, Massachusetts. Her father died soon after she was born, her mother was institutionalized, and she was raised by relatives. She attended Vassar College, where she began a lifelong friendship with the poet Marianne Moore. Bishop's first collection of poems, *North & South* (1946), won the Houghton Mifflin Poetry Award; her second volume, *Poems* (1955), was awarded the Pulitzer Prize; and *The Complete Poems* (1969) won the National Book Award. Bishop traveled extensively and lived at different times in Key West, Mexico, New York, and Boston, as well as the small town of Petrópolis, Brazil, which was her home from 1952 to 1971. A posthumous collection of her letters, *One Art*, was published in 1994, and a new collection of her poems, drafts, and fragments, *Edgar Allan Poe & The Juke-Box*, edited by Alice Quinn, was published in 2006. *Elizabeth Spires* is the author of five collections of poetry, most recently *Now the Green Black Rises* (2002). A recipient of fellowships from the Guggenheim and Whiting foundations, she is a professor of English at Goucher College in Baltimore, where she holds a Chair for Distinguished Achievement.

Jorge Luis Borges (1899–1986) was born in Buenos Aires, Argentina. In 1914 his family moved to Geneva, where he attended university, and then to Spain, where he began to publish poems in magazines. He returned to Argentina in 1921 and founded two literary magazines before publishing his first book, a volume of poems titled *Fervor de Buenos Aires* (1923). His first story collection, *A Universal History of Infamy* (1935), was followed by a second, *Ficciones* (1944), and in 1961 he shared the Prix Formentor, a major European publishers' award with Samuel Beckett. The next year *Ficciones* appeared in English translation, and Borges began traveling and lecturing across America, Europe, and Asia. Despite suffering nearly total blindness, the result of a hereditary condition, Borges continued to publish essays and stories into the 1980s, dictating to his secretaries or friends. *Ronald Christ*, the publisher of Lumen Books, is a translator, critic, and editor. He has received a translation grant from the National Endowment for the Arts, and the Kayden National Translation Award.

James M. Cain (1892–1977) was born in Annapolis, Maryland. He began working as a writer in 1917 as a reporter for *The Baltimore American*; the following year he switched to *The Baltimore Sun*. There he met H. L. Mencken, who eventually encouraged Cain to write for his new magazine, *The American Mercury*. Cain continued working as a journalist until the publication of his best-selling first novel, *The Postman Always Rings Twice* (1934), which was followed by *Double Indemnity* (1936), based on his early experience as an insurance salesman. Both books were made into films that are now considered classics of Hollywood noir, as was his fourth novel, *Mildred Pierce* (1941). Cain continued to write until the end of his life, publishing novels such as *The Moth* (1948), *Galatea* (1953), *Mignon* (1962), and *The Institute* (1976). *David L. Zinsser* interviewed James Cain while working at Penguin Books in 1977 and received a Ph.D. from New York University in 1981 for work on Raymond Chandler. He lives in New York City where he operates the bar Automatic Slim's.

Truman Capote (1924–84) was born Truman Streckfus Persons in New Orleans. His parents divorced when he was a young boy, and he was raised by various relatives across the South. He completed high school in Connecticut, living with his mother and stepfather, from whom he took the surname Capote. His first published short story, "Miriam," appeared in *Mademoiselle* in 1945 and won the O. Henry Memorial Award, and his first novel, *Other Voices, Other Rooms* (1948), earned him national attention as a writer of great promise. A collection of stories, *A Tree of Night*

(1949), was followed by the semiautobiographical novel *The Grass Harp* (1951) and the immensely popular novella *Breakfast at Tiffany's* (1958), which was made into a film. *In Cold Blood* (1966), Capote's account of the murder of a small-town Kansas family, was hailed by critics as a masterpiece. Capote continued to publish fiction and nonfiction sporadically for the next two decades. At the time of his death he was at work on a social satire titled *Answered Prayers*, published posthumously in 1987. *Pati Hill* lives in Burgundy, France. Her first works were published in *The Paris Review*. She met Truman Capote in Stonington, Connecticut, in 1951. She is an artist, and her last exhibition was "Vers Versailles," shown at the Lambinet Museum in Versailles in 2005.

Joan Didion was born in 1934 in Sacramento, California. After graduating from the University of California, Berkeley, she moved to New York City, where she worked at *Vogue* for seven years and began contributing essays to other publications, including the *National Review*. Her first novel, *Run River* (1963), was followed by a collection of nonfiction, *Slouching Towards Bethlehem* (1968), which established her reputation as an acute observer of the American scene. Didion is the author of four more novels—*Play It As It Lays* (1970), *A Book of Common Prayer* (1977), *Democracy* (1984), and *The Last Thing He Wanted* (1996)—and seven books of reportage, essays, and memoir, as well as numerous screenplays which she cowrote with her husband of nearly forty years, John Gregory Dunne. Didion's memoir of her marriage and widowhood, *The Year of Magical Thinking* (2005), won the National Book Award for nonfiction, and she received a Gold Medal from the American Academy of Arts and Letters. *Hilton Als* is a staff writer for *The New Yorker*.

T. S. Eliot (1888–1965), who was born Thomas Stearns Eliot in St. Louis, Missouri, was awarded the Nobel Prize for Literature in 1948. He graduated from Harvard College, then settled in England. His first volume of poetry, *Prufrock and Other Observations* (1917), was followed by *The Waste Land* (1922), a work that confirmed Eliot's role at the forefront of the modernist movement. Eliot published a first volume of essays in 1920, and he continued to write criticism and to publish the critical work of others while serving as editor of the quarterly review *The Criterion* from 1922 to 1939. His first play, *Sweeney Agonistes* (1932), was first performed in 1933, and he wrote for the stage through the 1950s. Eliot became a British subject in 1927, the same year he was confirmed in the Church of England. There, during the war, he published what is widely regarded as his masterpiece, *The Four Quartets* (1943). *Donald Hall* is a poet who lives in New Hampshire. He was the first poetry editor of *The*

Paris Review, from 1953 to 1961, and was named U.S. Poet Laureate in 2006.

Jack Gilbert was born in Pittsburgh, Pennsylvania, in 1925. His first book of poetry, *Views of Jeopardy* (1962), was published in the prestigious Yale Series of Younger Poets and was nominated for the Pulitzer Prize. He soon moved to Europe on a Guggenheim fellowship and lived for many years in Greece, England, and Denmark before returning to the United States. In 1975, he visited fifteen countries as a lecturer on American literature for the U.S. State Department. His second book, *Monolithos* (1984), was followed a decade later by *The Great Fires: Poems 1982–1992* (1994) which won him a Lannan Literary Award. His latest book, *Refusing Heaven* (2005) was awarded the National Book Critics Circle Award. *Sarah Fay* is a poet and essayist, and a recipient of the Avery Hopwood Award for Literature, as well as grants and fellowships from the Puffin Foundation and the MacDowell Colony.

Robert Gottlieb was born in New York City in 1931. He attended Columbia University and spent two postgraduate years at Cambridge University before taking a job as an editorial assistant at Simon and Schuster, where he eventually became editor in chief. Among his many noteworthy publishing discoveries was Joseph Heller's debut novel *Catch-22* (1961). In 1968 he became the publisher and editor in chief of Alfred A. Knopf, and in 1987 he succeeded William Shawn as editor of *The New Yorker.* Since leaving the magazine in 1992 he has worked as an editor at large at Knopf. *Larissa MacFarquhar* is a staff writer at *The New Yorker* and an editorial associate of *The Paris Review.*

Ernest Hemingway (1899–1961), who began writing for a living as a journalist and settled in Europe after World War I, was awarded the Nobel Prize for Literature in 1954. He was born in a suburb of Chicago and was an expatriate in Paris when he began publishing the short stories and vignettes that appeared in *In Our Time* (1925). His first novels, *The Sun Also Rises* (1926) and *A Farewell to Arms* (1929), secured his reputation as a powerful new voice in American literature. Hemingway's nonfiction, including *Death in the Afternoon* (1932), *Green Hills of Africa* (1935), and *A Moveable Feast* (1964), detailed a life of adventures from the battlefields and bullrings of Europe to the hunting and fishing grounds of Africa and the Caribbean. His last completed work of long fiction was *The Old Man and the Sea* (1952). *George Plimpton* was the editor of *The Paris Review* from 1953 until his death in 2003. He was the author of numerous books, including the best-selling works of participatory journalism *Paper Lion* (1966) and *Open Net* (1985).

Dorothy Parker (1893–1967) was born Dorothy Rothschild in the West End District of Long Branch, New Jersey. Her mother died when she was three, and she attended boarding school until the age of fourteen. Her first poem was published in 1914 in *Vanity Fair*, where several years later she replaced P. G. Wodehouse as drama critic. In the 1920s she became a central figure in the literary set known as the Algonquin Round Table, where she traded witticisms with friends and fellow writers including James Thurber, Harold Ross, Alexander Woollcott, Edna Ferber, and Harpo Marx. Soon after *The New Yorker* was founded in 1925, she began contributing short stories, and in 1927 she became the magazine's book reviewer. Her first collection of poems, *Enough Rope*, was published in 1926 and was followed by her first story collection, *Laments for the Living* (1930). She published fiction and poetry, as well as plays, for the next three decades and earned an Oscar nomination for her work on the screenplay for *A Star Is Born* (1937). *Marion Capron* is a former associate editor of *The Paris Review*. She lives and works in Florida.

Richard Price, who was born in the Bronx in 1949, is the author of six novels. His first, *The Wanderers* (1974), which he wrote while enrolled as a graduate writing student at Columbia University, and his second, *Bloodbrothers* (1976), both became the basis of feature films. Following the publication of his fourth novel, *The Breaks* (1983), Price began writing for film, and his screenplay for *The Color of Money* (1986) was nominated for an Oscar. Price has continued to write for television and film, adapting two of his own recent novels, *Clockers* (1992) and *Freedomland* (1998). In 1999 he received an award in literature from the American Academy of Arts and Letters. His most recent book is *Samaritan* (2003). *James Linville*, a former editor of *The Paris Review*, is a screenwriter and journalist based in London and New York.

Robert Stone was born in Brooklyn, New York, in 1937. He enlisted in the navy when he was seventeen and served for three years. Following his discharge, he worked as a copyboy for the *New York Daily News* and as a census taker in New Orleans before going to Stanford University as a Stegner graduate writing fellow in 1962. At Stanford he met and became closely involved with the author and psychedelic pioneer Ken Kesey. Stone's first novel, *A Hall of Mirrors* (1967), based on his experiences in New Orleans, was made into the film *WUSA*. A brief stint as a reporter in Vietnam in 1971 provided the basis for his next novel, *Dog Soldiers* (1974), which won the National Book Award and was adapted for the screen as *Who'll Stop the Rain*? Stone is the author of five more novels, *A Flag for Sunrise* (1981), *Children of Light* (1986), *Outerbridge Reach* (1992), *Damascus*

Gate (1998), and *Bay of Souls* (2003), as well as a collection of stories, *Bear and His Daughter* (1997). His latest book is a memoir of the sixties, *Prime Green* (2007). *William Crawford Woods* is the author of a novel, *The Killing Zone*, and a founder of the John Dos Passos Prize for Literature.

Kurt Vonnegut was born in Indianapolis in 1922. He began working as a writer for his high school paper, the *Shortridge High Echo*. He continued to write in college for the *Cornell Daily Sun*. In 1943 he enlisted in the army and was sent to Europe, where he was captured by the Germans during the Battle of the Bulge and sent to a POW camp in Dresden. His most famous work, *Slaughterhouse-Five* (1969), recounts the firebombing of Dresden, which Vonnegut survived by hiding in an underground shelter. Most of Vonnegut's stories and his early novels, including *Player Piano* (1952), *The Sirens of Titan* (1959), and *Cat's Cradle* (1963), were science fiction, and his fiction after *Slaughterhouse-Five* continued to engage with this tradition. After finishing *Timequake* (1996), Vonnegut announced that it would be his last novel. He has since published four collections of autobiographical essays; most recently, *A Man Without a Country* (2005). *David Hayman* is professor emeritus in the Department of Comparative Literature at the University of Madison, Wisconsin. He is the author of several books on Joyce and is currently writing a study of the creative evolution of Samuel Beckett's *Watt*; *David Michaelis*, an editorial associate of *The Paris Review*, is the author of a forthcoming biography of Charles M. Schulz and the award-winning *N. C. Wyeth: A Biography* (1998). *Richard Rhodes* is the author of twenty books of fiction, history, and letters. He received the Pulitzer Prize in nonfiction in 1988. *George Plimpton* also contributed to this interview.

Rebecca West (1892–1983), who was born Cicily Isabel Fairfield, graduated from London's Royal Academy of Dramatic Art and went to work as an actress. After appearing in Henrik Ibsen's *Rosmersholm*, she began writing for the suffragette magazine *Freewoman*, changing her given name to Rebecca West after a character in Ibsen's play. In 1916 she published her first book, a critical work on the writings of Henry James. Her first novel, *The Return of the Soldier* (1918), dealt with the psychology of battlefield trauma. After her second novel, *The Judge* (1922), West returned to criticism in *The Strange Necessity* (1928), a collection of essays on D. H. Lawrence, Sherwood Anderson, John Galsworthy, and other writers. West continued to alternate between fiction and nonfiction, and is perhaps best known for her historical travelogue and reportage on the Balkans, *Black Lamb and Grey Falcon* (1942), and her reports on the Nuremberg trials, which were collected in *A Train of Powder* (1955). *Marina Warner*'s recent books include a novel, *The Leto Bundle* (2001), and *Phantasmagoria: Spirit Visions, Metaphors, and Media* (2006).

Billy Wilder (1906–2002) was born in Sucha, Austria, now part of Poland. He worked briefly as a reporter in Berlin before turning his attention to the cinema, collaborating on the neorealist film *People on Sunday* (1929). In 1933 he immigrated to France and then to the United States, where he settled in Los Angeles and began the writing and directing career that would lead to twenty-one Academy Award nominations and six Oscars. His films range from noir to comedy and include *Double Indemnity* (1944, based on the novel by James M. Cain), *Sunset Boulevard* (1950), *The Seven Year Itch* (1955), and *Some Like It Hot* (1959). He received a lifetime achievement award from the American Film Institute in 1986 and the Irving G. Thalberg award from the Academy of Motion Picture Arts and Sciences in 1988. He was interviewed by *James Linville* (see Richard Price).

Acknowledgments

This book would not have been possible without the care and devotion of *The Paris Review*'s editorial staff, Radhika Jones, Nathaniel Rich, Meghan O'Rourke, Charles Simic, Sarah Stein, and Christopher Cox—and several seasons of superb interns, Petrina Crockford, Jessica Ferri, Hannah Goldfield, Elizabeth Gumport, Christopher Jennings, Evan McGarvey, Ryan McIlvain, and Zachary Sussman.

Special thanks also to the generations of *Paris Review* editors who presided over the genesis of the interviews in this volume during the past half century.

Special thanks to Frances Coady, David Rogers, Joshua Kendall, Eric Bliss, James Meader, and Tanya Farrell at Picador.

Special thanks to the Wylie Agency.

Saul Bellow manuscript page reprinted by permission of the Estate of Saul Bellow. Interview reprinted by permission of Gordon Lloyd Harper and *The Paris Review*.

Elizabeth Bishop manuscript page reprinted by permission of Farrar, Straus and Giroux, LLC, on behalf of the Elizabeth Bishop Estate. Interview reprinted by permission of Elizabeth Spires and *The Paris Review*.

Jorge Luis Borges manuscript page reprinted by permission of the Estate of Jorge Luis Borges. Interview reprinted by permission of Ronald Christ and *The Paris Review*.

James M. Cain manuscript page reprinted by permission of the Estate of

James M. Cain. Interview reprinted by permission of David L. Zinsser and *The Paris Review*.

Truman Capote manuscript page reprinted by permission of the Truman Capote Literary Trust. Interview reprinted by permission of Pati Hill and *The Paris Review*.

Joan Didion manuscript page reprinted by permission of Joan Didion. Interview reprinted by permission of Hilton Als and *The Paris Review*.

T. S. Eliot manuscript page reprinted by permission of the T. S. Eliot Estate. Interview reprinted by permission of Donald Hall and *The Paris Review*.

Jack Gilbert manuscript page reprinted by permission of Jack Gilbert. Interview reprinted by permission of Sarah Fay and *The Paris Review*.

Robert Gottlieb interview reprinted by permission of Larissa MacFarquhar and *The Paris Review*.

Ernest Hemingway interview reprinted by permission of the Estate of George A. Plimpton and *The Paris Review*.

Dorothy Parker interview and manuscript page reprinted by permission of Marion Capron and *The Paris Review*.

Richard Price manuscript page reprinted by permission of Richard Price. Interview reprinted by permission of James Linville and *The Paris Review*.

Robert Stone manuscript page reprinted by permission of Robert Stone. Interview reprinted by permission of William Crawford Woods and *The Paris Review*.

Kurt Vonnegut manuscript page reprinted by permission of Kurt Vonnegut. Interview reprinted by permission of David Hayman, David Michaelis, the Estate of George A. Plimpton, Richard Rhodes, and *The Paris Review*.

Rebecca West manuscript page reprinted by permission of the Estate of Rebecca West. Interview reprinted by permission of Marina Warner and *The Paris Review*.

Billy Wilder interview reprinted by permission of James Linville and *The Paris Review*.